I'M ON OUR 17th CUNARD CRUISE....

Bill Brennan

Bill Bresnan Speaks On Tax Planning Under The New Tax Law

. . . In Words Of One Syllable

ALSO BY THE SAME AUTHOR:

WABC 77AM Financial Expert Bill Bresnan Speaks on Real Estate . . . In Words of One Syllable

Bill Bresnan Speaks On Tax Planning Under The New Tax Law

. . . In Words Of One Syllable

Bill Bresnan

Prentice Hall
Englewood Cliffs, New Jersey 07632

Library of Congress Cataloging-in-Publication Data

Bresnan, Bill, (date)
Bill Bresnan speaks on tax planning under the new tax law: in words of one syllable / Bill Bresnan.
p. cm.
Bibliography: p.
Includes index.
ISBN 0-13-076472-8
1. Tax planning—United States—Popular works. I. Title.
II. Title: Tax planning under the new tax law.
KF6297.Z9B67 1987
343.7304—dc19
[347.3034]

Editorial/production supervision
and interior design: Sophie Papanikolaou
Cover design: Lundgren Graphics, Ltd.
Manufacturing buyer: Richard Washburn
Cover photo by Laima Druskis

This book is part of the Prentice-Hall/Institute of Certified Financial Planners Educational Foundation Series.

The publisher offers discounts on this book when ordered in bulk quantities. For more information, write:
Special Sales/College Marketing
Prentice Hall
College Technical and Reference Division
Englewood Cliffs, NJ 07632

Printed in the United States of America
10 9 8 7 6 5 4 3 2 1

ISBN 0-13-076472-8 025

Prentice-Hall International (UK) Limited, *London*
Prentice-Hall of Australia Pty. Limited, *Sydney*
Prentice-Hall Canada Inc., *Toronto*
Prentice-Hall Hispanoamericana, S.A., *Mexico*
Prentice-Hall of India Private Limited, *New Delhi*
Prentice-Hall of Japan, Inc., *Tokyo*
Simon & Schuster Asia Pte. Ltd., *Singapore*
Editora Prentice-Hall do Brasil, Ltda., *Rio de Janeiro*

Dedication

I dedicate this book to my wife, Kris.
Without her love, help, and encouragement
I would be unable to accomplish anything.

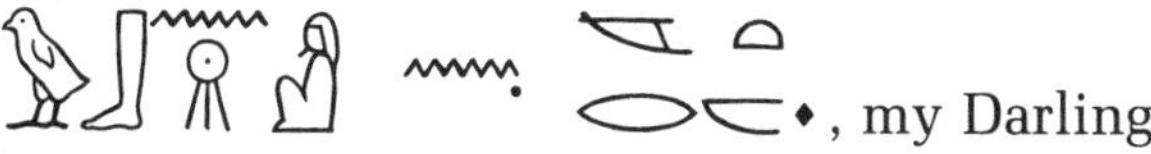, my Darling

XXXX ∞

Contents

SECTION I YOUR INCOME TAX UNDER THE NEW TAX LAW: THE LONG AND THE SHORT OF IT

SECTION II INVESTING UNDER THE NEW TAX LAW: MINIMIZING YOUR TAX BURDEN WHILE MAXIMIZING YOUR PROFITS

SECTION III EVERYTHING ELSE UNDER THE NEW TAX LAW . . . IN WORDS OF ONE SYLLABLE

Acknowledgments

During the more than two decades I spent in the financial community, as well as the years I spent teaching thousands of candidates to become licensed in that business, I was, quite frankly, a taker more than a giver. Each of those people who passed through my life left behind a little something, that when it is all added together, has become the author of this book.

Countless bits and pieces of the lore of Wall Street and the financial community were dropped into my hands by the owners, brokers, clerks, and others I worked directly and indirectly with on the "Street." The history and the rules of the game became a part of my being as a result of not only living it from day to day but of studying it in preparation for each class I conducted during that time. And, of course, as a result of living in such a highly-regulated environment I learned something that each of you can take into your own sphere . . . "If there are skeletons in the closet, leave the door open . . . " and when you make a mistake . . . "I did it . . . " not that mythical "they."

Following over five years in broadcasting my financial call-in show I can still say, in all honesty, that I'm still taking. Not only am I taking from those consummate professional fellow broadcasters I watch and listen to daily, but I am still taking from you, the audience.

Having acknowledged taking from those I've worked with would only be less than half the story. I have taken and taken from my family as well. In my previous book, I have acknowledged my mother, Nancy, and my wife, Kris, for their immeasurable contributions to my life and my being. I would like to add my two aunts, Dot and Babe, and thank them for a lifetime of encouragement, support, and that constant "nudge" that they always repeated, "You can do anything you really want to do." Without all of them I certainly wouldn't be where I am today.

In writing this series of books, I have drawn on the talents of both my editor, Jeff Krames, and production editor, Sophie Papanikolaou. They have not just drawn it all out of my head and mind but given it shape, purpose, and direction as well. I have said before and I'll say it again, "From the very first day we met, Jeff 'knew' that I was not to write just one book but at least as many as seven . . . " and he will drag each and every word out of me even if he has to employ every tool in his father's shop!

Introduction

"Anyone may so arrange his affairs that his taxes shall be as low as possible; he is not bound to choose the pattern which will best pay the treasury."

Judge Learned Hand

By the time this book is published and in the hands of the reading public, I will have conducted some 1,750 radio programs on which more than 25,000 listeners will have asked questions about their money. So far virtually every question has dealt with taxes in one form or another, and there is no reason to think that future questions will be any different.

The purpose of this book is to show you, by using real-life examples, that it is possible substantially to reduce your tax burden.

I like to use the example of many families and how they plan their two-week vacation:

Do we fly Delta, American, Pan Am, or which other airline?

Do we sit by the window or on the aisle?

Do we fly smoking or non-smoking?

Do we have the "mystery chicken" served to all passengers or do we order the "seafood meal," the "dietetic," or the "diabetic meal"?

Is the hotel on the ocean?

Does our room face the parking lot or the sunset view?

If you add up all the time and energy devoted to this process, and compare it to taking that shoebox full of receipts and tax records to your accountant on April 13 or 14, you see my point: Most people devote time and energy to anything and everything *but* using the maximum number of the tax rules to reduce their tax burden.

As I have often said, "The difference between most people and those who are rich isn't the amount of money they have but that they want to be rich and you don't." Simply put, the rich work every day at being rich, and you don't!

If you think that it is against the law to do everything in your power to be assessed the lowest tax, please carefully read this:

> "Anyone may so arrange his affairs that
> his taxes shall be as low as possible;
> he is not bound to choose the pattern
> which will best pay the treasury."
>
> Judge Learned Hand

In 1934, in a decision in the United States Court of Appeals, Judge Learned Hand said that we are under no legal, moral, or patriotic obligation to pay one cent more in taxes than we have to.

But keep in mind that you must do more than you ever did before to find out which rules apply to you and how best to use them. This book will deal with everyday situations facing the ordinary taxpayer, and will outline, in simple language, some solutions. This is not a technical discussion of the tax laws but a conversation with you, in words of one syllable, on how to lower your taxes and thereby achieve financial security and peace of mind.

To help you understand some of the terminology used in the world of taxation, a glossary is included. You will also find a section entitled "Do-It-Yourself Guides, Self-Help Workbooks, Handbooks, Answer Books, and Resources to Help You Prepare Your Own Tax Returns." It will help you to work out rough numbers and amounts before going to your Certified Public Accountant or tax preparer. It may even enable you to fill out the final tax returns on your own, if no unusual financial events have occurred within the last year. In any event, it is strongly suggested that every taxpayer consult a professional before filing his or her returns for 1987 and for those years' returns that will be most affected by tax reform.

AUTHOR'S NOTE

This book was written to make the subject of tax planning understandable to the layperson. The world of taxes and taxation is highly complicated and technical. It is essential that you consult your own Certified Financial Planner, Certified Public Accountant, or other tax expert to learn how the tax laws apply to your specific financial circumstances.

1

Testing Your NTLIQ (New Tax Law Intelligence Quotient)

A wise person once said that the only sure things in life are death and taxes. Thanks to The Tax Reform Act of 1986, only death is now for sure—taxes have become a "definite maybe." We still have to pay taxes, but some of the rules governing the way in which we pay taxes have dramatically changed. The goal of this book is to familiarize you with the new tax law so that you can learn which new rules will affect the filing of your future tax returns, and to help you transform this knowledge into a personal tax strategy that will reduce your tax burden in years to come.

Before you embark on your long journey down "New Tax-Law Lane," it is important to know how much you really understand about tax reform and its effect on your 1987 and 1988 returns. You will soon learn that Uncle Sam has scrambled the tax laws, and that many of the old rules no longer apply. Many of the deductions and exclusions allowed in 1986 are no longer allowed, and many others are being phased out. For example, the rules concerning the treatment of capital gains and the deductibility of IRAs are now severely restrictive; the tax advantages associated with limited partnerships (tax-shelters) and with income-producing properties have also been reduced; and perhaps most significantly, you are probably going to end up in a brand-new tax bracket, paying a different percentage of tax in 1987 and 1988 from what you paid in previous years.

At this point you may be asking yourself, "How much do I really know and understand about tax reform? Will I pay less tax under the new law? Are tax shelters gone forever?" These are all good questions, and will be answered in later chapters. Before planning this year's tax strategy, you must find out how much you know about The Tax Reform Act of 1986. Even if you retain a cracker-jack accountant, you should still have a basic understanding of the new tax law and its effect on your return. The informed taxpayer almost always pays less tax than the ignorant one (assuming similar incomes).

You can probably remember one teacher in school who insisted on giving a test the very first day of school. Well, I know I'm going to hate myself for this in the morning, but, that's right, it's quiz time. So find a hard pencil and a soft chair, kick off your shoes, and get ready for a tax quiz. I know you hate the thought of taking a test on the new tax law, but remember, only by finding out how much you know can you begin to improve your NTLIQ, New Tax Law Intelligence Quotient. It's a multiple choice exam, so if you get stuck on any one question, guess, and go on to the next question (it worked for me in college). Consider this a brief quiz; there will be a much longer one at the end of the book.

NTLIQ: NEW TAX LAW INTELLIGENCE QUIZ

1. A single adult, having a taxable income of $25,000 in 1987, would have a marginal tax rate of:
(a) 15%
(b) 28%
(c) 35%
(d) 38.5%

2. A married couple, filing jointly and with a taxable combined income of $40,000 in 1987, would have a marginal tax rate of:
(a) 15%
(b) 28%
(c) 35%
(d) 38.5%

3. Which of the following statements is true concerning Uncle Sam's treatment of short-term and long-term capital gains under the new tax law:
(a) The laws concerning capital gains have not changed.

- **(b)** Only those laws concerning short-term capital gains have changed.
- **(c)** In 1987 and 1988 there will no longer be made a distinction between short-term and long-term capital gains.
- **(d)** You may still write off a long-term capital loss of as much as $5,000.
- **(e)** none of the above.

4. Now that the new tax law is in effect, which statement regarding the deductibility of monies placed in IRA accounts is true?

- **(a)** To everyone's relief, Uncle Sam has not altered the tax on IRAs. All monies contributed to IRA accounts are still fully deductible.
- **(b)** Singles earning less than $25,000 *may not* take a full IRA deduction.
- **(c)** Couples earning less than $40,000 *may* still take a full IRA deduction in 1987.
- **(d)** Income levels have nothing to do with the deductibility of IRAs in 1987 and 1988.

5. Which of the following statements concerning deduction of medical expenses is true under the new tax law?

- **(a)** Uncle Sam has not changed the tax treatment of medical expenses. You may still deduct the total amount in excess of 5% of your adjusted gross income.
- **(b)** You may now deduct *all* of your medical expenses.
- **(c)** You may deduct only the amount of medical expenses in excess of 7.5% of your adjusted gross income.
- **(d)** You may deduct only the amount of medical expenses in excess of 10% of your adjusted gross income.

6. Under tax reform, the deductibility of consumer interest (interest on a car loan, credit card debt, installment loan and the like):

- **(a)** has not changed.
- **(b)** has been completely done away with.
- **(c)** will be phased out so that only 65% of consumer interest will be allowed in 1987 and 40% in 1988.
- **(d)** none of the above.

7. Now that the new tax law is in effect, which statement regarding the deductibility of monies placed in IRA accounts is true?
   (a) The new tax law has not affected the tax treatment of IRAs.
   (b) Single adults earning less than $40,000 may still take full deduction for an IRA.
   (c) Married couples, filing jointly and earning less than $50,000 per year, may still take full deduction for an IRA.
   (d) Single taxpayers earning $30,000 in 1987 will lose some of the deduction previously allowed.
8. If your total interest on consumer debt is $2,000 in 1987, you may deduct:
   (a) $2,000.
   (b) $1,500.
   (c) $1,300.
   (d) nothing, since deductions for consumer debt have disappeared under the new tax law.
9. If your total interest on consumer debt is $2,000 in 1988, you may deduct:
   (a) $2,000.
   (b) $1,200.
   (c) $800.
   (d) nothing, since you may no longer deduct interest on consumer debt.
10. Under tax reform, which of the following is true?
   (a) You may deduct no more than 30% of the interest on any home improvement loan.
   (b) You may deduct the interest on a home improvement loan only up to the cost basis.
   (c) You may deduct no more than 60% of the interest associated with a home improvement loan in 1987, and no more than 40% in 1988.
   (d) Deducting any of the interest on a home improvement loan will result in a minimum jail sentence of ten years.

11. Which of the following statements regarding capital gains is true?
   (a) Before the new tax law went into effect, 90% of all long-term capital gains were tax-free.
   (b) Before tax reform, the maximum effective tax rate on long-term capital gains was 25%.
   (c) From 1987 onward, all capital gains will be taxed as ordinary income.
   (d) In 1988, the maximum tax rate for a married couple realizing a long-term capital gain will be 33%.

12. Under the new tax law, the interest being earned on CDs (Certificates of Deposit) in 1987 is:
   (a) tax-free.
   (b) taxed at a maximum rate of 38.5%.
   (c) taxed as ordinary income.
   (d) both b and c.

13. Under the new tax law, the gains realized from the sale of a rare stamp collection will be:
   (a) tax-free in 1987.
   (b) taxed at a maximum rate of 38.5% in 1987.
   (c) taxed at a maximum rate of 28% in 1987 (assuming that the stamp collection was held for more than six months).
   (d) none of the above.

14. Under tax reform, the income earned on United States Treasury Bonds is:
   (a) tax-free.
   (b) subject to federal income taxes.
   (c) subject to state and local income taxes.
   (d) both b and c.

15. Which of the following statements regarding interest expense on securities held in margin accounts is false?
   (a) Before tax reform, only 50% of the interest expense on securities held in margin accounts was deductible.
   (b) Before tax reform, all the interest on securities held in margin accounts was fully deductible.

(c) Under the new tax law, the income from an investment is a major factor in determining how much of the interest on that security is deductible.
(d) The new tax law has cut down on the amount of interest you may deduct in 1987 and 1988.

The answers to the quiz follow this section. If you answered 12 or more questions correctly, you already have a good grasp of the new tax law; if you answered ten or more correctly, your knowledge of the vital tax questions is above average. If you answered between five and nine questions correctly, you still have a way to go. If you answered fewer than five questions correctly, this book may be the best investment you have made this year. Remember that there is a full exam at the end of the book.

It's time to boost your NTLIQ, so read on.

ANSWERS TO THE NEW TAX LAW INTELLIGENCE TEST

1. C
2. C
3. E
4. C
5. C
6. C
7. D
8. C
9. C
10. B
11. C
12. D
13. C
14. C
15. C

Filing That Form 1040EZ

The easiest form to fill out and perhaps the least painful to submit is the IRS Form 1040EZ. Although this form is not for each and every taxpayer who is single, you should at the very least review who may use this form before either getting the longer forms or taking the time, and unnecessarily spending the money, to have prepared for you a return which you could easily have handled yourself.

You may use Form 1040EZ if:

A. Your filing status is single.
B. You do not claim exemptions for being 65 or over.
C. You do not claim any dependents.
D. Your taxable income is less than $50,000.
E. You received only wages, salaries, and tips, and your income from interest was $400 or less, and did not receive any dividends or capital gains.

If you may not use IRS Form 1040EZ because you can't fulfill all these conditions, you *must* use Form 1040A or Form 1040 instead.

We will do a step-by-step, line-by-line review of the model Form 1040EZ printed here.

Name and address. If you received this form as a part of your tax package, read the label attached and make any corrections needed. Affix the corrected label to the top of the form or carefully print in the information required. If you do use the label, be sure that the Social Security number printed on it is yours. If it is wrong, enter your correct Social Security number in the space provided.

Filing That Form 1040EZ

Department of the Treasury - Internal Revenue Service

Form **1040EZ** **Income Tax Return for Single filers with no dependents** (0) **1986** OMB No. 1545-0675

Name & address

Use the IRS mailing label. If you don't have one, please print.
If your address is different from the one shown on your 1985 return, check here ☐.

Please print your numbers like this.

1234567890

Your social security number

Print your name above (first, initial, last)

Present home address (number and street). (If you have a P.O. box, see instructions.)

City, town, or post office, state, and ZIP code

Presidential Election Campaign Fund
Do you want $1 of your tax to go to this fund? ▶

Report your income

1 Total wages, salaries, and tips. This should be shown in Box 10 of your W-2 form(s). (Attach your W-2 form(s).) 1

2 Interest income of $400 or less. If the total is more than $400, you cannot use Form 1040EZ. 2

Attach Copy B of Form(s) W-2 here

3 Add line 1 and line 2. This is your **adjusted gross income.** 3

4 Enter your cash charitable contributions. See the instructions for line 4 on the back of this form. 4

5 Subtract line 4 from line 3. 5

6 Amount of your personal exemption. 6 1 080 00

7 Subtract line 6 from line 5. If line 6 is larger than line 5, enter 0 on line 7. This is your **taxable income.** 7

Figure your tax

8 Enter your Federal income tax withheld. This should be shown in Box 9 of your W-2 form(s). 8

9 Use the **single** column in the tax table on pages 31-36 of the Form 1040A instruction booklet to find the **tax** on your taxable income on **line 7**. Enter the amount of tax. 9

Refund or amount you owe

Attach tax payment here

10 If line 8 is larger than line 9, subtract line 9 from line 8. Enter the **amount of your refund.** 10

11 If line 9 is larger than line 8, subtract line 8 from line 9. Enter the **amount you owe.** Attach check or money order for the full amount, payable to "Internal Revenue Service." 11

Sign your return

I have read this return. Under penalties of perjury, I declare that to the best of my knowledge and belief, the return is true, correct, and complete.

Your signature Date

For Privacy Act and Paperwork Reduction Act Notice, see page 41. Form **1040EZ** (1986)

Presidential Election Campaign Fund. You are under no legal, moral, ethical, nor patriotic compulsion to contribute ($1.00 of your tax) to this fund. Look in the mirror. Answer to no one but yourself, and then check yes or no.

Line 1. Look at Box 10 on your W-2 FORM and on Line 1 enter that amount (your total wages, salaries and tips—from two or more W-2 Forms if you had more than one job). Be sure to attach any and all W-2 Forms to the form you file.

Line 2. Add up all interest income received from banks, savings and loans, credit unions, and the like. (All such income should have been reported to the IRS already by those institutions who paid it to you, and they in turn should have sent you a copy of Form 1099-INT showing the amount of that interest.)

Note: If your interest income was more than $400 from the sources named, you may not use IRS Form 1040EZ.

Line 3. The sum of Lines 1 and 2 will equal your adjusted gross income. Remember, it is taxable income, *not* adjusted gross income, that must be less than $50,000 if you are going to be eligible to use Form 1040EZ.

Line 4. Any amounts that you gave to charity (cash, checks, or money orders written to qualified charitable organizations) *could have been* deducted here for 1986, but tax reform requires you to use Form 1040 Schedule A to take such deductions in 1987 and thereafter.

Line 5. Since the charitable contributions cannot be used if you file Form 1040 EZ, the amount on Line 5 will be the same amount that appears on Line 3.

Line 6: Every taxpayer is entitled to take a personal exemption allowance of $1,900. This allowance will be $1,950 for 1988 and $2,000 for 1989.

Line 7: By subtracting personal exemptions from adjusted gross income, you will arrive at "Taxable Income."

To figure your tax:

Line 8: Refer to your various W-2 forms and enter the total federal income taxes withheld. Be sure to add up all sums if you had more than one employer during the year. The IRS will figure your tax for you if you wish to go no further.

Line 9. Using the amount on Line 7, "Taxable Income," and the tax tables in the Appendix, figure your tax (assuming you don't want the IRS to do it for you) and enter the amount of tax on Line 9.

Line 10. If the amount of tax on Line 9 is less than the amount of withholding tax entered on Line 8, enter the amount of your refund, sign the return, mail it in, and wait for the refund check.

Line 11. If the amount of tax on Line 9 is greater than the amount of withholding taxes paid on Line 8, enter the amount you owe the IRS, make out a check to them for that amount, sign the return, and mail it in on or before April 15.

Since the 1987 Federal Income Tax forms were not yet available as this book was being written, when reviewing any of the forms included in this book, please refer to the following list of changes that became effective after 1986:

REPEALED PROVISIONS

The dividend exclusion of up to $100 per taxpayer.

The 60% deduction for capital gains. After 1986, capital gains will be taxed as ordinary income.

The deduction for contributions to an individual retirement account for certain taxpayers who also participate in a pension plan provided by their employer.

The deduction for non-mortgage (personal) interest expense. The deduction for personal interest will be phased out. You will be allowed to deduct:

65% of your personal interest expenses in 1987;
40% of your personal interest expenses in 1988;
20% of your personal interest expenses in 1989;
10% of your personal interest expenses in 1990.

No deduction may be taken after 1990.

The deduction for state and local sales taxes.

The deduction for married couples when both work.

The extra personal exemptions for age and blindness. These

special exemptions are replaced by a standard deduction.

The partial exclusion of unemployment compensation. Amounts received after 1986 will be fully taxable.

The exclusion for scholarships and fellowships granted after August 16, 1986 that are not used for tuition and related expenses, or that are received by grantees who are not candidates for degrees.

The income-averaging method of computing the tax.

The deduction for adoption expenses for children with special needs.

The credit for political contributions.

The installment method of reporting certain income.

The reserve method for figuring bad-debt deductions of taxpayers other than financial institutions.

The items on this list apply only to repealed provisions. Many provisions have been amended. Some of those changes have been discussed elsewhere in this book, and in the instructions, workbooks, handbooks, and other resources listed, as well as in publications available to your personal financial planner or tax advisor. Please refer to those sources as well.

3

Filing That Income Tax Return Under The New Tax Law: Helpful Hints That Even Your Accountant Won't Tell You!

In this exciting, fast-paced chapter, you will learn:

* How the repeal of the dividend exclusion will affect your 1987 and 1988 tax returns.
* How the new tax law has significantly changed the treatment of capital gains.
* How Uncle Sam has limited the tax advantages associated with limited partnerships and income-producing properties.
* How the new tax law has limited IRA deductions.
* How charitable contributions are affected by tax reform.

Since under tax reform you are playing by a new set of rules, it makes sense to review your tax return, line by line, and see how tax reform affects it. Before deciding whether you are better off filing the "EZ" Short Form or taking the time and engaging a professional to help you prepare the long form, go step by step through this chapter where the changes raise or lower your taxes.

More help is available from your federal income tax packet as well as from the many sources listed in Appendix E.*

Wages, salaries, tips, etc. This item has not changed. The federal government expects you to report *all* of the money you made. Our tax system is predicated on voluntary compliance, and if you intentionally mis-state, under state, or otherwise do not state the true figures representing your wages, salary, etc., you could be guilty of tax fraud.

*"Do-It-Yourself Guides, Self-Help Workbooks, Handbooks, Answer Books and Resources to Help You Prepare Your Own Tax Returns."

1987, SINGLE PERSON

If Taxable Income Exceeds	You Will Pay	. . . As Well As This Percentage of Income More Than Figure In Col. 1
-0-	-0-	11.0%
$ 1,800	$ 198	15.0%
$16,800	$ 2,448	28.0%
$27,000	$ 5,304	35.0%
$54,000	$14,754	38.5%

1988, SINGLE PERSON (ASSUMING ONE EXEMPTION)

If Taxable Income Exceeds	You Will Pay	. . . As Well As This Percentage of Income More Than Figure In Col. 1
-0-	-0-	15.0%
$ 17,850	$ 2,678	28.0%
$ 43,140	$ 9,759	33.0%
$100,480	$28,681	28.0%

1987, MARRIED PERSONS FILING JOINTLY

If Taxable Income Exceeds	You Will Pay	. . . As Well As This Percentage of Income More Than Figure In Col. 1
-0-	-0-	11.0%
$ 3,000	$ 330	15.0%
$28,000	$ 4,080	28.0%
$45,000	$ 8,840	35.0%
$90,000	$24,590	38.5%

1988, MARRIED PERSONS FILING JOINTLY (ASSUMING TWO EXEMPTIONS)

If Taxable Income Exceeds	You Will Pay	. . . As Well As This Percentage of Income More Than Figure In Col. 1
-0-	-0-	15.0%
$ 29,750	$ 4,463	28.0%
$ 71,900	$16,265	33.0%
$171,090	$48,997	28.0%

Interest income. This item has not changed, so far as you are concerned, but note that all those entities and institutions paying interest to you have to report it to the IRS. Since the IRS already knows (or at least their computers already know) that you received the interest, collection of tax on interest may be more certain in the future. Remember that if you make an interest-free loan, and your return is audited, and the IRS finds out about the loan, it may tax you *on the interest you should have earned on that loan,* and make you pay a penalty and interest as well.

Dividends. Under the old rules, you were eligible for the dividend exclusion against a portion of dividend income received. The dividend exclusion has been repealed, so for 1987 and 1988 at least, all dividend income must be reported. As with interest income, those paying you a dividend are required to report it to the IRS, so remember that they already know you got it!

Taxable capital gains (deductible losses). Tax reform has changed the rules that apply to capital gains and losses. Formerly, you added up all your long-term capital gains (those realized after an asset was held for six months and one day, or longer, and then sold at a profit) and subtracted all your long-term capital losses (the same holding period applied) and showed either a net long-term gain or a net long-term loss. Then, you added up all your short-term capital gains (those realized after an asset was held for less than six months and then sold at a profit) and subtracted all your short-term capital losses (the same holding period applied) and showed either a net short-term capital gain or a net short-term capital loss. At the end of this process, you had some combination of the following:

A. Net long-term capital gains.
B. Net long-term capital losses.
C. Net short-term capital gains.
D. Net short-term capital losses.

Before adding gains or subtracting losses under the old rules one more step had to be taken. If you had:

1. Net long-term capital gains: 60% of those gains was tax-free and 40% was taxed as ordinary income.
2. Net short-term capital gains: they were added to ordinary income and taxed accordingly.
3. Net long-term capital losses: up to $3,000 could be deducted from ordinary income, counting $2.00 of loss for every dollar deducted, up to the $3,000 limit. The excess or unused long-term capital losses could be carried forward year after year until used up. They retained their "flavor" and remained long-term losses each year that they were carried forward.
4. Net short-term capital losses: these losses could be deducted from ordinary income, dollar for dollar, up to a maximum deduction of $3,000. Any unused short-term capital losses could be carried forward and used in later years. As was the case with the long-term losses carried forward, the short-term capital losses were carried forward as short term.
5. Net long-term capital gains and net short-term capital losses, or any other combination of long-term and short-term gains and losses: the two items would be netted out and the result would retain the "flavor" of the larger. For example, if you had a net long-term capital gain of $5,000 and a net short-term capital loss of $3,500, the difference, $1,500, would be treated as a net long-term capital gain. Sixty percent of that gain, or $900, would be tax-free. The remaining 40% or $600, would have been added to ordinary income and taxed accordingly.

In 1988, under tax reform, there is no distinction between long-term and short-term gains or losses. Regardless of how much time elapses between the purchase and the sale of an asset, the entire amount of the gains and $3,000 of the losses will be entered on this line of your return. Of course, the unused losses above $3,000 used in 1987 would be carried forward and used in 1988, and in following years.

Income (or loss) from limited partnerships (tax shelters) or income-producing properties. When the government wanted to encourage investment in income properties and in other limited partnerships, you could subtract all your losses from income and substantially reduce, or in some cases even eliminate, the taxes due. Now no one gets off the hook and those advantages are severely limited. Before any deduction is allowed for "passive losses" from limited partnerships, those passive losses must be subtracted from the passive gains realized. Then, if there are still net passive losses left over, you must take into account the phase-out that tax reform has imposed. In 1987, 35% of those passive losses will be disallowed and in 1988, 60%.

If you own no limited partnerships but only income-producing rental property, you can take deductions for mortgage interest, expenses, and depreciation, up to $25,000, plus the amount of income from the property. These deductions may be taken if your adjusted gross income for 1987 and for 1988 is under $100,000. Any amounts that are not deducted here may be treated as deductible losses subject to the same phase-out that applies to other losses. Sixty-five percent of such losses are deductible in 1987 and 40% will be in 1988. As your adjusted gross income climbs to over $100,000, that $25,000 deduction will slowly disappear. When your adjusted gross income exceeds $150,000, that deduction will be gone. Any passive losses used as a tax deduction should first be reviewed and calculated by your financial planner or tax advisor, because this is one area that the IRS will be interested in when considering whether to audit your return.

Other income is another section which has not been changed but which includes income that may have to be reported on schedules attached to your filing. Be sure to include:

1. Business income
2. Taxable income from pension and annuities
3. Income from Subchapter S Corporations

4. Farm income
5. Unemployment compensation
6. Recovery of a bad debt deducted in a prior year
7. Lottery, gaming, or related winnings
8. Social Security benefits
9. Recovery of medical expenses deducted in a prior year

The handbooks listed in the back of this book detail not only other forms of "Other Income" that must be added here but also describe the schedules that must also be attached.

Add up the following:

Wages, salaries, tips, etc.
Interest income
Dividends
Taxable gains (deductible losses)
Income from limited partnerships (tax shelters) minus losses
Income from investment properties minus losses
All other income

The sum—total income—sounds like a lot. You may think you are automatically in the highest tax bracket. But don't despair. You have many adjustments to income to make and deductions to take. It is here that expert help will make the biggest difference. The greater the deductions, the lower the taxable income and the lower the tax bracket. The greater the number of adjustments your accountant and financial planner can justify, the lower your income will be and the lower the tax bracket. Since you are expert at whatever it is you do for a living, ask someone who is expert in tax matters to handle your filing. I am probably the best example of this point. I have never looked under the hood of my car because I wouldn't know what should be there, much less how it worked. So I would go to you to have my car repaired or to have my children's teeth straightened or to have my plumbing unclogged. I therefore expect you to go to a tax expert for the help you need.

When you have calculated your total income, you can begin to make the following adjustments:

Employee business expenses. Check with your tax advisor and review the workbooks to determine which business expenses are deductible. Most of the business deductions you enjoyed in prior years will be treated as "miscellaneous deductions" and may be deducted only if they exceed 2% of your adjusted gross income. Therefore, the more adjustments you can justify under this section, the greater will be the effect of those deductions that are limited to the amount over 2% of adjusted gross income.

Deduction for the two-earner family. If yours was a two-earner family in 1986, one spouse earning $50,000 and the other $40,000, you were entitled to a deduction from gross income equal to 10% of the income of the lower-earning spouse. The maximum deduction was $3,000. Had the lower earner's income have been $25,000, the deduction would have been $2,500. Unfortunately, this deduction has been eliminated by the new tax law.

Keogh accounts. If in addition to your salary you also maintained another business (were self-employed), and it operated at a profit, substantial amounts of money could be salted away in a Keogh account. Those monies could not only be taken out of gross income, but could also be invested, tax deferred, until withdrawn after retirement. The new rules allow self-employed people who qualify to put as much as 20% of net business income into a Keogh account, up to a maximum of $30,000, even if they don't qualify for an IRA. (The new limitations will be discussed later.)

Before 1987, anyone who had earned income could put all of it, to a maximum of $2,000, into an IRA, and if married, $250 into the spousal account. All that has changed.

Beginning in 1987, the full IRA deduction may be taken if

the income for singles is less than $25,000 and less than $40,000 for married couples. Regardless of the amount of money earned by either a single person or a married couple, if they are not covered by a company retirement plan such as a pension, and are not putting money away in a Keogh, they would be allowed the full amount ($2,000 for a working spouse, $250 for a non-working spouse, $4,000 for a working couple) and be eligible to take the full deduction on those monies. If the single person makes more than $35,000, and the couple makes more than $50,000 and if either is covered by a company plan, then neither will be eligible to make tax-deductible deposits in those IRA accounts.

Note: See "IRA After Tax Reform: Don't Write Off That Deduction Yet" on page 51. Take a minute to add up:

Employee business expenses (Note: this will not go into effect until 1988)
Keogh savings (if any)
IRA savings (if any)
Alimony payments

The sum is the amount of adjustment you may make to total income to find adjusted gross income. That is simply total income minus adjustments. Even though adjusted gross income is much lower than total income, it still sounds like too much. But more can be taken off adjusted gross income before you arrive at taxable income. Now you can see why that professional is worth his or her tax-deductible fee. The fee paid in this case is a miscellaneous deduction, allowable if it exceeds 2% of adjusted gross income. The price of this book, as well as those listed in the bibliography and workbook section may also be deductible in the same way. Check with your personal advisor for the answer in your particular case.

Medical expenses. Of course you have kept and filed away records, receipts, canceled checks, and other supporting data for your medical expenses of the past year. Many of those expenses will be deductible and should be used in reducing the amount of your adjusted gross income.

The guides and workbooks mentioned will tell you the full range of deductible medical expenses; following are just a few:

Acupuncture
Alcoholism in-patient treatment
Back supports
Blood tests
Cardiographs
Chiropodist's fees
Contact lenses
Crutches
Eyeglasses
Hospital bills
Gynecologist's fees
Insulin
Metabolism tests
Oral surgery
Podiatrist's fees

Once you have figured the total dollar amount of your medical expenses, subtract 7.5% (formerly 5%) of adjusted gross income from that amount, and deduct what is left.

State and local taxes is one area that has not changed much under the new tax law. Itemized deductions for sales taxes are no longer allowed, *but* you may still deduct the following:

1. State and local income taxes
2. State and local personal property taxes
3. State and local real estate taxes

The deduction for real estate tax applies to both your principal residence and your second or vacation home. Of course, the deduction for the vacation home would be lost if it is rented out often enough to make the IRS look on it as a business property.

Your vacation home is considered a second home, for these purposes, if you use it at least 14 days per year or more than 10% of the time for which you rent it out, whichever is greater. To be absolutely certain that the full deduction may be taken and that the property cannot be classified as a rental property, let relatives or part-owners use it, as well as your own family. The more days of the year it is used this way, the less likely it will be to be classified as a rental unit. Why not keep a dated guest book in the foyer and have it signed by those in residence?

State and local sales taxes. State and local sales taxes are no longer deductible.

Mortgage interest. If you took out the mortgage against your principal residence before August 16, 1986, it doesn't matter whether the total amount borrowed is more than, the same as, or lower than your cost basis; all of the interest expenses on that mortgage remain fully deductible. The same applies to any home-equity financing done before that date (if you established a home-equity line of credit and didn't actually draw the money down before August 16, 1986, you didn't borrow the money and that rule would not apply). Home mortgages, mortgages against vacation homes, and home equity loans taken out after Aguust 16, 1986, will be deducted as follows:

A. Interest expenses are fully deductible for a mortgage, up to the cost basis of your principal residence (cost basis includes the purchase price, plus improvements, plus monies borrowed for necessary medical expenses, plus monies borrowed against the equity for education of your children).

B. Interest expenses are fully deductible for a mortgage and a home-equity loan against your principal residence, up to the cost basis (same conditions as in A.).

C. Interest expenses for a mortgage and/or home equity loan, up to the cost basis of your principal residence, are fully deductible. Interest expenses on monies borrowed above that cost basis, are deductible as consumer interest and will be phased out as follows:

65% is deductible in 1987.

40% is deductible in 1988.
20% is deductible in 1989.
10% is deductible in 1990.
No deduction may be taken for consumer interest beginning in 1991.

D. A mortgage held on a vacation home is treated as a mortgage on a second home and is deductible up to the cost basis.

Deductible interest (other than mortgage interest).

A. Consumer interest (interest on a car loan, credit card debt, college loans, installment loans, and the like) will be phased out:

1. 65% of consumer interest will be allowed in 1987.
2. 40% of consumer interest will be allowed in 1988.
3. 20% of consumer interest will be allowed in 1989.
4. 10% of consumer interest will be allowed in 1990.
5. No deduction for consumer interest will be allowed after 1990.

College *grants* are gifts and don't have to be repaid, much less repaid with interest.

B. Margin interest (monies borrowed to purchase securities or monies borrowed in a margin account against securities put up as collateral). For most people the interest expense will be offset by the income that the securities earn (the investment income) and no deduction may be taken, because, under the present rules, if you were to margin a security listed with the New York Stock Exchange, you may borrow only one-half the purchase price or one-half the market value. Clearly, if you are receiving dividend or interest income on all of the value, and are paying interest to borrow one-half of the value, the investment income minus the interest will probably equal either a wash or excess income. On the other hand, if the security pays a small dividend or yields little investment income and the margin interest exceeds that amount, the excess would be deducted as consumer interest, subject to the phase-out discussed in A.

C. Pre-paid interest. There are two schoools of thought regarding pre-paid interest. According to one, interest paid is interest paid and should be deductible, subject, of course, to the phase-out. Others hold that interest pre-paid may be deducted but that the deduction must be amortized over the life of the loan. Many people pre-paid interest in 1986 so as to be able to take the full deduction prior to tax reform. They may be audited, and if the IRS belongs to the second school of thought, it may exact a fine and a penalty.

Charitable contributions. This deduction will depend on whether or not you itemize your deductions beginning with 1987. If you don't itemize, the deduction will be lost. If you do itemize, you can deduct charitable contributions, but watch out for gifts of appreciated assets. If you give your favorite charity a stock that you bought years ago for $5,000 but which is now worth $10,000, the appreciated portion of that stock ($5,000) would have to be added back to your income, making you subject to the Alternative Minimum Tax. That is a flat tax of 21%. Furthermore, no gift to a non-profit organization that it cannot use for its non-profit activities will be allowed at all. Don't try to give Grandma's antique engagement ring to a non-profit educational foundation unless your accountant and financial planner have been consulted, both your regular and Alternative Minimum Tax have been computed, and the possible consequences have been considered carefully.

Miscellaneous expenses. The workbooks and resources listed at the end of this book will tell you of the many miscellaneous deductions that may be taken. Some of them are:

1. Adoption expenses
2. Education expenses
3. Employee business expenses
4. Investment expenses

5. Job-hunting expenses
6. Legal expenses
7. Professional and union dues
8. Tax preparation and advice and financial advice
9. Tools and equipment
10. Uniforms

Under the new rules, your deduction for miscellaneous items may be taken only if their cost exceeds 2% of your adjusted gross income.

Casualty losses. (These losses include those by theft.) Before taking this deduction at all, you must make a claim against any insurance you have to cover such losses. Then, the deduction will be for losses exceeding 10% of your adjusted gross income—after you were reimbursed by your insurance carrier, if any.

The sum of the following items will now be labeled Total Itemized Deductions. This figure is what will be added to your personal exemptions, and later subtracted from adjusted gross income, unless you take the standard deduction instead.

Medical expenses
State and local taxes
Mortgage interest expenses
Deductible interest expenses (other than mortgage interest)
Charitable contributions
Miscellaneous expenses
Casualty losses (including theft)

The following list of standard deductions will help you determine which, the Total Itemized Deduction or the standard deduction, will be to your greater advantage:

STANDARD DEDUCTIONS

	Single Taxpayer	Married Couple Filing Jointly
1987	$2,570	$3,800
1988	$3,000	$5,000

For both 1987 and 1988, if you are over 65 or are blind, you would take the standard deduction of $3,000 as a single taxpayer, plus $750 and $5,000 as a married couple filing jointly, plus $600. Otherwise you would use the higher itemized deductions if they result in the lower tax and are more than the standard deductions (shown above).

One more item remains to be considered before figuring that all-important amount known as taxable income: your personal exemptions. You are entitled to take an exemption for yourself, your spouse, and your dependents. The following is a list of relatives who would pass the "member of household" or "relationship" test:

You, the taxpayer, and your spouse
Your sons and daughters and their descendants
Your parents and their ancestors
Your aunts and uncles
Your step-brothers and step-sisters
Your brothers and sisters
Your nieces and nephews
Your step-father and step-mother
Your father-in-law and mother-in-law
Your brother-in-law and sister-in-law
Your son-in-law and daughter-in-law
Your step-son and step-daughter

In addition to the member-of-household and relationship tests, there are four other tests that must be passed before you can claim someone as an exemption.

Gross-income test. Your child who is under the age of 19 years or who is a full-time student (of any age) need not qualify under the gross-income test. "Your child" includes any of the following:

Your son
Your step-son
Your daughter
Your step-daughter
A legally adopted child
A foster child who lived with you all year

If you wish to take as an exemption a dependent who is not "your child," his or her gross taxable income must not exceed $1,900 in 1987, $1,950 in 1988, or $2,000 in 1989.

Citizenship test. Your dependents must be citizens of the United States, resident or national; be residents of Canada or Mexico for part of the year; or be citizens of Puerto Rico. Children are considered citizens of the parent's country.

Support test. During the tax year in question, you must have provided more than 50% of the dependent's total support. "Total support" is made up of the following items:

1. Expenses paid for that dependent
2. A share of the expenses paid for the entire household lived in (used) by that dependent
3. A share of the fair rental value of property occupied by you and that dependent

What happens when two or three adult children contribute to the support of an elderly parent but none contributes 50% or more? Even though you may have contributed less than 50% of that support, you may be able to take the parent as an exemption. By using IRS Form 2120, Multiple Support Declaration Form, one of the adult children may take the exemption one year, another the following year, and so on.

Joint return test. Even though you may have provided 50% of the support of a newly-married daughter, if she files a joint return with her new husband you have lost her as an exemption.

In summary, if a person passes the following five tests you may claim an exemption of $1,900 for each dependant in 1987, $1,950 in 1988, and $2,000 in 1989, this of course in addition to the $1,900 claimed for yourself and your spouse in 1987, the $1,950 each in 1988, and the $2,000 in 1989:

1. "Membership of household" or "relationship" test
2. Gross-income test
3. Support test
4. Citizenship test
5. Joint-return test

Now you have sufficient information to be able to calculate your taxable income.

	Total income
MINUS	(Adjustments to income)
EQUALS	Adjusted gross income
MINUS	(Total itemized deductions)
MINUS	(Exemptions)
EQUALS	Taxable income

In 1987, if your taxable income is more than $27,000 for a single taxpayer or $45,000 for a married couple filing a joint return, take 28% of net long-term capital gains (refer to the fourth item under Income) and subtract that amount from taxable income. The result is the figure to use to compute your tax.

If the amount of taxable income minus the capital gains tax in 1987 is $50,000 and you are a married couple filing a joint return, look up your tax on the tax table given earlier in this chapter. To compute the tax, follow down the column marked "If taxable income exceeds: " to "$45,000." If your taxable income is more than $45,000, the tax due is $8,840 plus 35% of the excess over $45,000. Thirty-five percent of the excess amount of $5,000 is $1,750. Simply add that $1,750 to $8,840 and to that sum add the special capital gains tax, and you will arrive at your tax.

Is this the amount of the check you must make out to Uncle Sam? Probably not! First of all, you have probably already made some payments and you are probably eligible for some tax credits as well. As a salaried employee, a certain portion of your pay has been withheld each week; a quick look at the federal income taxes withheld on your W-2 Form will ease the pain. If you used a tax preparer last year, or a financial planner, in all probability he or she recommended amounts to be withheld each week that would pretty well equal your tax bill. You may even have made quarterly estimated payments, and the combination of these two items could cover or at least substantially reduce your tax due. In any event, a look at all the tax credits available may lower your tax this year and aid in future planning after your first consultation with a professional.

The following credits, if you are eligible for them, will reduce the tax you must pay. The reductions are to be subtracted from the tax due, computed earlier:

Form 2441. Credit for child and dependent care expenses.

Schedule R. Credit for the elderly and permanently and totally disabled.

Form 5695. Residential energy credit.

Political contributions. This credit could be taken through 1986 but no longer.

Form 1116. Foreign tax credit.

General business credit. This credit may be taken by taxpayers required to file one or more of the following forms:

Form 3800
Form 3468
Form 5884
Form 6478

Handbooks and workboks listed at the back of this book give line-by-line instructions regarding all these items and the applicable forms and schedules. Be sure to mark those sections that discuss the forms and schedules covering payments made against the tax due. But you may already have covered that tax due with a combination of credits and payments.

Payments made could have come from any of the following:

1. Federal income taxes withheld
2. 1987 estimated tax payments and amounts applied from your 1986 return
3. Earned-income credit
4. Amounts paid by Form 4868
5. Excess Social Security tax and Railroad Retirement Act tax withheld (if you had two or more employers)
6. Credit for federal tax on gasoline and special fuels (Attach Form 4136.)
7. Regulated investment company credit (Attach Form 2439.)

Note: When preparing payments make sure that the following forms are attached to this section of your return:

Form W-2
Form W-2G
Form W-2P

At this point you are ready to fill in the final figure on your return. By taking your tax due before credits and payments and subtracting all of those items listed, you will arrive at your tax.

If your tax exceeds your payments, the balance due must be enclosed with the tax return you file. If your payments exceed your tax, you are entitled to file for a refund. You may either be issued that refund check, or instruct the IRS to keep all or part of it and apply it to next year's estimated tax.

It has been suggested that if you cannot pay the tax due at the same time you file your return, that you file the return anyway to avoid any late-filing penalty and let the IRS get in touch with you later. You will be charged interest on the unpaid amount. If there exists a true hardship you may request a meeting with the IRS, explain the problem, answer their questions concerning your financial hardship or other related factors, and perhaps negotiate a manageable schedule of payments (with interest added, of course). Don't think that this schedule of installment payments is available just because you feel like extending the payments over the next year or so. You have to prove to the satisfaction of the IRS that you cannot pay the amount due. You must also declare how much you can afford to pay and the IRS will accept or reject a payment plan.

Suppose that the refund you just calculated amounted to a few thousand dollars. Should you be patting yourself on the back? Absolutely not! That refund is a signal to you that some serious tax and financial planning is needed. (See Chapter 9 on "How to Find and Choose that Tax or Financial Professional.") If I were to ask you to lend me those thousands of dollars at *no interest* you would certainly have refused, but didn't you lend it to Uncle Sam *at no interest* over the last year or more? You actually started making that loan in January when the monies were withheld from your salary, and you have continued to do so not through December, not through April of the next year, but until that refund check arrives at your mailbox. That could be in June, July, or even August of the following year.

Do everything you can by using all of the resources discussed here to plan ahead and minimize that *interest-free* loan to the Government. Once the amount of that projected refund is known, go to your employer, change your W-4 withholding, and get that money every week in your pay envelope. And, if you are afraid of spending it because it was added to your take-home pay, let your employer deduct the added amounts from your check and *lend it back to the government,* but this time *at interest.* The easiest way to loan money back to the Government is to use your company's payroll deduction plan to purchase savings bonds.

Just look at the results. If you get that big refund in the summer of the following year, you have wasted as much as 18 months during which it could have been earning interest for you. Suppose that that extra $50 per paycheck (a pro-rata estimate of the added take-home pay you could expect instead of a refund of $2,500 or so in June) had been deducted by your employer and used to purchase a $100 Series EE savings bond every week. At the end of the year—December, not June of the following year—you would have $5,000 face value of bonds and would be receiving interest since the first week of January. And you would have accomplished all the following:

1. The government would still have the use of the money. Your patriotism would be intact.
2. Your investment would be as safe as it could be. The U.S. Government Series EE bonds are guaranteed by the full faith and credit of the United States Government. That is backed by their power to print money.
3. You would be earning interest on the money instead of having lent it out interest-free.
4. You would have a degree of liquidity where there was none before. After the first six months, you could cash in the bonds, collect any interest accrued, and spend the money.

There is one disadvantage that should be pointed out. These bonds would have to be redeemed to get at the money. Banks and other lenders do not accept Series EE bonds as collateral against loans—hardly a serious disadvantage but one that should be noted.

Should you be entitled to a refund this year and want to use the money before the IRS returns it to you, you might want to consider putting up your refund, soon to be received, as collateral for a loan that could be liquid today. Of course this will be only for this year. After you have read this book and used the techniques I outline, you will have the monies in your hands all along!

TAX FACTS TO REMEMBER UNDER THE NEW TAX LAW . . . in words of one syllable

1. The reporting of wages, salaries, and tips have not changed under tax reform.
2. The dividend exclusion has been repealed so that all dividend income must be reported in 1987 and in 1988.

3. The tax treatment of capital gains has dramatically changed; keep in mind that after 1987 the IRS no longer distinguishes between a long-term and short-term capital gain and loss.
4. The tax treatment of income (or loss) from limited partnerships (a.k.a. tax shelters) and income-producing properties has changed. Uncle Sam has severely curtailed the tax advantages associated with these investment vehicles.
5. Most of the business deductions taken in prior years will now be treated as "miscellaneous deductions," and only the amount in excess of 2% of adjusted gross income may be deducted.
6. The treatment of IRA deductions is significantly different. Now the eligibility for IRA deductions is dependent upon income level and in some cases your company's retirement plan.
7. The deductibility of medical expenses has changed. Now you can deduct only the amount of medical expense in excess of 7.5% of your adjusted gross income.
8. State and local sales taxes are no longer deductible.
9. If you do not itemize, you are not permitted to deduct any charitable contributions.
10. Remember that a large tax refund is not necessarily a good thing, but should be interpreted as a signal that thorough tax and financial planning is needed. A large tax refund means you are letting Uncle Sam play with your money *at no charge*! This money could have been invested in Series EE savings bonds or another interest-bearing investment vehicle.

4

Those Capital Gains Under Tax Reform: Don't Sell All Your Stocks And Bonds Just Because Uncle Sam Changes A Couple Of Rules

In this chapter, I discuss:

* How the new tax law affects your investments in stocks and bonds.
* How in 1988 and beyond all capital gains are now the same in the eyes of Uncle Sam.
* How the use of stop-loss orders can maximize your stock market profits and help minimize your losses.
* How the new tax law limits your deductions of interest associated with stock market margin accounts.
* How the new tax law affects the deductibility of charitable contributions.
* How the purchasing of municipal and savings bonds can help defer taxes in the future.

It used to be that the tax treatment of long-term capital gains was so favorable that investors actually waited out the year before selling appreciated securities. Then, the highest effective tax rate on long-term capital gains was limited to 20%, while income could be taxed at a rate as high as 50%. Those gains will now all be considered the same, for there is no longer a distinction between long-term, securities held six months and one day or longer, and short-term, securities held less than six months. All capital gains will be taxed at the rate of 28% in 1987 and as ordinary income from 1988 on out. Nineteen eighty-seven is the transitional year during which long-term gains will be taxed at the rate of 28% even if the taxpayer is in the 33% bracket or the 38.5% bracket. From 1988 until the next Tax Reform Act, all gains will be treated as ordinary income. From 1988 onwards, the highest rate could be as much as 33%.

What do you have to do to make money in the stock market? Do you keep those appreciated shares? Do you sell growth stocks and keep income stocks? Should you consider giving away appreciated securities?

For those of you who own stocks that have gone up in value, simply to sell them because the tax laws have been changed would be shortsighted, to say the least. First of all, no security should be sold before its time. If that sounds like a wine commercial, it should. If the wine isn't ready to drink, leave it in the cellar. If the stock hasn't done what you bought it to do, keep it, regardless of what happens to the tax laws.

Any investment can do only one of three things:

1. It can go up in value.
2. It can remain at its present value.
3. It can go down in value.

Suppose you bought a stock for growth and the company didn't grow. You would sell it and make another choice. If you bought a stock for appreciation and its price didn't go up, you would sell it and seek another. If you bought a stock for income and the board of directors discontinued the payment of dividends, you would sell it and buy another. None of these events has any bearing on the tax laws. But, if that same stock performed as you hoped, would you sell it? Maybe not.

Since no one knows just where the top is in the price or value of any investment, anyone who sells at the top does so only by accident, so the best you can hope for is to be as close to the top as possible.

The use of stop-loss orders is perhaps the one instrument or technique that assures an investor of getting as close to that top price as is reasonable to expect. The technique is really quite simple use.

Let's assume that you bought a stock at $25 per share and that that stock was listed on the New York Stock Exchange. As soon as you buy it, you decide how much of that $2,500 investment you are ready to lose. The price below which we can't stand to watch the value of our investments fall will be different for everyone. Although no one is ready to lose his or her entire investment, most people can tolerate a loss of 10% of any monies invested. (Of course your risk-tolerance level may be a lot higher than 10% or you may have more capital you can afford to lose. If so, your stop-loss orders will be further below the current market price of the stocks.)

In the case of a $25 purchase, a stop-loss order would be entered through your local brokerage house to sell that stock at $22½ G.T.C. (Good Till Canceled). What you have done is effectively stopped the losses on this investment if the stock falls to $22½ per share or if the value of your original $2,500 investment drops to $2,250. Should this be a stock you have owned for years and it cost you only $15 per share, that stop-loss order really becomes a "lock-in-the-gains order." The difference between your cost of $1,500 and the stopped price of $2,250 would lock in your gain of $750.

If the stock market trend goes lower, the stop price is not changed and remains in G.T.C., but if the market goes up and your stock appreciates in value, continue to upgrade that stop-loss order, daily, if necessary, to keep pace with the market. On a day when the stock goes from $25 per share to $27 per share, call your brokerage house and cancel the old stop-loss order at $22½ G.T.C. and enter a new one at $24½ and so on as the market moves up. Now, should the activity of the market be such that you have to sell that stock, consider the consequences to your tax.

During the balance of 1987, a stock held longer than six months and one day would result in a long-term gain that would be taxed at the rate of 28%. In 1988, regardless of the holding period of the securities, the difference between the cost price and the selling price (a gain) would be treated as ordinary income and could be taxed at a rate as high as 33%.

While you are waiting for those stop-loss orders either to stop your losses or to lock in your gains, the securities should be at work. There have been a few changes in the rules concerning borrowing against a security held in a margin account.

Before tax reform, the interest expense on securities held in margin accounts was fully deductible. Since tax reform, the amount of interest paid is first deducted from the investment income earned on the securities. The balance is treated as consumer interest subject to the phase-out discussed earlier. As long as the borrowed funds are working hard enough to recover the cost of borrowing them, they should be used. Again, leverage is probably your best bet. If you have $100,000 worth of securities in your margin account, you borrow $50,000 at the broker's loan rate plus 1½ percent, and you can put that $50,000 down on a piece of income-producing property, it pays to do so.

The $50,000 margin loan could cost you 9% interest annually. (No monthly payments are necessary against a margin loan, the interest simply being added onto the loan balance and repaid at the time the margined securities are sold.) With that down payment you were able to purchase a $150,000 piece of income-producing property at a flat cash flow. If the property has an 8% growth rate, it is appreciating by $12,000 per year on the average, while the loan is costing some $4,500 per year with some deduction to be taken. The $12,000 average annual appreciation is not taxed unless and until the property is sold; then it will be taxed at the rates prevailing, 28% top rate for the balance of 1987 and 33% top rate from 1988 until further notice.

The issue of keeping income stocks and selling growth stocks under tax reform, again, has to do with the treatment. If you keep an income stock and it is going up in price year in and year out, you will be taxed only on the income as received and can postpone paying the tax on the appreciation as long as you wish. But if you trade in the growth stock, which pays a small dividend, or none, you are immediately liable for a tax on both the small dividend received and the appreciation realized. In the first case, you keep the paper profit untaxed and pay a tax only on the income.

How about the notion of giving away appreciated assets so that the non-profit or charitable institution can receive the gain and you can get a tax deduction on the appreciated value? Maybe it should be that simple, but it isn't.

Under the old rules, if you bought an asset and it went up in value, you could give it away and in effect give away the gain. You could take a charitable deduction equal to the appreciated value of that asset. Under tax reform, you can still give away that appreciated asset, but watch out for the A.M.T. (Alternative Minimum Tax). The appreciation is added to your income in computing the A.M.T., a flat tax of 21% that assures that the well-to-do will pay their fair share. Furthermore, a gift of art, antiques, and collectibles could be disallowed entirely unless the gift is for a charitable purpose by the tax-exempt institution. Before you start giving away any appreciated assets, sit down with your CPA or financial planner and compute both your regular tax and the Alternative Minimum Tax. You may decide to keep that painting and give the charity cash instead.

One type of investment that could save you a lot of grief is a municipal bond bought at face value. But you have to make sure that the interest income is as free from tax as possible. The safest thing and your best bet would be to purchase general obligation bonds issued by the city in which you live.

Suppose you live in the City of New York and as a resident are subject to triple taxation. You file a federal return as well as a state and a city return. Your best bet would be a bond guaranteed by the full faith and credit of New York City (that means that the city can levy taxes to pay your interest and principal when due). It may have been issued two or three years ago and will mature (come due) in the year 2012. That would be a 25-year bond. If this bond were bought at par, that is, at face value, or 100 cents on the dollar, a $5,000 bond would cost $5,000. If it had a coupon of 8% that $5,000 bond would pay you semi-annual interest of $200 on which you would pay no federal, state, or city tax. For those now in the 33% tax bracket, that represents a federal taxable equivalent of 11.9%. In other words, you would have to earn 11.9% taxable interest to have 8% left over after a federal tax of 33% has been levied. It will obviously be a good deal more when the state and city levies are factored in. In addition to the rather high tax-free income from these bonds, you would also be free from any tax when the bonds mature (come due) in the year

2012. Since you purchased these bonds at par (their face value) and they mature at par (their face value), there is no difference between the purchase and the maturity value *to* tax.

I suggest that you use the whole world of municipal bond funds, unless you are planning to invest a minimum of $25,000 in five or more different municipal bond issues. A New Yorker might put together a portfolio like this: $5,000 in New York State General Obligation Bonds; $5,000 in New York State Power Authority Bonds; $5,000 in State of New York Urban Development Corporation Bonds; and $5,000 in Municipal Assistance Corporation Bonds. Investors elsewhere can put together their portfolios in a similar way.

The least-complicated investment anyone can make is in Savings Bonds. You know them as the old Series E or Series EE bonds that are bought at a discount from their face value and that go up in value every six months until maturity. Not only do these bonds have the guarantee of the full faith and credit of the federal government (that guarantee backed by the power to print money—nobody else can do that!), but they can be bought by anyone either through the payroll deduction plans at work or at any bank.

In addition to all of the above, any tax consequences which favor the small investor can be further enhanced by rolling over all income on the E and EE bonds. At maturity, the value of your savings bonds can be converted into another series of U.S. Government-guaranteed bonds known as the Series HH bonds. In this way all of the accrued interest earned on the older E and EE bonds, along with their purchase price, buys the same face value of the HH bonds. The HH bonds then pay semi-annual interest which *is* taxable, and pay their face value at maturity.

The zero coupon municipal bond is an investment that will be dealt with in a later chapter, but it carries far too many tax benefits to pass up. Since zero coupon municipal bonds ("zero munis") are suitable for the education funds started for small children, the benefits under tax reform will be covered in the section "Your Child's Education under Tax Reform."

TAX FACTS TO REMEMBER UNDER THE NEW TAX LAW . . . in words of one syllable

1. Under the "old" tax law, 60% of long-term capital gains (all gains held longer than six months and one day) were tax-free, and the remaining 40% of the gain was taxed as ordinary income. This ensured a maximum effective tax rate of 20% on long-term capital gains, while income could be taxed at a rate as high as 50%. In 1987, all capital gains will be taxed at a rate of 28%, regardless of tax bracket. In all years after 1987, all gains will be taxed as ordinary income.
2. Before tax reform, the interest expense on securities held in margin accounts was fully deductible. Now, in order to calculate the amount of deductible interest, you must deduct from the investment income earned by that security, the amount of interest paid. The balance is now treated as consumer interest, and the amount of that deductibility is being phased out as follows:

SCHEDULE FOR PHASING OUT CONSUMER INTEREST

Year	The Allowable Write-Off (%)
1987	65%
1988	40%
1989	20%
1990	10%
1991	-0-

By 1991, none of the interest expense associated with consumer debt will be deductible.

3. Before tax reform, you were allowed to take a charitable deduction equal to the appreciated value of an asset. Under the new tax law, the amount of the appreciation of that asset is added to your income, and Uncle Sam then calculates the A.M.T. (Alternative Minimum Tax), assuring that the well-to-do pay their fair share.

5

IRA After Tax Reform: Don't Write Off That Deduction Yet

In this fast-paced, information-packed chapter, you will learn:

* How the new tax laws have affected the deductibility of IRAs.
* How your company's pension plan may affect your deduction for monies paid into IRA accounts.
* How the new tax law has affected the deductibility of early withdrawals of IRAs.
* How putting your IRA money at some risk may substantially increase your retirement nest-egg.
* How mutual funds can be used to help build your retirement nest-egg.

Many people mistakenly think that under tax reform, Individual Retirement Accounts (a.k.a. IRAs) are dead. Nothing could be further from the truth, although the rules may have changed a bit. Some who could invest in IRAs in prior years and take a deduction may not be eligible for that deduction any longer. Some who could take a deduction in prior years may be eligible for only a partial deduction. And some who thought of the IRA as their only retirement fund will learn that it can be combined with others to make even more money available for those retirement years.

Before you learn about the many ways IRA monies can and should be invested, a quick review of the changes in rules may open your eyes.

A. Regardless of your income, if neither spouse is covered by a retirement plan elsewhere (Keogh Plan, company pension plan, or the like), you may deduct all of your IRA contributions (deposits) just as you could before tax reform.

B. If you are a married couple filing jointly and are covered by a company pension plan or Keogh, *and* your adjusted gross income is below $40,000, you may deduct all your IRA.

C. If you are single or a head of household and your adjusted gross income is less than $25,000, you may deduct all of your contributions.

D. If you are either single, or married and filing a joint return *and* your adjusted gross income falls into the following categories, you may no longer deduct IRA contributions:

1. A single taxpayer with adjusted gross income of between $25,000 and $35,000 would lose $10 of deduction for each $50 of income above $25,000.
2. A married couple filing a joint return, with adjusted gross income of between $40,000 and $50,000, would lose their deduction in the same manner as the single taxpayer, above. For each $50 above that $40,000 and up to the $50,000 limit earned, they would lose $10 of deduction as well.

E. Even if the monies contributed to the IRA couldn't be taken as a deduction, all income, dividends or gains realized in that account remain tax-deferred until withdrawn.

F. Withdrawals made before age 59½ are now subject to a two-tier tax.

1. Deductible contributions that have been tax-deferred are subject to ordinary income tax rates, plus a 10% tax penalty if withdrawn before you are age 59½.
2. Deductible contributions that have been combined with non-deductible contributions in the same account and that have grown in value would be taxed in proportion to the two amounts. If an early withdrawal were to be made from such an account that was ⅓ non-deductible contributions and ⅔ deductible contributions, the amount withdrawn would be taxed in the same proportions. The first ⅓ of the amount withdrawn would not be subject to

any tax since it was contributed from after-tax dollars. The second ⅔ would be fully taxed at that year's ordinary rate plus a 10 percent tax penalty, due to the withdrawal before you turn age 59½.

This schedule of withdrawal would of course apply to principal, withdrawn earnings, dividends, and gains on any monies in an IRA withdrawn as ordinary income, plus the 10% tax penalty if taken before you turn age 59½. It is suggested, if tax reform necessitates your dealing with both deductible and non-deductible monies, that you open a separate account for those non-deductible contributions.

G. Tax reform still allows the use of an IRA Rollover account for those monies that have been growing in a company or other retirement plan. If you leave a job and move on to another company, those monies that have accumulated for your retirement in the first company and that are eligible for the rollover can be rolled forward irrespective of the $2,000 yearly limitation, the $250 yearly spousal limitation, or the earnings limitations listed in B and C above.

With these rules in mind, you may ask, "Where is the money invested?" For those who have substantial sums in a company pension plan or a Keogh and have opted for a non-deductible IRA, you might want to consider this your "play money." Remember, you already have that company pension plan working, so this could be your risk portfolio. Even if put entirely at risk, this IRA portfolio would still grow, with the tax deferred; and you could do this at virtually any age. This means that if you took the entire account and put it into one of the following, and were right, the resulting gains would remain tax-deferred until withdrawn:

1. A growth-type mutual fund.
2. An aggressive growth-type mutual fund.
3. An emerging mutual fund.
4. An options fund.

5. An interest-rate options fund.
6. Individual stocks from the foregoing categories.
7. Penny stocks (under $5.00 per share).

If you are wrong, and the investments go against you, it was at-risk capital to begin with and you recognized and could afford the risk going in. If you are right, and the stocks or funds grow dramatically, those gains would not affect your tax situation because they would remain in the account and would be compounding until withdrawn at or after retirement, when your tax bracket should be your lowest. (Don't be surprised to see a few more versions of tax reform even if you are only a few years from retirement.)

The foregoing plan is great for those who have risk capital and who are covered under a company retirement or Keogh plan that is separate and apart from their non-deductible IRA account. But what if that is not the case for you? Suppose that you do fall into that category of those eligible for a deductible IRA and that that is your only retirement money apart from Social Security at age 62 or 65. Should you take that much risk? Should you treat your IRA account differently? The answer is a resounding *yes*! Using the following general age groups as a guide, you may want to consider patterning your IRA investments like this:

First job through age 35, single: A period of your financial life when risk-taking is OK. You probably still live at home and pay little or no rent. You probably have extra cash at the end of each week after paying your bills and putting something aside in savings. You certainly are free from responsibility, and time is on your side. For these and many other reasons, your IRA could be put in any of the seven areas of risk listed above. You could always make up losses out of extra earnings.

First job through age 35, married, starting a family: During this period of your financial life, accumulation, stability, nest-building, saving for the education of your children, and other obligations preclude your putting any substantial portion of your assets at risk, much less any of your accumulating retirement dollars. You have a mortgage to pay off; a car loan; perhaps credit-card debt; medical expenses; life insurance; and all those items that a family must consider before risk. In such a situation, you would be well advised to look at the following for your IRA accounts:

1. Blue-chip common-stock funds.
2. Billion-dollar diversified investment companies.
3. Common stocks issued by corporations that have been paying regular dividends for decades, such as Chrysler, General Motors, IBM, Sears, AT&T, and the like.
4. Balanced mutual funds (the portfolio balanced between common stocks and corporate bonds).
5. Individual United States Government Bonds or carefully watched U. S. Government Securities funds.

First job through age 35, married, no plans for family: In this case, the husband's IRA accound could be invested at risk as if single, and the wife's IRA account could be invested as if married and starting a family. In this way you would have the best of both worlds. If you were close in age, it wouldn't matter whose account was at risk. If one is older than the other, you might consider having the younger's account at risk and the older's account leaning toward the conservative.

Husband's Account	Wife's Account
Blue-chip common-stock funds.	Growth-type mutual funds.
Billion-dollar diversified investment companies.	Aggressive-growth-type mutual funds.
Blue chip individual common stocks.	Emerging-type mutual funds.
Balanced type mutual funds.	An options fund.
Individual U.S. Government bonds.	Interest-rate option funds.
	Individual growth or aggressive or emerging growth stocks.
	Penny stocks (under $5.00 per share).

Age 35 through 50, single: By this time you have been able to assess your skills as well as those of the professionals whose opinions you value. If you have a good record, and those areas of aggressive investment have produced the desired results, there is no reason not to continue along this path through your middle 50s. If you have been wrong, and both you and your financial professional have nothing but a history of losses, a new tack must be taken. That tack is to sail back to a pattern of conservativism. The portfolio outlined for the young married couple is the logical choice now.

Age 35 through 50, married with no plans for a family: Continue along the lines of the balanced portfolio of IRA investments started when you were younger. If by this time you have accumulated $50,000 to $75,000 in these accounts toward retirement, there would be nothing wrong with taking a risk occasionally. Perhaps the next year's contribution of $2,000 each could be put into a portfolio of stocks that have no earnings, pay no dividends, have no track record, but are in industries that weren't even around just five years ago. Maybe that $2,000 contribution for you could be invested entirely in stock-index futures and that of your spouse could go into 20,000 shares of a ten-cent stock from the Pink Sheets that could triple in value in a few months just as readily as it could disappear from the marketplace altogether.

Age 35 through 50, married with several children: This may be the only time during your financial life when you can be excused for skipping an IRA contribution. With all of your family responsibilities, and given the fact that you made the contributions while your family was in its early years, if the money is needed for a tuition payment or for books or other family necessities, a contribution skipped here and there will not cause you to live on dog food in retirement. Remain conservative, build principal, and re-invest dividends in the same funds or stocks that paid them inside the IRA account.

Note: If monies are put into an IRA on a regular basis by a husband alone and from time to time, whenever possible, by the spouse (working some years full-time, working some years part-time and not working at all some years); and the monies are working at an average of, say, 8% over a 30-year period, the couple can easily accumulate over a quarter of a million dollars for retirement, more, of course, if both can make the full $2,000 over that period. The key to remember if you fall into this age- and family-group is that you cannot afford to lose any of the money.

Over age 50, single, and until age 59½, 62 or even 65 and 70: You could begin to withdraw those IRA monies, without penalty, at age 59½ and might want to think of taking them out at age 62 (when you could also draw reduced Social Security), or at age 65 (when you would draw full Social Security). In each case the monies are not going to be used for their original purpose, your retirement income. Any contributions made during this period would be safest if invested in CDs (certificates of deposit) with maturity dates at age 59½, 62, 65, and 70. Should CDs not be available, United States Treasury Notes and United States Treasury Bonds are available to cover those years between 50 and 65 or 70. Since these treasury securities aren't always available in denominations to match the monies in your IRA account, the use of funds of such securities would suffice. Remember, you *must* begin to withdraw from your IRA when you reach age 70½.

Over age 50, married with no children: Your IRAs have been diversified for years and could remain so with just a little more emphasis on the Individual U.S. Government Bonds that have been in the portfolio since you were 35, plus any deposits you have continued to put into blue-chip stocks and blue-chip stock funds. What you have been doing by investing in individual stocks with part of your IRA funds is engaging in the best form of investing available, dollar-cost-averaging. You have flattened out all the peaks and valleys in the market by investing the same amount of money in the same securities year after year at different prices. The average price you paid over a period of 30 years or so will always keep you ahead of the market. Here's how dollar-cost-averaging has benefited you over time:

Investment	Price of Investment	Number of Units of Investment Bought	Year #
$ 1,000	$ 10	100	1
$ 1,000	$ 20	50	2
$ 1,000	$ 25	40	3
$ 1,000	$ 20	50	4
$ 1,000	$ 10	100	5
$ 1,000	$ 25	40	6
$ 1,000	$ 50	20	7
$ 1,000	$ 20	50	8
$ 1,000	$ 50	20	9
$ 1,000	$100	10	10
$10,000 Total Investment		480 Units Bought	

If you divide the number of units bought, that is, 480, into the total investment of $10,000, you will note that the average price per unit was $20.83. Even though the value of the units during that ten-year period fluctuated between $10 per unit and $100 per unit, by buying on a regular basis the same dollar amount of units regardless of their unit cost, you emerged the winner. If you were to turn around the day after you made the last investment at $100 per unit and sell the entire portfolio at or near $100, the proceeds would be close to $48,000 on that original $10,000 total investment. Investors who want to receive a particular return over a long period find this method the best there is.

Note: Dollar-cost-averaging works if you want to invest in debt instruments as well. The big difference would be the label. By buying bonds using this technique, you would be really interest-rate-averaging—buying fixed-income securities regularly, regardless of the coupon yield but always investing the same number of dollars.

Age over 50, married with family: People in our married-with-kids category, if they got into it when they were in their late twenties or early thirties, will have raised and educated most of those kids by the time they reach their fifties. If this was or will be your situation, by the time you are into your fifties you will have accomplished many of your goals. Those children will have been raised and educated; your house will have been paid for; your retirement account will have been fully funded, and you will be looking for a retirement house to buy in Florida, New Mexico, or Colorado. With all of these accomplishments, you could consider a little risk as you go through your fifties, but a little, not a lot! Take the contributions made for one of you over the next three or four years and diversify them among:

Growth-type mutual funds.
Aggressive-growth-type mutual funds.
Emerging-type mutual funds.
Options funds.

Notice that each of these at-risk categories involves mutual funds. Why? You raised children throughout your adult life. You made a living all of your adult life. You weren't studying investments. By using mutual funds instead of trying to pick the investments one by one yourself, you have bought:

A. Professional management. The portfolio managers of the mutual funds do nothing but manage money and certainly do it better than you could.
B. Mutual funds provide wide diversification. Even if you could plan the portfolio, you could never buy as many different investments as a billion-dollar fund can.
C. Liquidity. You can buy and sell mutual fund shares at the drop of a hat. All that is required to liquidate a position is a telephone call to the toll-free Shareholder's Services number printed in the prospectus.

IRA Rollovers, any age: Many of you have changed jobs and put all your retirement funds from the pension plans of the first job into an IRA rollover account. The reason you used the IRA rollover was to continue the tax-deferred status of the fund, but now you have to manage the money yourself. If your account, aside from your regular $2,000 annual IRA account, has any multiples of $25,000 in it, you should call your brokerage house and get as much information as possible on a new investment vehicle known as the "G.I.M." (the Government Investment Multiplier). By putting a series of G.I.M.s into that IRA rollover, or a pension fund, or any other tax-deferred account, you will not only buy yourself a guaranteed investment but also one that can be liquidated if you elect to retire early. The G.I.M. works like this:

> Each $25,000 investment buys an Individual Government National Mortgage Association instrument (a "Ginnie Mae") that matures the year you think you will retire. (This is not to be confused with a Ginnie Mae Fund.)
>
> That individual Ginnie Mae pays out by check an amount every month that is made up of both principal and interest.
>
> The monthly check is used to buy a piece of a United States Treasury Zero Coupon Bond that also matures the year you plan to retire.
>
> Both vehicles in the package are guaranteed by the full faith and credit of the United States Government.
>
> Any piece of the portfolio can be sold earlier if you elect to retire early.
>
> Since the marketability of the Ginnie Maes and the Zeros are in opposition to one another, no matter where the interest-rate market has taken rates, the monies in this package are intact.

Clearly the G.I.M. program is not for everyone any more than any investment is for everyone, but given the features described, you should call your local brokerage house and consult with someone you trust, to make certain you haven't missed out on something suitable for you.

TAX FACTS TO REMEMBER UNDER THE NEW TAX LAW . . . in words of one syllable

1. The old rules governing the deductibility of IRAs no longer apply; Uncle Sam has made some very definite changes that may affect you both this year and in years to come.

2. Singles earning less than $25,000, and married couples filing jointly and earning less than $40,000, are still entitled to a full IRA deduction.
3. If neither spouse is covered by a company Koegh plan, company pension plan or company retirement plan, the couple is entitled to full IRA deductions regardless of income level.
4. Single taxpayers earning between $25,000 and $35,000 will lose their deduction for IRAs; under tax reform they will lose $10 of deduction for each $50 of income above the $25,000. If this new rule is relevant to your situation, consult the following chart to learn how much you can deduct under the new tax law:

Income	IRA Contribution	IRA Deduction Allowed Under Tax Reform
$40,000	$2,000	$2,000
$41,000		$1,800
$42,000		$1,600
$43,000		$1,400
$44,000		$1,200
$45,000		$1,000
$46,000		$ 800
$47,000		$ 600
$48,000		$ 400
$49,000		$ 200
$50,000		-0-

5. Married couples filing a joint return with an adjusted gross income of between $40,000 and $50,000 will also lose deduction for IRAs; under tax reform they will lose $10 of deduction for each $50 of income above $25,000. Consult the chart on page 64 to find out how much can be deducted under the new tax law.
6. All income, dividends, or gains realized in an IRA account remain tax-deferred until withdrawn.
7. IRA withdrawals made before age 59½ are subject to a "two-tier" tax: deductible contributions that have been working

Income	IRA Contribution	IRA Deduction Allowed Under Tax Reform
$25,000	$2,000	$2,000
$26,000	↓	$1,800
$27,000		$1,600
$28,000		$1,400
$29,000		$1,200
$30,000		$1,000
$31,000		$ 800
$32,000		$ 600
$33,000		$ 400
$34,000		$ 200
$35,000		-0-

tax-deferred are now subject to ordinary income tax rates plus a 10% tax penalty (only for withdrawals made before you are 59½).

8. If tax reform makes it necessary for you to deal with both deductible and non-deductible IRA monies, I suggest that you open a separate account for those contributions that are non-deductible.
9. Tax reform still allows the use of an IRA rollover account for those monies that were growing in a company retirement plan or other retirement plan.
10. The use of G.I.Ms (Government Investment Multipliers) may offer you greater returns and liquidity than other investment vehicles. It is best to consult with a financial professional before taking this investment option.

6

The Investments To Look At Under The New Tax Law: A Smorgasbord Of Opportunities

In this chapter on investments, you will learn:

* How a diversified investment portfolio will build a solid return while keeping your risk at a minimum.
* How United States Treasury Bills, United States Treasury Notes, and United States Treasury Bonds can be used to help achieve your investment objectives.
* The difference in tax treatment of United States Treasury Bonds and Corporate Bonds.
* How the new tax law affects the gains realized from the sale of collectibles (e.g., rare stamps, coins, antiques, comic books, rugs, pictures).
* The pros and cons of investing in precious metals (e.g., silver, gold, platinum).

In earlier chapters you read about how tax reform has affected those capital gains and investments made in stocks and other assets that bring gains, as well as investments made into real property. There are other investments too that could be as suitable or even more suitable, given your unique investment picture. A discussion of these investments with your own professional advisor is advisable so that you and they can determine whether any of them meets the following criteria:

Investment Objectives. No investment is for you unless it meets *your* investment objectives. Even if a particular investment has just made the shoe-shine person rich, or your hairdresser has just made a killing in pork-bellies, that doesn't mean that it's for you. It may take two or three meetings with a financial planner, but if you can focus on a set of specific objectives such as growth, income, high yield, or high risk that will satisfy your needs, then pick those investments.

Diversification. No sane, logical investor puts all of his or her eggs into one basket. In order to spread risk, you must diversify. Investing in four or five companies that are in the same industry group makes more sense than investing four or five times the same amount of money in one company. Diversification allows you to take advantage of several management teams, different markets, larger sources of funding, greater marketing strength, and so on, as well as of a combination of well-known and little-known companies in the same field. If you diversify, make a mistake, and pick a loser, you don't lose your entire investment. Diversification affords a degree of liquidity. One company's stock might be traded on the New York Stock Exchange while another is traded on the American Stock Exchange and a third is traded over the counter. Each marketplace affords a different degree of liquidity.

Suitability. Is the investment suitable *for you*? One person doesn't care whether or not a company makes guns that kill, but maybe you do. Even if that company is highly profitable or growing rapidly, it isn't suitable for you. You may have strong feelings about nuclear energy. If so, don't buy public utilities that use nuclear power plants, regardless of their dividend payout. You can cite other examples of suitability based on your upbringing, religion, racial background, family experiences, and work history. Suffice it to say that if it isn't suitable for you, don't buy it.

What if you find an investment that meets your investment objectives but isn't suitable? What if that investment is suitable and meets your investment objectives, but doesn't offer diversification? What if you can't find what you are looking for? The only answer is you haven't looked far enough. There are thousands of stocks listed on the New York Stock Exchange, the American Stock Exchange and N.A.S.D.A.Q. (over-the-counter) as well as thousands of securities offered by the federal government, state and local governments, and even U.S. territories. The only reason you can't find one is, I repeat, you haven't looked far enough. Agents at the various brokerage house, and financial planners, accountants, lawyers, and other financial professionals know about investments that certainly will meet all three criteria listed above. Here are some to consider:

Certificates of Deposit. (CDs). Issued by the banking community, they represent loans made by you to the bank. They are available in amounts as small as $500 and as large as into the millions and they can be purchased to mature in as short a time as three months and in monthly maturities as long as the bank will make available. You can have CDs mature on the day college tuition is due, the date you plan to close on a mortgage, or virtually on any date you choose. Certificates of Deposit are backed, up to $100,000, by the Federal Deposit Insurance Corporation or the Federal Savings and Loan Insurance Corporation (F.D.I.C. and F.S.L.I.C, respectively), and actually, through these agencies, by the federal government. The interest income is taxed as ordinary income and with the tax brackets going down in 1987 and 1988, can be attractive, safe investments for almost anyone. Be sure to read the fine print when you open a CD so that you will know of possible penalties, should you need to break a CD prior to maturity.

U.S. Government Obligations. This group includes the following:

- **A.** United States Treasury Bills. The shortest-term borrowings by Uncle Sam, backed by the full faith and credit of the U.S. Treasury. T-bills can mature in 13, 26, or 52 weeks; there are no nine-month bills. They are available in denominations of $10,000 with multiples of $5,000 thereafter. They can be bought at a fee from banks or directly through the Federal Reserve, even by mail. Income is subject to federal income taxes but is exempt from state and local income taxes.
- **B.** United States Treasury Notes. Intermediate-term borrowings by Uncle Sam, backed by the full faith and credit of the U.S. Treasury. Notes have maturities ranging from two to ten years and may be bought in denominations as low as $1,000. Interest is paid semi-annually. These notes may be bought directly through the Federal Reserve or in the sec-

ondary market. Income is subject to federal income taxes but is free of state and local income taxes.

C. United States Treasury Bonds. Long-term borrowings by the federal government, backed by the full faith and credit of the U.S. Treasury. Bonds mature in from ten to thirty years and may be bought in denominations as low as $1,000 directly through the Federal Reserve or in the secondary market. Interest is paid semi-annually. Income is subject to federal income taxes but free of state and local income taxes.

D. Government National Mortgage Association Securities ("Ginnie Maes"). Not only is this the nickname given to my wife, Kris, by Alan Colmes (see "Acknowledgments" in the front of this book), but it is the nickname of an obligation of the Federal Government that is used to help the mortgage business in this country. The banking community makes mortgages available to the public, packages those mortgages, and sells them to the Federal National Mortgage Association. They in turn put those mortgages into pools and fund those pools by issuing Ginnie Mae certificates in denominations of $25,000. The federal government stands behind these securities. Your monthly check represents a combination of interest and principle should the mortgages in the pool being repaid before they fall due. Since few people have $25,000 or multiples thereof lying around, most Ginnie Maes are in mutual funds and you may invest as little as $1,000 in a fund of many different Ginnie Maes.

E. Corporate Bonds. These are mortgages issued by companies such as General Motors or IBM. You take the place of a bank if you buy such a bond. The big company has to pay you interest on that mortgage semi-annually and all of the principal at maturity. These issues are backed by the full faith and credit of the issuing company, so that the bigger the company is, and the stronger its credit history, the safer the bond and the lower the yield. Corporate bonds pay interest semi-annually, are available in denominations of $5,000 and in mutual funds. The income is taxable interest income.

A variation on a corporate is a corporate convertible (bond). With it, instead of being repaid the principal at maturity, the bondholder has the right to convert the bond into common shares of the corporation. In other words, you exchange your mortgage for shares of ownership. The two major rating services that rank bonds are Moody's and Standard & Poor's. Their highest ratings would be Aaa, Aa and A by Moody's, and AAA, AA and A by Standard and Poor's.

F. *Junk Bonds.* These are non-rated issues of corporate debt that are usually issued in connection with a take-over acquisition of a major company. They are non-rated because the risk you take as a bondholder is about as high as it can get, and in order to effect the transaction planned, the issuing corporation has probably extended itself beyond reason, or at least beyond the standards of the ratings company. Even though junk bonds are issued by some major companies, they are far down the pecking order when it comes to security and the ability of the company to make good. Risk, risk, risk . . . .

G. *Art, antiques, and "collectibles."* This area of investment requires the services of an expert. If you had a diamond put into one of your hands and a cubic zirconium into the other, you probably couldn't tell the real from the synthetic. Many jewelers can't either, so don't feel badly. The same thing goes for rare stamps, rugs, paintings, valuable coins, antiques, comic books, and the like. With a change in the tax laws, the gains realized from collectibles will be treated as income and with lower brackets for 1987 and 1988, are attractive. Two hints: Make sure that you carry sufficient additional insurance to cover these items (in some cases a "floater" may be needed); and, to get some extra return, be sure that the collectibles are something that you can enjoy and use. Put that fine rug on the living room floor and enjoy it; hang those pictures around the house and look at them. Play with those collectible trains, and drive that antique car.

H. *Municipal bonds.* If you want to live as much as possible a tax-free life (not forgetting the A.M.T., Alternative Minimum Tax); just want to sit at home and clip coupons; need the safety of the full faith and credit of a state or local government; and have no immediate use for the money, a portfolio of munis is the answer. Of course, munis are available in mutual fund form for those who don't even want to make the individual choices. For an investment under $25,000 or $35,000 I suggest that two or three different municipal bond funds be considered. For investments above those levels, a diversified portfolio of individual bonds would make more sense. These bonds are available in denominations of $5,000 and with $50,000 to invest you could achieve real diversification.

I. *Mutual funds.* Before worrying about whether the fund charges a sales load or is a no-load fund, you should look at the fund's prospectus and read up on the following areas:

1. *Investment objectives.* Does that fund have the same objectives you do? Is the portfolio made up of investments of many different companies in many different industries (a diversified fund)? Is it made up primarily of stocks of growing companies (a growth fund)? Is the portfolio made up of tax-exempt bonds and other tax-free instruments (a tax-exempt fund)? Is the portfolio made up half and half of investments in equities and in debt instruments (a balanced fund)? If the nature of the fund, as stated in its prospectus, is incompatible with your investment objectives, it is the wrong fund for you.
2. *Financial history or track record.* Another look at that prospectus will reveal whether or not the financial history of the fund over the last ten years has been good or poor. You don't need a team of high-priced CPAs to eyeball ten columns of figures and see that each one has a bigger total than the one before. If the financial history of the fund has been erratic, pick up the prospectus of another fund, and if its growth has been steady, read on.
3. *Management.* Who is minding the store? The prospectus of a mutual fund will give a history of the management and of its business background. It should be obvious that

if the portfolio manager of the fund you are examining was the manager of a beauty parlor in Bensonhurst, Brooklyn, for the past nine years and in charge of your fund's portfolio for the last year, you might want to look a little further. A history of having managed monies of the amounts in your fund will certainly put your mind at ease.

4. *Load* is another word for commission or sales charge. If all of the foregoing—your investment objectives, a good financial history, and quality management—can be gotten in a no-load fund, it would be plain stupid to buy a load fund. If, however, you must pay a commission or sales charge to get all those advantages, it should simply be viewed as the cost of doing business. The load on a typical mutual fund is 8% of the monies invested, but while shopping around you should certainly ask about the low-load funds.

J. *Precious metals.* A lot of people fear the "end of the world," "the collapse of the Market" or another "Depression-like economy," and it is usually out of such fears that precious metals are bought. Numbers of safeguards have been built into our system since the Great Depression, and fewer people are buying precious metals out of fear. More and more are viewing them as an investment vehicle. Keep in mind, though, that a bag of silver dollars or a few gold coins *don't pay any income.* They may go up in value over time but you receive nothing in the meantime and may even have to pay for their storage and protection.

The three precious metals you should be looking at are silver, gold, and platinum. There are many ways you can invest in these metals.

1. *Silver coins.* From time to time, silver medallions are made available, but perhaps the most common silver coins are those that were issued by the United States Treasury until the 1960s. The most popular is the U.S. silver dollar. These coins can be bought through dealers. You should have a working relationship with an expert

one, as there can be a night-and-day difference between the quality of one silver dollar and another, and a night-and-day difference in value.

2. *Silver bullion.* These are little bars of silver available through banks and dealers and are generally one ounce in weight. They have to be stored carefully, and if you own many bars this can be an expensive proposition. What most investors do is have their silver dealer store them, for a fee.
3. *Silver mining stocks.* Those companies mining the silver issue shares which are traded on the various exchanges and which may be bought in lots to meet your needs. Two examples of North American silver mining stocks, both traded on the New York Stock Exchange, are Hecla Mining and Callahan Mining.

   Many silver mining shares are also part of the portfolios of major mutual funds and may be invested in as part of the purchase of that fund.
4. *Gold coins* are available in medallion form (recently struck); in the older U.S. legal tender that was used during days of the gold standard; and in bullion coins. The most common of all the gold coins, apart from the older U.S. gold pieces, is probably the South African Krugerrand. Other gold coins you should look at are the Canadian Maple Leaf and the Panda Series from China.
5. *Gold bullion.* If you were to re-read *Goldfinger* you would be reminded that gold in bullion form is an "anonymous" investment. Bars of pure gold are unregistered and belong to the holder. They may readily be moved from bank to bank around the world and be accepted almost with reverence. Obviously, unless your name is Auric Goldfinger and you have a huge organization behind you, you would have to buy and sell your bullion through bullion dealers and probably never be in actual possession of the gold bars. Oh, you may want to have a one-ounce gold bar on your desk, or walk around with a $20 U.S. gold piece in your pocket, but it would not have been bought for investment, just show!

6. *Gold mining stocks.* Since most of the world's gold comes from South Africa, if you have a political or personal problem investing in that part of the world, *don't.* There are plenty of North American gold mining stocks available and if you don't find one that meets your objectives among the following examples, check with your brokerage house for other choices:

Campbell Red Lake (traded on the New York Stock Exchange)

Echo Bay (traded on the American Stock Exchange)

Agnico Eagle Mines (traded in the over-the-counter market)

Perhaps the most famous of the South African gold stocks is American South African, traded on the New York Stock Exchange.

7. *Platinum coins.* Every one of you is familar with gold coins and of course with all the silver coins that used to fill your pockets, but have you ever seen or held, much less owned, a platinum coin? Unlike the gold and silver coins which were, and in rare cases still are commonly used as currency, platinum coins are primarily collectible coins and not so readily available. For that matter, the metal itself is not so readily available as gold and silver. A visit to a reputable coin dealer will likely result in this suggestion regarding platinium coins: "Buy a few of the Nobels issued by the Isle of Man." The Isle of who? The Isle of Man. It is a small island in the Irish Sea, approximately 80 miles east of Liverpool, England, 20 miles south of Whithorn, Scotland, and some 80 miles northeast of Dublin, Ireland.

If you think you have exhausted all of the ways in which you could invest in precious metals, you are wrong. Gold coins may not be for you, but there are other ways to invest in gold. Silver coins may be too bulky to store in your vault. You may be afraid of buying just one gold mining stock or even a couple of silver mining stocks. The entire world of precious metal funds is wide open.

You may want to invest only in gold. There are a number of gold-only funds available whose portfolios are made up entirely of investments in gold mining stocks. Those stocks could be those of only North American gold mining companies; only South African gold mining companies; or a combination. A look at the investment objectives section of any mutual fund will tell you which fund has invested in precious metals and which has not. I suggest that you get in touch with The No-Load Mutual Fund Association. (Check with the toll-free 800 Information Operator in your area for the number to use.)

This organization will send you the names of hundreds of no-load mutual funds. From among them you can choose three or four no-load precious-metal or gold mining or silver mining funds and call for their respective prospectuses. Then review them in exactly the same way you would review those of any other kind of mutual fund you might be considering:

Does this fund meet *my* investment objectives?

Does this fund have a financial history or track record that shows it to have done what it was said to be able to do?

Is the ability of the manager what you want in the person managing your money?

After making such a review, you might invest in that fund by putting a small percentage of your investment capital to work this month. If the performance warrants, invest the same percentage next month, and so on. As soon as the fund stops performing as expected, liquidate and look for another fund. Should the fund continue to perform well (go up in value), keep adding to your holdings. You may have begun with an investment of $1,000. When the net asset value of the fund increased by 10%, you invested another $1,000, and so on, until all of your $10,000 of available capital was invested. But suppose that after the third investment of $1,000, the fund's net asset value had began to fall? Any time it drops 10% below the highest price it reached while you were buying, liquidate.

K. *Real estate.*This vehicle was discussed at length earlier, but one aspect of real estate investment has not been touched on at all.

L. *Real Estate Limited Partnerships.* Tax reform has made virtually obsolete those old deals where someone took your few bucks and leveraged them into a huge purchase, all the while promising you wonderful tax benefits (write-offs). The newer wave of real estate limited partnerships favors those who purchase property for cash. They don't promise great tax-sheltering but instead have you participating in the gains realized when the property is sold. These partnerships are sometimes referred to as non-leveraged real estate partnerships. Don't even try to read the prospectus sent by the sales organization covering a particular partnership. It wasn't written for you but for the lawyers. If your tax advisor in conjunction with your financial planner concludes that real estate limited partnerships are suitable for you, meet your investment objectives, and are a necessary part of your overall financial plan (help to diversify your portfolio), send a copy of the prospectus to your attorney for review and go right over to your public library. Your tax dollars pay for your library and there is a wealth of information to be had there, free.

With regard to limited partnerships in general and real estate limited partnerships specifically, you should find out what the Stanger Report says. Most major public libraries, many law firms, and many more accountants subscribe to this service. (It is not something you want on your nightstand to serve as bedtime reading.) In my opinion, if the Stanger Report hasn't reviewed the partnership you are considering, you should look for another one.

While at the library take a few minutes to look at three books on this subject of tax sheltering.

Stanger, Robert A., *Tax Shelters: The Bottom Line* (Fair Haven, New Jersey: Robert A. Stanger & Company, 1982).

Stanger, Robert A., with Keith D. Allaire, *How to Evaluate Real Estate Limited Partnerships* (Shrewsbury, New Jersey: Robert A. Stanger & Company, 1986).

Murray, Nick: *Shared Perceptions: The Art of Marketing Real Estate Limited Partnerships* (Shrewsbury, New Jersey: Robert A. Stanger & Company, 1986).

M. *Foreign currency.* The major world currencies may be traded as any stock. You buy the currency from a foreign exchange dealer when the exchange rates are favorable and re-sell them at a profit. The major currencies are:

1. Deutsch marks (West Germany)
2. Swiss francs (Switzerland)
3. British pound sterling (England)
4. Yen (Japan)
5. Dollar (United States of America)

There is some risk in the trading in currency. Ask your financial professional to discuss with you the advantages and disadvantages of investing in currency futures.

When you buy currency futures, instead of owning the actual currency, you have a "call" or right to purchase that currency in the future at a price established today. In other words, you are "betting" on what that price will be in the near future. The gains realized on such "bets" would be taxed as ordinary income under tax reform. *Please note:* You could lose all your money. Remember you are "betting" on the value of something in the future. You don't own it.

N. *Commodities options.* As with currency futures, you are betting on the future value of the commodity in question, and if you just take your contract and put it in the mattress, you could find yourself the proud owner of a boxcar full of eggs or sugar or soybeans. The best candidates for investing in commodity futures usually can use the commodity if it must become theirs at the end of the contract. Otherwise, you, the first investor, would hold the contract only until shortly before delivery and sell it to someone who needs it.

For example, you buy a contract for 5,000 bushels of corn today at $2.50 per bushel, and after three months, but still well before the month that that corn would have to be delivered to the holder of the contract, corn is worth $2.70 per bushel. You would simply sell your contract for 5,000 bushels to a farmer who needs that corn but who might have missed buying when you did.

Commodity futures are usually available for sugar, soybeans, corn, and lumber.

Remember, you are betting on the future value of something and are at high risk. "Playing" the commodity futures market is only for those who can stand to lose all of the monies they have commited.

The fourth book in this series, *Bill Bresnan Speaks on the Stock Market . . . In Words of One Syllable*, (soon to be published) will deal with many other types of investments, where they are traded, how they are traded, and their pros and cons. Your local bookstore or the publisher of this book (see the copyright page) can tell you when to expect publication.

TAX FACTS TO REMEMBER UNDER THE NEW TAX LAW . . . in words of one syllable

1. All income earned on CDs (Certificates of Deposit) will be taxed as ordinary income.
2. Income earned on United States Treasury Bills, United States Treasury Notes, and United States Treasury Bonds, is subject to federal tax, but *free* of state and local income tax.
3. The income earned by corporate bonds is treated as taxable interest income.
4. Before purchasing corporate bonds you should consult with a major rating service that ranks bonds; the two major rating services of bonds are Moody's and Standard & Poor's.
5. Remember to consult an expert before purchasing art, antiques, or collectibles for investment purposes. Failure to do so can lead to such disasters as investing in a $15,000 cubic zirconium even though the seller assured you of the flawless character of "that six-carat diamond."

7

That House Under Tax Reform: Look No Further Than Your Own Backyard For Tax Saving Tips

In this chapter concerning the effect of the new tax law on real estate, you will find a wealth of tax-saving tips, and also learn:

* That the new tax law has had little effect on the tax advantages associated with your principal residence and your vacation property.
* Whether the new tax law has affected the deductibility of home improvement loans.
* How senior citizens can use a one-time deduction to help offset real estate capital gains.
* How the deductibility of interest expenses on consumer debt is being phased out.
* How to use the new tax law to maximize your real estate wealth.
* How to use real-estate to help build tax-deferred equity.

In the introduction to this book, I quoted an opinion of a justice of a Court of Appeals who said, ". . . he is not bound to choose the pattern which will best pay the Treasury." Or to put it simply, you may legally use all the tax laws to reduce your tax burden to the minimum.

Since we want to pay only that tax which we absolutely *must* and not a penny more, let's explore some of the ways available to both rich and poor to reduce taxes. Remember, it is not because they are subject to a different set of tax laws that the rich are rich. The rich and the poor have the same rules to use. The difference lies in who uses the rules best.

Of all your possessions, perhaps the most expensive is your

house, *your* house, not the government's. And your house is probably the best tax shelter you will ever have.

Even after tax reform, the principal residence and even a second or vacation home has retained most of the tax advantages you previously enjoyed. Look no farther than your own backyard to see that you are surrounded by tax benefits.

Let's take a family who bought a principal residence five years ago and paid $100,000. At the time of purchase they had $25,000 to put down and they borrowed from a local bank a first mortgage of $75,000 to cover the balance. During the next five years the following happened:

1. Each year this family deducted the interest payments on the $75,000 mortgage which at a 10% annual rate amounted to an annual tax deduction of $7,500. This tax deduction lowered the family's tax bracket and increased their take-home pay over this period.
2. Each year this family deducted the real estate taxes paid to the local governments, further reduced their tax bracket, and increased their take home pay.
3. Over the five-year period the value of the house increased by an average of 8% per year and today is approximately $146,000. This increased equity over their purchase price amounts to a "paper profit" of some $46,000. No tax is due on this new equity.
4. They added a bedroom and a second garage and air-conditioned the entire house. These improvements cost $25,000 and were financed by using a home improvement loan. The interest expense on this loan was also deductible; the increased value of the property as a result of the improvements is a "paper profit" and isn't taxed either.
5. The property is now worth, with improvements, $175,000, and they decide to move.

The year this family has chosen to move is also the first year after tax reform. Should they move? Are they better off refinancing? Can they afford a more expensive house? What are the tax consequences of this situation? Will they lose all of the benefits they presently have? All these questions will be answered in this chapter.

The first item they should consider before selling, regardless of the tax consequences, is whether or not the move is necessary. Will the new community be closer to work? Do they have the same need for schools and other community facilities? Is a larger or smaller house needed to meet their family's current and future needs? Or do they simply want a change of scenery? Once the social aspects of the move are decided, they can focus on the tax consequences or tax advantages.

The good news is that the move will afford more advantages than consequences.

That the property has appreciated in value from $100,000 to its present improved value of $175,000 is of least concern. Since most people improve their status when they move, this family will in all likelihood be buying a more expensive house than the one being sold. If so, none of the increased value of the first house will be taxed. So long as they buy a new principal residence of equal or greater cost than the selling price of the previous one, the entire gain from the first house is rolled over into the new property. You don't even have to invest all of the proceeds in the new house.

When the first house is sold, the unpaid balance of the mortgage is paid from the proceeds of sale. The unpaid balance of the home improvement loan is paid from the proceeds of the sale, and all the expenses of sale (real estate commissions, closing costs, etc.) are paid as well. After all this, there remains some $70,000:

Proceeds of sale	$175,000
Balance of mortgage	(70,000)
Balance of home improvement loan	(20,000)
Closing costs plus commission	(15,000)
Balance available	$70,000

The owners bought this house originally with $25,000 of their own cash as the down payment and now have $70,000 in hand.

In order to get the advantages of rolling over the gain realized on the sale of this property, if you are the seller, you don't have to invest all of this remaining $70,000 in the new principal residence. Even though the new house will cost $200,000, you may decide to use $20,000 of the proceeds of the sale of your first house to repay consumer debt or buy some new furniture or to put into your child's education. You may want to put only $50,000 down on the new house and carry a $150,000 mortgage. You may find a seller so highly motivated that he or she is willing to hold a mortgage for $180,000 on his or her house so that you need only $20,000 of your cash to put down. All of these alternatives will still allow you to roll over the capital gain from House No. 1 into House No. 2. All of these alternatives will defer the tax consequences on the sale of your principal residence for as long as you like.

Even after you have bought and sold a succession of principal residences in the manner described and have a rollover of tens of thousands of dollars in capital gains, there still remains a way to reduce the size of the tax bite. After several houses you may finally reach the point where retirement looks good. At that point your accountant will compute the total of all of the capital gains rolled forward, house after house, and advise you of a deduction you may take on those gains.

The one-time deduction of $125,000 for a retiring senior citizen couple is available on all of those accumulated capital gains. Supposing you have accumulated $120,000 in gains and you are over 55 at the time you take this deduction. If the house being sold has been your principal residence three out of the five years prior to sale, your accountant would simply apply $120,000 of that deduction against $120,000 of accumulated gains and the tax would be wiped out. So too would the deduction. Remember it is a one-time event, and whether you use the entire $125,000 deduction or any part thereof, it is gone forever.

With the tax on the gain dealt with, the next area of concern becomes the deductibility of interest to be paid on the new house. The purchase price of the new principal residence was $200,000. That is the cost basis too. Every dollar of interest paid on the mortgage on this new house that has a cost basis of $200,000 is deductible under tax reform. As a matter of fact, if you found that motivated seller and you bought the new house with just $20,000 down and a $180,000 mortgage at 10%, the $18,000 of annual interest paid on that mortgage would all be deductible. Further, if the remaining $50,000 was used as the down payment on a vacation home costing $150,000 and carrying a $100,000 mortgage, the entire $10,000 annual interest expense on the vacation home would be deductible. Interest expenses up to the cost basis of that second home are deductible so long as you don't rent it out and earn income from tenants. Then it becomes a business and is treated as such.

Suppose you improve this new principal residence over the years by adding a swimming pool or upgrading the kitchen, taking out a home improvement loan to do so. Can you deduct the interest on that loan too? Yes. By increasing the value of the new house, you are increasing its cost basis and you may deduct interest expenses up to the cost basis. The cost basis may also be considered added to, if the monies borrowed against your principal residence are used for necessary medical expenses or for the education of your children.

As the value of your house goes up and as you increase the cost basis by the means discussed earlier, you should consider the new equity as your own personal bank. From time to time you may need money for expenditures such as a vacation, a new car, the purchase of high-ticket items, and the like, and you don't want to take cash from other investments or add to your credit-card balances. A home equity loan, up to the cost basis of your property, can be a handy solution. Once a line of credit against the equity in your principal residence has been established with a local lender, you have nothing more to do than to write a check. It should be noted, however, that this type of borrowing should be carefully monitored because most home equity lines of credit are made on an adjustable basis and the monthly payments can literally change from day to day. As this book is being written some voices in Congress are trying to eliminate or at the very least limit, this use of equity lines of credit. I suggest that you check with your personal financial planner before taking down substantial sums against the equity in your house and then deducting the interest expenses. In the meantime, so long as you keep the borrowing below the cost basis, you can go on deducting all the interest.

Does it make sense to borrow more than the deductible amount against your home equity? Again, yes. In this case such borrowing should produce results that offset the lost deductions.

When amounts are borrowed against the equity in your principal residence above the cost basis of the house, the easiest way to recover the lost deductions is to engage in a form of leverage. Suppose you borrow $50,000 more of the equity than you could deduct. You would pay non-deductible interest on this loan, and were you to re-invest just $50,000 at interest, the best you could hope to recover would be the cost of borrowing. But you would be ahead if you used that same $50,000 as the down payment on a $125,000 piece of rental property that would not only produce some income (rent exceeding the expenses on that house) but would grow also in value each year.

In this situation, the lost deduction of $5,000 (the interest on $50,000 borrowed at 10%) would be more than offset by the yearly appreciation (paper profit) of $10,000. Remembering that the appreciation is not taxed until realized and that the interest deduction is just that—a deduction and not a tax credit—you would be far better off giving up the deduction and gaining the paper profit.

Even if you did not buy property but used those deductible monies to repay less-than-fully-deductible debts, you would gain an advantage. Under tax reform the deductibility of interest expenses on car loans, college loans, credit-card debts, and other consumer debt will be phased out as follows:

In 1987 you will be able to write off only 65% of such interest.

In 1988 you will be able to write off only 40% of such interest.

In 1989 you will be able to write off only 20% of such interest.

In 1990 you will be able to write off only 10% of such interest.

In 1991 and afterward no deduction of such interest will be allowed.

But since you can borrow against your home equity at rates of 10% and 11% and you are paying rates of 18%, 19% and even 20% on those credit cards, aren't you better off in the long run? Of course you must always weigh the costs and expenses of these loans as well as the interst rates when deciding whether or not to repay or to re-finance.

For a further discussion on the topic of leveraging real property, I suggest that you read Chapter 4, "Owning Income-Producing Property: Leverage Yourself to Wealth!", in the first book in this series, *WABC TALK RADIO 77AM Financial Expert Bill Bresnan Speaks On Real Estate . . . In Words of One Syllable*, by Prentice-Hall, Inc., 1987.

Tax reform still allows the deductibility of expenses on that principal residence that exceed the interest on loans above the cost basis. Any interest paid on monies borrowed above the cost basis can still be deducted as consumer interest, given the phase-out outlined earlier in this chapter. In addition to the deductibility of these excess interest charges, tax reform has also preserved the deductibility of property taxes as well as of points paid to get a mortgage.

In the case of property taxes, the deductibility is the same as before tax reform. The entire amount of property taxes may be deducted.

In the case of points or up-front interest, you may deduct all the points you paid as interest on the first mortgage during the first year, but points paid on that second mortgage or any other type of refinancing are to be spread over the life of the loan. This is another area being argued in Congress as this book is being written, and again I suggest that you check with your financial planner or tax advisor before making a move.

Regarding the capital gain realized from a principal residence that is not rolled over, the following would apply:

Suppose that your principal residence was sold in 1987 and the monies not reinvested in another residence. Suppose also that you were not eligible for the one-time $125,000 exclusion. Then the gain would be taxed at the 28% rate. This would be a favorable treatment of that gain since the top bracket in 1987 could be 38.5%. In 1988, it makes no difference since all gains will be treated as ordinary income and taxed accordingly.

When thinking of real estate and taxes, the primary concern of the ordinary investor should be "What will the property be worth in the future?" In general, if the property pays for itself or has been bought for personal enjoyment and satisfaction, and there are only limited tax advantages available, your ultimate return will be at the time of resale. Not all property goes up at the same rate everywhere every day, but all property must go up in value over time if for no other reason than the old theory of supply and demand. No new property is being created, but the demand grows daily. It is reasonable to expect your property to appreciate at an average rate of 8% per year. This is an average rate. It could go up in value one year, remain level for several years, and drop slightly during another year, but on balance it will grow in value at the 8% average yearly rate. That means that property worth $200,000 today, and which may or may not be bringing you tax benefits, but which is being used and enjoyed, could be worth some $293,000 in just five short years. That new $93,000 in equity developed with tax deferred gains and may be used for future purchases.

TAX FACTS TO REMEMBER UNDER THE NEW TAX LAW . . . in words of one syllable

1. You may deduct all the interst on a home-mortgage-type obligation without restriction on all debt incurred prior to August 16, 1986.

2. You may deduct all the interest on a home improvement loan, up to the cost basis.
3. Interest paid on mortgages for principal residences and vacation properties is tax-deductible (up to the cost basis).
4. Under tax reform, the deductibility of interest expenses on car loans, college loans, credt-card debt, and other consumer debt will be phased out by 1991. Don't forget that in 1987 you can write off only 65% of the interest expense resulting from consumer debt.
5. Tax reform has preserved the deductibility of property taxes and the points paid to obtain a first mortgage.
6. Remember that in 1987 all capital gains will be taxed at a rate of 28%, and will be taxed as ordinary income in 1988 and beyond.

8

Your Child's Education Under The New Tax Reform: A Brief Look At The Long Road Ahead

In this brief, right-to-the point, but fact-filled chapter, you will learn:

* How the new tax law affects the monies deposited in your children's education fund.
* How you can put your child into a zero tax bracket.
* How zero coupon municipal bonds can help to finance your children's education in a tax-free environment.
* How Series EE Bonds can be used to finance your children's education.

Various studies have shown that to put a child born in 1987 through a four-year degree program at a public college can cost as much as $100,000. It only gets worse if you elect to send the child through the same degree program at a private college—it could cost you over $150,000. How are you expected to cover those costs? You certainly can't save $100,000 or more between now and the year 2005, and to make matters even worse, Uncle Sam isn't helping out a whole lot either, especially since tax reform.

Under tax reform, monies that are gifts to your children to pay for that college education program are treated as follows:

A. A husband and wife can each give each child $10,000 every year without having to pay any gift taxes. That means that the child's education fund may receive $20,000 each year without your having to pay a gift tax.

B. Monies invested in a child's name and working for the benefit of that child may be taxed if the income earned by a child under 14 years exceeds $1,000.

Any income earned by a child age 14 years or older will be fully taxed at the child's rate.

If under 14, the child would take a standard deduction on the first $500 of income, thereby eliminating the tax. The next $500 of income would be taxed at the child's rate (15%), and monies earned above $1,000 would be taxed at the parents' rate.

The best way to put a child into a zero tax bracket would be to invest that under-14-year-old's monies as follows:

A. The first $5,000 given to the child would be put into a high-yield U.S. Government or Ginnie Mae fund. If that fund earned at the rate of 10%, the $500 earned would be reduced by the child's standard deduction of $500 and no tax would be due.

B. The next $1,000 given to the child would be invested in a municipal bond fund yielding tax-free income and to which all of the earnings from Fund A (above) would be added. In this way, non-taxed dollars from Fund A would be compounding tax-free in Fund B. The combination of Funds A and B would result in the child's paying no tax.

C. The next $4,000 given to the child, and any monies in excess of this amount, would be invested in zero coupon municipals in the following manner:

1. One-fourth of the balance in a zero coupon municipal bond due to mature during the child's eighteenth year and available to pay the first year's tuition bill, along with any additional monies needed to be drawn from Funds A and B.
2. One-fourth of the balance in zero coupon municipal bonds due to mature during the child's nineteenth year and available as in Case 1, above.
3. One-fourth of the balance in a zero coupon municipal bond due to mature during the child's twentieth year and available as in Case 1 above.
4. One-fourth of the balance in a zero coupon municipal bond due to mature during the child's twenty-first year

and available as in Case 1 above. As you can see, the combination of Funds A, B and C produces no tax liability to the child at all.

If your primary worry is that this child will not go to college and instead just spend all those dollars on some nonsense, after 18 years you might want to have a look at a minor's trust. At least in this case you can keep the monies from the child until he or she is age 21. But more importantly, the $500 fee paid to set up this trust will not only assure that the child cannot touch the money until age 21, but also that:

A. The first $5,000 earned by the trust is taxed at 15 percent.
B. Amounts earned above $5,000 by the trust are taxed at the rate of 28%.

The self-employed might want to consider putting the child (at a reasonable age, of course) to work in their business at a salary. The salary paid to the child to perform reasonable tasks is a tax-deductible expense for your business, and the child may earn as much as:

$2,540 tax-free income in 1987,
$3,000 tax-free income in 1988.

Salary paid the child in excess of those levels would be taxed as his or her earned income, but certainly at a lower tax bracket than the parent's.

Don't overlook using those old reliable Series EE savings bonds for a child's education. Remember that the growth in their value is tax-deferred, and if you give your child $5,000 and he or she buys savings bonds with it, it will be worth almost $9,000 in just ten years. And what would happen to that same $5,000 if the child invested it in a single-premium life program? Five thousand dollars in a single-premium life program at an average rate of 8% would be worth over $10,000 in ten years.

As mentioned earlier, each and every homeowner "owns a bank" and that bank can be made to pay college expenses.

Monies borrowed against the equity built up in a principal residence, up to the cost basis, could be given to your child for college and you could deduct the interest expenses. You could even borrow above your cost basis and get the deduction. But be careful. Some in Washington take the position that monies borrowed for college expenses against the equity in your house, above the cost basis, must be spent the year in which the deductions are taken, while others simply say that whenever the monies are used for education, the deduction applies. Consult your financial planner or tax advisor before you do anything, and keep in mind that this one has yet to be tested.

TAX FACTS TO REMEMBER UNDER THE NEW TAX LAW . . . in words of one syllable

1. A husband and wife may give each child $10,000 every year without having to pay gift taxes. That means that each child's education fund can receive $20,000 each year without your having to pay a gift tax.
2. Under tax reform, the income earned by a child under the age of 14 will be taxed if it exceeds $1,000 at the parents' rate.
3. The income earned by a child 14 years or older will be fully taxed at the child's rate.
4. If you are self-employed, consider putting the child to work in your business on salary. The salary paid to the child to perform reasonable tasks is a tax-deductible expense for your business and the child can earn as much as $2,540 in tax-free income in 1987 and $3,000 tax-free income in 1988.

9

How To Find And Choose That Financial Professional: CPAs, CFPs, And Other Tax Professionals

Before you look at some of the professionals available to help you with your financial concerns as well as with preparation of tax returns, be sure that a professional is needed in the first place. Remember, a tax preparer could charge from $50 or $75 up to several hundred dollars just to fill out your forms and send them in.

In all probability, you will need the help of a professional if during the past year you did *any* of the following:

1. Sold a major piece of real estate.
2. Traded in the Market by buying and selling stocks and bonds.
3. Used tax shelters in an effort to lower your taxes and have carry-forward tax issues from prior years.
4. Received income not primarily from salary.
5. Were self-employed.
6. Found that business-related expenses accounted for a large percentage of your deductions.
7. Found that deductions and exemptions are quite different from last year's.

If none of these seven holds true for you, the package of forms you receive from the IRS and the instructions included, along with the sources and resources contained in this book, will be sufficient to allow you to complete your filing on your own. Otherwise, one of the following professionals can give you valuable help.

The first helper we needed and used, ourselves, was easy to find since we had only to look in the mirror, but the next expert needs to be carefully chosen. That professional is the financial planner.

We cannot, nay, must not, attempt tax planning, try filling out tax forms, or go out looking at houses unless and until we know exactly what we can afford now and what we will be able to afford later as our needs and financial picture change. To help us find out how far we can go, we must find that financial expert.

Financial planners seem to be as numerous as jelly beans at Eastertime, so we need to do a good deal of homework before we look for one for us. As with the medical or legal professions, the financial planning community has been turning out qualified individuals with good credentials who hold titles we all readily recognize. Start by looking for the following:

"CFP"—CERTIFIED FINANCIAL PLANNER™

In order to become a Certified Financial Planner, one must enroll in a financial planning course of study that has been reviewed and approved by The International Board of Standards and Practices For Certified Financial Planners (IBCFP), and must register with the IBCFP to take the CFP examination. The IBCFP authorizes the use of the marks CFP and Certified Financial Planner only after a candidate has passed all six CFP examinations, has provided full disclosure, and has agreed to adhere to the IBCFP code of ethics.

Study, testing, and continuing education all add to the stock of knowledge a CFP can bring to his or her clients. This designation is the one usually associated with financial planning in the minds of the general public, and in fact is on its way toward the status of the CPA (Certified Public Accountant) designation as the only designation for financial planners.

A good source of background information on the educational requirements of CFPs is found by writing to:

The International Board of Standards and Practices
For Certified Financial Planners
5445 DTC Parkway
Suite P-1
Englewood, CO 80111

CFP—Certified Financial Planner™

In order to receive a complete listing of the CFPs in your area, write to:

The Institute of Certified Financial Planners
Two Denver Highlands
10065 East Harvard Avenue
Suite 320
Denver, CO 80231

™CFP and Certified Financial Planner are certification marks of the IBCFP.

"CLU," CHARTERED LIFE UNDERWRITER

After an insurance agent has completed the required courses of study in life insurance and estate planning, normally a ten-part, two-year program, he or she may use the designation CLU. This professional may be consulted when you are thinking of buying a property, in much the same way you might consult a CFP. As a matter of fact, the CLU, as well as the CFP, are not only considered financial professionals but are also included by the International Association for Financial Planners in its efforts to establish industry-wide standards which these professionals will meet.

For background information on this group, write to:

The American Society of Chartered Life Underwriters
270 Bryn Mawr Avenue
Bryn Mawr, Pennsylvania 19010

"CFC" OR "CH.F.C.," CHARTERED FINANCIAL CONSULTANT

The American College, Bryn Mawr, Pennsylvania, not only awards the CLU designation discussed above but also prepares candidates for the Chartered Financial Consultant program. Although most of the Chartered Financial Consultants become insurance agents, their training qualifies them to guide you along paths of sanity toward financial planning. Recently more and more of them have concentrated their efforts in this area of financial planning and away from simply insurance sales. For information as well as a listing of the practitioners in your geographic area, write to:

The American College
Bryn Mawr, Pennsylvania 19010

Another good source of names of financial professionals that includes many of the CFPs, CLUs, CFCs and Ch.F.C.s already mentioned is:

The Registry of Financial Planning Practitioners
Two, Concourse Parkway
Suite 800
Atlanta, Georgia 30328

Ask for the current edition. All these materials and sources should be available for the asking, but should fees or expenses be incurred, remember to ask your own accountant how much, if any, of such expenses is deductible given your unique and personal financial picture.

"C.P.A.," CERTIFIED PUBLIC ACCOUNTANT

You may already be using a CPA to prepare your income taxes and to help you with tax planning in general. What better person to contact regarding your ability to support a house at "X" cost with "Y" expenses on "Z" income? He or she knows your financial history better than you do. Furthermore, the CPA credential itself tells you a great deal about this professional. Having met the licensing requirements of the state in which he or she practices, the CPA is required to pass a series of tests, to have reached a certain age, and even to have achieved a certain length of experience (it varies from state to state) before taking on clients. In addition to preparing tax returns and doing auditing and accounting, the CPA has had extensive experience in tax planning. Added together, this wealth of knowledge can only be a help to you in deciding whether or not the expenditure you are contemplating is within your budget. Only the accountant's expertise, coupled with your input, can come up with the formula that equals happiness and financial stability.

The International Association for Financial Planners is committed to lobbying for standards that would apply to all qualified practitioners of this profession:

1. MBAs, Masters of Business Administration
2. CLUs, Chartered Life Underwriters
3. CFPs, Certified Financial Planners
4. JDs. Many lawyers practice financial planning in conjunction with the practice of law. "JD" means doctor of jurisprudence or doctor of law.
5. CPAs, Certified Public Accountants

Information about all these should be sought directly through the IAFP. Write to:

The International Association for Financial Planners
Two, Concourse Parkway
Suite 800
Atlanta, Georgia 30328

Should you consider using a tax preparer who advertises in the TV schedule you find in the supermarket?

Is the tax-preparation desk at the shopping mall or in the department store lobby manned by professionals who can really help you?

Does that large chain of tax preparers who advertise during the midnight movie on TV really get big refunds for their customers, or is it all done with mirrors?

Can you be sure that a tax preparer who "guarantees" to get you a bigger refund will keep you out of trouble?

Obviously, the world of tax preparers is peopled with good and bad guys and you have to do a bit of sifting to separate them out. In general, if all you are doing is filing the shortest of forms, and your income and deductions are no different from what they have been for years, you can count on most tax preparers to do a good job.

But that is all you can expect. They will follow a step-by-step preparation manual, plug in your information, and grind out a completed form. You will receive no advice, no direction for next year, no suggestions on how to improve your tax picture, no planning, and certainly no follow-up for next year other than a reminder to come back again. Remember, such tax preparers are usually part-time help and they are really only picking up a few extra bucks during a busy period for tax preparers in general.

Another problem that could arise if you use a fly-by-night tax preparer is your inability to find him or her again if you were audited by the IRS. They may have taken deductions challenged in that audit and if you cannot locate your tax preparer, you will have to go to the IRS yourself. A firm of qualified CPAs would still be there and have at least someone on staff to answer questions during the audit. The CPA is probably the *one professional* on your financial team who can be truly relied upon when it comes to your taxes. Of course, a CPA will also be the most expensive to retain. Typical fees for a family with an annual income of $50,000 to $100,000 will be around $500 for the preparation of your income tax package of both federal and local returns.

Similar to a CPA but possessing an additional credential are the "Enrolled Agents." In *some* cases CPAs themselves, enrolled agents are former IRS auditors who have worked for the Service for several years, passed certain tests administered by the IRS, and charge hourly fees. To get a copy of their directory of agents in your area, call The National Association of Enrolled Agents Toll-Free (800) 424-4339.

Depending on the complexity of the year's financial activity, one or two consultations with both your CPA and your financial planner should be enough to help you set up your tax strategy for the year. Of course each of these sessions will involve hourly fees that can be deducted on your returns.

The very least you should expect from those employed for these purposes is as follows:

1. Tax-planning sessions held early enough in the year to ensure time to make whatever moves are required by your changing financial picture.
2. The person or firm must be available to you and not "always out to lunch, at a meeting, with a client, or out of town," every time you call or need them. This is probably the biggest problem most people have with professionals. They (you) let them treat you like nothing. Remember, when you hire *anyone* to do anything for you, he or she is *your employee* and must do what you are paying to have done. Would you still pay that cleaning person if on Thursday afternoon the house was still dirty?
3. The services advertised must be the services you get. If the CPA firm takes you on as a client and doesn't provide planning as already described; or if they promise big refunds but you are constantly being audited and the deductions are constantly being disallowed; if your returns are not filed on time and you are paying a penalty every year; or if you generally "feel" that they aren't doing what you hired them to do, they are wrong for you.

No matter which professional you hire, his or her job is to work for you and unless the person does what you want, look for a replacement. Look at Appendix B, "Guide to Tax-Free Services," and see whether it is possible for you to become your own tax professional and use outsiders only for long-range tax planning and perhaps once-or-twice-in-a-lifetime financial events such as a new house, a busy year in the stock market, or a dramatic change in income.

As your own tax expert, be sure that you keep good records. If you want to function as a professional, you have to act like one.

Some of the files and records the IRS itself recommends keeping include:

1. Copies of your old tax returns. If you have the space, why not keep all your old tax files? If not, those for the last seven years should be more than enough. If you cannot locate back filings, the IRS has them and will send you copies if you submit:

   Form 4506, Request For Copy of Tax Form

   In this way your home files can be complete and will be available for future reference not only by you but by your heirs as well.

2. Employee expenses. Travel, entertainment, gift, and other job-related records, as well as car expense records, should be kept. For a more complete discussion of which records you need to keep, go to the local IRS offices and pick up:

   Publication 463, Travel, Entertainment and Gift Expenses
   Publication 917, Business Use of a Car

   They discuss not only which records to keep but which deductions apply.

3. Business use of your home. If you work at home at the pleasure of your employer, or because you are self-employed, you must be able to prove all related expenses. The IRS has a publication that details not only the records you must be maintaining but also the calculations and rules that apply to your deductions. Ask for:

   Publication 587, Business Use of Your Home

4. Your home. Records from the date of purchase detailing all expenses that will ultimately constitute the cost basis should be kept as long as you own the home and for seven years following its sale. Again, it is not a bad idea to keep all tax-related records forever if you have the room. Storage of tax records and expenses related thereto is a deduction too. Two IRS publications will help you in this area:

   Publication 523, Tax Information on Selling Your Home
   IRS Form 2119, Sale or Exchange of Principal Residence
   (See Appendix A for copy of Form 2119 and instructions.)

Other related records that should be kept, if applicable to your situation, are those of:

Earnings for self-employment Social Security taxes.
Capital gains and losses.
Cost basis of property.
Reinvested dividends.
Services for charitable organizations.

You should also keep:

Canceled checks.
Receipts from charitable contributions for cash or goods.
The names of charities and their addresses.
The dates and location of property given away.
Descriptions of property given to charity.
W-2 Forms (federal, state and local).
Medical bills and related receipts.
Pay statements.
Divorce decrees.

A simple year-by-year filing system could save you thousands of dollars if you should be called by the IRS for an audit. Yes, I know, only a very small percentage of taxpayers get audited on a random basis, but isn't it worth devoting a file drawer in the basement to storing records that might save you a few hundred thousand dollars in penalties and interest?

10

The Bresnan New Tax Law Intelligence Test . . . In Words Of One Syllable: Now That You've Read The Book, Do You Know The Answers? Let's Find Out!

1. A single adult, earning $27,000 in 1987, would have a marginal tax rate of:
   (a) 15%
   (b) 28%
   (c) 35%
   (d) 38.5%
2. That same single adult, earning $27,000 in 1988, would have a marginal tax rate of:
   (a) 15%
   (b) 28%
   (c) 35%
   (d) 38%
3. The maximum tax rate for a single adult in 1987 is:
   (a) 28%
   (b) 35%
   (c) 38.5%
   (d) 50%
4. A married couple, filing jointly and earning a combined income of $45,000 in 1987, would have a marginal tax rate of:
   (a) 15%
   (b) 28%
   (c) 35%
   (d) 38.5%
5. That same married couple, filing jointly, still earning $45,000 in 1988, would have a marginal tax rate of:
   (a) 15%
   (b) 28%
   (c) 35%
   (d) 38.5%

6. For all practical purposes, the maximum tax rate for a single adult in 1988 is:
(a) 28%
(b) 33%
(c) 38%
(d) 38.5%

7. The maximum tax rate for a married couple, filing jointly in 1987, is:
(a) 28%
(b) 35%
(c) 38.5%
(d) 50%

8. For all practical purposes, the maximum tax rate for a married couple, filing jointly in 1988, is:
(a) 28%
(b) 33%
(c) 38%
(d) 38.5%

9. Which of the following statements is true concerning Uncle Sam's treatment of short-term and long-term capital gains, under the new tax law?
(a) the laws concerning capital gains have not changed.
(b) only those laws concerning short-term capital gains have changed.
(c) after 1987, there will no longer be a distinction between short-term and long-term capital gains.
(d) you can still write off a long-term capital loss of as much as $5,000.

10. Under the new tax law, the dividend exclusion allowed in years prior to 1987 has been:
(a) repealed.
(b) left as it was.
(c) changed significantly.
(d) a and c.

11. Employee business deductions enjoyed in prior years will now be treated as "miscellaneous deductions," and only the amount in excess of ____% of your adjusted gross income can be deducted.

(a) 1%
(b) 2%
(c) 3%
(d) 4%

12. Now that the new tax law is in effect, which statement regarding the deductibility of monies placed in IRA accounts is false?

(a) Uncle Sam has made some drastic changes in the tax laws governing the deductibility of IRAs.
(b) Single adults earning less than $25,000 can still take a full IRA deduction.
(c) married couples, filing jointly and earning less than $50,000 per year, can still take a full IRA deduction.
(d) your income level in 1987 may determine whether you are entitled to a full IRA deduction.

13. Which of the following statements concerning the deductibility of medical expenses is false under the new tax law?

(a) Uncle Sam has changed the tax treatment of medical expenses. You may no longer deduct the total medical expense in excess of 5% of your adjusted gross income.
(b) you may deduct all of your hospital bills.
(c) you may deduct only the amount of medical expense in excess of 7.5% of your adjusted gross income.
(d) you may deduct only the amount of medical expense in excess of 10% of your adjusted gross income.

14. Under tax reform, the deductibility of consumer interest (interest paid on a car loan, credit-card debt, installment loan, and the like):

(a) has not changed.
(b) has been completely done away with.
(c) will be gradually phased out so that only 65% of consumer interest will be allowed in 1987 and 40% of consumer interest will be allowed in 1988.
(d) will be phased out over a two-year period so that only

50% of consumer interest will be allowed in 1987 and no consumer interest will be allowed in 1988.

15. The treatment of charitable deductions under tax reform:
(a) has not changed.
(b) has been completely done away with; that is, charitable deductions are no longer tax deductible.
(c) makes charitable deductions still valid, but only 50% of the value of the contribution may be written off.
(d) is that they are still deductible, but only when you itemize each and every deduction.

16. Which statement concerning your house and the new tax law is false?
(a) when purchasing a new principal residence of equal or greater cost than the selling price of the previous one, the entire gain from property #1 is rolled over into property #2.
(b) interest paid on mortgages for principal residences and vacation properties are tax-deductible (up to the cost basis).
(c) you may deduct all of the interest on a home improvement loan up to the cost basis.
(d) under tax reform, you may deduct only 70% of the interest paid on home improvement loans.

17. Which of the following statements concerning the deductibility of interest expenses associated with consumer debt (car loans, college loans, credit-card debt, etc.) is true?
(a) you will be able to deduct 100% of the interest expenses paid on the above items in 1987.
(b) you will be able to write off only 65% of the interest expense paid for consumer debt in 1987.
(c) you will be able to write off only 40% of the interest expense paid for consumer debt in 1987.
(d) none of the above.

18. If your total interest expense resulting from consumer debt equals $5,000 in 1987, you will be allowed to deduct:
(a) $3,250

(b) $1,750
(c) $1,000
(d) $800

19. If your total interest expense resulting from consumer debt equals $5,000 in 1988, you will be allowed to deduct:
(a) $3,250
(b) $2,000
(c) $1,750
(d) $1,000

20. In 1988,
(a) only short-term capital gains will be taxed as ordinary income.
(b) only long-term capital gains will be taxed as ordinary income.
(c) all gains will be treated as ordinary income and taxed accordingly.
(d) the New York Giants will win the Super Bowl.

21. Under tax reform, which of the following is true?
(a) you may deduct *all* of the interest expense on a home improvement loan.
(b) you may deduct the interest expense on a home improvement loan only up to the cost basis.
(c) you may deduct no more than 60% of the interest expense associated with a home improvement loan in 1987, and no more than 40% in 1988.
(d) deducting any of the interest expense on a home improvement loan will result in a minimum jail sentence of five years.

22. Which of the following statements regarding the deductibility of interest payments on mortgages is false?
(a) interest payments on mortgages for principal residences are deductible up to the cost basis, under the new tax law.
(b) interest payments on vacation properties are still tax-deductible, up to the cost basis.

(c) in 1987, you may write off only 40% of the interest expense associated with all mortgages.

(d) both (b) and (c) are false.

23. Which of the following statements is false under the new tax law?

(a) the new tax law has had no effect on the treatment of property taxes; property tax payments are still fully deductible in 1987 and 1988.

(b) you may deduct all of the points paid as interest on the first mortgage for the first year of ownership.

(c) the deductibility of points paid on that second mortgage or any type of refinancing will now be spread over the entire life of the loan.

(d) points paid for any type of mortgage are no longer tax-deductible.

24. Which of the following statements regarding capital gains is true?

(a) under the old tax law, 90% of all long-term capital gains were tax-free.

(b) before tax reform, the maximum effective tax rate on long-term capital gains was 25%.

(c) from 1987 onward, all capital gains will be taxed as ordinary income.

(d) in 1988, the maximum tax rate for a married couple realizing a long-term capital gain will be 33%.

25. Which of the following statements regarding interest expense on securities held in margin accounts is false?

(a) before tax reform, only 50% of the interest expense on securities held in margin accounts was deductible.

(b) before tax reform, all of the interest expense on securities held in margin accounts was fully deductible.

(c) under the new tax law, the income earned on an investment is a major factor in determining the amount of deductibility of the interest expense associated with that security.

(d) the new tax law has reduced the amount of interest expense you may deduct in 1987 and 1988.

26. Under the new tax law, IRAs,
- **(a)** are still fully deductible, and have not been affected by tax reform.
- **(b)** are no longer tax-deductible.
- **(c)** are still fully tax-deductible for some people.
- **(d)** none of the above.

27. A married couple earns $55,000 in 1987 and files a joint return. They are not covered by any sort of company retirement or pension plan. Under tax reform:
- **(a)** they would be entitled to a full IRA deduction.
- **(b)** they would be entitled to a partial IRA deduction.
- **(c)** they are entitled to no IRA deduction.
- **(d)** none of the above.

28. A married couple earns $39,000 in 1987 and files a joint return. They are both covered by a company pension plan. Under tax reform:
- **(a)** they would be entitled to a full IRA deduction.
- **(b)** they would be entitled to a partial IRA deduction.
- **(c)** they are entitled to no IRA deduction.
- **(d)** none of the above.

29. A married couple earns $45,000 in 1987 and files a joint return; they are covered by a company retirement and pension plan. In 1987 they contribute $2,000 to their IRA. Under tax reform:
- **(a)** they are entitled to a full $2,000 deduction.
- **(b)** they may take only a $1,000 deduction.
- **(c)** they may not take any deduction because they are covered by a company retirement plan.
- **(d)** none of the above.

30. A married couple earns $75,000 in 1987 and files a joint return. Neither is covered by a company pension or retirement plan. Under the new tax law:
- **(a)** this couple may still take a full IRA deduction.
- **(b)** may be entitled to a partial IRA deduction.
- **(c)** this couple is not entitled to an IRA deduction.
- **(d)** none of the above.

31. A single adult earns $20,000 in 1987 and is covered by a company Keogh plan. Under the new tax law:
(a) he or she is entitled to a full IRA deduction.
(b) he or she is entitled only to a partial IRA deduction.
(c) this person is entitled to no deduction because he or she is covered by a company Keogh plan.
(d) none of the above.

32. A single adult earns $29,000 in 1987, is covered by a company pension plan, and holds $10,000 in various money-market accounts. In 1987 he contributes $2,000 to his IRA. Under tax reform:
(a) he is entitled to a full $2,000 deduction.
(b) he is entitled to take only a $1,200 deduction.
(c) he is entitled only to an $800.00 deduction.
(d) he is entitled to no IRA deduction.
(e) none of the above.

33. Under tax reform, all income, dividends, or gains realized in an IRA account prior to withdrawal:
(a) remain tax-deferred.
(b) are now taxed at 28%.
(c) are taxed at your ordinary rate.
(d) none of the above.

34. If tax reform makes it necessary for you to deal with both deductible and non-deductible IRA monies, the author suggests that you:
(a) keep all the money in one account.
(b) open a separate account for those contributions that are non-deductible.
(c) buy a new calculator because you are going to do more "figurin'" now than you ever did before in your whole life.
(d) purchase a zero coupon municipal bond.

35. A 35-year-old woman leaves her job at one company and moves to another. She has accumulated a significant amount of money in her company retirement plan, and a portion of that total is eligible for a rollover at the time of her move. Under the new tax law:

(a) she forfeits her right to roll over that money when she changes jobs.
(b) she may roll over 50% of the total amount eligible for rollover.
(c) only $2,000 of the total retirement plan may be rolled over.
(d) all the money eligible for rollover may be rolled over.

36. The author suggests that in some cases it is wise to use IRA money to purchase certain types of mutual funds. According to the author, mutual funds offer which of the following attractive benefits?
(a) professional Management: Portfolio managers manage these mutual funds and are usually much more knowledgeable than you in handling these investment vehicles.
(b) wide diversification.
(c) liquidity.
(d) returns that exceed those of penny stocks, in most cases.
(e) a, b, and c.

37. Under the new tax law, interest income earned on CDs (Certificates of Deposit) is:
(a) tax free.
(b) always taxed at a rate of 28%.
(c) taxed as ordinary income.
(d) none of the above.

38. In 1988, the gains realized from the sale of collectibles such as rare stamps, coins, antiques, comic books, rugs, and pictures will be:
(a) tax-free.
(b) taxed as ordinary income.
(c) both a and b.
(d) none of the above.

39. Under the new tax law, the income earned on United States Treasury Notes is:
(a) tax-free income.
(b) subject to federal, state, and local income taxes.
(c) subject to federal and state income taxes.

(d) subject to federal tax, but free of state and local income taxes.
(e) none of the above.

40. Interest from which of the following investment vehicles is subject to state and local income taxes?
(a) United States Treasury Bills.
(b) United States Treasury Notes.
(c) corporate bonds.
(d) United States Treasury Bonds.
(e) none of the above, they are all exempt from state and local taxes.

Now that wasn't so bad, was it? Now that you've completed the Bresnan New Tax Law Intelligence Test, it's time to find out how much you've learned about the new tax law. The answers to the test (if you haven't found them already) are on page 123. It's time to turn to the page and start grading your exam; and remember, no cheating—Uncle Sam is probably watching you right now.

Once you have calculated the number of correct answers, multiply that number by 2½ to get your total score and NEW TAX-LAW INTELLIGENCE QUOTIENT. If your total score is:

90-100: Congratulations! You are either a new-tax-law whiz or a CPA!

80-90: Great score. Rest assured that you will probably pay less in taxes than someone without your level of tax knowledge.

70-80: Not bad. You seem to have a pretty good working knowledge of how the new tax law will affect your payment of taxes in years to come.

60-70: Perhaps you used this book to help cure your insomnia. You may wish to go back and re-read portions of the book.

40-60: Did you really read the whole book or just skip to this test? In any event, I suggest you stay after school and review the relevant portions of the book. (I suggest that this time you read the chapters that come after the table of contents.)

Less than 40: If you scored less than 40, I suggest that you go back and review the book.

ANSWERS TO THE BRESNAN NEW TAX LAW INTELLIGENCE TEST

1. B
2. B
3. C
4. B
5. B
6. B
7. C
8. B
9. C
10. D
11. B
12. C
13. D
14. C
15. D
16. D
17. B
18. A
19. C
20. C
21. B
22. C
23. D
24. D
25. A
26. C
27. A
28. A
29. B
30. A
31. A
32. B
33. A
34. B
35. D
36. E
37. C
38. B
39. D
40. C

Appendix A

Commonly-Used IRS Forms, Publications And Selected Instructions

The Internal Revenue Service, like any other governmental agency, can function only by using a form for every purpose. Since each of you has a unique financial picture that changes from year to year, it would be impossible to cover every situation by using one common form, so whenever something new comes up probably another form will be required. The forms discussed here, by no means include every one that's available, but do include those which most of you will need during a normal lifetime.

Instructions are given so that you can review the tax situation each form deals with and how they should be filled out. Of course, as your tax problems become more complicated, the need for professional help becomes more obvious.

Copies of the following forms appear as part of this section:

Form W-4A Employee's Witholding Allowance Certificate (shorter version).

Form W-4 Employee's Withholding Allowance Certificate (long version)

Instructions for Form W-4 Employee's Withholding Allowance Certificate.

Form 709 United States Gift Tax Return.

Publication 919 Is My Withholding Correct?

Form 942 Employer's Quarterly Tax Return for Household Employees (includes general instructions).

Form 1040 U. S. Individual Income Tax Return.

Schedule A (Form 1040) Itemized Deductions.

Schedule B (Form 1040) Interest and Dividend Income.

Form 1040A Amended U. S. Individual Income Tax Return.

Form 1040X Amended U. S. Individual Income Tax Return.

Instructions for Form 1040X.

Schedule D (Form 1040X) Capital Gains and Losses.

Form 1120 S U. S. Income Tax Return for an S Corporation.

Form 2106 Employee Business Expenses.

Instructions for Form 2106 Employee Business Expenses.

Form 2119 Sale or Exchange of Principal Residence.

Instructions for Form 2119 Sale or Exchange of Principal Residence.

Form 2210 Underpayment of Estimated Tax by Individuals.

Form 2441 Credit for Child and Dependent Care Expenses.

Instructions for Form 2441 Credit for Child and Dependent Care Expenses.

Instructions for Form 2553 Election by a Small Business Corporation.

The purpose of this Form is to elect to be treated as an "S Corporation." (See Form 1120 S, above.)

Form 2688 Application for Additional Extension of Time to File.

Instructions for Form 2688 Application for Additional Extension of Time to File.

Form 3903 Moving Expenses (includes general instructions).

Form 4137 Computation of Social Security Tax on Unreported Tip Income (includes general instructions).

Form 4684 Casualty and Thefts.

Form 4768 Application for Extension of Time to File U. S. Estate Tax Return and/or Pay Estate Tax (general instructions included).

Form 4782 Employee Moving Expense Information (general instruction included).

Form 4798 Carryover of Pre-1970 Capital Losses (includes general instructions).

Form 4852 Substitute for Form W-2 Wage and Tax Statement or Form W2P, Statement for Recipients of Annuities, Pensions, Retired Pay or IRA Payments.

Form 4868 Applications for Automatic Extension of Time to File U. S. Individual Income Tax Return (includes general instructions).

Form 4952 Investment Interest Expense Deduction (includes general instructions).

Form 5305 Individual Retirement Trust Account (includes general instructions).

Form 5305-SEP Simplified Employee Pension—Individual Retirement Accounts Contribution Agreement (includes general instructions).

Form 5329 Return for Individual Retirement Arrangement Taxes.

Instructions for Form 5329 Return for Individual Retirement Arrangement Taxes.

Form 5695 Residential Energy Credit Carryforward (includes general instructions).

Form 6251 Alternative Minimum Tax Computation (includes general instructions).

Form 8283 Noncash Charitable Contributions.

Instructions for Form 8283 Noncash Charitable Contributions.

1987 Form W-4A

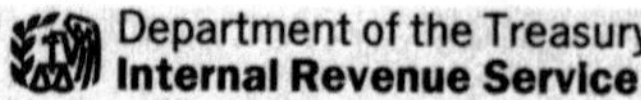

Department of the Treasury
Internal Revenue Service

What is Form W-4A? This form is an easier way to figure your withholding than the 4-page 1987 Form W-4. If you have already given your employer a Form W-4 this year, **do not** file a new Form W-4A unless you wish to change your withholding.

Caution: Form W-4A may cause more or less tax to be withheld from your wages than you wish because it adjusts your withholding only for pay you receive after it takes effect. If not enough tax was withheld earlier in the year, you can increase your withholding by reducing the allowances claimed on line 4 of the form or by requesting that more money be withheld on line 5 of the form.

Exemption From Withholding—Important Change in Law. If you are a dependent of another person (for example, a student who can still be claimed on your parents' return), you are not exempt if you have any nonwage income (such as interest on savings) **and** expect your total income to be more than $500.

What Do I Need To Do? Exempt employees can skip the Worksheet and go directly to line 6 of Form W-4A. All others must complete lines A through G. Many employees can stop at line G of the Worksheet.

Nonwage Income? If you have a large amount of income from other sources (such as interest or dividends), you should consider either using the 1987 Form W-4 or making estimated tax payments using Form 1040-ES. Call 1-800-424-3676 (in Hawaii and Alaska, check your local telephone directory) for copies of the 1987 Form W-4 and **Publication 919**, "Is My Withholding Correct?"

When Should I File? File as soon as possible to avoid underwithholding problems. If you do not file by October 1, 1987, your allowances may be adjusted to "1" if single or "2" if married and your take home pay may be reduced.

Two-Earner Couples? More Than One Job? To figure the number of allowances you may claim, combine allowances and wages from all jobs on one worksheet. File a Form W-4A with each employer, but do not claim the same allowances more than once. Your withholding will usually be more accurate if you claim all allowances on the highest paying job.

W-4A Worksheet To Figure Your Withholding Allowances

A Enter "1" for **yourself** if no one else can claim you as a dependent . . . . . A ______

B Enter "1" if:
- 1. You are single and have only one job; or
- 2. You are married, have only one job, and your spouse does not work; or
- 3. Your wages from a second job or your spouse's wages (the total of both) are $2,500 or less.

. . . . . B ______

C Enter "1" for your **spouse** if no one else claims your spouse as a dependent . . . . . C ______

D Enter number of **dependents** other than your spouse that you will claim on your return . . . . . D ______

E Enter "1" if you want to reduce your withholding because you or your spouse is at least **age 65 or blind** and you do not plan to itemize deductions . . . . . E ______

F Enter "1" if you want to reduce your withholding because you have at least $1,500 of **child or dependent care expenses** for which you plan to claim a credit . . . . . F ______

G Add lines A through F and enter total here . . . . . ▶ G ______

- If you plan to **itemize or claim other deductions** and wish to reduce your withholding, turn to the Deductions Worksheet on the back.
- If you have **more than one job or a working spouse** AND your combined earnings from all jobs exceed $25,000, or $15,000 if you are married filing a joint return, turn to the Two-Earner/Two-Job Worksheet on the back if you want to avoid having too little tax withheld.
- If **neither** of the above situations applies to you, **stop here** and enter the number from line G on line 4 of Form W-4A below.

------------------------ **Cut here and give the certificate to your employer. Keep the top portion for your records.** ------------------------

Form **W-4A**
Department of the Treasury
Internal Revenue Service

Employee's Withholding Allowance Certificate

▶ **For Privacy Act and Paperwork Reduction Act Notice, see reverse.**

OMB No. 1545-0010
1987

1 Type or print your full name	2 Your social security number
Home address (number and street or rural route)	3 Marital Status: ☐ Single ☐ Married ☐ Married, but withhold at higher Single rate. **Note:** *If married, but legally separated, or spouse is a nonresident alien, check the Single box.*
City or town, state, and ZIP code	

4 Total number of allowances you are claiming (from line G above, or from the Worksheets on back if they apply) . . . **4**

5 Additional amount, if any, you want deducted from each pay . . . . . **5** $

6 I claim exemption from withholding because (check boxes below that apply):

a ☐ Last year I did not owe any Federal income tax and had a right to a full refund of **ALL** income tax withheld, **AND**

b ☐ This year I do not expect to owe any Federal income tax and expect to have a right to a full refund of **ALL** income tax withheld. If both **a** and **b** apply, enter the year effective and "EXEMPT" here . . . . ▶ Year 19

c Are you a full-time student? . . . . . ☐ **Yes** ☐ **No**

Under penalties of perjury, I certify that I am entitled to the number of withholding allowances claimed on this certificate or, if claiming exemption from withholding, that I am entitled to claim the exempt status.

Employee's signature ▶ **Date ▶** , 1987

7 Employer's name and address **(Employer: Complete 7, 8, and 9 only if sending to IRS)**	8 Office code	9 Employer identification number

Form W-4A (1987) Page 2

Deductions Worksheet

NOTE: Use this Worksheet only if you plan to itemize or claim other deductions.

1. Enter an estimate of your 1987 itemized deductions. These include: home mortgage interest, 65% of personal interest, charitable contributions, state and local taxes (but not sales taxes), medical expenses in excess of 7.5% of your income, and miscellaneous deductions (most miscellaneous deductions are now deductible only in excess of 2% of your income) . . . 1 $
2. Enter: { $3,760 if married filing jointly or qualifying widow(er); $2,540 if single or head of household; $1,880 if married filing separately } . . . 2 $
3. **Subtract** line 2 from line 1. Enter the result, but not less than zero . . . 3 $
4. Enter an estimate of your 1987 adjustments to income. These include alimony paid and deductible IRA contributions . . . 4 $
5. **Add** lines 3 and 4 and enter the total . . . 5 $
6. Enter an estimate of your 1987 nonwage income (such as dividends or interest income) . . . 6 $
7. **Subtract** line 6 from line 5. Enter the result, but not less than zero . . . 7 $
8. **Divide** the amount on line 7 by $2,000 and enter the result here. Drop any fraction . . . 8
9. Enter the number from Form W-4A Worksheet, line G, on page 1 . . . 9
10. **Add** lines 8 and 9 and enter the total here. If you plan to use the Two-Earner/Two-Job Worksheet, also enter the total on line 1, below. Otherwise **stop here** and enter this total on Form W-4A, line 4 on page 1 . . . 10

Two-Earner/Two-Job Worksheet

NOTE: Use this Worksheet only if the instructions at line G on page 1 direct you here.

1. Enter the number from line G on page 1 (or from line 10 above if you used the Deductions Worksheet) . . . 1
2. Enter "1" if you are married filing a joint return and earnings from the lower paying jobs held by you or your spouse exceed $3,000. Otherwise enter "0" . . . 2
3. **Subtract** line 2 from line 1 and enter the result here. If you entered "1" on line 2 and combined earnings from all jobs are less than $40,000, enter the result on Form W-4A, line 4, page 1, and **do not** use the rest of this worksheet. Otherwise, continue . . . 3
4. Find the number in **Table 1** below that applies to the **LOWEST** paying job and enter it here . . . 4
5. If line 3 is **GREATER THAN OR EQUAL TO** line 4, **subtract** line 4 from line 3. Enter the result here (if zero, enter "0") and on Form W-4A, line 4, page 1. **Do not** use the rest of this worksheet . . . 5
6. If line 3 is **LESS THAN** line 4, enter "0" on Form W-4A, line 4, page 1, and enter the number from line 4 of this worksheet . . . 6
7. Enter the number from line 3 of this worksheet . . . 7
8. **Subtract** line 7 from line 6 . . . 8
9. Find the amount in **Table 2** below that applies to the **HIGHEST** paying job and enter it here . . . 9 $
10. **Multiply** line 9 by line 8 and enter the result here . . . 10 $
11. **Divide** line 10 by the number of pay periods each year. (For example, divide by 26 if you are paid every other week.) Enter the result here and on Form W-4A, line 5, page 1 . . . 11 $

Table 1: Two-Earner/Two-Job Worksheet

Married Filing Jointly		All Others	
If wages from **LOWEST** paying job are—	Enter on line 4, above	If wages from **LOWEST** paying job are—	Enter on line 4, above
0 - $6,000	0	0 - $4,000	0
6,001 - 10,000	1	4,001 - 7,000	1
10,001 - 13,000	2	7,001 - 11,000	2
13,001 - 16,000	3	11,001 - 14,000	3
16,001 - 20,000	4	14,001 - 17,000	4
20,001 - 23,000	5	17,001 - 23,000	5
23,001 - 26,000	6	23,001 - 30,000	6
26,001 - 29,000	7	30,001 and over	7
29,001 - 35,000	8		
35,001 - 50,000	9		
50,001 and over	10		

Table 2: Two-Earner/Two-Job Worksheet

Married Filing Jointly		All Others	
If wages from **HIGHEST** paying job are—	Enter on line 9, above	If wages from **HIGHEST** paying job are—	Enter on line 9, above
0 - $30,000	$300	0 - $17,000	$300
30,001 - 47,000	500	17,001 - 28,000	500
47,001 and over	700	28,001 and over	700

Privacy Act and Paperwork Reduction Act Notice.—We ask for this information to carry out the Internal Revenue laws of the United States. We may give the information to the Department of Justice for civil or criminal litigation and to cities, states, and the District of Columbia for use in administering their tax laws. You are required to give this information to your employer.

GPO : 1987 O - 183-427

Form **W-4** Department of the Treasury Internal Revenue Service

Employee's Withholding Allowance Certificate

▶ **For Privacy Act and Paperwork Reduction Act Notice, see instructions.**

OMB No. 1545-0010 **1987**

1 Type or print your full name | 2 Your social security number

Home address (number and street or rural route)

City or town, state, and ZIP code

3 Marital Status ☐ Single ☐ Married ☐ Married, but withhold at higher Single rate

Note: *If married, but legally separated, or spouse is a nonresident alien, check the Single box.*

4 Total number of allowances you are claiming (from the Worksheet on page 3) . . . . .

5 Additional amount, if any, you want deducted from each pay (see Step 4 on page 2) . . . . . $

6 I claim exemption from withholding because (see Step 2 above and check boxes below that apply):

a ☐ Last year I did not owe any Federal income tax and had a right to a full refund of **ALL** income tax withheld, **AND**

b ☐ This year I do not expect to owe any Federal income tax and expect to have a right to a full refund of **ALL** income tax withheld. If both a and b apply, enter the year effective and "EXEMPT" here . . . . ▶ Year 19

c If you entered "EXEMPT" on line 6b, are you a full-time student? . . . . . ☐ **Yes** ☐ **No**

Under penalties of perjury, I certify that I am entitled to the number of withholding allowances claimed on this certificate or, if claiming exemption from withholding, that I am entitled to claim the exempt status.

Employee's signature ▶ **Date ▶** , 19

7 Employer's name and address **(Employer: Complete 7, 8, and 9 only if sending to IRS)** | 8 Office code | 9 Employer identification number

Cut along this line and give this form to your employer. Keep the rest for your records.

Form **W-4** Department of the Treasury Internal Revenue Service

Employee's Withholding Allowance Certificate

▶ **For Privacy Act and Paperwork Reduction Act Notice, see instructions.**

OMB No. 1545-0010 **1987**

1 Type or print your full name | 2 Your social security number

Home address (number and street or rural route)

City or town, state, and ZIP code

3 Marital Status ☐ Single ☐ Married ☐ Married, but withhold at higher Single rate

Note: *If married, but legally separated, or spouse is a nonresident alien, check the Single box.*

4 Total number of allowances you are claiming (from the Worksheet on page 3) . . . . .

5 Additional amount, if any, you want deducted from each pay (see Step 4 on page 2) . . . . . $

6 I claim exemption from withholding because (see Step 2 above and check boxes below that apply):

a ☐ Last year I did not owe any Federal income tax and had a right to a full refund of **ALL** income tax withheld, **AND**

b ☐ This year I do not expect to owe any Federal income tax and expect to have a right to a full refund of **ALL** income tax withheld. If both a and b apply, enter the year effective and "EXEMPT" here . . . . ▶ Year 19

c If you entered "EXEMPT" on line 6b, are you a full-time student? . . . . . ☐ **Yes** ☐ **No**

Under penalties of perjury, I certify that I am entitled to the number of withholding allowances claimed on this certificate or, if claiming exemption from withholding, that I am entitled to claim the exempt status.

Employee's signature ▶ **Date ▶** , 19

7 Employer's name and address **(Employer: Complete 7, 8, and 9 only if sending to IRS)** | 8 Office code | 9 Employer identification number

References on the Form W-4 refer to Form W-4 Instructions.

☆ U.S. Government Printing Office: 1986—181-447/40019

Page 4

1987

 Department of the Treasury
Internal Revenue Service

Instructions for Form W-4

Employee's Withholding Allowance Certificate

Why Must I Complete a New Form W-4?

The Tax Reform Act of 1986 made many changes to the tax law that could affect your taxes for 1987. Therefore, the amount of tax that is now withheld from your pay may no longer be correct. So that your employer will not withhold too much or too little tax from your pay, give your employer a new Form W-4.

When Must I File the Form?

Give your employer a new Form W-4 **as soon as possible**. While the law requires you to file a new form before October 1, 1987, you are urged to file early to avoid incorrect withholding.

What Happens If I Do Not Complete the Form?

The amount of tax withheld from your pay may not be close to the amount of tax you will owe when you file your tax return. If you do not give your employer a new Form W-4, your employer will have to ignore any previous form you have filed, and the amount withheld will probably not be correct for your tax situation.

How Do I Complete the Form?

The following instructions tell you how to complete the Form W-4 on this page. Use the worksheet on page 3 to figure the number of withholding allowances you can claim on Form W-4.

Please Note: Most employees will have to complete ONLY lines A through E of the worksheet. But if you have a spouse who is also employed, or you have more than one job at the same time, or you have nonwage income, complete the rest of the worksheet. You should also complete the worksheet if you have itemized deductions, tax credits, adjustments to income, or the age or blindness deduction.

Should I Claim the Special Withholding Allowance?

Claim this allowance if you have only one job at a time and you don't have a working spouse. Take this allowance so that you won't have too much tax withheld from your pay. See line B of the worksheet on page 3.

Step-by-Step Instructions

Step 1—How To Complete Form W-4.— First, fill in the information asked for on lines 1 through 3 of the form. Then, if you think you might be exempt from withholding, read the instructions for Step 2 below. Otherwise, skip to Step 3 on page 2. If you want to have more money withheld from your pay, see Step 4 on page 2.

After your new Form W-4 takes effect, you should check to see if you are having the proper amount withheld. To do this, you may want to get **Publication 919,** Is My Withholding Correct? For more details on withholding, get **Publication 505**, Tax Withholding and Estimated Tax, and **Publication 553**, Highlights of 1986 Tax Law Changes. You can get these publications by calling 1-800-424-FORM (3676).

Note: ***If Your Allowances Change.***—*If the number of withholding allowances you are entitled to claim decreases to fewer than the number you claim on this Form W-4, you must file a new W-4 within 10 days.*

Step 2—Are You Exempt From Withholding?—You are exempt from withholding ONLY if:

1. Last year you did not have any Federal income tax liability; AND
2. This year you expect to have no Federal income tax liability.

Important Change in the Law.—If you can be claimed as a dependent on another person's tax return (for example, on your parent's return), you may not be exempt. You **cannot** claim exempt status if you have any nonwage income, such as interest on savings, and expect your wages plus this nonwage income to add up to more than $500.

If you are exempt, go to line 6 of Form W-4 and complete the appropriate boxes. Your exempt status will remain in effect until February 15 of the next year. If you still qualify for exempt status next year, complete and file a new form by that date.

(Continued on page 2)

Cut along this line and give this form to your employer. Keep the rest for your records.

Form **W-4** Department of the Treasury Internal Revenue Service

Employee's Withholding Allowance Certificate

► **For Privacy Act and Paperwork Reduction Act Notice, see instructions.**

OMB No. 1545-0010 **1987**

1 Type or print your full name	2 Your social security number
Home address (number and street or rural route)	3 Marital Status: ☐ Single ☐ Married ☐ Married, but withhold at higher Single rate. **Note:** *If married, but legally separated, or spouse is a nonresident alien, check the Single box.*
City or town, state, and ZIP code	

4 Total number of allowances you are claiming (from the Worksheet on page 3)

5 Additional amount, if any, you want deducted from each pay (see Step 4 on page 2) $

6 I claim exemption from withholding because (see Step 2 above and check boxes below that apply):

a ☐ Last year I did not owe any Federal income tax and had a right to a full refund of **ALL** income tax withheld, **AND**

b ☐ This year I do not expect to owe any Federal income tax and expect to have a right to a full refund of **ALL** income tax withheld. If both a and b apply, enter the year effective and "EXEMPT" here ► Year 19

c If you entered "EXEMPT" on line 6b, are you a full-time student? ☐ Yes ☐ No

Under penalties of perjury, I certify that I am entitled to the number of withholding allowances claimed on this certificate or, if claiming exemption from withholding, that I am entitled to claim the exempt status.

Employee's signature ► Date ► , 19

7 Employer's name and address **(Employer: Complete 7, 8, and 9 only if sending to IRS)**	8 Office code	9 Employer identification number

Step 3—Complete the Worksheet on Page 3.— By using this worksheet, the amount of tax withheld from your pay should closely match your tax liability for the year.

Please claim all the withholding allowances to which you are entitled. In certain cases, your employer must send copies of the Form W-4 to IRS. You may then be asked to verify your allowances. This applies if you claim more than 10 withholding allowances, or you claim exemption from withholding under Step 2 and your wages are expected to usually exceed $200 a week.

Penalty.—You may be fined $500 if, with no reasonable basis, you file a Form W-4 that results in less tax being withheld than is properly allowable. In addition, criminal penalties apply for willfully supplying false or fraudulent information or failing to supply information requiring an increase in withholding.

Line B—Special Withholding Allowance.— The Special Withholding Allowance is very important. Claim it if you qualify for it, because if you **do not**, too much tax may be withheld from your pay.

Claim this allowance if:

- You are single and have only one job at a time; OR
- You are married, have only one job at a time, and your spouse does not work; OR
- You have two jobs at a time and only one job paid more than $2,500; OR
- You are married, both you and your spouse work, and only one job paid more than $2,500.

Line E—Should I Stop Here?—You may stop here and enter the total from line E on Form W-4, line 4, **only** if you do not need to increase or decrease your allowances as explained between lines E and F of the worksheet.

Line F—Adjustments to Income.—Enter the total of the following:

- Qualified reimbursed employee business expenses (unreimbursed expenses are allowed only as an itemized deduction)
- Qualified alimony payments made
- Deductible business and investment losses
- Penalty on early withdrawal of savings
- Qualified contributions to an IRA account or Keogh plan. If either you or your spouse, if applicable, have an IRA and are covered by an employer's pension plan, your 1987 IRA deduction may be reduced or eliminated if your adjusted gross income is at least $40,000 ($25,000 if single, or $0 if married filing separately). Get **Publication 590**, Individual Retirement Arrangements (IRAs), for details.

Line G—Itemized Deductions.—Enter the total of the following:

- Medical expenses in excess of 7.5% of your AGI*
- State and local taxes (exclude **sales** taxes)
- Home mortgage interest and 65% of personal interest
- Qualified investment interest
- Charitable contributions
- Certain casualty and theft losses in excess of 10% of AGI*
- Moving expenses (if reimbursed, include only if your employer withheld tax on them)
- Miscellaneous deductions (most of these are now deductible only in excess of 2% of AGI*; see Publication 553)

* In general, your AGI (adjusted gross income) is your income less any adjustments to income included on line F of the worksheet.

Line J—Additional Standard Deduction for Age or Blindness.—If you do **not** expect to itemize deductions on your 1987 tax return **and** either you or your spouse is age 65 or over or blind, use the following table.

	If 65 or over **or** blind, enter on line J:	**If** 65 or over **and** blind, enter on line J:
Single	$1,210	$1,960
Head of Household	$2,610	$3,360
Married-Joint	$1,840 **	$2,440 **
Married-Separate	$1,220	$1,820
Qualifying Widow(er)	$1,840	$2,440

**If your spouse is 65 or over or blind, add $600 to this amount. Add $1,200 if spouse is both 65 or over and blind.

Line K—Tax Credits.— Enter the amount of any tax credits you expect to claim, such as the credit for child and dependent care expenses, the earned income credit (EIC), and other credits shown on the 1986 Form 1040. The amount of the EIC has increased for 1987. Get Publication 553 for details. Do not include the EIC if you are receiving advance payment of it.

Line O.— Round the result to the nearest whole number. Drop amounts under .50. Increase amounts from .50 to .99 to the next whole number. For example, 3.25 becomes 3, and 4.61 becomes 5.

Lines Q through T—Working Spouse? More Than One Job? Nonwage Income?— So that you will have enough tax withheld, you MUST complete any lines that apply to you.

Line U—Total Withholding Allowances.— If the number on line T is larger than the number on line P, you will probably owe more tax when you file your return and may have to pay a penalty unless you take further steps to have more tax withheld from your pay. You may use the instructions for Step 4 to estimate how much additional tax you should request your employer to withhold each pay period. As an alternative, you may use the 1987 **Form 1040-ES,** Estimated Tax for Individuals, to make this computation.

Step 4—Additional Amount You Want Deducted From Each Pay.—In some instances, you will be underwithheld, even if you do not claim any withholding allowances on Form W-4. This could occur if you have a working spouse, more than one job at a time, or nonwage income, AND the number on line T of the worksheet is larger than the number on line P.

To correct this problem, you may have more tax withheld by filling in a dollar amount on line 5 of Form W-4. A method of figuring this amount follows:

1. Enter the number from line T of the worksheet . . . . ________
2. Enter the number from line P of the worksheet . . . . ________
3. Subtract line 2 from line 1 . ________
4. Enter the amount from the table below that applies to you . . . . $________
5. Multiply line 3 by line 4 . . $________
6. Divide line 5 by the number of pay periods each year. Enter the result here and on Form W-4, line 5 . . . . . $________

Married Workers' Combined Annual Income	Line 4 Amount
Under $4,860	$209
$4,860 - $29,860	$285
$29,861 - $46,860	$532
$46,861 - $91,860	$665
$91,861 and over	$732

Unmarried Worker's Annual Income	Line 4 Amount
Under $2,440	$209
$2,440 - $17,440	$285
$17,441 - $27,640	$532
$27,641 - $54,640	$665
$54,641 and over	$732

Privacy Act and Paperwork Reduction Act Notice.—We ask for this information to carry out the Internal Revenue laws of the United States. We may give the information to the Department of Justice for civil or criminal litigation and to cities, states, and the District of Columbia for use in administering their tax laws. You are required to give this information to your employer.

Worksheet To Figure Your Withholding Allowances

Note: *If you have a working spouse or more than one job at a time, use only one worksheet to figure your total allowances, combining all income, deductions, and credits on the one worksheet.*

A Enter "1" **for yourself** unless you can be claimed as a dependent on another person's tax return . . . . A ______

B **Special Allowance.**—Enter "1" if:
- you are single and you have only one job; or
- you are married, you have only one job, and your spouse does not work; or
- wages earned by you on a second job or earned by your spouse (or both) are $2,500 or less.

. . B ______

C Enter "1" **for your spouse** unless your spouse can be claimed as a dependent on another person's tax return . . . . C ______

D Enter number of **dependents** other than your spouse that you expect to claim on your tax return . . . . D ______

E Add lines A through D and enter the total*—Read the following instructions to see if you should stop here . . . . ▶ E ______

You **MUST** complete lines Q through T if you have total income of $950 or more from the following sources:
- A Working Spouse • More Than One Job • Nonwage Income

You **SHOULD** complete lines F through P if you expect to have:
- Itemized Deductions • Tax Credits • Adjustments to Income • Age or Blindness Deduction

Otherwise, **STOP** here and enter the number from line E on Form W-4, line 4.

F Enter your estimated **adjustments to income** . . . . F $ ______

G Enter your estimated **itemized deductions** . . . . G $ ______

H Enter: { $3,760 if married filing jointly or qualifying widow(er) / $2,540 if single or head of household / $1,880 if married filing separately } H $ ______

I Subtract the amount on line H from line G. Enter the result, but not less than zero . . . . . I $ ______

J **Age 65 or Over? Blind?** If you do not plan to itemize deductions, enter your additional standard deduction from instructions for line J on page 2 . . . . J $ ______

K Enter your estimated **tax credits,** such as child and dependent care credit or earned income credit . . . . K $ ______

L If line K is zero, skip to line N. Otherwise, enter the number from the table below . . . . L ______

Married Filing Jointly or Qualifying Widow(er)			**Single or Married Filing Separately**			**Head of Household**		
If your combined estimated wages are—		Enter on line L	If your estimated wages are—		Enter on line L	If your estimated wages are—		Enter on line L
At least	But less than		At least	But less than		At least	But less than	
$0	$12,500	9	$0	$6,200	9	$0	$8,800	9
$12,500	$37,500	6.5	$6,200	$21,000	6.5	$8,800	$29,000	7
$37,500	$55,000	3.5	$21,000	$31,500	3.5	$29,000	$44,000	4
$55,000	$110,000	3	$31,500	$70,000	3	$44,000	$100,000	3
$110,000 or over		2.5	$70,000 or over		2.5	$100,000 or over		2.5

M Multiply the amount on line K by the number on line L and enter the total amount here . . M $ ______

N Add lines F, I, J, and M. Enter the total amount here . . . . N $ ______

O Divide the amount on line N by $1,900. Round to the nearest whole number (see instructions on page 2) . . . . ▶ O ______

P Add lines E and O and enter the total number here . . . . ▶ P ______

Q **Nonwage Income?**—Enter the estimated amount, if any, of all your nonwage income . . Q $ ______

R **Working Spouse? More Than One Job?**—Too little tax may be withheld if either of these situations applies. See page 4 for line R instructions and tables to figure the amount to enter on this line . . . . R $ ______

S Add amounts on lines Q and R and enter the total amount here . . . . S $ ______

T Divide the amount on line S by $1,900. Round to the nearest whole number (see instructions for line O) . . . . . ▶ T ______

U **Total Withholding Allowances.**—Subtract the number on line T from the number on line P. Enter the result here and on Form W-4, line 4.* If the result is zero or less, enter zero and see instructions for line U on page 2 . . . . ▶ U ______

** If you have more than one job or if your spouse works, you may claim all of your allowances on one job or you may claim some on each job, but you may **NOT** claim the same allowances more than once. Your withholding will usually be more accurate if you claim **all** allowances on the Form W-4 for the job with the largest wages and claim zero on all other Forms W-4.*

Form W-4 (1987) **Instructions and Tables for Line R of the Worksheet** Page **4**

1. Enter wages from the HIGHEST paying job (of either spouse, if married) $ ______
2. . . . . $1,900
3. Enter the number from line P of Worksheet on page 3 . . . × ______
4. Multiply line 2 by line 3. Enter the result here . . . . . . $ ______
5. Subtract line 4 from line 1. If zero or less, enter zero . . . . . . $ ______
6. Enter wages from the NEXT HIGHEST paying job . . . . . . $ ______
7. If married filing jointly, use Table A. Otherwise, use Table B.
8. Read ACROSS the table and find the column for the line 5 amount.
9. Read DOWN the left column and find the row for the line 6 amount.
10. Enter on line R of the Worksheet the amount in the table where the column and row meet.

Table A—For Married Couples Filing Joint Returns

Amount From Line 6 Above: At Least–	But Less Than–	Amount From Line 5 Above: Under $4,000	$4,000 And Under $18,000	$18,000 And Under $20,000	$20,000 And Under $22,000	$22,000 And Under $24,000	$24,000 And Under $26,000	$26,000 And Under $28,000	$28,000 And Under $30,000	$30,000 And Under $32,000	$32,000 And Under $34,000	$34,000 And Under $36,000	$36,000 And Under $38,000	$38,000 And Under $40,000	$40,000 And Under $42,000	$42,000 And Under $44,000	$44,000 And Under $46,000	$46,000 And Under $48,000	$48,000 And Under $50,000	$50,000 And Under $55,000	$55,000 And Under $60,000	$60,000 And Under $70,000	$70,000 Or Over
$0	$2,000	0	0	0	0	0	0	0	0	0	0	0	0	0	0	0	0	0	0	0	0	0	0
$2,000	$4,000	0	300	300	300	300	300	300	500	700	700	700	700	700	700	700	700	700	700	700	700	700	700
$4,000	$6,000	0	800	800	800	800	800	1,000	1,800	1,800	1,800	1,800	1,800	1,800	1,800	1,800	2,100	2,100	2,100	2,100	2,100	2,100	2,100
$6,000	$8,000	0	800	800	800	600	1,000	2,700	2,800	2,800	2,800	2,800	2,800	2,800	2,800	3,100	3,200	3,200	3,200	3,200	3,200	3,200	3,200
$8,000	$10,000	0	800	800	800	1,000	2,700	3,700	3,700	3,700	3,700	3,700	3,700	3,700	4,000	4,400	4,400	4,400	4,400	4,400	4,400	4,400	4,400
$10,000	$12,000	0	800	800	1,000	2,700	4,400	4,600	4,600	4,600	4,600	4,600	4,600	4,900	5,400	5,500	5,500	5,500	5,500	5,500	5,500	5,500	5,500
$12,000	$14,000	0	800	1,000	2,700	4,400	5,600	5,600	5,600	5,600	5,600	5,600	5,900	6,400	6,700	6,700	6,700	6,700	6,700	6,700	6,700	6,700	6,700
$14,000	$16,000	0	800	2,700	4,400	6,200	6,500	6,500	6,500	6,500	6,500	6,800	7,300	7,800	7,800	7,800	7,800	7,800	7,800	7,800	7,800	7,800	7,900
$16,000	$18,000	0	800	4,400	6,200	7,400	7,400	7,400	7,400	7,400	7,700	8,200	8,700	9,000	9,000	9,000	9,000	9,000	9,000	9,000	9,000	9,000	9,300
$18,000	$20,000	0	800	6,200	7,900	8,300	8,300	8,300	8,300	8,700	9,200	9,700	10,100	10,100	10,100	10,100	10,100	10,100	10,100	10,100	10,100	10,100	10,600
$20,000	$22,000	0	1,000	7,900	9,300	9,300	9,300	9,300	9,600	10,100	10,600	11,100	11,200	11,200	11,200	11,200	11,200	11,200	11,200	11,200	11,200	11,200	12,000
$22,000	$24,000	0	2,700	9,600	10,200	10,200	10,200	10,500	11,000	11,500	12,000	12,400	12,400	12,400	12,400	12,400	12,400	12,400	12,400	12,400	12,400	12,400	13,200
$24,000	$26,000	0	4,400	11,100	11,100	11,100	11,400	11,900	12,400	12,900	13,400	13,500	13,500	13,500	13,500	13,500	13,500	13,500	13,500	13,500	13,500	13,500	14,400
$26,000	$28,000	0	6,200	12,100	12,100	12,400	12,900	13,400	13,900	14,400	14,700	14,700	14,700	14,700	14,700	14,700	14,700	14,700	14,700	14,700	14,700	14,700	15,600
$28,000	$30,000	0	7,900	13,000	13,300	13,800	14,300	14,800	15,300	15,800	15,800	15,800	15,800	15,800	15,800	15,800	15,800	15,800	15,800	15,800	15,800	15,800	16,800
$30,000	$32,000	0	8,600	13,700	14,200	14,700	15,200	15,700	16,200	16,500	16,500	16,500	16,500	16,500	16,500	16,500	16,500	16,500	16,500	16,500	16,500	16,800	17,700
$32,000	$34,000	0	8,600	14,200	14,700	15,200	15,700	16,200	16,700	16,900	16,900	16,900	16,900	16,900	16,900	16,900	16,900	16,900	16,900	16,900	16,900	17,400	18,200
$34,000	$36,000	0	8,600	14,700	15,200	15,700	16,200	16,700	17,200	17,300	17,300	17,300	17,300	17,300	17,300	17,300	17,300	17,300	17,300	17,300	17,300	18,000	18,800
$36,000	$38,000	0	8,600	15,200	15,700	16,200	16,700	17,200	17,700	17,700	17,700	17,700	17,700	17,700	17,700	17,700	17,700	17,700	17,700	17,700	17,800	18,600	19,300
$38,000	$40,000	0	9,200	15,700	16,200	16,700	17,200	17,700	18,100	18,100	18,100	18,100	18,100	18,100	18,100	18,100	18,100	18,100	18,100	18,100	18,400	19,200	19,900
$40,000	$42,000	0	10,200	16,200	16,700	17,200	17,700	18,200	18,500	18,500	18,500	18,500	18,500	18,500	18,500	18,500	18,500	18,500	18,500	18,500	19,000	19,800	20,400
$42,000	$44,000	0	11,100	16,700	17,200	17,700	18,200	18,700	18,900	18,900	18,900	18,900	18,900	18,900	18,900	18,900	18,900	18,900	18,900	19,100	19,600	20,400	20,900
$44,000	$46,000	0	12,000	17,200	17,700	18,200	18,700	19,200	19,300	19,300	19,300	19,300	19,300	19,300	19,300	19,300	19,300	19,300	19,400	19,700	20,200	21,000	21,500
$46,000	$48,000	0	12,900	17,700	18,200	18,700	19,200	19,700	19,700	19,700	19,700	19,700	19,700	19,700	19,700	19,700	19,700	19,700	19,900	20,300	20,800	21,500	22,000
$48,000	$50,000	0	12,900	17,700	18,200	18,700	19,200	19,700	19,700	19,700	19,700	19,700	19,700	19,700	19,700	19,700	19,700	19,900	20,100	20,500	21,000	21,700	22,200
$50,000	$55,000	0	12,900	17,700	18,200	18,700	19,200	19,700	19,700	19,700	19,700	19,700	19,700	19,700	19,700	19,900	20,100	20,300	20,500	20,800	21,300	22,100	22,500
$55,000	$60,000	0	12,900	17,700	18,200	18,700	19,200	19,700	19,700	19,700	19,700	19,700	19,800	20,000	20,200	20,400	20,600	20,800	21,000	21,300	21,800	22,600	23,000
$60,000	$70,000	0	12,900	17,700	18,200	18,700	19,200	19,700	19,700	19,900	20,100	20,300	20,500	20,700	20,900	21,100	21,300	21,500	21,700	22,100	22,600	23,300	23,600
$70,000		0	12,900	18,300	19,100	19,800	20,600	21,000	21,200	21,400	21,600	21,800	22,000	22,200	22,400	22,600	22,800	23,000	23,200	23,600	24,100	24,800	25,000

Table B—For All Others

Amount From Line 6 Above: At Least–	But Less Than–	Amount From Line 5 Above: Under $10,000	$10,000 And Under $12,000	$12,000 And Under $14,000	$14,000 And Under $16,000	$16,000 And Under $18,000	$18,000 And Under $20,000	$20,000 And Under $22,000	$22,000 And Under $24,000	$24,000 And Under $30,000	$30,000 And Under $40,000	$40,000 And Under $50,000	$50,000 Or Over
$0	$4,000	0	0	0	0	0	0	0	0	0	0	0	0
$4,000	$6,000	0	0	0	0	1,000	1,000	1,000	1,000	1,400	1,400	1,400	1,600
$6,000	$8,000	0	0	0	1,500	1,900	1,900	1,900	2,100	2,600	2,600	2,600	2,800
$8,000	$10,000	0	0	1,500	2,900	2,900	2,900	3,000	3,500	3,700	3,700	3,700	4,000
$10,000	$12,000	0	1,500	[illegible]	3,800	3,800	3,900	4,400	4,900	4,900	4,900	4,900	5,300
$12,000	$14,000	0	3,300	[illegible]	4,700	4,900	5,400	5,900	6,000	6,000	6,000	6,200	6,500
$14,000	$16,000	0	5,000	5,700	5,800	6,300	6,800	7,200	7,200	7,200	7,200	7,500	7,700
$16,000	$18,000	1,500	6,600	6,700	7,200	7,700	8,200	8,300	8,300	8,300	8,300	8,800	8,900
$18,000	$20,000	1,900	6,900	7,400	7,900	8,400	8,900	8,900	8,900	8,900	8,900	9,600	9,600
$20,000		2,100	8,400	8,900	9,400	9,900	10,100	10,100	10,100	10,100	10,400	11,200	11,200

☆ U.S. Government Printing Office: 1986—493-393 23-0916750

Form **709** (Rev. June 1985) Department of the Treasury Internal Revenue Service

United States Gift Tax Return

(Section 6019 of the Internal Revenue Code) (For gifts made after December 31, 1981, and before January 1, 1988)

Calendar year 19 _____.

▶ **For "Privacy Act" Notice, see the Instructions for Form 1040.**

OMB No. 1545-0020 Expires 4-30-88

Donor's first name and middle initial	Donor's last name	Social security number
Address (number and street)		Domicile
City, State, and ZIP code		Citizenship

	Yes	No
If the donor died during the year, check here ▶ ☐ and enter date of death ______________, 19 _____. If you received an extension of time to file this Form 709, check here ▶ ☐ and attach the Form 4868, 2688, 2350 or extension letter.		
If you (the donor) filed a previous Form 709 (or 709-A), has your address changed since the last Form 709 (or 709-A) was filed?		
A Gifts by husband or wife to third parties.—Do you consent to have the gifts made by you and by your spouse to third parties during the calendar year considered as made one-half by each of you? (See instructions.)		
(If the answer is "Yes," the following information must be furnished and your spouse is to sign the consent shown below. If the answer is "No," skip lines 1-5 and go to Schedule A.)		
1a Name of consenting spouse — **1b** Social security number		
2 Were you married to one another during the entire calendar year? (see instructions)		
3 If the answer to 2 is "No," check whether ☐ married ☐ divorced or ☐ widowed, and give date (see instructions) ▶		
4 Will a gift tax return for this calendar year be filed by your spouse?		

5 **Consent of Spouse**—I consent to have the gifts made by me and by my spouse to third parties during the calendar year considered as made one-half by each of us. We are both aware of the joint and several liability for tax created by the execution of this consent.

Consenting spouse's signature ▶ **Date ▶**

Tax Computation

1	Enter the amount from Schedule A, line 13	1	
2	Enter the amount from Schedule B, line 3	2	
3	Total taxable gifts (add lines 1 and 2)	3	
4	Tax computed on amount on line 3 (see Table A in separate instructions)	4	
5	Tax computed on amount on line 2 (see Table A in separate instructions)	5	
6	Balance (subtract line 5 from line 4)	6	
7	Enter the unified credit from Table B (see instructions)	7	
8	Enter the unified credit against tax allowable for all prior periods (from Sch. B, line 1, col. (c))	8	
9	Balance (subtract line 8 from line 7)	9	
10	Enter 20% of the amount allowed as specific exemption after September 8, 1976, and before January 1, 1977 (see instructions)	10	
11	Balance (subtract line 10 from line 9)	11	
12	Unified credit (enter the smaller of line 6 or line 11)	12	
13	Credit for foreign gift taxes (see instructions)	13	
14	Total credits (add lines 12 and 13)	14	
15	Balance (subtract line 14 from line 6) (do not enter less than zero)	15	
16	Gift taxes prepaid with extension of time to file	16	
17	If line 16 is less than line 15, enter BALANCE DUE (see instructions)	17	
18	If line 16 is greater than line 15, enter AMOUNT TO BE REFUNDED	18	

Please attach check or money order here

Please attach the necessary supplemental documents; see instructions.

Under penalties of perjury, I declare that I have examined this return, including any accompanying schedules and statements, and to the best of my knowledge and belief it is true, correct, and complete. Declaration of preparer (other than donor) is based on all information of which preparer has any knowledge.

Donor's signature ▶ Date ▶

Preparer's signature (other than donor) ▶ Date ▶

Preparer's address (other than donor) ▶

For Paperwork Reduction Act Notice, see page 1 of the separate instructions to this form. Form **709** (Rev. 6-85)

Form 709 (Rev. 6-85) Page **2**

SCHEDULE A.—Computation of Taxable Gifts Gifts less political organization, medical and educational exclusions—see instructions

Item number	Donee's name and address and description of gift. If the gift was made by means of a trust, enter trust's identifying number below and attach a copy of the trust instrument. If the gift was securities, enter the CUSIP number(s), if available.	Donor's adjusted basis of gift	Date of gift	Value at date of gift
1				

1	Total gifts of donor (see instructions)	1	
2	One-half of items ________________ attributable to spouse (see instructions)	2	
3	Balance (subtract line 2 from line 1)	3	
4	Gifts of spouse to be included (from Schedule A, line 2 of spouse's return—see instructions)	4	
5	Total gifts (add lines 3 and 4)	5	
6	Total annual exclusions for gifts listed on Schedule A (including line 4) (see instructions)	6	
7	Total included amount of gifts, subtract line 6 from line 5	7	

Deductions (see instructions)

8	Gifts of interests to spouse for which a marital deduction will be claimed, based on items ________________ of Schedule A	8	
9	Exclusions attributable to gifts on line 8	9	
10	Marital deduction—subtract line 9 from line 8	10	
11	Charitable deduction, based on items ________ to ________ less exclusions	11	

12	Total deductions—add lines 10 and 11	12	
13	Taxable gifts (subtract line 12 from line 7)	13	

Terminable Interest Marital Deduction. (See instructions.)

☐ ◄ Check here if you elected, under the rules of section 2523(f), to include gifts of qualified terminable interest property on line 8, above. Enter the item numbers (from Schedule A, above) of the gifts for which you made this election ► ____________________________

SCHEDULE B.— Did you (the donor) file gift tax returns for prior periods? (If "Yes," see instructions for completing Schedule B below.) ☐ Yes ☐ No

(a) Calendar year or calendar quarter (see instructions)	(b) Internal Revenue office where prior return was filed	(c) Amount of unified credit against gift tax for periods after December 31, 1976	(d) Amount of specific exemption for prior periods ending before January 1, 1977	(e) Amount of taxable gifts

1	Totals for prior periods (without adjustment for reduced specific exemption)	1	
2	Amount, if any, by which total specific exemption, line 1, column (d), is more than $30,000	2	
3	Total amount of taxable gifts for prior periods (add amount, column (e), line 1, and amount, if any, on line 2)	3	

(If more space is needed, attach additional sheets of same size.)

★ U.S. Government Printing Office: 1985—461-495/10163

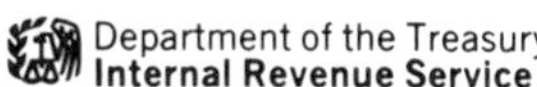

Department of the Treasury
Internal Revenue Service

Instructions for Form 709

(Revised June 1985)

United States Gift Tax Return

(For gifts made after December 31, 1981, and before January 1, 1988)

For Privacy Act Notice, see the Instructions for Form 1040

(Section references are to the Internal Revenue Code unless otherwise noted.)

If you are filing this form solely to elect gift-splitting for gifts of not more than $20,000 per donee, you may be able to use Form 709-A, United States Short Form Gift Tax Return, instead of this form. See the instructions for "Who Must File," below.

If you made gifts before January 1, 1982, do not use this Form 709 to report these gifts. Instead, use the November 1981 revision of Form 709.

Paperwork Reduction Act Notice.—We ask for this information to carry out the Internal Revenue laws of the United States. We need it to ensure that taxpayers are complying with these laws and to allow us to figure and collect the right amount of tax. You are required to give us this information.

General Instructions

Purpose of Form.—Form 709 is used to report transfers subject to the Federal gift tax and to figure the gift tax, if any, due on those transfers.

All gift taxes are computed and filed on a calendar year basis regardless of your income tax accounting period.

Transfers Subject to the Gift Tax.—Generally, the Federal gift tax applies to any transfer by gift of real or personal property, whether tangible or intangible, that you made directly, in trust, or by any other means to a donee.

The gift tax applies not only to the gratuitous transfer of any kind of property, but also to sales or exchanges, not made in the ordinary course of business, where money or money's worth is exchanged but the value of the money received is less than the value of what is sold or exchanged. The gift tax is in addition to any other tax, such as Federal income tax, paid or due on the transfer.

The exercise or release of a power of appointment may be a gift by the individual possessing the power.

The gift tax may also apply to the forgiveness of a debt, to interest-free (or below market interest rate) loans, to the assignment of the benefits of an insurance policy, to certain property settlements in divorce cases, and to certain survivorship annuities.

Bonds that are exempt from Federal income taxes are not exempt from Federal gift taxes unless specifically exempted by a gift tax provision of the Code.

Publication 448, Federal Estate and Gift Taxes, contains further information on the gift tax.

Transfers Not Subject to the Gift Tax.—Three types of transfers are not subject to the gift tax. These are: transfers to political organizations and payments that qualify for the educational and medical exclusions. These transfers are not "gifts" as that term is used on Form 709 and its instructions. You need not file a Form 709 to report these transfers and should not list them on Schedule A of Form 709.

Political organizations.—The gift tax does not apply to a gift to a political organization (defined in section 527(e)(1)) for the use of the organization.

Educational exclusion.—The gift tax does not apply to an amount you paid on behalf of an individual to a qualifying domestic or foreign educational organization as tuition for the education or training of the individual. A qualifying educational organization is one that normally maintains a regular faculty and curriculum and normally has a regularly enrolled body of pupils or students in attendance at the place where its educational activities are regularly carried on. See section 170(b)(1)(A)(ii) and its regulations.

The payment must be made directly to the qualifying educational organization and it must be for tuition. No educational exclusion is allowed for amounts paid for books, supplies, dormitory fees, board or other similar expenses that do not constitute direct tuition costs. To the extent that the payment to the educational institution was for something other than tuition, it is a gift to the individual for whose benefit it was made, and may be offset by the annual exclusion if it is otherwise available.

Medical exclusion.—The gift tax does not apply to an amount you paid on behalf of an individual to a person or institution that provided medical care for the individual. The payment must be to the care provider. The medical care must meet the requirements of section 213(d) (section 213(e) prior to January 1, 1984) (definition of medical care for income tax deduction purposes). Medical care includes expenses incurred for the diagnosis, cure, mitigation, treatment or prevention of disease, or for the purpose of affecting any structure or function of the body, or for transportation primarily for and essential to medical care. Medical care also includes amounts paid for medical insurance on behalf of any individual.

The medical exclusion does not apply to amounts paid for medical care that are reimbursed by the donee's insurance. If payment for a medical expense is reimbursed by the donee's insurance company, your payment for that expense, to the extent of the reimbursed amount, is not eligible for the medical exclusion and you have made a gift to the donee on the date the reimbursement is received by the donee.

To the extent that the payment was for something other than medical care, it is a gift to the individual on whose behalf the payment was made, and may be offset by the annual exclusion if it is otherwise available.

The medical and educational exclusions are allowed without regard to the relationship between you and the donee. For examples illustrating these exclusions, see regulations section 25.2503-6.

Disclaimers.—For the rules governing when a qualified disclaimer is not subject to the gift tax, see Publication 448.

Who Must File

Only individuals are required to file gift tax returns. If a trust, estate, partnership, or corporation makes a gift, the individual beneficiaries, partners, or stockholders are considered donors and may be liable for the gift tax.

If a donor dies before filing a return, the donor's executor must file the return.

A married couple may not file a joint gift tax return. However, see "Split Gifts" on page 2.

If a gift is of community property, it is considered made one-half by each spouse. For example, a gift of $100,000 of community property is considered a gift of $50,000 made by each spouse, and each spouse must file a gift tax return.

Citizens or Residents of the United States.—If you are a citizen or resident of the United States you must file a gift tax return (whether or not any gift tax is ultimately due) in the following situations:

Gifts to your spouse.—**Except as described below, you do not have to file a gift tax return to report gifts to your spouse regardless of the amount of these gifts and regardless of whether the gifts are present or future interests.**

However, you must file a gift tax return if you made any gift of a terminable interest that does not meet the "Life estate with power of appointment" exception described on page 3. You must also file a gift tax return to make a QTIP (Qualified Terminable Interest Property) election described on page 3.

Gifts to donees other than your spouse (including charitable donees).—You must file a gift tax return if you gave gifts to any such donee that are not fully excluded under the $10,000 annual exclusion (as described below). Thus, you must file a gift tax return to report any gift of a future interest (regardless of amount) or to report gifts to any donee that total more than $10,000 for the year.

Gift splitting.—You must file a gift tax return to split gifts (regardless of their amount) with your spouse as described on page 2.

The term *citizen of the United States* includes a person who, at the time of making the gift:

- was domiciled in a possession of the United States;
- was a U.S. citizen; and
- became a U.S. citizen for a reason other than being a citizen of a U.S. possession or being born or residing in a possession.

Annual Exclusion.—The first $10,000 of gifts of present interests to each donee during the calendar year is subtracted in figuring the amount of taxable gifts.

All of the gifts made during the calendar year to a donee are **fully excluded under the annual exclusion** if they are all gifts of *present interests* and if they altogether total $10,000 or less.

No part of a gift of a *future interest* can ever be excluded under the annual exclusion.

A gift is considered a *present interest* if the donee has all immediate rights to the use, possession, and enjoyment of the property and income from the property. A gift is considered a *future interest* if the donee's rights to the use, possession, and enjoyment of the property and income from the property will not begin until some future date. Future interests include reversions, remainders, and other similar interests or estates.

In the case of transfers for the benefit of a minor and for the transitional rules for certain trusts with a power of appointment referenced to the annual exclusion, see Publication 448.

Nonresident Aliens.—Nonresident aliens are subject to gift taxes for gifts of tangible property situated in the United States. Under certain circumstances they are also subject to gift taxes for gifts of certain intangible property. (See section 2501(a).)

If you are a nonresident alien who made a gift subject to gift tax, you must file a gift tax return if (1) you gave *any* gifts of future interests or if (2) your gifts of present interests to *any donee* (including your spouse) total more than $10,000.

When To File

Form 709 is an annual return.

Generally, you must file Form 709 on or after January 1 but not later than April 15 of the year following the calendar year when the gifts were made.

If the donor of the gifts died during the year in which the gifts were made, the executor must file the donor's Form 709 not later than the *earlier* of (1) the due date (with extensions) for filing the donor's estate tax return, or (2) April 15 of the year following the calendar year when the gifts were made. Under this rule, Form 709 may be due before April 15 if the donor died before July 15 of the year in which the gifts were made. If the donor died after July 14, the due date for Form 709 (without extensions) will always be April 15 of the following year. If no estate tax return is required to be filed, the due date for Form 709 (without extensions) is April 15. For more information, see regulations section 25.6075-1.

Extension of Time To File.— There are two methods of extending the time to file the gift tax return. *Neither method extends the time to pay the gift tax.* If you want an extension of time to pay the gift tax, you must request that separately. (See regulations section 25.6161-1.)

(1) By letter.—You can request an extension of time to file your gift tax return by writing to the district director or service center for your area. You must explain the reasons for the delay; or

(2) By form.—Any extension of time granted for filing your calendar year income tax return will also extend the time to file any gift tax return. Income tax extensions are made by using Forms 4868, 2688 or 2350, which have check boxes for Form 709.

Any extension of time to file will not extend the April 15 deadline for making a QTIP election (explained on page 3).

Where To File

File Form 709 with the Internal Revenue Service center where you would file your Federal income tax return. See the Form 1040 instructions for a list of filing locations.

Penalties

The law provides for penalties for both late filing of returns and late payment of tax unless you have reasonable cause. There are also penalties for valuation understatements that cause an underpayment of the gift tax, willful failure to file a return on time, and for willful attempt to evade or defeat payment of tax.

Joint Tenancy

If you buy property with your own funds and have it titled with yourself and the donee as joint tenants with right of survivorship and if either you or the donee may give up those rights by severing your interest, you have made a gift to the donee in the amount of half the value of the property. If you create a joint bank account for yourself and the donee (or a similar kind of ownership by which you can get back the entire fund without the donee's consent), you have made a gift to the donee when the donee draws on the account for his or her own benefit. The amount of the gift is the amount that the donee took out without any obligation to repay you. If you buy a U.S. savings bond registered as payable to yourself or the donee, there is a gift to the donee when he or she cashes the bond without any obligation to account to you.

Transfer of Certain Life Estates

If you received a qualifying terminable interest from your spouse for which a marital deduction was elected on your spouse's estate or gift tax return, you will be subject to the gift tax if you dispose of (by gift, sale or otherwise) all or part of your life income interest.

The entire value of the property involved, less the amount you received on the disposition, and less the amount (if any) of the life income interest you retained after the transfer, will be treated as a taxable gift. That portion of the property's value that is attributable to the remainder interest is a gift of a future interest for which no annual exclusion is allowed. To the extent you made a gift of the life income interest, you may claim an annual exclusion, treating the person to whom you transferred the interest as the donee for purposes of computing the $10,000 limitation.

Specific Instructions

Gifts by Husband or Wife to Third Parties—Split Gifts

A married couple may not file a joint gift tax return.

If you and your spouse agree, all gifts either of you make to third parties during the calendar year may be considered as made one-half by each of you if:

- you and your spouse were married to one another at the time of the gift;
- you did not remarry during the rest of the calendar year;
- neither of you was a nonresident alien at the time of the gift; and
- you did not give your spouse a general power of appointment over the property interest transferred.

If you transferred property partly to your spouse and partly to third parties, you can only split the gifts if the interest transferred to the third parties is ascertainable at the time of the gift.

If you meet these requirements and want your gifts to be considered made one-half by you and one-half by your spouse, check the "Yes" box on line A, page 1; complete lines 1 through 4; and have your spouse sign the consent on line 5. If you are not married or do not wish to split gifts, skip to Schedule A.

Line 2.—If you were married to one another for the entire calendar year, check the "Yes" box and skip to line 4. If you were married for only part of the year, check the "No" box and go to line 3.

Line 3.—Check the box that explains the change in your marital status during the year and give the date you were either married, divorced, or widowed.

Consent of Spouse

To have your gifts considered as made one-half by each of you, your spouse must sign the consent. The consent may generally be signed at any time after the end of the calendar year. However, there are two exceptions. They are:

1. The consent may not be signed after April 15 following the end of the year. (But, if neither you nor your spouse has filed a gift tax return for the year on or before that date, the consent must be made on the first gift tax return for the year filed by either of you.)
2. The consent may not be signed after a notice of deficiency for the gift tax for the year has been sent to either you or your spouse.

The executor for a deceased spouse or the guardian for a legally incompetent spouse may sign the consent.

The consent is effective for the entire calendar year; therefore, all gifts made by both you and your spouse to third parties during the calendar year (while you were married) must be split.

If the consent is effective, the liability for the entire gift tax of each spouse is joint and several.

When the consenting spouse must also file a gift tax return.—If the spouses elect gift splitting (described under "Split Gifts," above), then both the donor spouse and the consenting spouse must each file separate gift tax returns unless all the requirements of either Exceptions 1 or 2 below are met:

Exception 1.—During the calendar year:

- Only one spouse made any gifts;
- The total value of these gifts to each third-party donee does not exceed $20,000, and
- All of these gifts constitute present interests.

Exception 2.—During the calendar year:

- Only one spouse (the donor spouse) made gifts of more than $10,000 but not more than $20,000 to any third-party donee;
- The only gifts made by the other spouse (the consenting spouse) were gifts of not more than $10,000 to third-party donees other than those to whom the donor spouse made gifts, and
- All of the gifts by both spouses constitute present interests.

If either of Exceptions 1 or 2 is met, only the donor spouse needs to file a return and the consenting spouse signifies consent on that return. This return may probably be made on **Form 709-A,** United States Short Form Gift Tax Return. This form is much easier to complete than Form 709, and you should consider filing it whenever your gifts to each third-party donee are not more than $20,000 for the year.

Schedule A.—Computation of Taxable Gifts

Do not enter on Schedule A any gift or part of a gift that qualifies for the political organization, educational or medical exclusions. In the instructions below, "gifts" means gifts (or parts of gifts) that do not qualify for the political organization, educational or medical exclusions.

Gifts to donees other than your spouse.—You must always enter all gifts of *future interests* that you made during the calendar year regardless of their value.

If you do not elect gift splitting.—If the total gifts of *present interests* to any donee are more than $10,000 in the calendar year, then you must enter *all such gifts* that you made during the year to or on behalf of that donee, including those gifts that will be excluded under the annual exclusion. If the total is $10,000 or less you need not enter on Schedule A any gifts (except gifts of future interests) that you made to that donee.

If you elect gift splitting.—Enter on Schedule A the entire value of every gift you made during the calendar year while you were married, even if the gift's value will be less than $10,000 after it is split on line 2.

Gifts to your spouse.—If you were a citizen or resident during the entire calendar year, you do not need to enter any of the gifts to your spouse on Schedule A unless you gave a gift of a terminable interest to your spouse. If you gave your spouse any terminable interest that does not qualify as a life estate with power of appointment (defined below), you must report on Schedule A *only* gifts of terminable interests you made to your spouse during the year. You should not report any gifts you made to your spouse that are not terminable interests; however, you must report all terminable interests, whether or not they can be deducted.

Charitable remainder trusts.—If you make a gift to a charitable remainder trust and your spouse is the only noncharitable beneficiary (other than yourself), the interest you gave to your spouse is not considered a terminable interest and therefore should not be shown on Schedule A. For rules and definitions concerning these trusts, see section 2056(b)(8)(B).

Nonresident aliens.—If you were a nonresident alien at any time during the year, you must enter *all* gifts you made to your spouse during the year.

If you need more space than that provided, attach a separate sheet, using the same format as Schedule A.

Group the gifts in four categories: gifts made to your spouse; gifts made to third parties that are to be split with your spouse; charitable gifts (if you are not splitting gifts with your spouse); and other gifts. If a transfer results in gifts to two individuals (such as a life estate to one with remainder to the other), list the gift to each separately.

Number and describe all gifts (including charitable, public, and similar gifts) in the columns provided in Schedule A. Describe each gift in enough detail so that the property can be easily identified, as explained below.

For real estate provide:

- a legal description of each parcel;
- the street number, name, and area if the property is located in a city; and
- a short statement of any improvements made to the property.

Page 2

For bonds, give:

- the number of bonds transferred;
- the principal amount of each bond;
- name of obligor;
- date of maturity;
- rate of interest;
- date or dates when interest is payable;
- series number if there is more than one issue;
- exchanges where listed; principal business office of corporation, if unlisted; and
- CUSIP number, if available. The CUSIP number is a nine digit number assigned by the American Banking Association to traded securities.

For stocks:

- give number of shares;
- state whether common or preferred;
- if preferred, give the issue, par value, quotation at which returned, and exact name of corporation;
- if unlisted, give location of principal business office, State in which incorporated, and date of incorporation;
- if listed, give principal exchange where sold; and
- give CUSIP number, if available. The CUSIP number is a nine digit number assigned by the American Banking Association to traded securities.

For interests in property based on the length of a person's life, give the date of birth of the person.

For life insurance policies, give the name of the insurer and the policy number.

Donor's Adjusted Basis of Gifts.—Show the basis you would use for income tax purposes if the gift were sold or exchanged. Generally, this means cost plus improvements, less applicable depreciation, amortization, and depletion.

For more information on adjusted basis, please see **Publication 551,** Basis of Assets.

Date and Value of Gift.—The value of a gift is the fair market value of the property on the date the gift is made. The fair market value is the price at which the property would change hands between a willing buyer and a willing seller, when neither is forced to buy or to sell, and when both have reasonable knowledge of all relevant facts. Fair market value may not be determined by a forced sale price, nor by the sale price of the item in a market other than that in which the item is most commonly sold to the public. The location of the item must be taken into account wherever appropriate.

Stock of close corporations or inactive stock must be valued on the basis of net worth, earnings, earning and dividend capacity, and other relevant factors.

Supplemental Documents.—To support the value of your gifts, you must provide information showing how it was determined.

For stock of close corporations or inactive stock, attach balance sheets, particularly the one nearest the date of the gift, and statements of net earnings or operating results and dividends paid for each of the five preceding years.

For each life insurance policy, attach **Form 712,** Life Insurance Statement.

Note for single premium or paid-up policies: *In certain situations, for example, where the surrender value of the policy exceeds its replacement cost, the true economic value of the policy will be greater than the amount shown on line 56 of Form 712. In these situations you should report the full economic value of the policy on Schedule A. See Rev. Rul. 78-137, 1978-1 C.B. 280 for details.*

If the gift was made by means of a trust, attach a certified or verified copy of the trust instrument.

Also attach appraisal lists, such as any appraisal used to determine the value of real estate.

If you do not attach this information, you must include in Schedule A full information to explain how the value was determined.

Line 1.—Add the value of all your gifts. Enter the total on line 1.

Line 2.—If you are not splitting gifts with your spouse, skip this line and enter the amount from line 1 on line 3. If you are splitting gifts with your spouse, show half of the gifts you made to third parties on line 2. On the dotted line indicate which numbered items from the top of Schedule A you treated this way.

Line 4.—If you are not splitting gifts, skip this line and go to line 5. If you gave all of the gifts, and your spouse is only filing to show his or her half of those gifts, you need not enter any gifts on line 4 of your return, or include your spouse's half anywhere else on your return. Your spouse should enter the amount from Schedule A, line 2 of your return on Schedule A, line 4 of his or her return. If both you and your spouse make gifts for which a return is required, the amount each of you shows on Schedule A, line 2 of his or her return must be shown on Schedule A, line 4 of the other's return.

Line 6.—Enter the total annual exclusions you are claiming for the gifts listed on Schedule A (including gifts listed on line 4). See "Annual Exclusion," on page 1. If you split a gift with your spouse, the annual exclusion you claim against that gift may not be more than your half of the gift.

Deductions

Line 8.—Enter on line 8 all of the terminable interest gifts to your spouse which you listed on Schedule A and for which you are claiming a marital deduction. **Do not enter any gift that you did not include on Schedule A.** On the dotted line on line 8 indicate which numbered items from the top of Schedule A are gifts to your spouse for which you are claiming the marital deduction.

Nonresident aliens.—If you were a nonresident alien for the entire calendar year, enter "-0-" in line 8. If you were a citizen or resident of the U.S. for part of the calendar year you may claim a marital deduction for gifts you made to your spouse while you were a citizen or resident of the U.S. even if your spouse was a nonresident alien. You may deduct all gifts of nonterminable interests made during this time that you entered on Schedule A regardless of amount, and certain gifts of terminable interests as outlined below. **Do not enter on line 8 any gifts to your spouse that were made while you were a nonresident alien.**

Citizens or residents of the U.S.—Only terminable interest gifts to your spouse should have been listed on Schedule A. They are deducted according to the rules below.

Terminable interests.—Generally, you cannot take the marital deduction if the gift to your spouse is a terminable interest.

Some examples of terminable interests are:

- a life estate;
- an estate for a specified number of years; or
- any other property interest that after a period of time will terminate or fail.

If you transfer an interest to your spouse as sole joint tenant with yourself or as a tenant by the entirety, the interest is not considered a terminable interest just because the tenancy may be severed. A retiring Federal employee who receives a reduced annuity so that his or her spouse can get a survivor annuity after he or she dies, gives a terminable interest to the spouse when he or she retires. In that case, no marital deduction election would be allowed and no amount could be deducted for the annual exclusion because the gift of the survivor annuity is a future interest. Refer to **Publication 721,** Comprehensive Tax Guide to U.S. Civil Service Retirement Benefits, for additional information concerning the gift of a Federal annuity.

Life estate with power of appointment.—You may deduct, without an election, a gift of a terminable interest if all four requirements below are met:

1. your spouse is entitled for life to all of the income from the entire interest;
2. the income is paid yearly or more often;
3. your spouse has the unlimited power, while he or she is alive or by will, to appoint the entire interest in all circumstances; and
4. no part of the entire interest is subject to another person's power of appointment (except to appoint it to your spouse).

If only part of the property interest meets the above, see Publication 448 for the part that qualifies for the marital deduction.

Election to deduct qualified terminable interest property (QTIP).—You may *elect* to deduct a gift of a terminable interest if it meets requirements 1, 2, and 4 above, even though it does not meet requirement 3.

Make the election by checking the block above Schedule B and entering the appropriate item numbers from Schedule A. You must make this election before April 15 of the year following the year in which you made the gifts to your spouse. You may not make the election on a late filed Form 709. You may not make the election on a Form 709 filed after April 15 even if you have received an extension of time to file.

If you make this election, the terminable interest property involved will be included in your spouse's gross estate upon his or her death (section 2044). If your spouse disposes (by gift or otherwise) of all or part of the qualifying life income interest, he or she will be considered to have made a transfer of the entire property that is subject to the gift tax (see "Transfer of Certain Life Estates," above).

Line 9.—Enter the value of the annual exclusion that was claimed against the gifts you listed on line 8.

Line 11.—You may deduct from the total gifts made during the calendar year all gifts you gave to or for the use of:

- The United States, a State or political subdivision of a State or the District of Columbia, for public purposes only.
- Any corporation, trust, community chest, fund, or foundation organized and operated only for religious, charitable, scientific, literary, or educational purposes, or to prevent cruelty to children or animals, or to foster national or international amateur sports competition (if none of its activities involve providing athletic equipment (unless it is a qualified amateur sports organization)), as long as no part of the earnings benefits any one person, no substantial propaganda is produced, and no lobbying or campaigning for any candidate for public office is done.
- A fraternal society, order, or association operating under a lodge system, if the transferred property is to be used only for religious, charitable, scientific, literary, or educational purposes including the encouragement of art and the prevention of cruelty to children or animals.
- Any war veterans organization organized in the United States (or any of its possessions), or any of its auxiliary departments or local chapters or posts, as long as no part of any of the earnings benefits any one person.

On line 11, show your total charitable, public, or similar gifts (minus exclusions allowed). On the dotted line indicate which numbered items from the top of Schedule A are charitable gifts.

See Publication 448 for more information.

Schedule B

If you did not file gift tax returns for previous periods, check the "No" box at the top of Schedule B and skip to the Tax Computation on page 1. If you filed gift tax returns for previous periods, check the "Yes" box and complete Schedule B by listing the years or quarters in chronological order as described below. If you need more space than that provided, attach a separate sheet, using the same format as Schedule B.

If you filed returns for gifts made before 1971 or after 1981, show the calendar years in column (a). If you filed returns for gifts made after 1970 and before 1982, show the calendar quarters.

In column (b), identify the Internal Revenue Service office where you filed the returns. If you have changed your name, be sure to list any other names under which the returns were filed. If there was any other variation in the names under which you filed, such as the use of full given names, instead of initials, please explain.

In column (e), show the correct amount (the amount finally determined) of the taxable gifts for each earlier period.

Tax Computation

Line 7.—If you are a citizen or resident of the United States, you must take any available unified credit against gift tax for gifts made after December 31, 1976. If you are not a citizen or resident of the United States, you may not claim a unified credit.

Using Table B below, figure the amount of unified credit according to when you made the gift. Report the total credit for the period for which you are filing this return on line 7.

Line 10.—Enter 20% of the amount allowed as a specific exemption for gifts made after September 8, 1976, and before January 1, 1977. (These amounts will be among those listed in column (d) of Schedule B, for gifts made in the third and fourth quarters of 1976.)

Line 13.—Gift tax conventions are in effect with France, the United Kingdom, Australia and Japan. If you are claiming a credit for payment of foreign gift tax, figure the credit on an attached sheet and attach evidence that the foreign taxes were paid. See the applicable convention for details of computing the credit.

Line 17.—Make check or money order payable to "Internal Revenue Service" and write the donor's social security number on it.

Signature.—You as donor must sign the return. If you pay another person, firm, or corporation to prepare your return, that person must also sign the return as preparer, unless he or she is your regular full-time employee.

Table A—Table for Computing Tax

Column A	Column B	Column C	Column D
Taxable amount over—	Taxable amount not over—	Tax on amount in Column A	Rate of tax on excess over amount in Column A
--------	$10,000	--------	18%
$10,000	20,000	$1,800	20%
20,000	40,000	3,800	22%
40,000	60,000	8,200	24%
60,000	80,000	13,000	26%
80,000	100,000	18,200	28%
100,000	150,000	23,800	30%
150,000	250,000	38,800	32%
250,000	500,000	70,800	34%
500,000	750,000	155,800	37%
750,000	1,000,000	248,300	39%
1,000,000	1,250,000	345,800	41%
1,250,000	1,500,000	448,300	43%
1,500,000	2,000,000	555,800	45%
2,000,000	2,500,000	780,800	49%
2,500,000	See Table A(1), A(2) or A(3) for year in which the gift was made.		

Table A(1)—Gifts Made in 1982

Column A	Column B	Column C	Column D
Taxable amount over—	Taxable amount not over—	Tax on amount in Column A	Rate of tax on excess over amount in Column A
$2,500,000	$3,000,000	$1,025,800	53%
3,000,000	3,500,000	1,290,800	57%
3,500,000	4,000,000	1,575,800	61%
4,000,000	----------	1,880,800	65%

Table A(2)—Gifts Made in 1983

Column A	Column B	Column C	Column D
Taxable amount over—	Taxable amount not over—	Tax on amount in Column A	Rate of tax on excess over amount in Column A
$2,500,000	$3,000,000	$1,025,800	53%
3,000,000	3,500,000	1,290,800	57%
3,500,000	----------	1,575,800	60%

Table A(3)—Gifts Made in 1984, 1985, 1986 or 1987

Column A	Column B	Column C	Column D
Taxable amount over—	Taxable amount not over—	Tax on amount in Column A	Rate of tax on excess over amount in Column A
$2,500,000	$3,000,000	$1,025,800	53%
3,000,000	----------	1,290,800	55%

Table B

Maximum Unified Credit Against Gift Tax	
For gifts made in—	The credit is—
1981 and earlier	Use the November 1981 revision of Form 709
1982	$62,800
1983	79,300
1984	96,300
1985	121,800
1986	155,800
1987 and later	192,800

☆ U.S. Government Printing Office: 1985—461-495/10164

Department of the Treasury
Internal Revenue Service

Publication 919
(January 1987)

Is My Withholding Correct?

(For use in figuring whether your income tax withholding is too little or too much)

After you have given your employer a 1987 Form W-4, *Employer's Withholding Allowance Certificate,* you should check to see if the new amount of tax withheld is sufficient. In some instances, the amount of tax withheld may be too little or too much.

This publication will help you determine whether you are having the right amount withheld. It will help you compare the amount of tax you expect to show on your 1987 tax return with the amount of tax to be withheld during 1987. The publication also includes worksheets, a filled-in example, and blank 1987 Forms W-4.

Too Little Tax Withheld?

If too little tax is withheld, you may owe tax at the end of the year. In that case, you should give your employer a new 1987 Form W-4 showing an additional amount of money to be withheld from your pay.

You will most likely have too little tax withheld and owe tax at the end of the year if any one of the following situations applies to you:

1) You are married and both you and your spouse work;
2) You have more than one job at a time; or
3) You have nonwage income, such as interest, dividends, etc., in addition to your wages.

Too Much Tax Withheld?

If too much tax is withheld, you may receive a refund when you file your tax return. If you do not want a refund, you may be able to decrease the amount being withheld by giving your employer a new 1987 Form W-4. See the 1987 Form W-4 instructions to find out if you can decrease your withholding by claiming more allowances, including the special withholding allowance, that you may be entitled to and have not already claimed.

What To Do

When you receive a pay slip for a full pay period in 1987 that shows that tax was withheld based on the 1987 Form W-4 you filed, you can use the following worksheets to see if you are having the right amount of tax withheld.

1987 Withholding Worksheet

(Enter combined amounts if married filing joint return.)

1) Complete the *1987 Tax Worksheet* on page 2 and enter your total taxes from line 13 of that worksheet . . . ______
2) Total federal income tax withheld to date in 1987 (includes all jobs) . . . ______
3) Tax withholding expected for the rest of 1987:

   For each job, multiply the amount of federal income tax now being withheld each payday by the number of paydays remaining in 1987 and enter the combined amount for all jobs. . . . . ______
4) Total expected withholding tax for all paydays in 1987. Add lines 2 and 3 . ______
5) Too little tax withheld. Subtract line 4 from line 1. (If line 1 is smaller than line 4, you will be overwithheld. See *Too Much Tax Withheld?*) . . . . . ______
6) Additional amount to be withheld. Divide line 5 by the number of paydays remaining in 1987 that will be covered by another 1987 Form W-4 when it takes effect. Ask your employer which payday will be the first to be covered . . . . ______

More than one job. If too little tax is withheld on line 5 above and you have more than one job (or you are married filing jointly and your spouse also works):

1) You may file a new 1987 Form W-4 for only one of the jobs, showing the total additional amount (the amount on line 5 above divided by the number of paydays remaining in 1987 for that job); or
2) You may file a new 1987 Form W-4 for each job. First, divide the amount on line 5 above between the jobs any way you wish. Then, for each job to which you apply an amount, divide the amount by the number of paydays remaining in 1987 for that job. This will give you the additional amount to enter on line 5 of the new Form W-4 you will file for that job.

Completing Form W-4. Enter on line 5 of the new 1987 Form W-4 the additional amount from line 6 of the worksheet. Also, be sure to enter on the 1987 Form W-4 the same number of allowances you claimed on your last 1987 Form W-4.

Give the completed Form W-4 to your employer right away so that the additional amount will be withheld by the first payday covered on line 6 of the worksheet.

(Continued on page 3)

1987 Tax Worksheet *(Enter combined amounts if married filing joint return.)*

1) Enter amount of Adjusted Gross Income (AGI) you expect in 1987. (AGI means wages, interest, dividends, alimony received, and all other income **minus** certain adjustments to income, such as alimony paid and qualified contributions to an IRA.)	1	
2) If you plan to itemize deductions, enter the estimated total of your deductions. These include items such as charitable contributions, real estate taxes, home mortgage interest, and 65% of other personal interest. If you do not plan to itemize deductions, enter the amount for your filing status shown in the *1987 Standard Deduction Chart* below.	2	
3) Subtract line 2 from line 1. Enter the difference here. (If zero or less, enter zero.)	3	
4) Exemptions (Multiply $1,900 by the number of exemptions.)	4	
5) Subtract line 4 from line 3. (If zero or less, enter zero.)	5	
6) Tax. (Figure your tax on line 5 by using Tax Rate Schedule X, Y, or Z below. DO NOT use the Tax Table or Tax Rate Schedule X, Y, or Z in the 1986 tax return instructions.)	6	
7) Enter any additional taxes	7	
8) Add lines 6 and 7	8	
9) Credits	9	
10) Subtract line 9 from line 8. (If zero or less, enter zero.)	10	
11) Self-employment tax. Estimate of 1987 self-employment income $________; if $43,800 or more, enter $5,387.40; If less than $43,800, multiply self-employment income by .123	11	
12) Other taxes	12	
13) Total taxes. Add lines 10 through 12. (Enter the total here and on line 1 of the *1987 Withholding Worksheet* on page 1.)	13	

1987 Standard Deduction Chart ***(Caution:** Do Not use this chart to figure your 1986 taxes.)*

Filing Status	If NOT Elderly or Blind, Enter on Line 2	If Age 65 or Over, or Blind, But Not Both, Enter on Line 2	If Age 65 or Over AND Blind, Enter on Line 2
Married filing jointly, or Qualifying widow(er)	$3,760	$5,600*	$6,200*
Head of household	2,540	5,150	5,900
Single	2,540	3,750	4,500
Married filing separately	1,880	3,100	3,700

*If your spouse is 65 or over, or blind, but not both, add $600 to this amount. If your spouse is both 65 or over and blind, add $1,200.

1987 Tax Rate Schedules ***(Caution:** Do Not use these schedules to figure your 1986 taxes.)*

SCHEDULE X—Single Taxpayers

If line 5 is: Over—	but not over—	Enter on line 6	of the amount over—
$0	$1,800	0 + 11%	$0
1,800	16,800	$198 + 15%	1,800
16,800	27,000	2,448 + 28%	16,800
27,000	54,000	5,304 + 35%	27,000
54,000	-------	14,754 + 38.5%	54,000

SCHEDULE Z—Heads of Household

If line 5 is: Over—	but not over—	Enter on line 6	of the amount over—
$0	$2,500	0 + 11%	$0
2,500	23,000	$275 + 15%	2,500
23,000	38,000	3,350 + 28%	23,000
38,000	80,000	7,550 + 35%	38,000
80,000	-------	22,250 + 38.5%	80,000

SCHEDULE Y—Married Taxpayers and Qualifying Widows and Widowers

Married Filing Joint Returns and Qualifying Widows and Widowers

If line 5 is: Over—	but not over—	Enter on line 6	of the amount over—
$0	$3,000	0 + 11%	$0
3,000	28,000	$330 + 15%	3,000
28,000	45,000	4,080 + 28%	28,000
45,000	90,000	8,840 + 35%	45,000
90,000	-------	24,590 + 38.5%	90,000

Married Filing Separate Returns

If line 5 is: Over—	but not over—	Enter on line 6	of the amount over—
$0	$1,500	0 + 11%	$0
1,500	14,000	$165 + 15%	1,500
14,000	22,500	2,040 + 28%	14,000
22,500	45,000	4,420 + 35%	22,500
45,000	-------	12,295 + 38.5%	45,000

Page 2

(Continued from page 1)

Example

The following example shows how to check your withholding by comparing it to your tax liability. All amounts are rounded off.

John and Mary are married, have two dependent children, and both work for the Ajax Company. They are paid every other week (26 paydays a year). John is paid $975 ($25,350 a year) and Mary is paid $925 ($24,050 a year) for combined annual wages of $49,400. The only other income they expect to receive in 1987 is savings account interest of $61. Thus, they expect 1987 adjusted gross income of $49,461. They do not expect to itemize their deductions in 1987.

On the last Forms W-4 they filed in 1985, John and Mary each claimed two withholding allowances. They both filed 1987 Forms W-4 in January of 1987. John checked the "Married" box on his Form W-4 and claimed the same number of withholding allowances (two) as on his last form. Mary checked the "Married" box and claimed "0" withholding allowances on her Form W-4.

The 1987 Forms W-4 took effect for the third payday in 1987. Since John's withholding allowances did not change from his previous Form W-4, the amount of federal income tax to be withheld from his pay on each of the remaining 24 paydays covered by the 1987 Form W-4 will be the same as the amount withheld on each of the first two paydays covered by the previous Form W-4. The Ajax Company will withhold $108 from John's pay on each of the 26 paydays in 1987.

Mary's withholding allowances changed from her previous Form W-4. She had $102 withheld on each of the first two 1987 paydays (covered by her previous Form W-4), and $124 will be withheld on each of the remaining 24 paydays (covered by the 1987 Form W-4).

To see if enough tax will be withheld from their pay, John and Mary compare the amount of tax they expect to show on their 1987 joint tax return with the actual amount of tax that will be withheld for the year. First, to figure the amount of tax they expect to show on their 1987 return, they completed the applicable items on the *1987 Tax Worksheet* on page 2 as follows:

1) Expected 1987 adjusted gross income	$49,461
2) Standard deduction (from page 2)	3,760
3) Subtract line 2 from line 1	$45,701
4) Exemptions ($1,900 × 4)	7,600
5) Subtract line 4 from line 3	$38,101
6) Tax (from Tax Rate Schedule Y on page 2)	$6,908
(Lines 7 through 12 do not apply to John and Mary.)	
13) Total tax	$ 6,908

John and Mary then completed the *1987 Withholding Worksheet* on page 1 to determine how much tax will be withheld in 1987 and to determine if any additional tax need be withheld.

1987 Withholding Worksheet

1) Complete the *1987 Tax Worksheet* on page 2 and enter your total taxes from line 13 of that worksheet	$6,908
2) Total federal income tax withheld to date in 1987 (includes all jobs)	$420
[*John's withholding ($108 X 2 paydays = $216)* *Mary's withholding ($102 X 2 paydays = $204)*]	
3) Tax withholding expected for the rest of 1987: For each job, multiply the amount of federal income tax now being withheld each payday by the number of paydays remaining in 1987 and enter the combined amount for all jobs	5,568
[*John's withholding ($108 X 24 paydays = $2,592)* *Mary's withholding ($124 X 24 paydays = $2,976)*]	
4) Total expected withholding tax for all paydays in 1987. Add lines 2 and 3	$5,988
5) Too little tax withheld. Subtract line 4 from line 1	$920
6) Additional amount to be withheld. Divide line 5 by the number of paydays remaining in 1987 that will be covered by another 1987 Form W-4 when it takes effect	$46
[*The Ajax Company tells John and Mary that 20 paydays will be covered ($920 ÷ 20 = $46)*]	

John and Mary choose to divide the $46 equally.* John checks the "Married" box on his 1987 Form W-4 and on line 4 claims two withholding allowances, the same as on his previous 1987 Form W-4. In addition, he enters $23 on line 5.

Mary checks the "Married" box on her 1987 Form W-4 and on line 4 claims "0" withholding allowances, the same as on her previous 1987 Form W-4. In addition, she enters $23 on line 5. John and Mary file their new 1987 Forms W-4 with the Ajax Company right away so that the additional amount will be withheld for the rest of the year.

*John and Mary would not divide the $46 equally if the number of paydays remaining in 1987 were different (for example, 20 paydays remaining for John and 10 paydays for Mary). Instead, they would figure the additional amount for each by using the method under *More than one job*, on page 1.

Form **942** (Rev. January 1986) Department of the Treasury Internal Revenue Service

Employer's Quarterly Tax Return for Household Employees

(For Social Security and Withheld Income Taxes)

OMB No. 1545-0034 Expires 9-30-88

YOUR COPY

Name .... Date quarter ended ....

Address .... Employer identification number ....

IMPORTANT: Keep this copy and a copy of each related schedule or statement.

Before filing the return, be sure to enter on this copy your name, address, employer identification number, and the period for which you are filing the return.

Make check or money order payable to, and mail to, Internal Revenue Service.

Social security taxes are due for each household employee to whom you paid cash wages of $50 or more in the calendar quarter covered by this return. For income tax withholding, see page 2.

			Dollars	Cents
1	Total cash wages ▶	1		
2	Social security taxes (multiply line 1 by 14.3% (.143))	2		
3	Federal income tax withheld (if requested by your employee)	3		
4	Total taxes (add lines 2 and 3)	4		
5	Advance earned income credit (EIC) payments, if any (see **Notes** on page 1)	5		
6	Total taxes due (subtract line 5 from line 4). Pay to the Internal Revenue Service	6		

If you will **NOT** need to file Form 942 in the future, check here ☐. **If no tax is due, write NONE on line 6.** ▲
Important: Form W-2 must be given to each employee and filed with the **Social Security Administration**—see page 4.

Employee Information (Optional).—The schedule below will help you complete Forms W-2 for your employees. Fill in the spaces that apply each quarter; add the quarterly amounts for each individual employee at the end of the year; and complete Forms W-2. You may keep this schedule as part of your records.

Employee's name (as shown on social security card), address, and ZIP code				Advance earned income credit (EIC) payments (if any)
Employee's social security number	Federal income tax withheld (if any)	Wages subject to income tax (cash and noncash, before tax deductions)	Employee social security tax	Wages subject to social security taxes (cash wages only, before tax deductions)
Employee's name (as shown on social security card), address, and ZIP code				Advance earned income credit (EIC) payments (if any)
Employee's social security number	Federal income tax withheld (if any)	Wages subject to income tax (cash and noncash, before tax deductions)	Employee social security tax	Wages subject to social security taxes (cash wages only, before tax deductions)
Employee's name (as shown on social security card), address, and ZIP code				Advance earned income credit (EIC) payments (if any)
Employee's social security number	Federal income tax withheld (if any)	Wages subject to income tax (cash and noncash, before tax deductions)	Employee social security tax	Wages subject to social security taxes (cash wages only, before tax deductions)
Employee's name (as shown on social security card), address, and ZIP code				Advance earned income credit (EIC) payments (if any)
Employee's social security number	Federal income tax withheld (if any)	Wages subject to income tax (cash and noncash, before tax deductions)	Employee social security tax	Wages subject to social security taxes (cash wages only, before tax deductions)

Keep this copy

General Instructions

Purpose of Form.—Use this form to report and pay employer and employee social security taxes, and any income tax withheld at the employee's request, on wages paid to household employees.

Who Must File.—File Form 942 if you paid a household employee cash wages of $50 or more in a calendar quarter for household work in or about your private home. Also file Form 942 if you have household employees who asked to have income tax withheld from pay for household work.

Social Security Taxes.—Both the employer and the employee must pay social security taxes on cash wages the employee receives for household work in or about the employer's private home (not including a private home on a farm operated for profit). Generally, it includes services by cooks, waiters, waitresses, butlers, housekeepers, governesses, maids, cleaning people, valets, babysitters, janitors, laundresses, caretakers, handymen, gardeners, and drivers of cars for family use. The combined employer and employee social security tax rate is 14.3% (7.15% employer tax plus 7.15% employee tax) and applies ONLY to the first $42,000 of cash wages for 1986.

How To Determine if Social Security Taxes Are Due. The $50-a-quarter Test.—Social security taxes are due if you pay an employee cash wages of $50 or more in a calendar quarter for household work. The taxes apply to all cash wages paid in the quarter regardless of when earned. The $50-a-quarter test applies separately to each household employee. You are not required to pay social security taxes on workers who are not your employees, such as carpenters, painters, or plumbers working for you as independent contractors. If you are not sure whether the taxes apply to a worker, you should see Circular E.

Employers with workers on a farm operated for profit should see **Circular A**, Agricultural Employer's Tax Guide, for more information. Other business employers should see Circular E. You can get these free from the IRS.

What Are Wages Subject to Social Security Taxes?—Social security taxes apply only to cash wages paid to household employees who meet the $50-a-quarter test. Checks, money orders, etc., are the same as cash. The value of food, lodging, clothing, bus tokens, and other noncash items given to household employees are not subject to social security taxes. Cash given in place of these items is considered wages. It does not matter whether payments are based on the hour, day, week, month, or year, or on piecework.

Social security taxes do not apply to wages for work in your home by your spouse, or by your son or daughter under the age of 21.

Also, these taxes do not apply to wages for domestic work in your home by your mother or father unless both of the following apply:

- You have in your home a son or daughter who is under age 18 or has a physical or mental condition that requires the personal care of an adult for at least 4 continuous weeks in the quarter, and
- You are a widow or widower, or are divorced, or have a spouse in your home who, because of a physical or mental condition, cannot care for your son or daughter for at least 4 continuous weeks in the quarter.

When you report cash wages on your quarterly return, show the full amount before tax was deducted.

Deducting Employee Social Security Tax.— In 1986 deduct 7.15% from each cash wage payment if you expect the employee to meet the $50-a-quarter test. (See the table on page 4.) Payments in 1986 of fourth quarter 1985 wages must be withheld at the 7.15% rate. Even if you are not sure the $50-a-quarter test will be met when you pay the wages, you may still deduct the tax.

If you do not deduct employee social security tax, or if you deduct too little tax, correct the mistake by deducting it from a later payment to the same employee. If you deduct tax when no tax is due, or if you deduct too much, you should repay your employee.

If you would rather pay the employee's share of social security tax without deducting it from his or her wages, you may do so. If you do not deduct the tax, you must still pay it. Any employee social security tax you pay is additional income to the employee. You must include it in box 10 on the employee's Form W-2 (see *Forms W-2 and W-3* on page 4), but do not count it as cash wages for social security purposes.

Income Tax.—An employee who wants you to withhold Federal income tax from wages must give you a completed **Form W-4**, Employee's Withholding Allowance Certificate.

If an employee asks you to withhold income tax and you agree, you must withhold an amount from each payment based on the Form W-4 the employee gives you. Show the total amount on line 3 of Form 942.

Any income tax withholding you pay for an employee without deducting it from the employee's wages is additional income. You must include it in boxes 10 and 13 on the employee's Form W-2.

See Circular E for Federal income tax withholding tables and other information. You can get Form W-4 and Circular E from the IRS.

What Are Wages Subject to Income Tax Withholding?—They consist of everything paid to your employee for work done. The word "wages" covers all pay, including:

- salaries
- vacation allowances
- bonuses
- meals (unless furnished on your premises and for your convenience)
- lodging (unless furnished on your premises, for your convenience, and as a condition of employment)
- clothing
- bus tokens
- other noncash items.

Measure wages you pay in any form other than money by the value of the goods, lodging, meals, or other consideration you give. See Circular E for details.

Employee's Social Security Number.—When you hire a household employee, record the name and social security number exactly as they appear on the employee's social security card.

An employee who does not have a number must apply for one on **Form SS-5**, Application for a Social Security Number Card. Form SS-5 is available from the Social Security Administration and Internal Revenue Service.

Employer Identification Number.—Your Form 942 should show the number assigned to you as an employer of household employees. If you do not have a number, write NONE in the space for the number. IRS will then assign you a number and send you a Form 942 each quarter. It is important that you keep a record of your employer identification number.

When To File.—File starting with the first quarter in which you—

- pay wages subject to social security taxes, or
- withhold income tax if requested by your employee.

Due Dates for Returns

Quarter	Ending	Due Date
Jan.-Feb.-Mar.	Mar. 31	Apr. 30
Apr.-May-June	June 30	July 31
July-Aug.-Sept.	Sept. 30	Oct. 31
Oct.-Nov.-Dec.	Dec. 31	Jan. 31

If the due date for filing a return falls on a Saturday, Sunday, or a legal holiday, you may file the return on the first day afterward that is not a Saturday, Sunday, or legal holiday.

If you receive Form 942 for a quarter when you did not pay any taxable wages, write NONE on line 6, and sign and return Form 942 to IRS.

Final Return.—If you do not expect to pay taxable wages in the future, check the box below line 6 on the return. If you start paying taxable wages again, notify IRS.

Paying the Taxes.—Make your check or money order payable to the Internal Revenue Service and write your employer identification number and "Form 942" on it. You may pay by mail or in person. To avoid loss, do not mail cash.

Where To File.—

If you are in ▼	File with the Internal Revenue Service Center at ▼
Alabama, Florida, Georgia, Mississippi, South Carolina	Atlanta, GA 31101
New Jersey, New York City and counties of Nassau, Rockland, Suffolk, and Westchester	Holtsville, NY 00501
New York (all other counties), Connecticut, Maine, Massachusetts, Minnesota, New Hampshire, Rhode Island, Vermont	Andover, MA 05501
Illinois, Iowa, Missouri, Wisconsin	Kansas City, MO 64999
Delaware, District of Columbia, Maryland, Pennsylvania	Philadelphia, PA 19255
Kentucky, Michigan, Ohio, West Virginia	Cincinnati, OH 45999
Kansas, Louisiana, New Mexico, Oklahoma, Texas	Austin, TX 73301
Alaska, Arizona, California (counties of Alpine, Amador, Butte, Calaveras, Colusa, Contra Costa, Del Norte, El Dorado, Glenn, Humboldt, Lake, Lassen, Marin, Mendocino, Modoc, Napa, Nevada, Placer, Plumas, Sacramento, San Joaquin, Shasta, Sierra, Siskiyou, Solano, Sonoma, Sutter, Tehama, Trinity, Yolo, and Yuba), Colorado, Idaho, Montana, Nebraska, Nevada, North Dakota, Oregon, South Dakota, Utah, Washington, Wyoming	Ogden, UT 84201
California (all other counties), Hawaii	Fresno, CA 93888
Arkansas, Indiana, North Carolina, Tennessee, Virginia	Memphis, TN 37501
If you have no legal residence in any state	Philadelphia, PA 19255

Keeping Records.—Keep your copies of Forms 942, W-2, and W-3. Also keep a record of each employee's social security number and name, dates and amounts of cash and noncash wage payments, and employee social security tax and income tax (if any) deducted.

Penalties.—Avoid penalties and interest by filing returns on time and paying tax when due. The law provides a penalty for filing a return late or paying tax late unless you show good reason for the delay. If you cannot avoid filing a return late or paying the tax late, attach an explanation to your return. The law also provides a penalty for not giving Forms W-2 to your employees.

(Continued on page 4)

Form **942** (Rev. January 1986) Department of the Treasury Internal Revenue Service 4242

Employer's Quarterly Tax Return for Household Employees

(For Social Security and Withheld Income Taxes)

OMB No. 1545-0034
Expires 9-30-88

Your name, address, employer identification number, and calendar quarter of return. (If not correct, please change.)

Name | Date quarter ended
Address and ZIP code | Employer identification number

FOR IRS USE ONLY

If address is different from prior return, check here ☐

Social security taxes are due for each household employee to whom you paid cash wages of $50 or more in the calendar quarter covered by this return. For income tax withholding, see page 2.

			Dollars	Cents
1	Total cash wages	1		
2	Social security taxes (multiply line 1 by 14.3% (.143))	2		
3	Federal income tax withheld (if requested by your employee)	3		
4	Total taxes (add lines 2 and 3)	4		
5	Advance earned income credit (EIC) payments, if any (see **Notes** below)	5		
6	Total taxes due (subtract line 5 from line 4). Pay to the Internal Revenue Service	6		

If you will **NOT** need to file Form 942 in the future, check here ☐. **If no tax is due, write NONE on line 6.**

Important: Form W-2 must be given to each employee and filed with the **Social Security Administration**—see page 4.

Under the penalties of perjury, I declare that I have examined this return, and to the best of my knowledge and belief it is true, correct, and complete.

Signature of employer ▶ Date ▶

Paperwork Reduction Act Notice.—We ask for this information to carry out the Internal Revenue laws of the United States. We need it to ensure that taxpayers are complying with these laws and to allow us to figure and collect the right amount of tax. You are required to give us this information.

Making Entries on Form 942.—When making entries on lines 1 through 6, **print** the amounts (do not use dollar signs), use a **soft lead pencil**, and keep the numbers inside the boxes. (If you use whole dollar amounts, enter a "0" in each of the "Cents" columns of lines 1 through 6.)

Please print your numbers like this.

1 2 3 4 5 6 7 8 9 0

Notes:

Under social security, your employees may qualify for:

- Monthly payments for themselves and their eligible dependents when they reach age 65 (reduced benefits are payable at age 62).
- Monthly payments for themselves and their eligible dependents (after a waiting period) when they become disabled.
- Monthly payments for their families when they die.
- Health insurance benefits at age 65 or (after a waiting period) when disabled.

For 1986, the maximum amount of cash wages subject to social security taxes is $42,000.

The law provides that an employee will be given a quarter of social security coverage, up to four quarters, for each $440 of wages paid to the employee in 1986.

For 1986, social security tax rates are 7.15% each for the employer and the employee. A 7.15% employee social security tax deduction table for 1986 is on page 4.

Household employers must also file **Form W-2**, Wage and Tax Statement, and (except those with only one employee during the year) **Form W-3**, Transmittal of Income and Tax Statements. For examples and filled-in copies of Forms W-2 and W-3 for household employees, please get **Publication 503**, Child and Dependent Care Credit, and Employment Taxes for Household Employers. This publication is available from the IRS.

Advance Earned Income Credit (EIC) Payments.—In certain cases, employees who qualify can choose to receive advance earned income credit (EIC) payments with their wages. Make the payments from social security taxes (and any withheld income taxes) that would otherwise be paid to IRS. Employees who are eligible can make this election by giving you annually a completed **Form W-5**, Earned Income Credit Advance Payment Certificate. Employees who work for you and any other employers should be advised that employees can have only one certificate in effect with a current employer at one time. **Circular E**, Employer's Tax Guide, has tables and instructions for figuring advance EIC payments. You can get this circular from the IRS. (Do not continue advance EIC payments to any employee on wages exceeding $11,000.)

Federal Unemployment (FUTA) Tax.— The Federal Unemployment Tax Act (FUTA) covers certain employees doing household work in a private home. If you paid cash wages of $1,000 or more for household work in any calendar quarter in 1985 or 1986, the employees you have in 1986 are covered under FUTA and you must file **Form 940**, Employer's Annual Federal Unemployment (FUTA) Tax Return. Form 940 is due by January 31 for the previous calendar year. (For an example and a filled-in copy of Form 940 for a household employer, please get Publication 503.)

Important: Send this form and your payment **ONLY** to your Internal Revenue Service Center (see instructions on *Where To File*). Form **942** (Rev. 1-86)

Form 942 (Rev 1-86) Page **4**

How To Fill In Form 942.—

Line 1. Total cash wages.—Show the total cash wages you paid in the quarter to all your employees who met the $50-a-quarter test.

Line 2. Social security taxes.—Multiply the cash wages on line 1 by 14.3% (.143).

Line 3. Federal income tax withheld.—Show the total Federal income tax withheld in the quarter, if any.

Line 4. Total taxes.—Add line 2 (Social security taxes) to line 3 (Federal income tax withheld).

Line 5. Advance earned income credit (EIC) payments, if any.—Show the total advance EIC payments you made to employees in the quarter.

Line 6. Total taxes due.—Subtract line 5 (Advance earned income credit (EIC) payments, if any) from line 4 (Total taxes).

Please sign and date the return, and include your employer identification number and "Form 942" on your check or money order.

Forms W-2 and W-3.—You must give the appropriate copies of Form W-2, Wage and Tax Statement, for the calendar year to each employee by February 2, 1987. If an employee stops working for you before the end of a year, give him or her Form W-2 any time after employment ends but no later than January 31 of the following year. However, if the employee asks you for Form W-2, give him or her the completed form within 30 days of the request or the last wage payment, whichever is later.

By March 2, 1987, send Copy A of Forms W-2 with Form W-3 to the Social Security Administration. (If you are sending only one Form W-2, Form W-3 is not needed.) Forms W-2 and W-3 will be mailed to you in the fourth quarter of 1986, and the SSA addresses are in the instructions for Form W-3. If you are a new household employer, Forms W-2 and W-3 can be obtained from the IRS. Copy A of Form W-2 has three forms on a page. If possible, Form W-2 should have no erasures, whiteouts, or strikeovers on Copy A. If you make a mistake, put an "X" in the "Void" square and use the next form. **Send the whole page even if one or two forms are blank or void.** If you file a final Form 942 before the end of a year, you can get Forms W-2 and W-3 from the IRS.

How To Fill In Form W-2.—If any entry does not apply to you, leave it blank. In most cases, only the following boxes on the 1986 Form W-2 will apply:

Boxes 2 and 3.—Show your name, address, and ZIP code in box 2, and your employer identification number in box 3.

Box 5.—Check the square titled "942 emp." if you had only one household employee during 1986.

Box 7.—Show the total advance earned income credit (EIC) payments made in the year, if any. (See *Advance Earned Income Credit (EIC) Payments* on page 1.)

Boxes 8, 12, and 15.—Show your employee's social security number in box 8, name in box 12, and address and ZIP code in box 15.

Box 9.—Show any Federal income tax withheld.

Box 10.—Show wages paid subject to income tax, whether or not income tax was withheld. (See *What Are Wages Subject to Income Tax Withholding?* on page 2.)

Box 11.—Show employee social security tax deducted or paid by you for the employee. (See *Deducting Employee Social Security Tax* on page 2.)

Box 13.—Show wages paid subject to social security taxes. (See *What Are Wages Subject to Social Security Taxes?* on page 2.)

How To Fill In Form W-3.—In most cases, only the following boxes on the 1986 Form W-3 will apply:

Boxes 2 and 3.—Check the squares titled "942" in box 2, and "W-2" in box 3.

Box 7.—Show the total advance earned income credit (EIC) payments, if any, for all employees.

Boxes 5, 15, 17, and 19.—Show the number of Forms W-2 you are sending with Form W-3 in box 5, your employer identification number in box 15, your name in box 17, and your address and ZIP code in box 19.

Boxes 9, 10, 11, and 13.—Add separately the amounts in boxes 9, 10, 11, and 13 of all Forms W-2 and show the totals in boxes 9, 10, 11, and 13, respectively, on Form W-3.

Note: *Be sure the amounts on void Forms W-2 are NOT included in the totals on Form W-3.*

Correcting Mistakes on Form 942 and Form W-2.—If, after filing Form 942, you find you paid more than the correct social security tax, you may subtract the difference on your next quarterly return. If you paid less than the correct social security tax and have not received a bill for the additional payment, add the difference to your next quarterly return. In either case, attach an explanation to the return on which you make the correction.

You may use **Form W-2c**, Statement of Corrected Income and Tax Amounts, and **Form W-3c**, Transmittal of Corrected Income and Tax Statements, to correct errors on previously filed Forms W-2. Please see the instructions for those forms for more information.

Optional Use of Whole Dollar Amounts for Social Security Taxes.—You may round off cash wages paid to the nearest whole dollar in determining whether the $50-a-quarter test is met, figuring employee tax deductions, and reporting wages on your return. For example, if you paid from $104.50 to $105.49, you may report $105 as the taxable wage. If you use this method in a quarter, you must use it for all wage payments to household employees in that quarter.

1986 Employee Social Security (7.15%) Tax Deduction Table. (See Circular E for income tax withholding tables.)

Note: You may use this table to figure how much employee social security tax to deduct from each wage payment in 1986. For example, if you pay total wages of $120 during the quarter, the employee tax is $8.58 ($7.15 tax for $100, plus $1.43 for $20 wages). The tax you report in 1986 on Form 942, line 2, would be $17.16 ($120 x .143 (7.15% employee tax plus 7.15% employer tax)).

If wage payment is—	The employee tax to be deducted is—	If wage payment is—	The employee tax to be deducted is—	If wage payment is—	The employee tax to be deducted is—	If wage payment is—	The employee tax to be deducted is—	If wage payment is—	The employee tax to be deducted is—
$1	$0.07	**$21**	$1.50	**$41**	$2.93	**$61**	$4.36	**$81**	$5.79
2	.14	**22**	1.57	**42**	3.00	**62**	4.43	**82**	5.86
3	.21	**23**	1.64	**43**	3.07	**63**	4.50	**83**	5.93
4	.29	**24**	1.72	**44**	3.15	**64**	4.58	**84**	6.01
5	.36	**25**	1.79	**45**	3.22	**65**	4.65	**85**	6.08
6	.43	**26**	1.86	**46**	3.29	**66**	4.72	**86**	6.15
7	.50	**27**	1.93	**47**	3.36	**67**	4.79	**87**	6.22
8	.57	**28**	2.00	**48**	3.43	**68**	4.86	**88**	6.29
9	.64	**29**	2.07	**49**	3.50	**69**	4.93	**89**	6.36
10	.72	**30**	2.15	**50**	3.58	**70**	5.01	**90**	6.44
11	.79	**31**	2.22	**51**	3.65	**71**	5.08	**91**	6.51
12	.86	**32**	2.29	**52**	3.72	**72**	5.15	**92**	6.58
13	.93	**33**	2.36	**53**	3.79	**73**	5.22	**93**	6.65
14	1.00	**34**	2.43	**54**	3.86	**74**	5.29	**94**	6.72
15	1.07	**35**	2.50	**55**	3.93	**75**	5.36	**95**	6.79
16	1.14	**36**	2.57	**56**	4.00	**76**	5.43	**96**	6.86
17	1.22	**37**	2.65	**57**	4.08	**77**	5.51	**97**	6.94
18	1.29	**38**	2.72	**58**	4.15	**78**	5.58	**98**	7.01
19	1.36	**39**	2.79	**59**	4.22	**79**	5.65	**99**	7.08
20	1.43	**40**	2.86	**60**	4.29	**80**	5.72	**100**	7.15

☆U.S. G.P.O. 1986-463-818

Form **1040** Department of the Treasury—Internal Revenue Service
U.S. Individual Income Tax Return **1986** (0)

For the year January 1-December 31, 1986, or other tax year beginning , 1986, ending , 19 | OMB No. 1545-0074

Use IRS label. Otherwise, please print or type.

Your first name and initial (if joint return, also give spouse's name and initial) | Last name | **Your social security number**

Present home address (number and street or rural route). (If you have a P.O. Box, see page 4 of Instructions.) | **Spouse's social security number**

City, town or post office, state, and ZIP code | If this address is different from the one shown on your 1985 return, check here ▶ ☐

Presidential Election Campaign ▶ Do you want $1 to go to this fund? . . . Yes | No
If joint return, does your spouse want $1 to go to this fund? . . . Yes | No
Note: *Checking "Yes" will not change your tax or reduce your refund.*

For Privacy Act and Paperwork Reduction Act Notice, see Instructions.

Filing Status

Check only one box.

1 ☐ Single
2 ☐ Married filing joint return (even if only one had income)
3 ☐ Married filing separate return. Enter spouse's social security no. above and full name here. ______
4 ☐ Head of household (with qualifying person). (See page 5 of Instructions.) If the qualifying person is your unmarried child but not your dependent, enter child's name here. ______
5 ☐ Qualifying widow(er) with dependent child (year spouse died ▶ 19). (See page 6 of Instructions.)

Exemptions

Always check the box labeled Yourself. Check other boxes if they apply.

6a ☐ Yourself ☐ 65 or over ☐ Blind
b ☐ Spouse ☐ 65 or over ☐ Blind
} Enter number of boxes checked on 6a and b ▶ ☐

c First names of your dependent children who lived with you ______ } Enter number of children listed on 6c ▶ ☐

d First names of your dependent children who did not live with you (see page 6). ______ (If pre-1985 agreement, check here ▶ ☐ .) } Enter number of children listed on 6d ▶ ☐

e Other dependents:

(1) Name	(2) Relationship	(3) Number of months lived in your home	(4) Did dependent have income of $1,080 or more?	(5) Did you provide more than one-half of dependent's support?

Enter number of other dependents ▶ ☐

f Total number of exemptions claimed (also complete line 36) . . . Add numbers entered in boxes above ▶ ☐

Income

Please attach Copy B of your Forms W-2, W-2G, and W-2P here.

If you do not have a W-2, see page 4 of Instructions.

Please attach check or money order here.

7 Wages, salaries, tips, etc. *(attach Form(s) W-2)* . . . 7
8 Interest income *(also attach Schedule B if over $400)* . . . 8
9a Dividends *(also attach Schedule B if over $400)* ______ , 9b Exclusion ______
c Subtract line 9b from line 9a and enter the result . . . 9c
10 Taxable refunds of state and local income taxes, if any, from the worksheet on page 9 of Instructions . 10
11 Alimony received . . . 11
12 Business income or (loss) *(attach Schedule C)* . . . 12
13 Capital gain or (loss) *(attach Schedule D)* . . . 13
14 40% of capital gain distributions not reported on line 13 (see page 9 of Instructions) . . . 14
15 Other gains or (losses) *(attach Form 4797)* . . . 15
16 Fully taxable pensions, IRA distributions, and annuities not reported on line 17 (see page 9) . 16
17a Other pensions and annuities, including rollovers. Total received | 17a |
b Taxable amount, if any, from the worksheet on page 10 of Instructions . . . 17b
18 Rents, royalties, partnerships, estates, trusts, etc. *(attach Schedule E)* . . . 18
19 Farm income or (loss) *(attach Schedule F)* . . . 19
20a Unemployment compensation (insurance). Total received . . | 20a |
b Taxable amount, if any, from the worksheet on page 10 of Instructions . . . 20b
21a Social security benefits (see page 10) . . . | 21a |
b Taxable amount, if any, from worksheet on page 11 . { Tax-exempt interest ______ } . . . 21b
22 Other income (list type and amount—see page 11 of Instructions) ______ 22
23 Add the amounts shown in the far right column for lines 7 through 22. This is your **total income** . ▶ 23

Adjustments to Income

(See Instructions on page 11.)

24 Moving expenses *(attach Form 3903 or 3903F)* . . . 24
25 Employee business expenses *(attach Form 2106)* . . . 25
26 IRA deduction, from the worksheet on page 12 . . . 26
27 Keogh retirement plan and self-employed SEP deduction . . 27
28 Penalty on early withdrawal of savings . . . 28
29 Alimony paid (recipient's last name ______ and social security no. ______) . . . 29
30 Deduction for a married couple when both work *(attach Schedule W)* 30
31 Add lines 24 through 30. These are your **total adjustments** . . . ▶ 31

Adjusted Gross Income

32 Subtract line 31 from line 23. This is your **adjusted gross income.** *If this line is less than $11,000 and a child lived with you, see "Earned Income Credit" (line 58) on page 16 of Instructions. If you want IRS to figure your tax, see page 13 of Instructions* . . . ▶ 32

Form 1040 (1986) Page 2

Tax Computation (See Instructions on page 13.)

33 Amount from line 32 (adjusted gross income) . . . 33

34a If you itemize, attach Schedule A (Form 1040) and enter the amount from Schedule A, line 26 . . 34a

Caution: If you have unearned income and can be claimed as a dependent on your parents' return, see page 13 of Instructions and check here ▶ ☐ . Also see page 13 if you are married filing a separate return and your spouse itemizes deductions, or you are a dual-status alien.

b If you do not itemize but you made charitable contributions, enter your cash contributions here. (If you gave $3,000 or more to any one organization, see page 14.) . . . 34b

c Enter your noncash contributions *(you must attach Form 8283 if over $500)* 34c

d Add lines 34b and 34c. Enter the total . . . 34d

35 Subtract line 34a or line 34d, whichever applies, from line 33 . . . 35

36 Multiply $1,080 by the total number of exemptions claimed on line 6f (see page 14) . . . 36

37 **Taxable income.** Subtract line 36 from line 35. Enter the result (but not less than zero) . . . 37

38 Enter tax here. Check if from ☐ Tax Table, ☐ Tax Rate Schedule X, Y, or Z, or ☐ Schedule G 38

39 Additional taxes (see page 14 of Instructions). Enter here and check if from ☐ Form 4970, ☐ Form 4972, or ☐ Form 5544 . . . 39

40 Add lines 38 and 39. Enter the total . . . ▶ 40

Credits (See Instructions on page 14.)

41 Credit for child and dependent care expenses *(attach Form 2441)* 41

42 Credit for the elderly or for the permanently and totally disabled *(attach Schedule R)* . . . 42

43 Partial credit for political contributions for which you have receipts 43

44 Add lines 41 through 43. Enter the total . . . 44

45 Subtract line 44 from line 40. Enter the result (but not less than zero) . . . 45

46 Foreign tax credit *(attach Form 1116)* . . . 46

47 General business credit. Check if from ☐ Form 3800, ☐ Form 3468, ☐ Form 5884, ☐ Form 6478, or ☐ Form 6765 47

48 Add lines 46 and 47. Enter the total . . . 48

49 Subtract line 48 from line 45. Enter the result (but not less than zero) . . . ▶ 49

Other Taxes (Including Advance EIC Payments)

50 Self-employment tax *(attach Schedule SE)* . . . 50

51 Alternative minimum tax *(attach Form 6251)* . . . 51

52 Tax from recapture of investment credit *(attach Form 4255)* . . . 52

53 Social security tax on tip income not reported to employer *(attach Form 4137)* . . . 53

54 Tax on an IRA *(attach Form 5329)* . . . 54

55 Add lines 49 through 54. This is your **total tax** . . . ▶ 55

Payments Attach Forms W-2, W-2G, and W-2P to front.

56 Federal income tax withheld . . . 56

57 1986 estimated tax payments and amount applied from 1985 return 57

58 Earned income credit (see page 16) . . . 58

59 Amount paid with Form 4868 . . . 59

60 Excess social security tax and RRTA tax withheld (two or more employers) . . . 60

61 Credit for Federal tax on gasoline and special fuels *(attach Form 4136)* 61

62 Regulated investment company credit *(attach Form 2439)* . . . 62

63 Add lines 56 through 62. These are your **total payments** . . . ▶ 63

Refund or Amount You Owe

64 If line 63 is larger than line 55, enter amount **OVERPAID** . . . ▶ 64

65 Amount of line 64 to be **REFUNDED TO YOU** . . . ▶ 65

66 Amount of line 64 to be applied to your 1987 estimated tax . . . ▶ 66

67 If line 55 is larger than line 63, enter **AMOUNT YOU OWE.** Attach check or money order for full amount payable to "Internal Revenue Service." Write your social security number, daytime phone number, and "1986 Form 1040" on it . . . ▶ 67

Check ▶ ☐ if Form 2210 (2210F) is attached. See page 17. **Penalty:** $

Please Sign Here

Under penalties of perjury, I declare that I have examined this return and accompanying schedules and statements, and to the best of my knowledge and belief, they are true, correct, and complete. Declaration of preparer (other than taxpayer) is based on all information of which preparer has any knowledge.

Your signature	Date	Your occupation
Spouse's signature (if joint return, BOTH must sign)	Date	Spouse's occupation

Paid Preparer's Use Only

Preparer's signature	Date	Check if self-employed ☐	Preparer's social security no.
Firm's name (or yours, if self-employed) and address		E.I. No.	
		ZIP code	

☆ U.S. GOVERNMENT PRINTING OFFICE: 1986-493-074

SCHEDULES A&B (Form 1040)
Department of the Treasury
Internal Revenue Service (O)

Schedule A—Itemized Deductions

(Schedule B is on back)

▶ Attach to Form 1040. ▶ See Instructions for Schedules A and B (Form 1040).

OMB No. 1545-0074
1986
Attachment Sequence No. **07**

Name(s) as shown on Form 1040 | **Your social security number**

Medical and Dental Expenses (Do not include expenses reimbursed or paid by others.) (See Instructions on page 19.)	1	Prescription medicines and drugs; and insulin	1	
	2 a	Doctors, dentists, nurses, hospitals, insurance premiums you paid for medical and dental care, etc.	2a	
	b	Transportation and lodging	2b	
	c	Other (list—include hearing aids, dentures, eyeglasses, etc.) ▶	2c	
	3	Add lines 1 through 2c, and enter the total here	3	
	4	Multiply the amount on Form 1040, line 33, by 5% (.05)	4	
	5	Subtract line 4 from line 3. If zero or less, enter -0-. **Total** medical and dental ▶		5
Taxes You Paid (See Instructions on page 20.)	6	State and local income taxes	6	
	7	Real estate taxes	7	
	8 a	General sales tax (see sales tax tables in instruction booklet)	8a	
	b	General sales tax on motor vehicles	8b	
	9	Other taxes (list—include personal property taxes) ▶	9	
	10	Add the amounts on lines 6 through 9. Enter the total here. **Total** taxes ▶		10
Interest You Paid (See Instructions on page 20.)	11 a	Home mortgage interest paid to financial institutions (report deductible points on line 13)	11a	
	b	Home mortgage interest you paid to individuals (show that person's name and address) ▶	11b	
	12	Total credit card and charge account interest you paid	12	
	13	Other interest you paid (list payee's name and amount) ▶	13	
	14	Add the amounts on lines 11a through 13. Enter the total here. **Total** interest ▶		14
Contributions You Made (See Instructions on page 21.)	15 a	Cash contributions. (If you gave $3,000 or more to any one organization, report those contributions on line 15b.)	15a	
	b	Cash contributions totaling $3,000 or more to any one organization. (Show to whom you gave and how much you gave.) ▶	15b	
	16	Other than cash. (You must attach Form 8283 if over $500.)	16	
	17	Carryover from prior year	17	
	18	Add the amounts on lines 15a through 17. Enter the total here. **Total** contributions ▶		18
Casualty and Theft Losses	19	Total casualty or theft loss(es). (You must attach Form 4684 or similar statement.) (See page 21 of Instructions.) ▶		19
Miscellaneous Deductions (See Instructions on page 22.)	20	Union and professional dues	20	
	21	Tax return preparation fee	21	
	22	Other (list type and amount) ▶	22	
	23	Add the amounts on lines 20 through 22. Enter the total here. **Total** miscellaneous ▶		23
Summary of Itemized Deductions (See Instructions on page 22.)	24	Add the amounts on lines 5, 10, 14, 18, 19, and 23. Enter your answer here		24
	25	If you checked Form 1040 { Filing Status box 2 or 5, enter $3,670; Filing Status box 1 or 4, enter $2,480; Filing Status box 3, enter $1,835 }		25
	26	Subtract line 25 from line 24. Enter your answer here and on Form 1040, line 34a. (If line 25 is more than line 24, see the Instructions for line 26 on page 22.) ▶		26

For Paperwork Reduction Act Notice, see Form 1040 Instructions. **Schedule A (Form 1040) 1986**

Schedules A&B (Form 1040) 1986 — OMB No. 1545-0074 — Page 2

Name(s) as shown on Form 1040. (Do not enter name and social security number if shown on other side.) | Your social security number

Schedule B—Interest and Dividend Income

Attachment Sequence No. 08

Part I Interest Income

(See Instructions on pages 8 and 22.)

Also complete Part III.

If you received more than $400 in interest income, you must complete Part I and list ALL interest received. If you received, as a nominee, interest that actually belongs to another person, or you received or paid accrued interest on securities transferred between interest payment dates, see page 22.

Interest Income		Amount
1 Interest income from seller-financed mortgages. (See Instructions and list name of payer.) ▶	1	
2 Other interest income (list name of payer) ▶	2	
3 Add the amounts on lines 1 and 2. Enter the total here and on Form 1040, line 8 . ▶	3	

Part II Dividend Income

(See Instructions on pages 8 and 22.)

Also complete Part III.

If you received more than $400 in gross dividends and/or other distributions on stock, complete Part II. If you received, as a nominee, dividends that actually belong to another person, see page 23.

Dividend Income				Amount
4 Dividend income (list name of payer—include on this line capital gain distributions, nontaxable distributions, etc.) ▶			4	
5 Add the amounts on line 4. Enter the total here			5	
6 Capital gain distributions. Enter here and on line 13, Schedule D.*	6			
7 Nontaxable distributions. (See Schedule D Instructions for adjustment to basis.)	7			
8 Add the amounts on lines 6 and 7. Enter the total here			8	
9 Subtract line 8 from line 5. Enter the result here and on Form 1040, line 9a . ▶			9	

**If you received capital gain distributions for the year and you do not need Schedule D to report any other gains or losses, do not file that schedule. Instead, enter 40% of your capital gain distributions on Form 1040, line 14.*

Part III Foreign Accounts and Foreign Trusts

(See Instructions on page 23.)

If you received more than $400 of interest or dividends, OR if you had a foreign account or were a grantor of, or a transferor to, a foreign trust, you must answer both questions in Part III.	Yes	No
10 At any time during the tax year, did you have an interest in or a signature or other authority over a financial account in a foreign country (such as a bank account, securities account, or other financial account)? (See page 23 of the Instructions for exceptions and filing requirements for Form TD F 90-22.1.)		
If "Yes," enter the name of the foreign country ▶		
11 Were you the grantor of, or transferor to, a foreign trust which existed during the current tax year, whether or not you have any beneficial interest in it? If "Yes," you may have to file Forms 3520, 3520-A, or 926		

For Paperwork Reduction Act Notice, see Form **1040 Instructions.** — Schedule B (Form 1040) 1986

☆ U.S. Government Printing Office: 1986—483-082 23-0016750

Form **1040A**

Department of the Treasury—Internal Revenue Service
U.S. Individual Income Tax Return (0) **1986**

Step 1 Name and address

Use the IRS mailing label. If you don't have one, print or type: OMB No. 1545-0085

Your first name and initial (if joint return, also give spouse's name and initial) | Last name | Your social security no.

Present home address (number and street). (If you have a P.O. Box, see page 7 of the instructions.) | Spouse's social security no.

City, town or post office, state, and ZIP code | If this address is different from the one shown on your 1985 return, check here ☐

Presidential Election Campaign Fund
Do you want $1 to go to this fund? . . . . ☐ Yes ☐ No
If joint return, does your spouse want $1 to go to this fund?. ☐ Yes ☐ No

Step 2 Check your filing status (Check only one)

1 ☐ Single (See if you can use Form 1040EZ.)
2 ☐ Married filing joint return (even if only one had income)
3 ☐ Married filing separate return. Write spouse's social security number above and spouse's full name here. ______
4 ☐ Head of household (with qualifying person). If the qualifying person is your unmarried child but not your dependent, write this child's name here. ______

Step 3 Figure your exemptions

Attach Copy B of Form(s) W-2 here

Always check the exemption box labeled Yourself. Check other boxes if they apply.

5a ☐ Yourself ☐ 65 or over ☐ Blind
b ☐ Spouse ☐ 65 or over ☐ Blind — Write number of boxes checked on 5a and b ____
c First names of your dependent children who lived with you ______ — Write number of children listed on 5c ____
d First names of your dependent children who did not live with you (see page 11). (If pre-1985 agreement, check here ☐ .) ______ — Write number of children listed on 5d ____
e Other dependents:

1. Name	2. Relationship	3. Number of months lived in your home.	4. Did dependent have income of $1,080 or more?	5. Did you provide more than one-half of dependent's support?

Write number of other dependents listed on 5e ____

f Total number of exemptions claimed. (Also complete line 18.) — Add numbers entered on lines above ☐

Step 4 Figure your total income

Attach check or money order here

6 Total wages, salaries, tips, etc. This should be shown in Box 10 of your W-2 form(s). (Attach Form(s) W-2.) — 6
7 Interest income. (If the total is over $400, also attach Schedule 1, Part III.) — 7
8a Dividends. (If the total is over $400, also attach Schedule 1, Part IV.) Total. 8a ____ **8b** Exclusion (see page 16). 8b ____
c Subtract line 8b from line 8a. Write the result on line 8c. — 8c
9a Unemployment compensation (insurance), from Form(s) 1099-G. Total received. — 9a
b Taxable amount, if any, from the worksheet on page 17 of the instructions. — 9b
10 Add lines 6, 7, 8c, and 9b. Write the total. This is your **total income**. ▶ 10

Step 5 Figure your adjusted gross income

11 Individual retirement arrangement (IRA) deduction, from the worksheet on page 19. — 11
12 Deduction for a married couple when both work. Complete and attach Schedule 1, Part I. — 12
13 Add lines 11 and 12. Write the total. These are your **total adjustments**. — 13
14 Subtract line 13 from line 10. Write the result. This is your **adjusted gross income**. ▶ 14

For **Privacy Act and Paperwork Reduction Act Notice**, see page 41. Form **1040A** (1986)

1986 Form 1040A Page 2

Step 6
Figure your taxable income

15	Write the amount from line 14.		15 .
16a	If you made charitable contributions, write your cash contributions. (If $3,000 or more to any one organization, see page 21.)	16a .	
b	Write your noncash contributions. If over $500, you must attach Form 8283.	16b .	
c	Add lines 16a and 16b. Write the total.		16c .
17	Subtract line 16c from line 15. Write the result.		17 .
18	Multiply $1,080 by the total number of exemptions claimed on line 5f. See the chart on page 22 of the instructions.		18 .
19	Subtract line 18 from line 17. Write the result. This is your **taxable income.** ▶		19 .

Step 7
Figure your tax, credits, and payments (including advance EIC payments)

If You Want IRS to Figure Your Tax, See Page 22 of the Instructions.

20	Find the tax on the amount on line 19. Use the tax table, pages 31-36.		20 .
21a	Credit for child and dependent care expenses. Complete and attach Schedule 1, Part II.	21a .	
b	Partial credit for political contributions for which you have receipts. See page 24 of the instructions.	21b .	
22	Add lines 21a and 21b. Write the total.		22 .
23	Subtract line 22 from line 20. Write the result. (If line 22 is more than line 20, write -0- on line 23.) This is your **total tax**. ▶		23 .
24a	Total Federal income tax withheld. This should be shown in Box 9 of your W-2 form(s). (If line 6 is more than $42,000, see page 25 of the instructions.)	24a .	
b	Earned income credit, from the worksheet on page 27 of the instructions. See page 26 of the instructions.	24b .	
25	Add lines 24a and 24b. Write the total. These are your **total payments**. ▶		25 .

Step 8
Figure your refund or amount you owe

26	If line 25 is larger than line 23, subtract line 23 from line 25. Write the result. This is the **amount of your refund**.	26 .
27	If line 23 is larger than line 25, subtract line 25 from line 23. Write the result. This is the **amount you owe**. Attach check or money order for full amount payable to "Internal Revenue Service." Write your social security number, daytime phone number, and "1986 Form 1040A" on it.	27 .

Step 9
Sign your return

Under penalties of perjury, I declare that I have examined this return and accompanying schedules and statements, and to the best of my knowledge and belief, they are true, correct, and complete. Declaration of preparer (other than the taxpayer) is based on all information of which the preparer has any knowledge.

Your signature	Date	Your occupation
X		
Spouse's signature (if joint return, both must sign)	Date	Spouse's occupation
X		

Paid preparer's use only

Preparer's signature	Date	Preparer's social security no.
X		
Firm's name (or yours, if self-employed)		Employer identification no.
Address and ZIP code		Check if self-employed ☐

1986 Schedule 1 (Form 1040A)

OMB No. 1545-0085

Name(s) as shown on Form 1040A. (Do not complete if shown on other side.) | Your social security number

Part III **Interest Income** (see page 15)

Complete this part and attach Schedule 1 to Form 1040A if you received over $400 in interest income.

1 List name of payer	Amount
	$.
	$.
	$.
	$.
	$.
	$.
	$.
	$.
	$.
	$.
	$.
	$.
	$.
	$.
	$.
	$.
	$.
	$.
	$.
	$.

2 Add amounts on line 1. Write the total here and on Form 1040A, line 7. 2

Part IV **Dividend Income** (see page 16)

Complete this part and attach Schedule 1 to Form 1040A if you received over $400 in dividends.

1 List name of payer	Amount
	$.
	$.
	$.
	$.
	$.
	$.
	$.
	$.
	$.
	$.
	$.
	$.
	$.
	$.
	$.
	$.
	$.
	$.
	$.
	$.

2 Add amounts on line 1. Write the total here and on Form 1040A, line 8a. 2 .

*U.S. G.P.O. 1986-493-120

1986 Schedule 1 (Form 1040A)

OMB No. 1545-0085

Name(s) as shown on Form 1040A | Your social security number

You MUST complete and attach Schedule 1 to Form 1040A only if you:

- Claim the deduction for a working married couple (complete **Part I**)
- Claim the credit for child and dependent care expenses (complete **Part II**)
- Have over $400 of interest income (complete **Part III**)
- Have over $400 of dividend income (complete **Part IV**)

Part I — Deduction for a married couple (filing a joint return) when both work (see page 20)

Complete this part to figure the amount you can deduct on Form 1040A, line 12. Attach Schedule 1 to Form 1040A.

		(a) You	(b) Your spouse
1	Wages, salaries, tips, etc., from Form 1040A, line 6.	1 .	.
2	IRA deduction, if any, from Form 1040A, line 11.	2 – .	– .
3	Subtract line 2 from line 1. Write the result.	3 = .	= .
4	Write the amount from line 3, column (a) or (b) above, whichever is smaller.		4 .
5	Percentage used to figure the deduction (10%).		5 × .10
6	Multiply the amount on line 4 by the percentage on line 5. Write your answer here and on Form 1040A, line 12.		6 =

Part II — Credit for child and dependent care expenses (see page 23)

Complete this part to figure the amount of credit you can take on Form 1040A, line 21a. Attach Schedule 1 to Form 1040A.

Note: *If you paid cash wages of $50 or more in a calendar quarter to an individual for services performed in your home, you must file an employment tax return. Get* ***Form 942*** *for details.*

1 Write the number of qualifying persons who were cared for in 1986. (See the instructions for the definition of a qualifying person.) — 1

2 Write the amount of **qualified** expenses you incurred and actually paid in 1986 for the care of the qualifying person. (See the instructions for which expenses qualify for the credit.) DO NOT write more than $2,400 ($4,800 if you paid for the care of two or more qualifying persons). — 2 .

3 a You **must** write your earned income on line 3a. — 3a .

b If you are married, filing a joint return for 1986, you must write your spouse's earned income on line 3b. — 3b .

c If you are married, compare the amounts on lines 3a and 3b, and write the **smaller** of the two amounts on line 3c. — 3c .

4 • If you were unmarried at the end of 1986, compare the amounts on lines 2 and 3a, and write the **smaller** of the two amounts on line 4.

• If you are married, filing a joint return for 1986, compare the amounts on lines 2 and 3c, and write the **smaller** of the two amounts on line 4. — 4 .

5 Write the percentage from the table below that applies to the amount on Form 1040A, line 15.

If line 15 is: Over—	But not over—	Percentage is:	If line 15 is: Over—	But not over—	Percentage is:
$0	10,000	30% (.30)	$20,000	22,000	24% (.24)
10,000	12,000	29% (.29)	22,000	24,000	23% (.23)
12,000	14,000	28% (.28)	24,000	26,000	22% (.22)
14,000	16,000	27% (.27)	26,000	28,000	21% (.21)
16,000	18,000	26% (.26)	28,000		20% (.20)
18,000	20,000	25% (.25)			

5 × .

6 Multiply the amount on line 4 by the percentage on line 5. Write the result here and on Form 1040A, line 21a. — 6 = .

Form **1040X** (Rev. October 1986) (O)

Department of the Treasury—Internal Revenue Service

Amended U.S. Individual Income Tax Return

OMB No. 1545-0091
Expires 4-30-88

This return is for calendar year ▶ 19 , OR fiscal year ended ▶ , 19 .

Please print or type

Your first name and initial (if joint return, also give spouse's name and initial) Last name	**Your social security number**
Present home address (number and street or rural route). (If you have a P.O. Box, see Instructions.)	**Spouse's social security number**
City, town or post office, state, and ZIP code	Telephone number (optional) ( )

Enter below name and address as shown on original return (if same as above, write "Same"). If changing from separate to joint return, enter names and addresses used on original returns. (**Note:** *You cannot change from joint to separate returns after the due date has passed.*)

a Service center where original return was filed

b Has original return been changed or audited by IRS? ☐ Yes ☐ No
If "No," have you been notified that it will be? ☐ Yes ☐ No
If "Yes," identify IRS office ▶

c Are you amending your return to include any item (loss, credit, deduction, other tax benefit, or income) relating to a tax shelter required to be registered? ☐ Yes ☐ No
If "Yes," you **MUST** attach **Form 8271,** Investor Reporting of Tax Shelter Registration Number.

d Filing status claimed. (**Note:** *You cannot change from joint to separate returns after the due date has passed.*)
On original return ▶ ☐ Single ☐ Married filing joint return ☐ Married filing separate return ☐ Head of household ☐ Qualifying widow(er)
On this return ▶ ☐ Single ☐ Married filing joint return ☐ Married filing separate return ☐ Head of household ☐ Qualifying widow(er)

	Income and Deductions		**A.** As originally reported or as adjusted (see Instructions)	**B.** Net change—Increase or (Decrease)—explain on page 2	**C.** Correct amount
	1 Total income (see Instructions)	1			
	2 Adjustments to income (see Instructions)	2			
	3 Adjusted gross income (subtract line 2 from line 1)	3			
	4 Deductions (see Instructions)	4			
	5 Subtract line 4 from line 3	5			
	6 Exemptions (see Instructions)	6			
	7 Taxable income (subtract line 6 from line 5)	7			
Tax Liability	8 Tax (see Instructions). (Method used in col. C ....)	8			
	9 Credits (see Instructions)	9			
	10 Subtract line 9 from line 8. Enter the result, but not less than zero	10			
	11 Other taxes (such as self-employment tax, alternative minimum tax)	11			
	12 Total tax liability (add line 10 and line 11)	12			
Payments	13 Federal income tax withheld and excess FICA and RRTA tax withheld	13			
	14 Estimated tax payments	14			
	15 Earned income credit	15			
	16 Credits for Federal tax on gasoline and special fuels, regulated investment company, etc.	16			
	17 Amount paid with Form 4868, Form 2688, or Form 2350 (application for extension of time to file)			17	
	18 Amount paid with original return, plus additional tax paid after it was filed			18	
	19 Total of lines 13 through 18, column C			19	

Refund or Amount You Owe

20 Overpayment, if any, as shown on original return (or as previously adjusted by IRS)	20	
21 Subtract line 20 from line 19 (see Instructions)	21	
22 **AMOUNT YOU OWE.** If line 12, col. C, is more than line 21, enter difference. Please pay in full with this return.	22	
23 **REFUND** to be received. If line 12, column C, is less than line 21, enter difference.	23	

Please Sign Here

Under penalties of perjury, I declare that I have filed an original return and that I have examined this amended return, including accompanying schedules and statements, and to the best of my knowledge and belief, this amended return is true, correct, and complete. Declaration of preparer (other than taxpayer) is based on all information of which the preparer has any knowledge.

▶ Your signature Date ▶ Spouse's signature (if filing jointly, BOTH must sign)

Paid Preparer's Use Only

Preparer's signature ▶	Date	Check if self-employed ☐	Preparer's social security no.
Firm's name (or yours, if self-employed) and address ▶		E.I. No.	
		ZIP code	

For Paperwork Reduction Act Notice, see page 1 of separate Instructions. **BE SURE TO COMPLETE PAGE 2**

Form 1040X (Rev. 10-86) Page 2

Part I **Exemptions (see Form 1040 or Form 1040A Instructions)**
If claiming more exemptions, complete lines 1–9.
If claiming fewer exemptions, complete lines 1–6.

			A. Number originally reported	B. Net change	C. Correct number
1	Exemptions—yourself and spouse, 65 or over, blind	1			
2	Your dependent children who lived with you	2			
3	For tax years beginning after 1984, your dependent children who did not live with you	3			
4	Other dependents	4			
5	Total exemptions (add lines 1 through 4)	5			
6	Multiply $1,080 ($1,040, for tax year 1985; $1,000, for tax years beginning before 1985) by the number of exemptions claimed on line 5. Enter the result here and on page 1, line 6	6			

7 First names of your dependent children who lived with you and were not claimed on original return: **Enter number ▶** ☐

8 For tax years beginning after 1984, first names of your dependent children who did not live with you and were not claimed on original return (see Instructions). (If pre-1985 agreement, check here ☐ .) **Enter number ▶** ☐

9 Other dependents not claimed on original return:

(a) Name	(b) Relationship	(c) Number of months lived in your home	(d) Did dependent have income of at least $1,080 ($1,040, for tax year 1985; $1,000, for tax years beginning before 1985)?	(e) Did you provide more than one-half of dependent's support?

Enter number ▶ ☐

Part II **Explanation of Changes to Income, Deductions, and Credits**

Enter the line number from page 1 for each item you are changing and give the reason for each change. Attach all supporting forms and schedules for items changed. Be sure to include your name and social security number on any attachments.

If the change pertains to a net operating loss carryback, a general business credit carryback, or for tax years beginning before 1986, a research credit carryback, attach the schedule or form that shows the year in which the loss or credit occurred. See the Instructions. Also, check here ▶ ☐

Part III **Presidential Election Campaign Fund**

Checking below will not increase your tax or reduce your refund.

If you did not previously want to have $1 go to the fund, but now want to . . . check here ▶ ☐

If joint return and your spouse did not previously want to have $1 go to the fund, but now wants to . . . check here ▶ ☐

☆ U.S.G.P.O.: 1986 -493-144

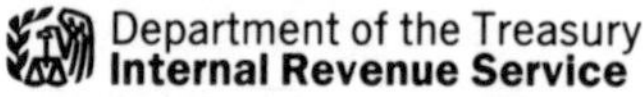

Instructions for Form 1040X

(Revised October 1986)

Amended U.S. Individual Income Tax Return

General Instructions

Paperwork Reduction Act Notice.—We ask for this information to carry out the Internal Revenue laws of the United States. We need it to ensure that taxpayers are complying with these laws and to allow us to figure and collect the right amount of tax. You are required to give us this information.

Purpose of Form.—Use Form 1040X to correct **Form 1040**, **Form 1040A**, or **Form 1040EZ.** Please note that it often takes 2 to 3 months to process Form 1040X. If you are changing your Federal return, you may also have to change your state return.

Filing Form 1045.—You may use **Form 1045**, Application for Tentative Refund, instead of Form 1040X if:

- you are applying for a refund resulting from a net operating loss or credit carryback (other than a foreign tax credit carryback), **AND**
- less than one year has elapsed since the end of the year in which the loss or credit arose.

Carryback Claims.—You must attach copies of the following to Form 1040X if it is used as a carryback claim.

- Pages 1 and 2 of Form 1040 for the year of the loss or credit from which the carryback results.
- Any Schedules K-1 you received from any partnership, S corporation, estate, or trust for the year of the loss or credit which contribute to the loss or credit carryback.
- Any form or schedule from which the carryback results (such as Form 3468 or Schedule C or F).
- The forms or schedules for items refigured in the carryback year.

All information described above must be attached to your Form 1040X, if applicable, or your Form 1040X will be returned for the attachments.

Net Operating Loss.—Attach a computation of your net operating loss using **Schedule A (Form 1045).**

A refund based on a net operating loss should not include the refund of any self-employment tax reported on line 11 of Form 1040X. For more information, get **Publication 536,** Net Operating Losses and the At-Risk Limits.

Information on Income, Deductions, etc.—If you have questions, such as what income is taxable or what expenses are deductible, the instructions for the return you are amending may help you. Be sure to use the Tax Table or Tax Rate Schedules for the right year to figure the corrected tax. The related schedules and forms may also help you.

Death of Taxpayer.—If you are filing a claim for refund for a deceased person, write "deceased" after the deceased's name and show the date of death in the name and address space at the top of Form 1040X. Also write "**DECEASED**" across the top of Form 1040X.

If you are claiming a refund as a surviving spouse filing a joint return with the deceased spouse, also write "Filing as surviving spouse" in the area where you sign the return. If someone else is the personal representative, he or she must also sign. No other form is needed to have the refund issued to you. However, all other filers who request a refund due a deceased taxpayer must file **Form 1310,** Statement of Person Claiming Refund Due a Deceased Taxpayer, to claim the refund.

If you want more details, get **Publication 559,** Tax Information for Survivors, Executors, and Administrators.

When To File.—File Form 1040X after you file your original return. Generally, Form 1040X must be filed within 3 years after the date the original return was due or 3 years after the date you filed it, whichever was later. A Form 1040X based on a net operating loss carryback, general business credit carryback, or, for tax years beginning before 1986, research credit carryback generally must be filed within 3 years after the due date of the return for the tax year of the net operating loss or unused credit.

Where To File. —Please use the address for your state. Mail your return to the **Internal Revenue Service Center** for the place where you live. No street address is needed.

If you are located in: ▼	Use this address: ▼
Alabama, Florida, Georgia, Mississippi, South Carolina	Atlanta, GA 31101
New Jersey, New York City and counties of Nassau, Rockland, Suffolk, and Westchester	Holtsville, NY 00501
Connecticut, Maine, Massachusetts, Minnesota, New Hampshire, New York (all other counties), Rhode Island, Vermont	Andover, MA 05501
Illinois, Iowa, Missouri, Wisconsin	Kansas City, MO 64999
Delaware, District of Columbia, Maryland, Pennsylvania	Philadelphia, PA 19255
Kentucky, Michigan, Ohio, West Virginia	Cincinnati, OH 45999
Kansas, Louisiana, New Mexico, Oklahoma, Texas	Austin, TX 73301
Arkansas, Indiana, North Carolina, Tennessee, Virginia	Memphis, TN 37501
Alaska, Arizona, California (counties of Alpine, Amador, Butte, Calaveras, Colusa, Contra Costa, Del Norte, El Dorado, Glenn, Humboldt, Lake, Lassen, Marin, Mendocino, Modoc, Napa, Nevada, Placer, Plumas, Sacramento, San Joaquin, Shasta, Sierra, Siskiyou, Solano, Sonoma, Sutter, Tehama, Trinity, Yolo, and Yuba), Colorado, Idaho, Montana, Nebraska, Nevada, North Dakota, Oregon, South Dakota, Utah, Washington, Wyoming	Ogden, UT 84201
California (all other counties), Hawaii	Fresno, CA 93888
American Samoa	Philadelphia, PA 19255
Guam	Commissioner of Revenue and Taxation Agana, GU 96910
Puerto Rico (or if excluding income under section 933) Virgin Islands: Nonpermanent residents	Philadelphia, PA 19255
Virgin Islands: Permanent residents	V.I. Bureau of Internal Revenue P.O. Box 3186 St. Thomas, VI 00801
Foreign country: U.S. citizens and those filing Form 2555 or Form 4563, even if you have an A.P.O. or F.P.O. address	Philadelphia, PA 19255
A.P.O. or F.P.O. address of:	Miami—Atlanta, GA 31101 New York—Holtsville, NY 00501 San Francisco—Fresno, CA 93888 Seattle—Ogden, UT 84201

Preparer Information.—If you fill in your own return, the Paid Preparer's space should remain blank. If someone else prepares your return and does not charge you, that person should **not** sign your return.

Generally, anyone who is paid to prepare your tax return must sign your return and fill in the other blanks in the Paid Preparer's Use Only area of your return.

If you have questions about whether a preparer is required to sign your return, please contact an IRS office.

The person required to sign your return **MUST** complete the required preparer information and:

- Sign it, by hand, in the space provided for the preparer's signature. (Signature stamps or labels are not acceptable.)
- Give you a copy of your return in addition to the copy to be filed with IRS.

Tax return preparers should be familiar with their responsibilities. They should get **Publication 1045,** Information and Order Blanks for Preparers of Federal Income Tax Returns, for more details.

Line-by-Line Instructions

Page 1

Above your name, enter the calendar year or fiscal year of the return you are amending.

Name and Social Security No.—If amending a joint return, list your names and social security numbers in the same order as shown on the original return.

If changing from a separate to joint return and your spouse did not file an original return, enter your name and social security number first.

P.O. Box.—If your post office does not deliver mail to your street address, enter your P.O. box number instead of your street address.

Item d—Filing Status.—If you are changing from separate returns to a joint return, both of you must sign Form 1040X. If there is any tax due, it must be paid in full.

Column A.—Enter the amounts from your return as originally filed or as you later amended it. If your return was changed or audited by IRS, enter the amounts as adjusted.

Column B.—Enter the net increase or net decrease for each line you are changing. Bracket all decreases. Explain each change on page 2, Part II, and attach any related schedule or form. For example, if you are amending your return to income average, attach **Schedule G (Form 1040).**

Column C.—Add the increase in column B to the amount in column A, or subtract the column B decrease from column A. Show the result in column C. For any item you do not change, enter the amount from column A in column C.

Note: *If you are changing only credits or other taxes, skip lines 1–7 and start with line 8. If changing only payments, skip lines 1–11 and start with line 12.*

Line 1.—To figure this amount, add income from all sources, such as wages, interest, dividends, and net profit from business. On Form 1040, for 1983, use line 22. For 1984–1986, use line 23.

On Form 1040A, use line 10.

On Form 1040EZ, use line 3.

If you are correcting wages or other employee compensation, attach the first copy or Copy B of all additional or corrected Forms W-2 that you got after you filed your original return.

Line 2.—Enter all adjustments to income, such as the deduction for a married couple when both work, moving expenses, or employee business expenses. On Form 1040, for 1983, use lines 23–30. For 1984–1986, use lines 24–30. Be sure to include as an adjustment to income any write-in adjustment. For more details, see your Form 1040 instructions.

On Form 1040A, use lines 11 and 12.

Line 4.—If you itemize deductions on **Schedule A (Form 1040),** enter on line 4 the amount, if any, of your excess itemized deductions. On Schedule A, for 1983, use line 28. For 1984–1986, use line 26.

If you do not itemize, enter zero. However, if you claim a deduction for charitable contributions, enter the amount of the deduction on line 4 of Form 1040X.

Note: *If you are amending your 1985 or 1986 Form 1040 or Form 1040A to claim the contribution deduction for nonitemizers, also complete the applicable lines on page 2 of Form 1040 or Form 1040A, whichever applies, and attach that page to Form 1040X.*

If you made an entry on line 4 of the worksheet on page 13 of the Form 1040 instructions for 1983–1986, enter the amount from line 4 of the worksheet on line 4 of Form 1040X. Add lines 3 and 4 instead of subtracting, and enter the result on line 5.

Caution: *Some changes you make to income or deductions can cause other amounts to increase or decrease. For example, increasing your income may decrease your medical expense deduction. It also may increase the allowable deduction for charitable contributions or sales tax. You should refigure these items whenever you change your return.*

Line 6.—If you are changing your exemptions, complete the applicable lines in Part I on page 2 to figure the amounts to enter on line 6.

If you are not changing your exemptions, enter in columns A and C of line 6 the amount you claimed for exemptions on your original return. On Form 1040, use line 36.

On Form 1040A, use line 18.

On Form 1040EZ, use line 6.

Line 8.—Enter your income tax before subtracting any credits. Show on this line the method you use in column C to figure your tax. For example, if you use the Tax Rate Schedules, write "TRS." If you use income averaging, write "Sch. G."

Figure the tax on the taxable income you reported on line 7, column C. Attach the appropriate schedules or forms. Include on line 8 any additional taxes from **Form 4970, Form 4972,** and **Form 5544.** Also, for 1983, include any section 72 penalty tax on this line. For 1984–1986, include any section 72 tax in the total for line 11 of Form 1040X. The forms and instructions for the right year will help you with line 8.

Line 9.—Enter your total credits, such as the credit for the elderly or for the permanently and totally disabled, or credit for child and dependent care expenses. On Form 1040, for 1983, use lines 41–47. For 1984 and 1985, use lines 41–44, 47, and 48. For 1986, use lines 41–43, 46, and 47. Include as a credit any write-in credit. For more details, see your Form 1040 instructions.

On Form 1040A, use lines 21a and 21b.

Line 11.—Include other taxes, such as tax from recapture of investment credit, alternative minimum tax, self-employment tax, or advance earned income credit payments. On Form 1040, for 1983, use lines 50–55. For 1984 and 1985, use lines 51–55. For 1986, use lines 50–54. Be sure to include any write-in tax. For more details, see your Form 1040 instructions.

On Form 1040A, use advance earned income credit (EIC) payments received.

Lines 13–17.—Enter on the applicable lines your payments and credits. On Form 1040, for 1983–1985, use lines 57–63. For 1986, use lines 56–62. Also, include the amount of any overpaid windfall profit tax on line 16 of Form 1040X and write on the dotted line "OWPT."

On Form 1040A, use lines 24a and 24b.

On Form 1040EZ, use line 8.

Line 13.—If you change these amounts, attach the first copy or Copy B of all additional or corrected Forms W-2 that you got since you filed your original return.

Line 14.—Enter the estimated tax payments you claimed on your return. If you filed Form 1040C, include the amount you paid as the balance due with the return.

Line 18.—Enter the amount you paid on the "Balance Due" or "Amount You Owe" reported on your original return. Also include any additional tax that may have resulted if your original return was changed or examined. **Do not include payments of interest or penalties.**

Line 20.— Enter the overpayment from your original return. On Form 1040A and Form 1040EZ, it is called "amount of your refund." On Form 1040 it is called "amount overpaid."

That amount must be considered in preparing Form 1040X since any refund you have not yet received from your original return will be refunded separately from any additional refund claimed on your Form 1040X. If your original return was changed or audited by IRS and, as a result of the change or audit, there was an additional overpayment of tax, also include that amount on line 20. **Do not** include any interest you received on any refund.

Lines 21–22.—***Caution:*** *If line 21 is a minus figure, add it to line 12, column C, instead of subtracting. Enter the result on line 22.*

We will figure the interest due and send you a bill.

Line 23.—If you are entitled to a larger refund than you claimed on your original return, show only the additional amount due you. This will be refunded separately from the amount claimed on your original return (see the instructions for line 20). We will figure the interest and include it in your refund.

Page 2

Part I—Exemptions.—If you are claiming more exemptions, complete lines 1–9, as they apply. If you are claiming fewer exemptions, complete lines 1–6.

In column A, enter the number of exemptions claimed on your original return. In column B, enter any changes to exemptions claimed on your original return. Enter in column C the corrected number of exemptions you are claiming.

If claiming a child under the special rules for children of divorced or separated parents, you must either attach **Form 8332,** or similar statement, **OR** check the box **on line 8** for pre-1985 agreements. For details, see your 1986 Form 1040 instructions for line 6d or Form 1040A instructions for line 5d.

Part III—Presidential Election Campaign Fund.—You may use Form 1040X to have $1 go to the Presidential Election Campaign Fund if you (or your spouse on a joint return) did not do so on your original return. This must be done within 20 1/2 months after the original due date for filing the return. For the calendar year 1986, this period ends on December 31, 1988.

Note: *A "Yes" designation cannot be changed.*

☆ U.S. Government Printing Office: 1986—493-145 23-0916750

Page 2

SCHEDULE D
(Form 1041)
Department of the Treasury
Internal Revenue Service

Capital Gains and Losses

► File with Form 1041. See the separate instructions.

OMB No. 1545-0092

1986

Name of estate or trust | Employer identification number

Do not report section 644 gains on Schedule D; see Form 1041 instruction for line 25b.

Part I **Short-Term Capital Gains and Losses—Assets Held Six Months or Less**

(a) Description of property (Example, 100 shares 7% preferred of "Z" Co.)	(b) Date acquired (mo., day, yr.)	(c) Date sold (mo., day, yr.)	(d) Gross sales price	(e) Cost or other basis, as adjusted, plus expense of sale (see instructions)	(f) Gain or (loss) (col. (d) less (e))
1					

2 Short-term capital gain from installment sales from Form 6252	2	
3 Enter the net short-term gain or (loss) from partnerships, S corporations, and other fiduciaries	3	
4 Net gain or (loss), (combine lines 1 through 3)	4	
5 Short-term capital loss carryover (see instructions)	5	( )
6 Net short-term gain or (loss), (combine lines 4 and 5). Enter here and on line 15 below ►	6	

Part II **Long-Term Capital Gains and Losses—Assets Held More Than Six Months**

7					

8 Long-term capital gain from installment sales from Form 6252	8	
9 Enter the net long-term gain or (loss) from partnerships, S corporations, and other fiduciaries	9	
10 Capital gain distributions	10	
11 Enter gain, if applicable, from Form 4797	11	
12 Net gain or (loss), (combine lines 7 through 11)	12	
13 Long-term capital loss carryover (see instructions)	13	( )
14 Net long-term gain or (loss), (combine lines 12 and 13). Enter here and on line 16 below ►	14	

Part III **Summary of Parts I and II**		(a) Beneficiaries	(b) Fiduciary	(c) Total
15 Net short-term gain or (loss) from line 6, column (f) above	15			
16 Net long-term gain or (loss) from line 14, column (f) above	16			
17 Total net gain or (loss), (combine lines 15 and 16) ►	17			

If line 17, column (c), is a net gain, enter the gain on Form 1041, line 6, and complete Part IV. If line 17, column (c), is a net (loss), complete Part V.

For Paperwork Reduction Act Notice, see page 1 of the Instructions for Form 1041. **Schedule D (Form 1041) 1986**

Part IV Computation of Capital Gain Deduction

18	Net long-term capital gain shown on line 16, column (c)	18	
19	Net short-term capital loss shown on line 15, column (c)	19	( )
20	Excess of line 18 over line 19	20	
21	Net long-term capital gains taxable to beneficiaries	21	
22	Balance (subtract line 21 from line 20) (see instructions) ▶	22	
23	Enter 60% of the amount on line 22 here and on Form 1041, line 21 *(If this amount is other than zero, you may be liable for the alternative minimum tax. See Form 6251.)*	23	

Part V Computation of Capital Loss Limitation

24	If losses are shown on both lines 13 and 14 which are the result of a long-term capital loss carryover from years beginning before 1970, check here ▶ ☐ and compute the net capital loss on a separate sheet and attach it to this return. See sections 1.1211-1 and 1.1212-1 of the regulations. Enter on line 24a the net capital loss computed on the separate sheet. **Otherwise** **a** Enter one of the following amounts if there is no long-term capital loss carryover from years beginning before 1970: *(i)* If amount on line 15, column (c), is zero or a net gain, enter 50% of amount on line 17, column (c); *(ii)* If amount on line 16, column (c), is zero or a net gain, enter amount on line 17, column (c); **or** *(iii)* If amounts on line 15, column (c), and line 16, column (c), are net losses, enter amount on line 15, column (c), added to 50% of amount on line 16, column (c)	24a	
	b Enter here and enter as a (loss) on Form 1041, line 6, the smallest of: *(i)* The amount on line 24a; *(ii)* $3,000; **or** *(iii)* Taxable income computed without regard to capital gains and losses and the deduction for exemption ▶	24b	( )

Part VI Computation of Post-1969 Capital Loss Carryovers From 1986 to 1987

(Complete this part if the loss on line 24a is more than the loss on line 24b)

Section A.—Short-Term Capital Loss Carryover

25	Enter loss shown on line 6; if none, enter zero and skip lines 26 through 29 and go to line 30	25	
26	Enter gain shown on line 14. If that line is blank or shows a loss, enter zero	26	
27	Reduce any loss on line 25 to the extent of any gain on line 26	27	
28	Enter smaller of line 27 or line 24b	28	
29	Subtract line 28 from line 27. This is your short-term capital loss carryover from 1986 to 1987	29	

Section B.—Long-Term Capital Loss Carryover

(Complete this part if there is a loss on line 14)

30	Subtract line 28 from line 24b (**Note:** *If you skipped lines 26 through 29, enter amount from line 24b)*	30	
31	Enter loss from line 14	31	
32	Enter gain shown on line 6. If that line is blank or shows a loss, enter zero	32	
33	Reduce any loss on line 31 to the extent of any gain on line 32	33	
34	Multiply amount on line 30 by 2	34	
35	Subtract line 34 from line 33. This is your long-term capital loss carryover from 1986 to 1987	35	

☆ U.S. Government Printing Office: 1986—493-148 23-0916750

Form **1120S** Department of the Treasury Internal Revenue Service

U.S. Income Tax Return for an S Corporation

For the calendar year 1986 or tax year beginning ...., 1986, ending ...., 19 ....

▶ For Paperwork Reduction Act Notice, see page 1 of the instructions.

OMB No. 1545-0130

1986

A Date of election as an S corporation	Use IRS label. Otherwise, please print or type.	Name	C Employer identification number
		Number and street	D Date incorporated
B Business Code No. (see Specific Instructions)		City or town, state, and ZIP code	E Total assets (see Specific Instructions) Dollars / Cents $

F. Check applicable boxes: (1) ☐ Final return (2) ☐ Change in address (3) ☐ Amended return

1986-87 fiscal year corporations see Specific Instructions before completing page 1.

Income

1a	Gross receipts or sales .... b Less returns and allowances .... Balance ▶	1c
2	Cost of goods sold and/or operations (Schedule A, line 7)	2
3	Gross profit (subtract line 2 from line 1c)	3
4	Taxable interest and nonqualifying dividends	4
5	Gross rents	5
6	Gross royalties	6
7	Net gain or (loss) from Form 4797, line 17, Part II	7
8	Other income (see instructions—attach schedule)	8
9	TOTAL income (loss)—Combine lines 3 through 8 and enter here ▶	9

Deductions

10	Compensation of officers	10
11a	Salaries and wages .... b Less jobs credit .... Balance ▶	11c
12	Repairs	12
13	Bad debts (see instructions)	13
14	Rents	14
15	Taxes	15
16a	Total deductible interest expense not claimed elsewhere on return (see instructions) — 16a	
b	Interest expense required to be passed through to shareholders on Schedule K-1, lines 9, 13a(2), and 13a(3) — 16b	
c	Subtract line 16b from line 16a	16c
17a	Depreciation from Form 4562 (attach Form 4562) — 17a	
b	Depreciation claimed on Schedule A and elsewhere on return — 17b	
c	Subtract line 17b from line 17a	17c
18	Depletion (**Do not deduct oil and gas depletion.** See instructions)	18
19	Advertising	19
20	Pension, profit-sharing, etc. plans	20
21	Employee benefit programs	21
22	Other deductions (attach schedule)	22
23	TOTAL deductions—Add lines 10 through 22 and enter here ▶	23
24	Ordinary income (loss)—Subtract line 23 from line 9	24

Tax and Payments

25	Tax:	
a	Excess net passive income tax (attach schedule) — 25a	
b	Tax from Schedule D (Form 1120S), Part IV — 25b	
c	Add lines 25a and 25b	25c
26	Payments:	
a	Tax deposited with Form 7004 — 26a	
b	Credit for Federal tax on gasoline and special fuels (attach Form 4136) — 26b	
c	Add lines 26a and 26b	26c
27	**TAX DUE** (subtract line 26c from line 25c). See instructions for Paying the Tax ▶	27
28	**OVERPAYMENT** (subtract line 25c from line 26c) ▶	28

Please Sign Here

Under penalties of perjury, I declare that I have examined this return, including accompanying schedules and statements, and to the best of my knowledge and belief, it is true, correct, and complete. Declaration of preparer (other than taxpayer) is based on all information of which preparer has any knowledge.

▶ Signature of officer — Date — ▶ Title

Paid Preparer's Use Only

Preparer's signature ▶	Date	Check if self-employed ▶ ☐	Preparer's social security number
Firm's name (or yours, if self-employed) and address ▶		E.I. No. ▶	
		ZIP code ▶	

Form **1120S** (1986)

Schedule A **Cost of Goods Sold and/or Operations** (See instructions for Schedule A)

1 Inventory at beginning of year	1	
2 Purchases	2	
3 Cost of labor	3	
4 Other costs (attach schedule)	4	
5 Total—Add lines 1 through 4	5	
6 Inventory at end of year	6	
7 Cost of goods sold and/or operations—Subtract line 6 from line 5. Enter here and on line 2, page 1	7	

8a Check all methods used for valuing closing inventory:

(i) ☐ Cost

(ii) ☐ Lower of cost or market as described in Regulations section 1.471-4 (see instructions)

(iii) ☐ Writedown of "subnormal" goods as described in Regulations section 1.471-2(c) (see instructions)

(iv) ☐ Other (Specify method used and attach explanation) ▶ ....

b Check this box if the LIFO inventory method was adopted this tax year for any goods (if checked, attach Form 970) ☐

c If the LIFO inventory method was used for this tax year, enter percentage (or amounts) of closing inventory computed under LIFO **8c** ____

d If you are engaged in manufacturing, did you value your inventory using the full absorption method (Regulations section 1.471-11)? ☐ Yes ☐ No

e Was there any change in determining quantities, cost, or valuations between opening and closing inventory? ☐ Yes ☐ No
If "Yes," attach explanation.

Additional Information Required

	Yes	No
G Did you at the end of the tax year own, directly or indirectly, 50% or more of the voting stock of a domestic corporation? (For rules of attribution, see section 267(c).)		
If "Yes," attach a schedule showing:		
(1) Name, address, and employer identification number;		
(2) Percentage owned;		
(3) Highest amount owed by you to such corporation during the year: and		
(4) Highest amount owed to you by such corporation during the year.		
(Note: *For purposes of G(3) and G(4), "highest amount owed" includes loans and accounts receivable/payable.)*		
H Refer to the listing of Business Activity Codes at the end of the Instructions for Form 1120S and state your principal: Business activity ▶ ....; Product or service ▶		
I Were you a member of a controlled group subject to the provisions of section 1561?		
J Did you claim a deduction for expenses connected with:		
(1) Entertainment facilities (boat, resort, ranch, etc.)?		
(2) Living accommodations (except for employees on business)?		
(3) Employees attending conventions or meetings outside the North American area? (See section 274(h).)		
(4) Employees' families at conventions or meetings?		
If "Yes," were any of these conventions or meetings outside the North American area? (See section 274(h).)		
(5) Employee or family vacations not reported on Form W-2?		
K At any time during the tax year, did you have an interest in or a signature or other authority over a financial account in a foreign country (such as a bank account, securities account, or other financial account)? (See instructions for exceptions and filing requirements for form TD F 90-22.1.)		
If "Yes," write the name of the foreign country ▶		
L Were you the grantor of, or transferor to, a foreign trust which existed during the current tax year, whether or not you have any beneficial interest in it? If "Yes," you may have to file Forms 3520, 3520-A, or 926		
M During this tax year did you maintain any part of your accounting/tax records on a computerized system?		
N Check method of accounting: **(1)**☐ Cash **(2)**☐ Accrual **(3)**☐ Other (specify) ▶		
O Check this box if the S corporation has filed or is required to file Form 8264, Application for Registration of a Tax Shelter ▶☐		
P Check this box if the corporation issued publicly offered debt instruments with original issue discount ▶☐ If so, the corporation may have to file Form 8281.		

Form 1120S (1986) Page 3

Schedule K Shareholders' Share of Income, Credits, Deductions, etc. (See Instructions.)

(a) Distributive share items		(b) Total amount
Income (Losses) and Deductions		
1a Ordinary income (loss) (page 1, line 24) *	**1a**	
b Income (loss) from rental real estate activity(ies) (FY corporations only)	**1b**	
c Income (loss) from other rental activity(ies) (FY corporations only)	**1c**	
d Portfolio income not reported elsewhere on Schedule K (FY corporations only)	**1d**	
2 Dividends qualifying for the exclusion	**2**	
3 Net short-term capital gain (loss) (Schedule D (Form 1120S)) *	**3**	
4 Net long-term capital gain (loss) (Schedule D (Form 1120S)) *	**4**	
5 Net gain (loss) under section 1231 (other than due to casualty or theft) *	**5**	
6 Other income (loss) (attach schedule)	**6**	
7 Charitable contributions	**7**	
8 Section 179 expense deduction (FY corporations attach schedule)	**8**	
9 Other deductions (attach schedule)	**9**	
Credits		
10a Jobs credit *	**10a**	
b Low-income housing credit (FY corporations only)	**10b**	
c Qualified rehabilitation expenditures related to rental real estate activity(ies) (FY corporations only) (attach schedule)		
d Other credits related to rental real estate activity(ies) other than on line 10b and 10c (FY corporations only) (attach schedule)	**10d**	
11 Other credits (attach schedule) *	**11**	
Tax Preference and Adjustment Items		
12a Accelerated depreciation on nonrecovery real property or 15, 18, or 19-year real property placed in service before 1-1-87	**12a**	
b Accelerated depreciation on leased personal property or leased recovery property, other than 15, 18, or 19-year real property, placed in service before 1-1-87	**12b**	
c Accelerated depreciation on property placed in service after 12-31-86 (FY corporations only)	**12c**	
d Depletion (other than oil and gas)	**12d**	
e **(1)** Gross income from oil, gas, or geothermal properties	**12e(1)**	
(2) Gross deductions allocable to oil, gas, or geothermal properties	**12e(2)**	
f **(1)** Qualified investment income included on page 1, Form 1120S	**12f(1)**	
(2) Qualified investment expenses included on page 1, Form 1120S	**12f(2)**	
g Other items (attach schedule)	**12g**	
Investment Interest		
13a Interest expense on: **(1)** Investment debts incurred before 12-17-69	**13a(1)**	
(2) Investment debts incurred before 9-11-75 but after 12-16-69	**13a(2)**	
(3) Investment debts incurred after 9-10-75	**13a(3)**	
b **(1)** Investment income included on page 1, Form 1120S	**13b(1)**	
(2) Investment expenses included on page 1, Form 1120S	**13b(2)**	
c **(1)** Income from "net lease property"	**13c(1)**	
(2) Expenses from "net lease property"	**13c(2)**	
d Excess of net long-term capital gain over net short-term capital loss from investment property	**13d**	
Foreign Taxes		
14a Type of income		
b Name of foreign country or U.S. possession		
c Total gross income from sources outside the U.S. (attach schedule)	**14c**	
d Total applicable deductions and losses (attach schedule)	**14d**	
e Total foreign taxes (check one): ▶ ☐ Paid ☐ Accrued	**14e**	
f Reduction in taxes available for credit (attach schedule)	**14f**	
g Other (attach schedule)	**14g**	
Other Items		
15 Total property distributions (including cash) other than dividend distributions reported on line 17	**15**	
16 Other items and amounts not included in lines 1 through 15 that are required to be reported separately to shareholders (attach schedule).		
17 Total dividend distributions paid from accumulated earnings and profits contained in other retained earnings (line 26 of Schedule L)	**17**	

* Calendar year filers are not required to complete lines 1a, 10a, and 11. Completion of these lines is optional because the amounts which would appear in column (b) appear elsewhere on Form 1120S or on other IRS forms or schedules which are attached to Form 1120S. See Specific Instructions for Schedules K and K-1.

Form 1120S (1986) Page 4

Schedule L Balance Sheets

Assets	Beginning of tax year (a)	(b)	End of tax year (c)	(d)
1 Cash				
2 Trade notes and accounts receivable				
a Less allowance for bad debts				
3 Inventories				
4 Federal and state government obligations				
5 Other current assets (attach schedule)				
6 Loans to shareholders				
7 Mortgage and real estate loans				
8 Other investments (attach schedule)				
9 Buildings and other depreciable assets				
a Less accumulated depreciation				
10 Depletable assets				
a Less accumulated depletion				
11 Land (net of any amortization)				
12 Intangible assets (amortizable only)				
a Less accumulated amortization				
13 Other assets (attach schedule)				
14 Total assets				
Liabilities and Shareholders' Equity				
15 Accounts payable				
16 Mortgages, notes, bonds payable in less than 1 year				
17 Other current liabilities (attach schedule)				
18 Loans from shareholders				
19 Mortgages, notes, bonds payable in 1 year or more				
20 Other liabilities (attach schedule)				
21 Capital stock				
22 Paid-in or capital surplus				
23 Accumulated adjustments account				
24 Other adjustments account				
25 Shareholders' undistributed taxable income previously taxed				
26 Other retained earnings (see instructions). Check this box if the corporation has subchapter C earnings and profits at the close of the tax year ▶ ☐ (see instructions)				
27 Total retained earnings per books—Combine amounts on lines 23 through 26, columns (a) and (c) (see instructions)				
28 Less cost of treasury stock		( )		( )
29 Total liabilities and shareholders' equity				

Schedule M **Analysis of Accumulated Adjustments Account, Other Adjustments Account, and Shareholders' Undistributed Taxable Income Previously Taxed (If Schedule L, column (c), amounts for lines 23, 24, or 25 are not the same as corresponding amounts on line 9 of Schedule M, attach a schedule explaining any differences. See instructions.)**

	Accumulated adjustments account	Other adjustments account	Shareholders' undistributed taxable income previously taxed
1 Balance at beginning of year			
2 Ordinary income from page 1, line 24			
3 Other additions			
4 Total of lines 1, 2, and 3			
5 Distributions other than dividend distributions			
6 Loss from page 1, line 24			
7 Other reductions			
8 Add lines 5, 6, and 7			
9 Balance at end of tax year—Subtract line 8 from line 4			

★ U.S. GOVERNMENT PRINTING OFFICE-1987 493-199

Form **2106**

Department of the Treasury
Internal Revenue Service (O)

Employee Business Expenses

▶ See instructions on back.
▶ Attach to Form 1040.

OMB No. 1545-0139
1986
Attachment Sequence No. **54**

Your name	Social security number	Occupation in which expenses were incurred

Part I Employee Business Expenses Deductible in Figuring Adjusted Gross Income

1 Vehicle expenses from Part II, lines 15 or 22	1	
2 Parking fees, tolls, and business portion of certain interest and taxes (see instructions)	2	
3 Local transportation including train, cabs, bus, airplane, etc.	3	
4 Travel expenses while away from home overnight including meals, lodging, airplane, car rental, taxi, etc.	4	
5 **Employees who are not outside salespersons:** Enter your expenses, not included on lines 1 through 4, for entertainment, gifts, and other business expenses, up to the amount you were reimbursed by your employer. Use Schedule A (Form 1040) for these expenses that were more than your reimbursement	5	
6 **Outside salesperson's expenses:** Enter your total expenses for entertainment, gifts, and other business expenses not included on lines 1 through 4	6	
7 Add lines 1 through 6	7	
8 Enter reimbursements from employer on this line if the reimbursements were not included on Form W-2	8	
9 If line 7 is more than line 8, enter difference here and on Form 1040, line 25	9	
10 If line 8 is more than line 7, enter difference here and include it on Form 1040, line 7	10	

Part II Vehicle Expenses (Use either your actual expenses or the standard mileage rate.)

Section A.—General Information

		Vehicle 1	Vehicle 2
1 Enter the date vehicle was placed in service	1	/ /	/ /
2 Total mileage vehicle was used during 1986	2	miles	miles
3 Miles included on line 2 that vehicle was used for business	3	miles	miles
4 Percent of business use (divide line 3 by line 2)	4	%	%
5 Average daily round trip commuting distance	5	miles	miles
6 Miles included on line 2 that vehicle was used for commuting	6	miles	miles
7 Other personal mileage (subtract line 6 plus line 3 from line 2)	7	miles	miles

8 Do you (or your spouse) have another vehicle available for personal purposes? ☐ Yes ☐ No
9 If your employer provided you with a vehicle, is personal use during off duty hours permitted? ☐ Yes ☐ No ☐ Not applicable
10 Do you have evidence to support your deduction? ☐ Yes ☐ No. If yes, is the evidence written? ☐ Yes ☐ No

Section B.—Standard Mileage Rate (Do not use this section unless you own the vehicle.)

11 Enter the smaller of Part II, line 3 or 15,000 miles	11	miles
12 Subtract line 11 from Part II, line 3	12	miles
13 Multiply line 11 by 21¢ (.21) (see instructions for a fully depreciated vehicle)	13	
14 Multiply line 12 by 11¢ (.11)	14	
15 Add lines 13 and 14. Enter total here and on Part I, line 1	15	

Section C.—Actual Expenses

		Vehicle 1	Vehicle 2
16 Gasoline, oil, repairs, vehicle insurance, etc.	16		
17 Vehicle rentals	17		
18 Value of employer-provided vehicle (applies only if included on Form W-2 at 100% fair rental value, see instructions)	18		
19 Add lines 16 through 18	19		
20 Multiply line 19 by the percentage on Part II, line 4	20		
21 Depreciation from Section D, column (f) (see instructions)	21		
22 Add lines 20 and 21. Enter total here and on Part I, line 1	22		

Section D.—Depreciation of Vehicles

(Depreciation can only be claimed for a vehicle you own. If a vehicle is used 50 percent or less in a trade or business, the Section 179 deduction is not allowed and depreciation must be taken using the straight line method over 5 years. For other limitations, see instructions.)

	Cost or other basis (a)	Basis for depreciation (Business use only—see instructions) (b)	Method of figuring depreciation (c)	Depreciation deduction (d)	Section 179 expense (e)	Total column (d) + column (e) (f)
Vehicle 1						
Vehicle 2						

For Paperwork Reduction Act Notice, see Instructions. Form **2106** (1986)

Items You Should Note:

- If you are an employee and claim any deduction for the business use of a vehicle, you must use Form 2106 and complete Part II, Section A, including questions 8 through 10.
- If the vehicle was used more than 50 percent for business in the first year it was placed in service, and used 50 percent or less in a later year, part of the depreciation, Section 179 deduction, and investment credit will have to be recaptured in the later year. Figure the amount of depreciation and Section 179 deduction to be recaptured on **Form 4797**, Gains and Losses From Sales or Exchanges Of Assets Used in a Trade or Business and Involuntary Conversions. Figure the amount of investment credit to be recaptured on **Form 4255**, Recapture of Investment Credit.
- Recent legislation provides a new method that reduces the allowable depreciation deduction for automobiles placed in service after 12/31/86. However, you may elect to use that method for automobiles placed in service after 7/31/86. See **Publication 534**, Depreciation, for more information.

Instructions

Paperwork Reduction Act Notice.—We ask for this information to carry out the Internal Revenue laws of the United States. We need it to ensure that taxpayers are complying with these laws and to allow us to figure and collect the right amount of tax. You are required to give us this information.

Who Must File.—File this form if you are an employee and are deducting the following expenses attributable to your job:

- Outside salesperson expenses.
- Travel and transportation expenses.
- For employees, other than outside salespersons, any other business expenses, but only up to the amount of employer reimbursements.

Exception: You need not complete this form if you account to your employer by means of an account book, diary or similar statement, and your business expenses are equal to your reimbursement.

For deduction of education expenses as a business expense, including transportation, see **Publication 508**, Educational Expenses.

Line-by-Line Instructions

Part I

For lines 1 through 4 and 6, enter the total expenses applicable to each of those lines. For line 5, only enter the expenses up to the amount of your employer's reimbursement.

Line 2.—Enter any parking fees or tolls you paid in connection with using your vehicle for business. If you purchased the vehicle this year, and paid sales tax, multiply Part II, line 4 by the total sales tax, and include the result on this line. If you paid interest on the vehicle, multiply Part II, line 4 by that interest and include the result on this line. The remaining sales tax and interest should be deducted on Schedule A (Form 1040).

Line 3.—If you use transportation for business such as a taxicab, bus, or train, enter the cost. Also, enter any airplane fares that did not involve overnight travel. Do not include transportation while commuting to and from work.

Line 4.—Enter your meals, lodging, and transportation expenses paid while traveling away from your tax home overnight on business including temporary business assignments.

Instead of actual cost, you may include your expenses for meals at $14 a day when you are in one general area less than 30 days and at $9 a day for all the days, if you are in one general area 30 days or more. Get **Publication 463**, Travel, Entertainment, and Gift Expenses, for more details.

Lines 5 and 6.—You are an outside salesperson if you do your selling away from your employer's place of business. You are not an outside salesperson if your main duties are service and delivery or if you sell at your employer's place of business. If you are reimbursed by your employer one amount to cover travel or transportation expenses as well as other business expenses, allocate your reimbursement for purposes of line 5. Do this by dividing the expenses reportable on line 5 by your total expenses, and multiplying the result by your reimbursement.

Line 8.—Do not include reimbursements on this line if included on Form W-2.

Part II

If you used 2 vehicles for business during the year, use a separate column for each vehicle in Sections A and C. If you used more than 2, attach a computation following the format in Sections A, C, and D.

Line 1.—Date placed in service is the date you first start using your car for any purpose, whether personal or business. For example, if you first start using a car for personal use in February and convert it to business use in October, the car is considered placed in service in February, even though you cannot start depreciating it until October.

Line 2.—Enter the total mileage each vehicle was driven for all purposes during the year.

Caution: If you changed jobs during the year to one in which you first started using a vehicle in your job, enter only the total mileage for the months the vehicle was used in your job. After entering your business miles on line 3, figure your percentage of business use by dividing line 3 by line 2. Multiply that percentage by the number of months the car was used in your job, and divide the result by 12. Enter this percentage on line 4.

Line 3.—Do not include commuting mileage on this line.

Line 5.—Enter your average daily round trip commuting distance. If you go to a different business location each day, figure the average. Commuting mileage is the mileage from home to your first stop and from your last stop to home even if you do not go to the same location each day, or whether or not you are self-employed.

Line 6.—You may figure your total commuting mileage by multiplying line 5 by the number of days during the year you used each vehicle to and from work.

Section B—Standard mileage rate.—You may use the standard mileage rate instead of using actual expenses in figuring the deductible costs of operating a passenger car, including a van, pick-up or panel truck. You cannot use the standard mileage rate if you ever took depreciation on that car using a method other than straight line. You may not use the standard mileage rate unless you used that method the first year you start using the car for business. If you listed more than one vehicle on line 3, get **Publication 917**, Business Use of a Car.

Line 13.—If your vehicle is fully depreciated, multiply line 11 by 11¢ a mile (.11) instead of 21¢. A vehicle is considered fully depreciated after 60,000 miles of business use at the maximum standard mileage rate.

Line 16.—Enter your total expenses for the year, for gasoline, oil, repairs, insurance, tires, license plates, or similar items.

Line 17.—If you rented or leased a vehicle during the year instead of using one that you own, enter the cost of renting. However, you may have to include an amount in income. See Publication 917. Also, include on this line any temporary vehicle rentals, such as when your car was being repaired.

Line 18.—If your employer provided you a vehicle during the year that you used for business, and included the value on your Form W-2 at 100 percent of the fair rental value, enter that amount on this line. If less than the full rental value was included on your W-2, such as where your employer reduced the value for business use based on your records, do not include any amount on this line, but see Publication 917.

Section D.—Depreciation

Depreciation is an amount you can deduct over a certain number of years. In some cases, you may elect to expense, under Internal Revenue Code Section 179, part of your vehicle in the year of purchase. For more information on depreciation and the Section 179 deduction, including the limitations and their effective dates, get **Publication 917.**

Limitations.—For purposes of figuring the amounts to enter in columns (d), (e), and (f):

- *Vehicles placed in service after April 2, 1985.* —Depreciation plus Section 179 deduction is limited to $3,200 the first year, multiplied by the percent of business use (line 4, Part II), and $4,800 the second year multiplied by Part II, line 4.
- *Vehicles placed in service after June 18, 1984 and before April 3, 1985.*— Depreciation is limited to $6,200 ($6,000 if placed in service before January 1, 1985.)the second and third year, multiplied by Part II, line 4.

Column (a).—Enter the vehicle's actual cost or other basis. If you traded in your vehicle, see Publication 917 for the computation of basis. Reduce your basis by any diesel fuel tax credit.

Column (b).—Multiply column (a) by the percentage in Part II, line 4. From that result, subtract any Section 179 expense, and one-half of investment credit taken (if applicable,unless you took the reduced credit).

Column (c).— Use one of the following methods for figuring depreciation under ACRS.

Method 1. Enter "ACRS" and 25%, the first year placed in service; 38%, the second year; and 37%, the third year; or

Method 2. Enter "SL" and your choice of 3, 5, or 12 years; or

Method 3. You must use this method if the vehicle was placed in service after June 18, 1984, and Part II, line 4 shows 50% or less. Enter "SL" and 10%, the first year; and 20%, the second and third year.

Column (d).—Multiply column (b) by column (c) unless you used method 2 above. In that case divide column (b) by column (c), and if this is the first or last year of depreciating the vehicle, divide the result by 2.

Column (e).—If this is the first year the vehicle was placed in service, and you are taking a deduction under Section 179, enter the cost multiplied by Part II, line 4, but not more than $3,200 multiplied by Part II, line 4. If Part II, line 4 shows 50 percent or less, enter zero.

Column (f).—Add columns (d) and (e), but do not enter more than the limitation listed above. If you sold or exchanged your vehicle during the year, enter zero in column (f) for that vehicle.

*U.S. GOVERNMENT PRINTING OFFICE: 1986-493-207

Form **2119**

Department of the Treasury
Internal Revenue Service (0)

Sale or Exchange of Principal Residence

▶ See instructions on back.

▶ Attach to Form 1040 for year of sale (see instruction B).

OMB No. 1545-0072

1986

Attachment Sequence No. **21**

Name(s) as shown on Form 1040.

Your social security number

Do not include expenses that you deduct as moving expenses.

		Yes	No
1 a	Date former residence sold ▶		
b	Enter the face amount of any mortgage, note (for example, second trust), or other financial instrument on which you will receive periodic payments of principal or interest from this sale ▶		
2 a	If you bought or built a new residence, enter date you occupied it; otherwise enter "None" ▶		
b	Are any rooms in either residence rented out or used for business for which a deduction is allowed? (If "Yes," see instructions)		
3 a	Were you 55 or over on date of sale?		
b	Was your spouse 55 or over on date of sale? If you answered "No" to 3a and 3b, do not complete 3c through 3f and Part II.		
c	Did the person who answered "Yes" to 3a or 3b own and use the property sold as his or her principal residence for a total of at least 3 years (except for short absences) of the 5-year period before the sale?		
d	If you answered "Yes" to 3c, do you elect to take the once in a lifetime exclusion of the gain on the sale?		
e	At time of sale, was the residence owned by: ☐ you, ☐ your spouse, ☐ both of you?		
f	Social security number of spouse, at time of sale, if different from number on Form 1040 ▶ (Enter "None" if you were not married at time of sale.)		

Part I Computation of Gain

4	Selling price of residence less expense of sale. (Do not include personal property items.)	4	
5	Basis of residence sold	5	
6	Gain on sale (subtract line 5 from line 4). If zero or less, enter zero and do not complete the rest of form. Enter the gain from this line on Schedule D, line 3 or 10*, unless you bought another principal residence or checked "Yes" to 3d. Then continue with this form	6	

If you haven't replaced your residence, do you plan to do so within the replacement period? ☐ Yes ☐ No
(If "Yes" see instruction B.)

Part II Age 55 or Over One-Time Exclusion

Complete this part only if you checked "yes" to 3(d) to elect the once in a lifetime exclusion; otherwise, skip to Part III.

7	Enter the smaller of line 6 or $125,000 ($62,500, if married filing separate return)	7	
8	Gain (subtract line 7 from line 6). If zero, do not complete rest of form. Enter the gain from this line on Schedule D, line 10*, unless you bought another principal residence. Then continue with this form	8	

Part III Gain To Be Postponed and Adjusted Basis of New Residence

Complete this part if you bought another principal residence.

9	Fixing-up expenses (see instructions for time limits)	9	
10	Adjusted sales price (subtract line 9 from line 4)	10	
11	Cost of new residence	11	
12	Gain taxable this year (subtract line 11 plus line 7 (if applicable) from line 10). If result is zero or less, enter zero. Do not enter more than line 6 or line 8 (if applicable). Enter the gain from this line on Schedule D, line 3 or 10*	12	
13	Gain to be postponed (subtract line 12 from line 6. However, if Part II applies, subtract line 12 from line 8)	13	
14	Adjusted basis of new residence (subtract line 13 from line 11)	14	

***Caution:** If you completed Form 6252 for the residence in 1a, do not enter your taxable gain from Form 2119 on Schedule D.

For Paperwork Reduction Act Notice, see back of form.

Form **2119** (1986)

Instructions

Paperwork Reduction Act Notice.—We ask for this information to carry out the Internal Revenue laws of the United States. We need it to ensure that taxpayers are complying with these laws and to allow us to figure and collect the right amount of tax. You are required to give us this information.

A. Who Must File.—Use Form 2119 to report gain from selling your principal residence, whether or not you buy another. A loss is not deductible. Use this form to postpone gain and make the one-time election to exclude it from your income. All filers must complete lines 1 through 6 except as explained in Instruction B.

If you sold your residence on the installment method, complete **Form 6252,** Computation of Installment Sale Income, in addition to Form 2119.

For more information, see **Publication 523,** Tax Information on Selling Your Home.

Principal Residence.—Postponement or exclusion of gain applies only to the sale of your principal residence. Usually, the home where you live is your principal residence. It can be, for example, a house, houseboat, housetrailer, cooperative apartment, or condominium. If you have more than one residence, your principal residence is the one you physically occupy most of the time.

B. When to File.—File Form 2119 for the year of sale whether or not you replaced your principal residence.

In the following cases file 2 Forms 2119:

If you plan to replace your residence but have not done so by the time you file your return, and the replacement period has not expired, attach Form 2119 to Form 1040 for the year of sale. In this case complete lines 1, 2 and Part I only, but do not include the gain on Schedule D. If you replace your residence after you file your return, within the replacement period, and the new residence costs as much as the adjusted sales price of your old residence, write to notify the Director of the Internal Revenue Service Center where you filed your return. Attach a new Form 2119 for the year of sale.

If you replace your residence after you file your return, within the replacement period, and the new one costs less than the adjusted sales price of the old one, or you do not replace it within the replacement period, file **Form 1040X,** Amended U.S. Individual Income Tax Return, with a Schedule D and a new Form 2119 for the year of sale. Show the gain then. Interest will be charged on the additional tax due.

If you paid tax on the gain from selling your old residence and then buy a new one within the replacement period, file Form 1040X with Form 2119 to claim a refund.

C. Excluding Gain from Income (Part II).—You can elect to exclude from your income part or all of the gain from the sale of your principal residence if you meet the following tests:

1. You were 55 or over on the date of the sale.
2. Neither you nor your spouse has already elected this exclusion.
3. You owned and occupied your residence for periods totaling at least 3 years within the 5 years ending on the date of sale.

The exclusion election is a once-in-a-lifetime election, so you may choose not to make it now.

The gain excluded from your income is never taxed. The rest of your gain is taxed in the year of sale, unless you replace the residence and postpone that part of the gain. Generally, you can make or revoke the exclusion election within 3 years from the date the return for the year you sold the residence was due, including extensions. Use Form 1040X to amend your return.

Married Taxpayers.—If you and your spouse own the property jointly and file a joint return, only one of you must meet the age, ownership, and use tests for electing the exclusion. If you do not own the property jointly, the owner must meet these tests, regardless of your filing status on Form 1040.

If you are married at the time of sale, both you and your spouse must make the election to exclude the gain. If you do not file a joint return with that spouse, that spouse must consent to the election by writing in the bottom margin of Form 2119 or on an attached statement, "I consent to Part II election," and signing.

The election does not apply separately to you and your spouse. If you and your spouse make an election during marriage and later divorce, no further elections are available to either of you or to your new spouse if you remarry.

D. Postponing Gain on Sale of Principal Residence (Part III).—You may have to postpone gain if you buy or build, and occupy another principal residence within 2 years before or after the sale.

If, after you sell your old residence, you are on active duty in the U.S. Armed Forces for more than 90 days, or you live and work outside the U.S., see Publication 523 for a longer replacement period.

If you sell the new residence in a later year and do not replace it, the postponed gain will be taxed then. If you do replace it, you may continue to postpone the gain. If you bought more than one principal residence during the replacement period, only the last residence you bought qualifies as your new residence for postponing gain. During the replacement period, any sale after the first does not qualify for postponing gain, unless you sold the residence because of a job relocation and are allowed a moving expense deduction.

E. Applying Separate Gain to Basis of New Residence.—If you own the old residence separately, but you and your spouse own the new residence jointly (or vice versa) you and your spouse may elect to divide the gain and the adjusted basis if both of you:

1. use the old and new residences as your principal residence; and
2. sign a consent that says, "We consent to reduce the basis of the new residence by the gain from selling the old residence." Write this statement in the bottom margin of Form 2119 or on an attached sheet, and sign it. If you both do not sign the consent, determine the recognition of gain in the regular way with no division.

Line-By-Line Instructions

Line 2b. If you rent out any rooms, or use a portion of your residence for business, for which a deduction is allowed, do not include that portion on this form. Instead, include that part of the gain on Form 4797. You cannot postpone gain or take the exclusion on that portion.

Line 4. Selling Price of Residence Less Expense of Sale.—Enter the amount of money you received, the amount of all notes, mortgages, or other liabilities to which the property was subject, and the fair market value of any other property you received.

Reduce the selling price by any expense of sale such as sales commissions, advertising expenses, attorney and legal fees, etc., incurred in order to sell the old residence. Loan charges, such as "loan placement fees" or "points" charged the seller are selling expenses.

Note: *Report interest from a note as income for the tax year in which the interest is received.*

Line 5. Basis of Residence Sold.—Include the original cost of the property, commissions, and other expenses incurred in buying it, plus the cost of improvements. Subtract any casualty loss or energy credit you took on the residence, and the postponed gain on the sale or exchange of a previous principal residence. For more information, see **Publication 551,** Basis of Assets.

Line 9. Fixing-up Expenses.—These are decorating and repair expenses incurred only to help sell the old property. You must have incurred the expenses for work performed within 90 days before the contract to sell was signed and paid for them within 30 days after the sale. Do not include capital expenditures for permanent improvements or replacements that are added to the basis of the property sold.

Line 11. Cost of New Residence.—The cost of your new residence includes one or more of the following:

(a) cash payments;
(b) the amount of any mortgage or other debt on the new residence;
(c) commissions and other purchase expenses you paid that were not deducted as moving expenses;
(d) construction costs (when you build your own residence) made within 2 years before and 2 years after the sale of the old residence;
(e) if you buy rather than build your new residence, all capital expenditures made within 2 years before and 2 years after the sale of the old residence.

★ U.S.G.P.O.: 1986 -493-209

Form **2210**

Department of the Treasury
Internal Revenue Service (O)

Underpayment of Estimated Tax by Individuals

▶ See separate instructions
▶ Attach to Form 1040

OMB No. 1545-0140
1986
Attachment Sequence No. **56**

Name(s) as shown on Form 1040 | **Social security number**

Part I **Figuring Your Underpayment**

1	1986 tax after credits (from Form 1040, line 49)			1	
2	Other taxes (see instructions)			2	
3	Add lines 1 and 2			3	
4	Earned income credit	4			
5	Credit for Federal tax on gasoline and special fuels	5			
6	Credit for overpaid windfall profit tax attributable to amounts withheld	6			
7	Add lines 4, 5, and 6			7	
8	Subtract line 7 from line 3			8	
9	Multiply line 8 by 80% (.80)	9			
10	Withholding taxes from 1986 Form 1040, lines 56 and 60. (Include any credit from Form 4469.)			10	
11	Subtract line 10 from line 8. If the result is less than $500, do not complete rest of form			11	
12	Enter your 1985 tax (see instructions)			12	
13	Enter the smaller of line 9 or line 12			13	

			Payment Due Dates (a) Apr. 15, 1986	(b) June 15, 1986	(c) Sept. 15, 1986	(d) Jan. 15, 1987
14	Divide line 13 by four (4) and enter the result in each column. However, if you use the annualized income installment method, complete the worksheet in the instructions and enter the amount from line 26 in each column of line 14	14				
	Complete lines 15 through 22 for one column before completing the next column.					
15	Estimated tax paid and tax withheld. (For column (a) only, enter the amount from line 15 on line 19)	15				
16	Enter amount, if any, from line 22 of previous column	16				
17	Add lines 15 and 16	17				
18	Add amounts on lines 20 and 21 of the previous column and enter the result	18				
19	Enter line 17 minus line 18. If zero or less, enter zero. (For column (a) only, enter the amount from line 15).	19				
20	Remaining underpayment from previous period. If the amount on line 19 is zero, enter line 18 minus line 17	20				
21	UNDERPAYMENT. If line 14 is larger than or equal to line 19, enter line 14 minus line 19. Then go to line 15 of next column. Otherwise, go to line 22	21				
22	OVERPAYMENT. If line 19 is larger than line 14, enter line 19 minus line 14. Then go to line 15 of next column	22				

For Paperwork Reduction Act Notice, see page 1 of separate instructions.

Form **2210** (1986)

Form 2210 (1986) Page 2

Part II Figuring the Penalty

		Payment Due Dates			
		(a) Apr 15, 1986	(b) June 15, 1986	(c) Sept 15, 1986	(d) Jan 15, 1987
23 Underpayment from line 21, page 1	23				
Rate Period 1 - 10% (April 15, 1986—June 30, 1986)					
24a Computation starting date for this period	24a	Apr. 15, 1986	June 15, 1986		
b Number of days FROM the date on line 24a TO the date line 23 was paid or June 30, 1986, whichever is earlier. If June 30 is earlier, enter 76 and 15, respectively	24b	Days	Days		
c (Number of days on line 24b / 365) × 10% × underpayment on line 23 (see instructions)	24c	$	$		
Rate Period 2 - 9% (July 1, 1986—April 15, 1987)					
25a Computation starting date for this period	25a	June 30, 1986	June 30, 1986	Sept 15, 1986	Jan 15, 1987
b Number of days FROM the date on line 25a TO the date line 23 was paid or April 15, 1987, whichever is earlier. If April 15 is earlier, enter 289, 289, 212, and 90 in columns (a) - (d), respectively	25b	Days	Days	Days	Days
c (Number of days on line 25b / 365) × 9% × underpayment on line 23 (see instructions)	25c	$	$	$	$

26 Penalty (add all amounts on lines 24c and 25c in all columns). Check the box below line 67 on Form 1040 and show this amount in the space provided. If you owe tax, add the penalty to your tax and show the total on line 67. If you are due a refund, subtract the penalty from the overpayment on line 64 . . . 26 $

☆ U.S. Government Printing Office: 1986—493-211 23-0916750

Form **2441**

Department of the Treasury
Internal Revenue Service (O)

Credit for Child and Dependent Care Expenses

▶ **Attach to Form 1040.**
▶ **See instructions below.**

OMB No. 1545-0068
1986
Attachment Sequence No. **23**

Name(s) as shown on Form 1040 | **Your social security number**

Note: *If you paid cash wages of $50 or more in a calendar quarter to an individual for services performed in your home, you must file an employment tax return. Get **Form 942**, Employer's Quarterly Tax Return for Household Employees, for details.*

1	Enter the number of qualifying persons who were cared for in 1986. (See the instructions below for the definition of qualifying persons.) ▶	1	
2	Enter the amount of **qualified** expenses you incurred and actually paid in 1986 for the care of the qualifying person. (See **What Are Qualified Expenses** in the instructions.) **Do not** enter more than $2,400 ($4,800 if you paid for the care of two or more qualifying persons)	2	
3a	You **must** enter your earned income on line 3a. See the instructions for line 3 for the definition of earned income	3a	
b	If you are married, filing a joint return for 1986, you must enter your spouse's earned income on line 3b	3b	
c	If you are married filing a joint return, compare the amounts on lines 3a and 3b, and enter the **smaller** of the two amounts on line 3c	3c	
4	• If you were unmarried at the end of 1986, compare the amounts on lines 2 and 3a, and enter the **smaller** of the two amounts on line 4 • If you are married filing a joint return, compare the amounts on lines 2 and 3c, and enter the **smaller** of the two amounts on line 4	4	
5	Enter the percentage from the table below that applies to the adjusted gross income on Form 1040, line 33	5	

If line 33 is: Over—	But not over—	Percentage is:	If line 33 is: Over—	But not over—	Percentage is:
$0	10,000	30% (.30)	$20,000	22,000	24% (.24)
10,000	12,000	29% (.29)	22,000	24,000	23% (.23)
12,000	14,000	28% (.28)	24,000	26,000	22% (.22)
14,000	16,000	27% (.27)	26,000	28,000	21% (.21)
16,000	18,000	26% (.26)	28,000		20% (.20)
18,000	20,000	25% (.25)			

6	Multiply the amount on line 4 by the percentage shown on line 5, and enter the result	6	
7	Multiply any child and dependent care expenses for 1985 that you paid in 1986 by the percentage that applies to the adjusted gross income on your 1985 Form 1040, line 33, or Form 1040A, line 15. Enter the result. (See line 7 instructions for the required statement.)	7	
8	Add amounts on lines 6 and 7. Enter the total here and on Form 1040, line 41. This is the maximum amount of your credit for child and dependent care expenses	8	

General Instructions

Paperwork Reduction Act Notice.—We ask for this information to carry out the Internal Revenue laws of the United States. We need it to ensure that taxpayers are complying with these laws and to allow us to figure and collect the right amount of tax. You are required to give us this information.

What Is the Child and Dependent Care Expenses Credit?

You may be able to take a tax credit for amounts you paid someone to care for your child or other qualifying person so you could work or look for work in 1986. The credit will lower the amount of your tax. The credit is based on a percentage of the amount you paid during the year. The most the credit may be is $720 for the care of one qualifying person, or $1,440 for the care of two or more qualifying persons.

Additional information.—For more information about the credit, please get **Publication 503**, Child and Dependent Care Credit, and Employment Taxes for Household Employers.

Who Is a Qualifying Person?

A qualifying person is any one of the following persons:

- Any person under age 15 whom you claim as a dependent (but see the special rule later for **Children of divorced or separated parents**).
- Your disabled spouse who is mentally or physically unable to care for himself or herself.
- Any disabled person who is mentally or physically unable to care for himself or herself and whom you claim as a dependent, or could claim as a dependent except that he or she had income of $1,080 or more.

Note: *You must have shared the same home with any person you claim as a qualifying person.*

Children of divorced or separated parents.—If you were divorced, legally separated, or lived apart from your spouse during the last 6 months of 1986, you may be able to claim the credit even if your child is not your dependent. If your child is not your dependent, he or she is a qualifying person if **all five** of the following apply:

1. You had custody of the child for the longer period during the year; and

2. The child received over half of his or her support from one or both of the parents; and

3. The child was in the custody of one or both of the parents over half of the year; and

4. The child was under age 15, or was physically or mentally unable to care for himself or herself; and

(Continued on back)

5. The child is not your dependent because—

- **a.** As the custodial parent, you have signed **Form 8332**, Release of Claim to Exemption for Child of Divorced or Separated Parents, or a similar statement, agreeing not to claim the child's exemption for 1986; or
- **b.** You were divorced or separated before 1985 and your divorce decree or written agreement states that the other parent can claim the child's exemption, and the other parent provides at least $600 in child support during the year. **Note:** *This rule does not apply if your decree or agreement was changed after 1984 to specify that the other parent cannot claim the child's exemption.*

Who May Take the Credit?

To claim the credit, **all five** of the following must apply:

1. You paid for the care so you (and your spouse if you were married) could work or look for work (but see the rules at the line 3 instructions for **Spouse who is a full-time student or is disabled).**

2. You and the qualifying person(s) lived in the same home.

3. You (and your spouse if you were married) paid over half the cost of keeping up your home. The cost includes: rent; mortgage interest; property taxes; utilities; home repairs; and food eaten at home.

4. The person you paid to provide the care was not your spouse or a person you could claim as a dependent.

Note: *If the person you paid to provide the care was your child, he or she must have been 19 or over by the end of 1986.*

5. If you were married at the end of 1986, generally, you must file a joint tax return. However, there are two exceptions to this rule. You will be treated as unmarried and still be eligible to take the credit if:

- **a.** You were legally separated; or
- **b.** You were living apart from your spouse during the last 6 months of the year, and:
  - the qualifying person lived with you in your home over 6 months, and
  - you provided over half the cost of keeping up your home.

What Are Qualified Expenses?

Qualified expenses include amounts paid for household services and care of the qualifying person while you work or look for work. For more information on qualified expenses, see Publication 503.

Household services.—These services must be needed to care for the qualifying person as well as to run the home. They include, for example, the services of a cook, maid, babysitter, housekeeper, governess, or cleaning person if the services were partly for the care of the qualifying person. Do not include services of a chauffeur or gardener.

Note: *If you paid cash wages of $1,000 or more for household services in any calendar quarter in 1985 or 1986, you should file a* ***Form 940,*** *Employer's Annual Federal Unemployment (FUTA) Tax Return, for 1986 by February 2, 1987.*

Care of the qualifying person.—Care includes the cost of services for the qualifying person's well-being and protection. It does not include the cost of clothing or entertainment.

Generally, care also does not include food or schooling expenses. However, if these items are included as part of the total care, and they are incident to, and cannot be separated from, the total cost, you may count the total payment. However, you may not count the cost of schooling for a child in the first grade or above.

Care outside the home.—You may count care provided outside your home if the care was for:

- **a.** Your dependent under age 15; or
- **b.** Any other qualifying person who regularly spends at least 8 hours each day in your home.

Care that is provided by a dependent care center may be counted if the center complies with all applicable state and local laws and regulations. A dependent care center is a place that provides care for at least seven persons (other than persons who live there), and receives a fee, payment, or grant for providing the services for any of those persons, regardless of whether the center is run for profit.

Medical expenses.—Some dependent care expenses may qualify as medical expenses. If you itemize deductions, you may want to take all or part of these medical expenses on Schedule A (Form 1040). If you cannot use all the medical expenses on Form 2441 because of the dollar limit or earned income limit (explained later), you may take the rest of these expenses on Schedule A. But if you deduct the medical expenses first on Schedule A, you may not use any part of these expenses on Form 2441.

Specific Instructions

The following are specific instructions for most of the lines on the form. Lines which have no instructions here are self-explanatory.

Line 2. Dollar limit.—On line 2, enter the amount of qualified child and dependent care expenses you incurred and actually paid in 1986. However, the most you may figure the credit on is $2,400 a year for one qualifying person, or $4,800 a year for two or more qualifying persons. Do not include amounts paid or incurred by your employer if, and to the extent, such amounts are excluded from your gross income.

Note: *Do not include on line 2 qualified expenses that you incurred in 1986 but did not pay until 1987. Instead, you may be able to increase the amount of your 1987 credit when you pay the 1986 expenses in 1987.*

Line 3. Earned income limit.—Figure your earned income limitation on line 3. The amount of your qualified expenses **may not** be more than your earned income or, if married filing a joint return, the **smaller** of your earned income or your spouse's earned income.

In general, earned income is wages, salaries, tips, and other employee compensation. It also includes net earnings from self-employment. This is usually the amount shown on Schedule SE (Form 1040), line 9. For more information on what is earned income for purposes of the credit, see Publication 503.

Unmarried taxpayers.—If you were unmarried at the end of 1986 or are treated as being unmarried at the end of the year, enter your earned income on line 3a.

Married taxpayers.—If you are married, filing a joint return, figure each spouse's earned income separately and disregard community property laws. Enter your earned income on line 3a and your spouse's earned income on line 3b. Then, enter the smaller of your earned income or your spouse's earned income on line 3c.

Spouse who is a full-time student or is disabled.—If your spouse was a full-time student or was mentally or physically unable to care for himself or herself, figure your spouse's earned income on a monthly basis to determine your spouse's earned income for the year. For each month that your spouse was disabled or a full-time student, your spouse is considered to have earned income of not less than $200 a month ($400 a month if more than one qualifying person was cared for in 1986).

If, in the same month, both you and your spouse were full-time students and did not work, you may not use any amount paid that month to figure the credit. The same applies to a couple who did not work because neither was capable of self-care.

A full-time student is one who was enrolled in a school for the number of hours or classes that the school considers full time. The student must have been enrolled at least 5 months during 1986.

Self-employment income.—You must reduce your earned income by any loss from self-employment. If your net earnings from self-employment are less than $1,600, and you use the optional method to figure your self-employment tax, you may be able to increase your net earnings to $1,600 for this credit. Get **Publication 533,** Self-Employment Tax, for details. If you only have a loss from self-employment, or your loss is more than your other earned income and you do not use the optional method, you may not take the credit.

Line 7.—If you had qualified expenses for 1985 that you did not pay until 1986, you may be able to increase the amount of credit you may take in 1986. To do this, multiply the 1985 expenses you paid in 1986 by the percentage from the table on line 6 that applies to the adjusted gross income shown on your 1985 Form 1040, line 33, or Form 1040A, line 15. Your 1985 expenses must be within the 1985 limits. Attach a computation showing how you figured the increase. (Use the example in Publication 503 as a guide.)

*U.S. G.P.O. 1986-493-221

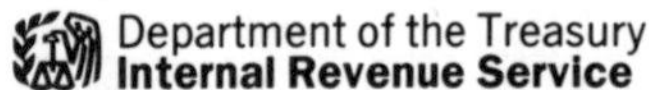

Instructions for Form 2553

(Revised February 1987)

Election by a Small Business Corporation

(Section references are to the Internal Revenue Code, unless otherwise specified.)

Paperwork Reduction Act Notice.—We ask for this information to carry out the Internal Revenue laws of the United States. We need it to insure that you are complying with these laws and to allow us to figure and collect the right amount of tax. You are required to give us this information.

A. Purpose.—To elect to be treated as an "S Corporation," a corporation must file Form 2553. The election permits the income of the S corporation to be taxed to the shareholders of the corporation except as provided in Subchapter S of the code. (See section 1363.)

B. Who May Elect.—Your corporation may make the election only if it meets the following tests:

1. It is a domestic corporation.
2. It has no more than 35 shareholders. A husband and wife (and their estates) are treated as one shareholder for this requirement. All other persons are treated as separate shareholders.
3. It has only individuals, estates, or certain trusts as shareholders. See instruction I for details regarding qualified subchapter S trusts.
4. It has no nonresident alien shareholders.
5. It has only one class of stock. See sections 1361(c)(4) and (5) for additional details.
6. It is not an ineligible corporation as defined in section 1361(b)(2). See section 6(c) of Public Law 97-354 for additional details.
7. It has a calendar tax year or other permitted tax year as explained in instruction G.
8. Each shareholder consents as explained in the instructions for Column D.

See sections 1361, 1362 and 1378 for additional information on the above tests.

C. Where to File.—File this election with the Internal Revenue Service Center where the corporation will file **Form 1120S**, U.S. Income Tax Return for an S Corporation. See the Instructions for Form 1120S for Service Center addresses.

D. When to Make the Election.—Complete Form 2553 and file it either: (1) at any time during that portion of the first tax year the election is to take effect which occurs before the 16th day of the third month of that tax year (or at any time during that year, if that year does not extend beyond the period described above) or (2) in the tax year before the first tax year it is to take effect. An election made by a small business corporation after the 15th day of the third month but before the end of the tax year is treated as made for the next year. For example, if a calendar tax year corporation makes the election in April 1987, it is effective for the corporation's 1988 calendar tax year.

For purposes of this election, a newly formed corporation's tax year starts when it has shareholders, acquires assets, or begins doing business, whichever happens first.

E. Acceptance or Non-acceptance of Election.—IRS will notify you if your election is accepted and when it will take effect. You should generally receive determination on your election within 60 days after you have filed Form 2553. Do not file Form 1120S until you are notified that your election is accepted. If you are now required to file **Form 1120**, U.S. Corporation Income Tax Return, or any other applicable tax return, continue filing it until your election takes effect.

You will also be notified if your election is not accepted.

Care should be exercised to ensure the election is received by Internal Revenue Service. If you are not notified of acceptance or non-acceptance of your election within 3 months of date of filing (date mailed), you should take follow-up action by corresponding with the service center where the election was filed. If filing of Form 2553 is questioned, an acceptable proof of filing is: (1) Certified receipt (timely filed); (2) Form 2553 with accepted stamp; (3) Form 2553 with stamped IRS received date; or (4) IRS letter stating that Form 2553 had been accepted.

F. End of Election.—Once the election is made, it stays in effect for all years until it is terminated. During the 5 years after the election has been terminated under section 1362(d), the corporation can make another election on Form 2553 only if the Commissioner consents. See section 1362(g) and Revenue Ruling 86-141, IRB 1986-49 page 6, for more information. See sections 1362(d), (e), and (f) for rules regarding termination of election.

G. Permitted Tax Year.—Section 1378 provides that no corporation may make an election to be an S corporation for any tax year unless the tax year is a permitted tax year. A permitted tax year is a tax year ending December 31 or any other tax year for which the corporation establishes a business purpose to the satisfaction of IRS.

H. Investment Credit Property.—Although the corporation has elected to be an S corporation under section 1362, the tax imposed by section 47 in the case of early disposition of investment credit property will be imposed on the corporation for credits allowed for tax years for which the corporation was not an S corporation. The election will not be treated as a disposition of the property by the corporation. See section 1371(d).

I. Qualified Subchapter S Trusts.—When a qualified subchapter S trust consents to the election on Form 2553, an additional election must be made by the trust beneficiary in accordance with section 1361(d)(2) and temporary regulations section 18.1361-1(a). Failure to make and file the section 1361(d)(2) election in a timely manner will invalidate the election under section 1362 (Form 2553 election). See section 1361(d) and temporary regulations section 18.1361-1(a) for other details.

Specific Instructions

Part I.—Part I must be completed by all corporations.

Name and Address of Corporation.—If the corporation's mailing address is the same as someone else's such as a shareholder's, please enter this person's name below the corporation's name.

Employer Identification Number.—If you have applied for an employer identification number (EIN) but have not received it, enter "applied for." If the corporation does not have an EIN, you should apply for one on **Form SS-4**, Application for Employer Identification Number, available from most IRS or Social Security Administration offices. Send Form SS-4 to the IRS Service Center where Form 1120S will be filed.

Principal Business Activity and Principal Product or Service.—Use the Codes for Principal Business Activity contained in the Instructions for Form 1120S. Your principal business activity is the one that accounts for the largest percentage of total receipts. Total receipts are gross receipts plus all other income.

Also state the principal product or service. For example, if the principal business activity is "grain mill products," the principal product or service may be "cereal preparation."

Number of Shares Issued and Outstanding.—Enter only one figure. This figure will be the number of shares of stock that have been issued to shareholders and have not been reacquired by the corporation. This is the number of shares all shareholders own, as reported in column E, Part I.

Item B.—The selected tax year must be a permitted tax year as defined in instruction G.

A newly formed corporation may automatically adopt a tax year ending December 31.

Generally, an existing corporation may automatically change to a tax year ending December 31, if all of its principal shareholders have tax years ending December 31, or if all of its principal shareholders are concurrently changing to such tax year. If a corporation is automatically changing to a tax year ending December 31, it is not necessary for the corporation to file **Form 1128**, Application for Change in Accounting Period. A shareholder may not change his or her tax year without securing prior approval from IRS. For purposes of the automatic change, a principal shareholder is a shareholder who owns 5% or more of the issued and outstanding stock of the corporation. See temporary regulations section 18.1378-1 for additional details.

If a corporation wants to change to a tax year ending December 31, but does not qualify for an automatic change as explained above, it may want to complete Part IV and indicate in an attached statement that it wants to change to a tax year ending December 31.

If a corporation selects a tax year ending other than December 31, it must complete Part II or IV in addition to Part I.

Column D.—Shareholders' Consent Statement.—Each person who is a shareholder at the time the election is made must consent to the election. If the election is made during the corporation's first tax year for which it is effective, any person who held stock at any time during that portion of that year which occurs before the time the election is made must consent to the election although the person may have sold or transferred his or her stock before the election is made. Each shareholder consents by signing in column D or signing a separate consent statement, described below.

The election by a small business corporation is considered made for the following tax year if one or more of the persons who held stock at any time during that portion of that year which occurs before the time the election is made did not consent to the election. See section 1362(b)(2).

If a husband and wife have a community interest in the stock or in the income from it, both must consent. Each tenant in common, joint tenant, and tenant by the entirety also must consent.

A minor's consent is made by the minor or the legal guardian. If no legal guardian has been appointed, the natural guardian makes the consent (even if a custodian holds the minor's stock under a law patterned after the Uniform Gifts to Minors Act).

Continuation Sheet or Separate Consent Statement.—If you need a continuation sheet or use a separate consent statement, attach it to Form 2553. The separate consent statement must contain the name, address, and employer identification number of the corporation and the shareholder information requested in columns C through G of Part I.

If you wish, you may combine all the shareholders' consents in one statement.

Column E.—Enter the number of shares of stock each shareholder owns and the dates the stock was acquired. If the election is made during the corporation's first tax year for which it is effective, do not list the shares of stock for those shareholders who sold or transferred all of their stock before the election was made but who still must consent to the election for it to be effective for the tax year.

Column G.—Enter the month and day that each shareholder's tax year ends. If a shareholder is changing his or her tax year, enter the tax year the shareholder is changing to. If the election is made during the corporation's first tax year for which it is effective, you do not have to enter the tax year of shareholders who sold or transferred all of their stock before the election was made but who still must consent to the election for it to be effective for the tax year.

Signature.—Form 2553 must be signed by the president, treasurer, assistant treasurer, chief accounting officer, or other corporate officer (such as tax officer) authorized to sign.

Part II.—Items H and I of Part II are to be completed by a corporation that selects a tax year ending other than December 31, and that qualifies under section 4.02, or 4.04 of Revenue Procedure 83-25, 1983-1 C.B. 689. (**Note:** Section 4.03 of Rev. Proc. 83-25 was suspended for S corporation elections made after November 5, 1986. See Announcement 86-113, IRB 1986-47 page 46, for details.) Items H and I are completed in place of the additional statement asked for in section 7.01 of the procedure. Sections 4.02, and 4.04 provide for expeditious approval of certain corporations' requests to adopt, retain, or change to a tax year ending other than December 31. The representation statements in Part II of Form 2553 highlight the requests provided for in sections 4.02 and 4.03 of the revenue procedure. A corporation adopting, retaining, or changing its accounting period under the procedure must comply with or satisfy all applicable conditions of the procedure.

The revenue procedure applies only to the tax years of corporations which are electing S corporation status by filing Form 2553. A corporation is permitted to adopt, retain, or change its tax year only once under the procedure. It is not necessary for the corporation to file Form 1128 when adopting or changing its tax year under the procedure.

Items H and J of Part II are to be completed by a corporation that is making a request as specified in section 8 of the procedure. Section 8 provides that if a corporation wants to adopt, retain, or change to a tax year not specified under section 4.02, or 4.04 of the procedure or certain paragraphs of temporary regulations section 18.1378-1, it should attach a statement to Form 2553 pursuant to the ruling request requirements of Revenue Procedure 87-1, IRB 1987-1 page 7. (Changes to this revenue procedure are usually incorporated annually into a new revenue procedure as the first revenue procedure of the year.) The statement must show the business purpose for the desired tax year.

Approval of tax year selections made under section 4.02, or 4.04 of Revenue Procedure 83-25 are generally automatic; however, a request under section 8 is not automatic. If a request is made under section 8, the corporation may want to make the back-up request under Part III. See section 8 of the procedure for details.

Part III.—Check the box in Part III to make the back-up request provided by temporary regulations section 18.1378-1(b)(2)(ii)(A). This section provides that corporations requesting to retain (or adopt) a tax year ending other than December 31, may make a back-up request to adopt or change to a tax year ending December 31, in case the initial request for a fiscal year is denied. In order to make the back-up request, a corporation requesting to retain its tax year ending other than December 31, must qualify for an automatic change of its tax year under temporary regulations section 18.1378-1(b)(1).

Part IV.—Check the box in Part IV to request the IRS to determine your permitted tax year under the provisions of temporary regulations section 18.1378-1(d). If you check the box in Part IV, enter "See Part IV" in the space in item B, Part I, for month and year.

You may attach a schedule to Form 2553 showing any additional information you want the IRS to consider in making the determination. IRS will notify you of the permitted tax year determination. The tax year determination by IRS is final.

☆ U.S. Government Printing Office: 1987—181-447/40084

Form **2688**
Department of the Treasury
Internal Revenue Service

Application for Additional Extension of Time To File U.S. Individual Income Tax Return

(See back for filing instructions. Be sure to complete all items.)

OMB No. 1545-0066
1986
Attachment Sequence No. **59**

Please type or print. File the original and one copy by the due date for filing your return.	Your first name and initial (if joint return, also give spouse's name and initial) Last name	**Your social security number**
	Present home address (number and street or rural route). (If you have a P.O. Box, see the instructions.)	**Spouse's social security number**
	City, town or post office, state, and ZIP code	

If you expect to file a gift tax return (Form 709 or Form 709-A) for 1986, generally due by April 15, 1987, check this box. . . . ▶ ☐

1 I request an extension of time until ____________, 19 ____, to file Form 1040A or Form 1040 for the calendar year 1986, or other tax year ending ____________, 19 ____.

2 Were you previously granted an extension of time to file for this tax year? . . . ☐ Yes ☐ No

3 Previous extension granted to (date) . . . ________

4 State in detail why you need an extension. ____________

Signature and Verification

Under penalties of perjury, I declare that I have examined this form, including accompanying schedules and statements, and to the best of my knowledge and belief, it is true, correct, and complete; and, if prepared by someone other than the taxpayer, that I am authorized to prepare this form.

Signature of taxpayer ▶ ____________ Date ▶ ____________

Signature of spouse ▶ ____________ Date ▶ ____________

Signature of preparer other than taxpayer ▶ ____________ Date ▶ ____________

IRS will show below whether or not your application is approved and will return the copy.

Notice to Applicant—To Be Completed by IRS

☐ We **HAVE** approved your application. (Please attach this form to your return.)

☐ We **HAVE NOT** approved your application. (Please attach this form to your return.)
However, because of your reasons stated above, we have granted a 10-day grace period from the date shown below or due date of your return, whichever is later. This grace period is considered to be a valid extension of time for elections otherwise required to be made on returns filed on time.

☐ We **HAVE NOT** approved your application. After considering your reasons stated above, we cannot grant your request for an extension of time to file. (We are not granting the 10-day grace period.)

☐ We cannot consider your application because it was filed after the due date of your return.

☐ Other ____________

____________ Director

____________ Date By: ____________

For Paperwork Reduction Act Notice, see back of form. Form **2688** (1986)

Form 2688 (1986) Page **2**

If the copy of this form is to be returned to you at an address other than that shown on page 1, or to an agent acting for you, please enter the name of the agent and/or the address where the copy should be sent.

Please Type or Print	Name	
	Number and street (or P.O. Box number if mail is not delivered to street address)	
	City, town or post office, state, and ZIP code	

Note:

A. You may not choose to have IRS figure your income tax if you file your return after the regular due date.

B. This is not an extension of time to pay tax. You will be charged a penalty for late payment of tax unless you show reasonable cause for not paying the tax when due.

General Instructions

Paperwork Reduction Act Notice.—We ask for this information to carry out the Internal Revenue laws of the United States. We need it to ensure that taxpayers are complying with these laws and to allow us to figure and collect the right amount of tax. You are required to give us this information.

Purpose of Form.—Use Form 2688 to ask for an additional extension of time to file **Form 1040A** or **Form 1040** if you have already filed **Form 4868,** Application for Automatic Extension of Time To File U.S. Individual Income Tax Return, to get an automatic 4-month extension of time, but still need more time. Except in cases of undue hardship, do not file Form 2688 unless you have first filed Form 4868.

You must file Form 2688 on time and show reasonable cause why you cannot file your return within the 4-month extension period allowed by properly filing Form 4868. Generally, we will consider your application based on your efforts to meet the filing requirements, rather than on the convenience of your tax return preparer. However, if your tax return preparer is not able to complete the return by the due date for reasons beyond his or her control, or if in spite of reasonable efforts you cannot get professional help in time to file, we will generally grant the additional extension.

Note: *Any extension of time granted for filing your 1986* ***calendar*** *year income tax return also extends the time for filing a gift tax return for 1986.*

Filing Form 2350.—If you are a U.S. citizen or resident alien living abroad who expects to qualify for special tax treatment, file Form 2350, Application for Extension of Time To File U.S. Income Tax Return, to ask for an extension of time to file your Form 1040. See **Publication 54,** Tax Guide for U.S. Citizens and Resident Aliens Abroad, for more information.

Period of Extension.—We cannot grant an extension of more than 6 months if you live in the United States. The 6-month extension period granted includes the 4 months granted if Form 4868 was previously filed.

When To File.—File Form 2688 by the due date of your return (April 15, 1987, for a 1986 calendar year return), or extended due date if Form 4868 was previously filed. U.S. citizens and resident aliens living or traveling outside the United States and Puerto Rico on the due date of their return are automatically allowed a 2-month extension (to June 15 for a calendar year return).

File early enough so that we will have time to act on your application before your return's regular or extended due date.

Where To File.—File the original and one copy of Form 2688 with the Internal Revenue Service Center where you are required to file your return.

Penalties.—You may be charged one or both of the following penalties.

Late payment penalty.—Form 2688 does not extend the time to pay income, gift, or generation-skipping transfer taxes. Generally, a penalty of 1/2 of 1% of any tax (other than estimated tax) not paid by the regular due date is charged for each month, or part of a month, that the tax remains unpaid, unless you can show reasonable cause for not paying on time. The penalty is limited to 25%.

Late filing penalty.—A penalty is charged if your return is filed after the due date (including extensions) unless you can show reasonable cause for filing late. The penalty is 5% of the tax not paid by the **regular** due date for each month, or part of a month, that your return is late. The penalty is limited to 25%. If your return is more than 60 days late, the penalty will not be less than $100 or the balance of tax due on your return, whichever is smaller.

Interest.—Interest is charged on the tax not paid by the regular due date of your return until it is paid. It will be charged even if you have been granted an extension, or if you can show reasonable cause for not paying the tax on time.

Specific Instructions

Name, address, and social security numbers.—At the top of this form, fill in the spaces for your name, address, social security number, and spouse's social security number if you are filing a joint return. If the post office does not deliver mail to your street address and you have a P.O. Box, enter your P.O. Box number on the line for your present home address instead of your street address.

If you expect to file a gift tax return **(Form 709** or **Form 709-A)** for 1986, check the box on the front of this form.

Line 4.—Clearly describe the reasons that will cause your delay in filing your return. We cannot accept incomplete reasons, such as "illness" or "practitioner too busy," without adequate explanations. If it is clear that an application was made for no important reason, but only to gain time, both the application and the 10-day grace period will be denied.

If, because of undue hardship, you use this form to ask for an extension of time beyond the regular due date of your return, clearly explain your reasons and attach all supporting information to the form.

Caution: *If an extension is granted and the IRS later determines that the statements made on this form are false and misleading, the extension is null and void. You will be subject to the late filing penalty, explained above.*

Signature by Taxpayers.—Generally, both spouses must sign this form for the extension to be valid if a joint return is to be filed. But if one spouse cannot sign because of illness, absence, or other good cause, the other spouse may sign for both, provided a proper explanation is attached explaining why that spouse cannot sign this form.

Signature by Other than Taxpayer.—Persons who may sign for the taxpayers include attorneys or certified public accountants qualified to practice before the IRS, enrolled agents, or any person holding a power of attorney. If the taxpayer cannot sign because of illness, absence, or other good cause, a person in close personal or business relationship to the taxpayer may sign provided a proper explanation is attached as to why the taxpayer cannot sign this form. It is not necessary that such person hold a power of attorney.

How To Claim Credit for Payment Made With This Form.—If you file Form 1040A and are making a payment with Form 2688, include the amount of the payment in the total on Form 1040A, line 25. Also write "Form 2688" and the amount paid in the space to the left of line 25. If you file Form 1040 and are making a payment with Form 2688, include the amount of the payment on Form 1040, line 59. Also write "Form 2688" and the amount paid in the space to the left of line 59.

☆ U.S. Government Printing Office: 1986—493-224 23-0916750

Form **3903**

Department of the Treasury
Internal Revenue Service (O)

Moving Expenses

▶ Attach to Form 1040.

OMB No. 1545-0062

1986

Attachment Sequence No. **62**

Name(s) as shown on Form 1040 | Your social security number

a Enter the number of miles from your **old** residence to your **new** work place	a	
b Enter the number of miles from your **old** residence to your **old** work place	b	
c Subtract line **b** from line **a.** Enter the result (but not less than zero) ▶	c	

If line **c** is 35 or more miles, complete the rest of this form. If line **c** is less than 35 miles, you may not take a deduction for moving expenses. This rule does not apply to members of the armed forces.

1	Transportation expenses in moving household goods and personal effects			1	
2	Travel, meal, and lodging expenses in moving from old to new residence			2	
3	Pre-move travel, meal, and lodging expenses in looking for a new residence after getting your job	3			
4	Temporary living expenses in new location or area during any 30 days in a row after getting your job	4			
5	Add lines 3 and 4	5			
6	Enter the smaller of line 5 or $1,500 ($750 if married, filing a separate return, and, at the end of the tax year, you lived with your spouse who also started work during the tax year)		6		
7	Expenses of (check one): **a** ☐ selling or exchanging your old residence; or **b** ☐ if renting, settling an unexpired lease on your old residence		7		
8	Expenses of (check one): **a** ☐ buying your new residence; or **b** ☐ if renting, getting a lease on your new residence		8		
9	Add lines 6, 7, and 8		9		
10	Enter the smaller of line 9 or $3,000 ($1,500 if married, filing a separate return, and, at the end of the tax year, you lived with your spouse who also started work during the tax year)			10	
	Note: *Use any amount on line **7a** not deducted because of the $3,000 (or $1,500) limit to decrease the gain on the sale of your residence. Use any amount on line **8a** not deducted because of the limit to increase the basis of your new residence. See **No Double Benefit** in the instructions.*				
11	Add lines 1, 2, and 10. This is your moving expense deduction. Enter here and on Form 1040, line 24. **(Note:** *If your employer paid for any part of your move (including the value of any services furnished in kind), report that amount on **Form 1040, line 7.** See **Reimbursements** in the instructions.)* ▶			11	

General Instructions

Paperwork Reduction Act Notice.—We ask for this information to carry out the Internal Revenue laws of the United States. We need it to ensure that taxpayers are complying with these laws and to allow us to figure and collect the right amount of tax. You are required to give us this information.

Purpose of Form.—Use Form 3903 if you moved to a new principal work place within the United States or its possessions and you qualify to deduct your moving expenses.

Note: *Use **Form 3903F,** Foreign Moving Expenses, instead of this form if you are a U.S. citizen or resident alien who moved to a new principal work place outside the United States or its possessions.*

Additional Information.—For more information about moving expenses, please get **Publication 521,** Moving Expenses.

Who May Deduct Moving Expenses.—If you moved your residence because of a change in the location of your job, you may be able to deduct your moving expenses. You may qualify for a deduction whether you are self-employed or an employee. However, you must meet certain tests of distance and time, explained below.

Distance Test.—Your new work place must be at least 35 miles farther from your old residence than your old work place was. For example, if your old work place was 3 miles from your old residence, your new work place must be at least 38 miles from that residence. If you did not have an old work place, your new work place must be at least 35 miles from your old residence. (The distance between two points is the shortest of the more commonly traveled routes between the points.)

Time Test.—If you are an employee, you must work full time for at least 39 weeks during the 12 months right after you move. If you are self-employed, you must work full time for at least 39 weeks during the first 12 months and a total of at least 78 weeks during the 24 months right after you move.

You may deduct your moving expenses for 1986 even if you have not met the time test before your 1986 return is due. You may do this if you expect to meet the 39-week test by the end of 1987 or the 78-week test by the end of 1988. If you have not met the test by then, you will have to do one of the following:

- Amend your 1986 tax return on which you deducted moving expenses. To do this, use **Form 1040X,** Amended U.S. Individual Income Tax Return; or
- Report as income on your tax return for the year you cannot meet the test the amount you deducted on your 1986 return.

If you do not deduct your moving expenses on your 1986 return, and you later meet the time test, you may file an amended return for 1986, taking the deduction. To do this, use Form 1040X.

Exceptions to the Distance and Time Tests.—You do not have to meet the time

Form **3903** (1986)

test in case of death or if your job ends because of disability, transfer for your employer's benefit, or layoff or other discharge besides willful misconduct.

You do not have to meet the time test if you meet the requirements, explained below, for retirees or survivors living outside the United States.

If you are in the armed forces, you do not have to meet the distance and time tests if the move is due to a permanent change of station. A permanent change of station includes a move in connection with and within 1 year of retirement or other termination of active duty. In figuring your moving expenses, do not deduct any moving expenses for moving services that were provided by the military or that were reimbursed to you and that you did not include in income. However, you may deduct your unreimbursed moving expenses, subject to the dollar limits. If you and your spouse and dependents are moved to or from different locations, treat the moves as a single move.

Qualified Retirees or Survivors Living Outside the United States.—If the requirements below are met, retirees or survivors who move to a U.S. residence are treated as if they moved to a new work place located in the United States. You are subject to the dollar limits and distance test explained on this form. Use this form instead of Form 3903F to claim your moving expenses.

Retirees.—You may deduct moving expenses for a move to a new residence in the United States when you actually retire, if both your old principal work place and your old residence were outside the United States.

Survivors.—You may deduct moving expenses for a move to a residence in the United States if you are the spouse or dependent of a person whose principal work place at the time of death was outside the United States. In addition, the expenses must be: (1) for a move that begins within 6 months after the decedent's death; and (2) must be from a former residence outside the United States that you lived in with the decedent at the time of death.

Moving Expenses in General.—You may deduct most, but not all, of the reasonable expenses you incur in moving your family and dependent household members. You may not include moving expenses for employees such as a servant, governess, or nurse.

Examples of expenses you **MAY** deduct are:

- Travel, meal, and lodging expenses during the move to the new residence;
- Temporary living expenses in the new location; and
- Pre-move travel expenses.

Examples of expenses you **MAY NOT** deduct are:

- Loss on the sale of your residence;
- Mortgage penalties;
- Cost of refitting carpets and draperies; and
- Losses on quitting club memberships.

Reimbursements.—You must include any reimbursement of, or payment for, moving expenses in gross income as compensation for services. If your employer paid for any part of your move, you must report that amount as income on **Form 1040, line 7.** Your employer should include the amount paid in your total income on Form W-2. However, if you are not sure that the reimbursements have been included in your Form W-2, check with your employer. Your employer must give you a statement showing a detailed breakdown of reimbursements or payments for moving expenses. Your employer may use **Form 4782,** Employee Moving Expense Information, to give you the required breakdown of reimbursements, or your employer may use his or her own form.

No Double Benefit.—You may not take double benefits. For example, you may not use the moving expenses on line 7 that are part of your moving expense deduction to lower the amount of gain on the sale of your old residence. In addition, you may not use the moving expenses on line 8 that are part of your moving expense deduction to add to the cost of your new residence. (Use **Form 2119,** Sale or Exchange of Principal Residence, to figure the gain, if any, you must report on the sale of your old residence and the adjusted cost of the new one.)

Dollar Limits.—Lines 1 and 2 (costs of moving household goods and travel expenses to your new residence) are not limited to any amount. All the other expenses (lines 3, 4, 7, and 8) together may not be more than $3,000. In addition, line 3 (househunting trip expenses) and line 4 (temporary living expenses) together may not be more than $1,500. These are overall per-move limits.

There are some special situations:

- If both you and your spouse began work at new work places and shared the same new residence at the end of the tax year, you must treat this as one move rather than two. If you file separate returns, each of you is limited to a total of $1,500 for lines 3, 4, 7, and 8; and to a total of $750 for lines 3 and 4.
- If both you and your spouse began work at new work places but each of you moved to separate new residences, this is treated as two separate moves. If you file a joint return, lines 3, 4, 7, and 8 are limited to a total of $6,000; and lines 3 and 4 are limited to a total of $3,000. If you file separate returns, each of you is limited to a total of $3,000 for lines 3, 4, 7, and 8; and to a total of $1,500 for lines 3 and 4.

Line-by-Line Instructions

To see if you meet the distance test, complete lines **a** through **c** at the top of the form. If line **c** is at least 35 miles, or you are a member of the armed forces, continue with the items that follow.

We have provided specific instructions for most of the lines on the form. Those lines that do not appear in these instructions are self-explanatory.

Line 1.—Enter the actual cost of packing, crating, moving, storing in transit, and insuring your household goods and personal effects.

Line 2.—Enter the costs of travel from your old residence to your new residence. These include transportation, meals, and lodging on the way, including costs for the day you arrive. You may only include expenses for one trip. However, all the members of your household do not have to travel together or at the same time. If you use your own car, you may figure the expenses in either of the following two ways:

- Actual out-of-pocket expenses for gas and oil (keep records to verify the amounts); or
- At the rate of 9 cents a mile (keep records to verify your mileage).

You may add parking fees and tolls to the amount claimed under either method.

Line 3.—Include the costs of travel before you move in order to look for a new residence. You may deduct the costs only if:

- You began the househunting trip after you got the job;
- You returned to your old residence after looking for a new one; and
- You traveled to the general location of the new work place primarily to look for a new residence.

There is no limit on the number of househunting trips made by you and members of your household that may be included on this line. Your househunting does not have to be successful to qualify for this deduction. If you used your own car, figure transportation costs the same way as in the instructions for line 2. If you are self-employed, you may deduct these househunting costs only if you had already made substantial arrangements to begin work in the new location.

Line 4.—Include the costs of meals and lodging while occupying temporary quarters in the area of your new work place. You may include these costs for any period of 30 days in a row after you get the job, but before you move into permanent quarters. If you are self-employed, you may count these temporary living expenses only if you had already made substantial arrangements to begin work in the new location.

Lines 7 and 8.—You may include most of the costs to sell or buy a residence or to settle or get a lease. Examples of expenses you **MAY** include are:

- Sales commissions;
- Advertising costs;
- Attorney's fees;
- Title and escrow fees;
- State transfer taxes; and
- Costs to settle an unexpired lease or to get a new lease.

Examples of expenses you **MAY NOT** include are:

- Costs to improve your residence to help it sell;
- Charges for payment or prepayment of interest; and
- Payments or prepayments of rent.

Check the appropriate box, **a** or **b,** for lines 7 and 8 when you enter the amounts for these two lines.

☆ U.S. Government Printing Office: 1986—493-230 23-0916750

Form **4137**

Department of the Treasury
Internal Revenue Service

Computation of Social Security Tax on Unreported Tip Income

(Under Federal Insurance Contributions Act)

▶ **Attach to Form 1040.**

OMB No. 1545-0059

1986

Attachment Sequence No. **64**

Name of person who received tip income. Enter name as shown on social security card. | **Social security number**

Names of employers:

1	Total cash and charge tips **received** in 1986. (**Note:** *Include December 1985 tips reported to your employer from January 1, 1986, through January 10, 1986. Do not include December 1986 tips reported to your employer from January 1, 1987, through January 10, 1987.*) See **"When Tips Are Taxable"** in the instructions		1	
2	Total cash and charge tips **reported** to your employer in 1986		2	
3	Balance (subtract line 2 from line 1). Enter here and include in total on Form 1040, line 7		3	
4	Cash and charge tips you received but did not report to your employer because the total was less than $20 in a calendar month		4	
5	Balance (subtract line 4 from line 3)		5	
6	Largest amount of wages (including tips) subject to social security tax	6 42,000 00		
7	Total social security wages shown on Form W-2 or railroad retirement compensation shown on statement. (Include covered wages you received as an agricultural or household employee.)	7		
8	Balance (subtract line 7 from line 6). If line 7 is more than line 6, you do not owe this tax. Do not complete the rest of this form or Schedule U below		8	
9	Unreported tips subject to social security tax. Enter here and on Schedule U below, the amount from line 5 or line 8, whichever is smaller		9	
10	Multiply line 9 by .0715. Enter here and on Form 1040, line 53 ▶		10	

For Paperwork Reduction Act Notice, see instructions on back. Form **4137** (1986)

Do Not Detach

SCHEDULE U (Form 1040)

Department of the Treasury
Internal Revenue Service

U.S. Schedule of Unreported Tip Income

For crediting to your social security record

1986

Important: The amounts reported below are for your social security record. This record is used in figuring any benefits, based on your earnings, payable to you, your dependents, and your survivors. Fill in each item accurately and completely.

Print or type name of person who received tip income. Enter name as shown on social security card. | **Social security number**

Address (number and street) | Occupation

City or town, state, and ZIP code

Unreported tips subject to social security tax. Enter amount from line 9 above ▶ $

Please do not write in this space

DLN—

Instructions

Paperwork Reduction Act Notice.—We ask for this information to carry out the Internal Revenue laws of the United States. We need it to ensure that taxpayers are complying with these laws and to allow us to figure and collect the right amount of tax. You are required to give us this information.

Purpose of Form.—Form 4137 is used to figure the social security tax on unreported tip income and to figure the amount of tip income to be reported on your tax return and social security record.

Who Must File.—File this form if you received cash and charge tips of $20 or more in any month and did not report all of those tips to your employer. You must also file this form if you are reporting any part of the allocated tips shown on your Form W-2 as income on line 7 of Form 1040.

Tips You Must Report To an Employer.—You must give your employer a written statement of cash and charge tips if you receive $20 or more in tips during a month. If, in any month you work for two or more employers and receive tips while working for each, the $20 test applies separately for the tips you received for your work for each employer and not to the total you receive. You must report these tips to your employers by the 10th day of the month after the month you receive them.

Certain Tips You Do Not Report on This Form.—Do not report on this form tips received:

- for work covered by the Railroad Retirement Tax Act (contact any Railroad Retirement Board office for information on how to get railroad retirement credit for tips not reported to railroad employers); or
- while working for state or local governments.

When Tips Are Taxable.—If you report tips to your employer as required by the 10th day of the month after the month you receive them, those tips are considered income to you in the month you report them. For example, tips you receive in December of 1986 that you report to your employer between January 1, 1987, and January 10, 1987, are considered income in 1987 and should be included on your 1987 Form W-2. (Do not include these tips on line 1 of this form.)

Tips you did not report to your employer on time or did not report at all are considered income to you in the month you actually received them. For example, tips you received in December of 1986 that are reported to your employer after January 10, 1987, are considered income in 1986 because you did not report to your employer on time. (Include these tips on line 1 of this form.) Also include on line 1 of this form and on line 7 of Form 1040, any allocated tips shown on your Form W-2 unless you can show that you did not receive this amount. See **Publication 531**, Reporting Income From Tips, for more information.

Payment of Tax.—Tips you report to your employer are subject to social security or railroad retirement tax and income tax withholding. Your employer collects these taxes from wages (excluding tips) or other funds of yours available to cover them. If your wages are not enough to cover these taxes, you may give your employer the additional amounts needed. Your Form W-2 will include the tips you reported to your employer and the taxes withheld. If there was not enough money to cover the social security or railroad retirement tax, your Form W-2 will also show the tax due.

Penalty for Not Reporting Tips.—If you do not report the tips you are required to report to your employer, you may be charged a penalty equal to 50% of the social security tax due on those tips. Therefore, you should attach a statement to your return explaining why you did not report them.

For more information, see Publication 531 and **Publication 505**, Tax Withholding and Estimated Tax, available from most Internal Revenue Service offices.

Form **4684**

Department of the Treasury
Internal Revenue Service

Casualties and Thefts

► See separate instructions.
► To be filed with Form 1040, 1041, 1065, 1120, etc.
Use a separate Form 4684 for each different casualty or theft.

OMB No. 1545-0177
1986
Attachment Sequence No.: **35**

Name(s) as shown on tax return | **Identifying number**

SECTION A.—Personal Use Property *(Casualties and thefts to property **not** used in a trade or business or for income-producing purposes.)*

1 Description of Properties (Show kind, location, and date of purchase for each)
Property A ....
Property B ....
Property C ....
Property D ....

	Properties (Use a separate column for each property lost or damaged from one casualty or theft.)			
	A	B	C	D
2 Cost or other basis of each property				
3 Insurance or other reimbursement you received or expect to receive for each property **Note:** *If line 2 is more than line 3, skip line 4*				
4 Gain from casualty or theft. If line 3 is more than line 2, enter difference here and skip lines 5 through 13				
5 Fair market value before casualty or theft				
6 Fair market value after casualty or theft				
7 Subtract line 6 from line 5				
8 Enter smaller of line 2 or line 7				
9 Subtract line 3 from line 8				

10 Casualty or theft loss. Add amounts from line 9 for all columns

11 Enter the amount from line 10 or $100, whichever is smaller

12 Subtract line 11 from line 10
Caution: *Use only one Form 4684 for lines 13 through 18.*

13 Add the line 12 amounts from all Forms 4684, Section A

14 Add the line 4 amounts from all Forms 4684, Section A

15 If line 14 is more than line 13, enter difference here and on Schedule D, and do not complete the rest of form (see instructions). Otherwise, enter zero and complete lines 16 through 18. If line 14 is equal to line 13, do not complete the rest of form

16 If line 13 is more than line 14, enter difference

17 Enter 10% of adjusted gross income (Form 1040, line 33). Estates and trusts, see instructions

18 Subtract line 17 from line 16. If zero or less, enter zero. Enter on Schedule A (Form 1040), line 19. Estates and trusts, enter on the "other deductions" line of your tax return

For Paperwork Reduction Act Notice, see page 1 of separate instructions. Form **4684** (1986)

Form 4684 (1986) 35 Page 2

Name(s) as shown on tax return (Do not enter name and identifying number if shown on other side)	Identifying number

SECTION B.—Business and Income-Producing Property

(Casualties and thefts to property used in a trade or business or for income-producing purposes.)

Part I Casualty or Theft Gain or Loss (Use a separate Part I for each different casualty or theft.)

1 Description of Properties (Show kind, location, and date of purchase for each)

Property A ....

Property B ....

Property C ....

Property D ....

	Properties (Use a separate column for each property lost or damaged from one casualty or theft.)			
	A	B	C	D
2 Cost or adjusted basis of each property				
3 Insurance or other reimbursement you received or expect to receive for each property **Note:** *If line 2 is more than line 3, skip line 4*				
4 Gain from casualty or theft. If line 3 is more than line 2, enter difference here and on line 11 or 16, column (c). However, see instructions for line 15. Also, skip lines 5 through 10				
5 Fair market value before casualty or theft				
6 Fair market value after casualty or theft				
7 Subtract line 6 from line 5				
8 Enter smaller of line 2 or line 7 **Note:** *If the property was totally destroyed by a casualty, or lost from theft, enter on line 8, in each column, the amount from line 2.*				
9 Subtract line 3 from line 8				

10 Casualty or theft loss. Add amounts from line 9 for all columns. Enter here and on line 11 or 16 . . . . . . | |

Part II Summary of Gains and Losses (From separate Parts I)

	(a) Identify casualty or theft	(b) Losses from casualties or thefts (i) Trade, business, rental or royalty property	(ii) Income-producing property	(c) Gains from casualties or thefts includible in income
	Casualty or Theft of Property Held 6 Months or Less			
11				
12	Totals. Add amounts on line 11 for each column			
13	Combine line 12, columns (b)(i) and (c). Enter the net gain or (loss) here and on Form 4797, Part II, line 13. (If Form 4797 is not otherwise required, see instructions.)			
14	Enter the amount from line 12, column (b)(ii) here and on Schedule A (Form 1040), line 19. Partnerships, S Corporations, Estates and Trusts, see instructions			
	Casualty or Theft of Property Held More Than 6 Months			
15	Casualty or theft gains from Form 4797, Part III, line 31			
16				
17	Total losses. Add amounts on line 16, columns (b)(i) and (b)(ii)			
18	Total gains. Add lines 15 and 16, column (c)			
19	Add amounts on line 17, columns (b)(i) and (b)(ii) *Partnerships, enter the amount from line 20 or line 21 on your Schedule K-1, line 7. S Corporations, enter the amount from line 20 on your Schedule K-1, line 6.*			
20	If the loss on line 19 is more than the gain on line 18:			
	a Combine line 17, column (b)(i) and line 18. Enter the net gain or (loss) here and on Form 4797, Part II, line 13. (If Form 4797 is not otherwise required, see instructions.)			
	b Enter the amount from line 17, column (b)(ii) here and on Schedule A (Form 1040), line 19. Estates and Trusts, enter on the "other deductions" line of your tax return			
21	If the loss on line 19 is equal to or smaller than the gain on line 18, combine these lines and enter here and on Form 4797, Part I, line 2			

☆ U.S. Government Printing Office: 1986—493-242 23-0916750

Form **4768**
(Rev. January 1985)
Department of the Treasury
Internal Revenue Service

Application for Extension of Time to File U.S. Estate Tax Return and/or Pay Estate Tax

(Sections 6081 and/or 6161 of the Internal Revenue Code)

OMB No. 1545-0181
Expires 7-31-87

Part I Identification

Decedent's first name and middle initial	Decedent's last name	Date of death
Name of application filer		Decedent's social security number
Address of application filer (Number and street)		Estate tax return due date
City, State, and ZIP code		

Part II Extension of Time to File (Sec. 6081)

You must attach your written statement to explain in detail why it is impossible or impractical to file a reasonably complete return within nine months after the date of the decedent's death.	Extension date requested

Part III Extension of Time to Pay (Sec. 6161)

You must attach your written statement to explain in detail why it is impossible or impractical to pay the full amount of the estate tax by the estate tax return due date.	Extension date requested
1 Amount of estate tax estimated to be due	
2 Amount of cash shortage claimed	
3 **Balance due (subtract line 2 from line 1) (Pay with this application.)**	

Signature and Verification

If filed by executor—Under penalties of perjury, I declare that to the best of my knowledge and belief, the statements made herein and attached are true and correct.

Executor's signature ______ Title ______ Date ______

If filed by someone other than the executor—Under penalties of perjury, I declare that to the best of my knowledge and belief, the statements made herein and attached are true and correct, that I am authorized by the executor to file this application, and that I am (check box(es) that applies):

- ☐ A member in good standing of the bar of the highest court of (specify jurisdiction) ▶ ______
- ☐ A certified public accountant duly qualified to practice in (specify jurisdiction) ▶ ______
- ☐ A person enrolled to practice before the Internal Revenue Service.
- ☐ A duly authorized agent holding a power of attorney. (The power of attorney need not be submitted unless requested.)

Filer's signature (other than the executor) ______ Date ______

Part IV Notice to Applicant—To be completed by Internal Revenue Service

1 The application for extension of time to file (Part II) is:
- ☐ Approved
- ☐ Not approved because ______
- ☐ Other ______

2 The application for extension of time to pay (Part III) is:
- ☐ Approved
- ☐ Not approved because ______
- ☐ Other ______

Internal Revenue Service official	Date	Internal Revenue Service official	Date

For Paperwork Reduction Act Notice, see instructions on the back of this form. Form **4768** (Rev. 1-85)

General Instructions

(Section references are to the Internal Revenue Code, unless otherwise noted.)

Paperwork Reduction Act Notice.—We ask for the information to carry out the Internal Revenue laws of the United States. We need it to ensure that taxpayers are complying with these laws and to allow us to figure and collect the right amount of tax. You are required to give us this information.

A. Who May File.—The executor who is required to file the estate tax return for the decedent's estate may file Form 4768 to apply for an extension of time to file under section 6081 and/or an extension of time to pay the estate tax under section 6161. Executor means the executor, executrix, administrator, administratrix or personal representative of the decedent's estate; if no executor, executrix, administrator, administratrix or personal representative is appointed, qualified and acting within the United States, executor means any person in actual or constructive possession of any property of the decedent. Also, an authorized attorney, certified public accountant, enrolled agent, or agent holding power of attorney may use this form to apply for an extension of time on behalf of the executor.

The form must be signed by the person filing the application. If filed by an attorney, certified public accountant, enrolled agent, or agent holding a power of attorney, the appropriate box must be checked.

B. When to File.—Please file Form 4768 in adequate time to permit the Internal Revenue Service to consider the application and reply before the estate tax due date. Except for certain section 6166 elections (closely held business), an application for an extension of time to pay estate tax received after the estate tax due date will not be considered by the Internal Revenue Service.

C. How and Where to File.—If only Part II or only Part III is completed, please file Form 4768 in duplicate; if both Part II and Part III are completed, please file Form 4768 in quadruplicate with the Internal Revenue Service office where the estate tax return will be filed. All applications relating to **Form 706NA**, United States Estate Tax Return, Estate of nonresident not a citizen of the United States, must be filed with the Internal Revenue Service Center, Philadelphia, PA 19255.

D. Interest.—Interest from the estate tax due date must be paid on the part of the estate tax for which an extension of time to pay is approved.

E. Penalties.—Penalties may be imposed for failure to file the estate tax return within the extension period granted, or failure to pay the balance of the estate tax due within the extension period granted.

F. Bond.—If an extension of time to pay is granted, the executor may be required to furnish a bond.

G. Form 706NA.—If you are applying for an extension with respect to Form 706NA, please write "Form 706NA" at the top of Form 4768.

H. Form 706-A.—If you are applying for an extension with respect to **Form 706-A,** United States Additional Estate Tax Return, please write "Form 706-A" at the top of Form 4768. You should substitute "qualified heir(ess)" for "executor" wherever "executor" appears in Form 4768 and its instructions.

Specific Instructions

1. Estate Tax Return Due Date.—The due date is nine months after the decedent's death. If there is no numerically corresponding day in the ninth month, the last day of the ninth month is the due date. When the due date falls on Saturday, Sunday, or a legal holiday, the due date is the next succeeding week day which is not a legal holiday.

2. Part II, Extension of Time to File (Sec. 6081).—The time to file extension may not exceed 6 months unless the executor is out of the country.

The application must establish sufficient cause why it is impossible or impractical for the executor to file a reasonably complete return by the estate tax return due date.

If the application is for an extension of time to file only, the amount of the estate tax estimated to be due must be shown on the "Balance due" line in Part III and a check or money order payable to the Internal Revenue Service included with the application. Please write the decedent's social security number on the check or money order.

The Internal Revenue Service will complete Part IV and return a copy to the applicant. If the application is approved, please attach the copy to the estate tax return that is filed. The estate tax return must be filed before the expiration of the period granted for extension of time to file and cannot be amended after the expiration of the extension period, although supplemental information may subsequently be filed which may result in a different amount of tax.

A time to file extension does NOT extend the time to pay date.

3. Part III, Extension of Time to Pay (Sec. 6161).—An extension of time to pay under section 6161(a)(1) may not exceed 12 months. A discretionary extension of time to pay for reasonable cause under section 6161(a)(2) may not exceed 10 years. Different extension periods may be applicable to extensions of time granted for a deficiency, a section 6163 election (reversionary or remainder interest) or a section 6166 election (closely held business).

The application must establish why it is impossible or impractical for the executor to pay the full amount of the estate tax by the estate tax return due date. Examples of reasonable cause provided in section 20.6161-1 of the regulations include the following:

(a) An estate includes sufficient liquid assets to pay the estate tax when otherwise due. The liquid assets, however, are located in several jurisdictions and are not immediately subject to the control of the executor. Consequently, such assets cannot readily be marshalled by the executor even with the exercise of due diligence.

(b) An estate is comprised in substantial part of assets consisting of rights to receive payments in the future (i.e., annuities, copyright royalties, contingent fees, or accounts receivable). These assets provide insufficient present cash with which to pay the estate tax when otherwise due and the estate cannot borrow against these assets except upon terms that would inflict loss upon the estate.

(c) An estate includes a claim to substantial assets which cannot be collected without litigation. Consequently, the size of the gross estate is unascertainable at the time the tax is otherwise due.

(d) An estate does not have sufficient funds (without borrowing at a rate of interest higher than that generally available) with which to pay the entire estate tax when otherwise due, to provide a reasonable allowance during the remaining period of administration of the estate for the decedent's surviving spouse and dependent children, and to satisfy claims against the estate that are due and payable. Furthermore, the executor has made a reasonable effort to convert assets in the executor's possession (other than an interest in a closely held business to which section 6166 applies) into cash.

In general, an extension of time to pay will be granted only for the amount of the cash shortage. You must show on Part III the amount of the estate tax (attach a copy of the return if it has already been filed; otherwise estimate the tax), the amount of the cash shortage, including a statement of the current assets in the estate and the assets already distributed, a plan for partial payments during the extension period and the balance due. You must attach a check or money order payable to the Internal Revenue Service for the balance due. Please write the decedent's social security number on the check or money order.

The Internal Revenue Service will complete Part IV and return a copy to the applicant. If the application that is approved has different extension dates in Parts II and III, the Internal Revenue Service will return two copies to the applicant. Please attach one of the copies to the estate tax return that is filed. Please submit the other copy with the separate payment.The part of the estate tax for which the extension is granted must be paid with interest from the estate tax due date before the expiration of the extension granted.

A time to pay extension does NOT extend the time to file date.

If an application for extension of time to pay is denied, a written appeal may be made to the regional commissioner within 10 days from the time the denial is mailed; for additional information see section 20.6161-1(b) of the regulations.

★U.S. Government Printing Office: 1985—461-495/10113

Form **4782** (Rev. March 1985) Department of the Treasury Internal Revenue Service

Employee Moving Expense Information

Payments made during the calendar year 19 ....

OMB No. 1545-0182 Expires 3-31-88

Do not file. Keep for your records.

Name of employee	**Social security number**

Moving Expense Payments

Type of expense	a. Amount paid to employee	b. Amount paid to a third party for employee's benefit and value of services furnished in-kind	c. Total (Add columns a. and b.)
1 Transportation expenses in moving household goods and personal effects (including storage expenses for a foreign move)			
2 Travel, meal, and lodging expenses in moving from old to new residence			
3 Pre-move travel, meal, and lodging expenses in looking for a new residence after obtaining employment			
4 Temporary living expenses in new location or area during any 30 days in a row after obtaining employment (90 days in a row for a foreign move)			
5 Qualified expenses of selling, buying, or leasing a residence			
6 All other payments (specify) -----			
7 Total moving expense payments. Add lines 1 through 6 ▶			

Instructions for Employer

Paperwork Reduction Act Notice.—This information is required to carry out the Internal Revenue laws of the United States. It is needed to ensure that taxpayers are complying with these laws. You are required to provide this information.

Purpose of Form.—You are required to give your employees a statement showing a detailed breakdown of reimbursements or payments of moving expenses. Form 4782 may be used for this purpose or you may use your own form as long as it provides the same information as Form 4782. A separate form is required for each move made by an employee for which reimbursement or payment is made.

These amounts must also be included in box 10, "Wages, tips, other compensation," on the employee's Form W-2.

When To Give the Information.—You must give Form 4782 (or your own form) to your employee by January 31 following the calendar year in which the employee received the reimbursement or payment. However, if the employee stops working for you before December 31 and he or she submits a written request to receive the form earlier, you must give the completed form to the former employee within 30 days after you receive the request if the 30-day period ends before January 31.

Note: ***Publication 15,*** *Circular E, Employer's Tax Guide, explains the conditions under which these reimbursements or payments are not subject to withholding.*

General Information for Employees

Purpose of Form.—This form is furnished by your employer to give you the necessary information to help you figure your moving expense deduction. The form shows the amount of any reimbursement made to you, payments made to a third party for your benefit, and the value of services furnished in-kind for moving expenses. You should receive a separate form for each move that you made during the calendar year for which you receive any reimbursement or during which payment is made for your benefit.

Allowance of Deduction.—If you meet the "distance and time" tests explained below, you may deduct the reasonable expenses you paid or incurred during the tax year to move to a new principal place of work. If the expenses shown on this form qualify as deductible moving expenses, you may include them in figuring your moving expense deduction.

For moves within or to the United States, use **Form 3903**, Moving Expense Adjustment, to claim the deduction. Use **Form 3903F**, Foreign Moving Expense Adjustment, to claim the deduction if you moved outside the United States or its possessions.

See the form instructions and **Publication 521**, Moving Expenses, for detailed moving expense information, including which expenses qualify and what are reasonable expenses.

Conditions for Allowance.—Generally, you must meet the following tests to deduct moving expenses:

Distance Test.—Your new work place must be at least 35 miles farther from your old residence than your old work place was.

Time Test.—If you are an employee, you must work full time for at least 39 weeks during the 12 months right after you move.

Form **4782** (Rev. 3-85)

*U.S. GOVERNMENT PRINTING OFFICE: 1986-491-308 E.I. NO. 43-1400716

Form **4798**

Department of the Treasury
Internal Revenue Service

Carryover of Pre-1970 Capital Losses

(Computation of Capital Loss Carryovers and Summary of Capital Gains and Losses if Pre-1970 Capital Losses Are Carried to 1986.)

► **See instructions on page 2.**
► **Attach to Form 1040.**

OMB No. 1545-0185

1986

Attachment Sequence No. **69**

Name(s) as shown on Form 1040 | **Your social security number**

Part I Capital Gains and Losses

Section A.—Summary of Capital Gains and Losses

Short-term	1	Amount from your 1986 Schedule D (Form 1040), Part I, line 8	1			
	2	Pre-1970 short-term capital loss carryover to 1986 from your 1985 Form 4798, Part II, line 17	2	( )		
	3	Net short-term gain or (loss), combine lines 1 and 2			3	
Long-term	4	Amount from your 1986 Schedule D (Form 1040), Part II, line 17	4			
	5	Pre-1970 long-term capital loss carryover to 1986 from your 1985 Form 4798, Part II, line 23	5	( )		
	6	Net long-term gain or (loss), combine lines 4 and 5			6	
	7	Combine lines 3 and 6, and enter the net gain or (loss) here *If line 7 is a gain, complete lines 8 through 10. If line 7 is a loss, skip to line 11.*			7	
	8	If line 7 shows a gain, enter the smaller of line 6 or line 7. Enter zero if there is a loss or no entry on line 6	8			
	9	Enter 60% of line 8 *If line 9 is more than zero, you may be liable for the alternative minimum tax. See Form 6251.*			9	
	10	Subtract line 9 from line 7. Enter here and on Form 1040, line 13, and write "Form 4798"			10	
	11	If line 7 shows a loss—If losses are shown on both lines 5 and 6, omit line 11 and go to line 12. **Otherwise,** enter one of the following amounts: **a** If line 3 is zero or a net gain, enter 50% of line 7; **b** If line 6 is zero or a net gain, enter amount from line 7; or **c** If line 3 and line 6 are net losses, enter amount on line 3 added to 50% of amount on line 6			11	
		Note: *If there is an entry on line 11, skip lines 12 through 28 and go to line 29.*				
	12	Enter loss from line 3; if line 3 is zero or a gain, enter zero			12	
	13	Enter loss from line 6			13	
	14	Enter gain, if any, from line 3; if line 3 is zero or a loss, enter zero			14	
	15	Reduce loss on line 13 by any gain on line 14			15	
	16	Combine amounts on 1986 Schedule D (Form 1040), lines 8 and 17, without regard to any carryover on lines 6 and 15 of Schedule D (Form 1040). If gain, enter gain. If zero or a loss, enter zero **Note:** *If the entry on line 16 is zero, skip lines 17 through 23 and enter on line 24 the loss shown on line 5.*	16			
	17	Enter gain, if any, from 1986 Schedule D (Form 1040), line 17, without regard to any carryover on line 15 of Schedule D (Form 1040). If zero or a loss, enter zero	17			
	18	Enter line 16 or line 17, whichever is smaller	18			
	19	Subtract line 18 from line 16	19			
	20	Enter loss from line 2; if line 2 is blank, enter zero	20			
	21	Reduce gain on line 19 by loss on line 20 (see Instruction B)	21			
	22	Enter loss from line 5	22			
	23	Add the gain(s) on line(s) 18 and 21	23			
	24	Reduce the loss on line 22 by any gain on line 23 (see Instruction C)			24	
	25	Enter line 24 or line 15, whichever is smaller (if line 24 is zero, enter zero)			25	
	26	Subtract amount on line 25 from the loss on line 15			26	
	27	Enter 50% of the amount on line 26			27	
	28	Add lines 12, 25, and 27			28	
	29	Enter the amount from line 11 or line 28, whichever applies	29			
	30	Enter here and enter as a (loss) on Form 1040, line 13, and write "Form 4798," the smallest of: **a** Amount on line 29; **b** $3,000 (Married taxpayers filing separate returns, see Instruction D); or **c** Taxable income, as adjusted (see instructions for Schedule D (Form 1040))			30	( )

Form **4798** (1986)

Form 4798 (1986) Page 2

Section B.—Complete if You Are Married Filing a Separate Return and Losses Are Shown on Lines 2 and 7 of Part I

31	Combine amounts on 1986 Schedule D (Form 1040), lines 8 and 17, without regard to any carryover on lines 6 and 15 of Schedule D (Form 1040). If a gain, enter gain; if zero or a loss, enter zero	31	
	Note: *If the entry on line 31 is zero, SKIP lines 32 through 38, and enter on line 39 the loss shown on line 2.*		
32	Enter gain, if any, from 1986 Schedule D (Form 1040), line 8, without regard to any carryover on line 6 of Schedule D (Form 1040). If zero or a loss, enter zero	32	
33	Enter line 31 or line 32, whichever is smaller	33	
34	Subtract line 33 from line 31	34	
35	Enter loss from line 5; if line 5 is blank, enter zero	35	
36	Reduce any gain on line 34 by any loss on line 35 (see Instruction B)	36	
37	Enter loss from line 2	37	
38	Add the gain(s) on line(s) 33 and 36	38	
39	Reduce the loss on line 37 by any gain on line 38 (see Instruction C)	39	

Part II Pre-1970 and Post-1969 Capital Loss Carryovers From 1986 to 1987
(Complete This Part if the Amount in Part I, Line 29, Is Larger Than the Loss in Part I, Line 30.)

40	Enter loss shown on line 3; if none, enter zero and skip lines 41 through 44, then go to line 45	40	
41	Enter gain shown on line 6. If that line is blank or shows a loss, enter zero	41	
42	Subtract line 41 from line 40	42	
43	Enter smaller of line 30 or line 42	43	
44	Subtract line 43 from line 42. This is your short-term capital loss carryover from 1986 to 1987	44	
45	Subtract line 43 from line 30. (Note: If you skipped lines 41 through 44, enter amount from line 30.)	45	
46	Enter loss from line 6; if none, enter zero and skip lines 47 through 50	46	
47	Enter gain shown on line 3. If that line is blank or shows a loss, enter zero	47	
48	Subtract line 47 from line 46	48	
49	Multiply amount on line 45 by 2	49	
50	Subtract line 49 from line 48. This is your long-term capital loss carryover from 1986 to 1987	50	

Instructions

Paperwork Reduction Act Notice.—We ask for this information to carry out the Internal Revenue laws of the United States. We need it to ensure that taxpayers are complying with these laws and to allow us to figure and collect the right amount of tax. You are required to give us this information.

A Change You Should Note

After 1986, you will not have to keep separate records of pre-1970 and post-1969 net long-term capital loss carryovers. 1986 is the last year you will need Form 4798.

If, after completing Part I of Form 4798, line 29 is larger than the loss on line 30, complete Part II of Form 4798. Next year, you can enter the carryover to 1987 directly on your 1987 Schedule D (Form 1040).

A. Purpose of Form.—Use this form only if you have a pre-1970 capital loss carryover to 1986 from your 1985 Form 4798, Part II, line 17 or 23. If so, first fill in your 1986 Schedule D (Form 1040), lines 1 through 17. Then complete Form 4798, Part I. Use Part II of Form 4798 to figure your capital loss carryover from 1986 to 1987.

B. Part I, Line 21 or 36.—If the loss is more than the gain, enter zero. If there is a gain and no loss, enter the gain.

C. Part I, Line 24 or 39.—If the gain is more than the loss, enter zero. If there is a loss and no gain, just enter the loss.

D. Married Taxpayers Filing Separate Returns.—If you are married, filing a separate return, and losses are shown on lines 2 and 7 of Part I, complete Section B of Part I. If losses are shown on lines 5 and 7 of Part I, complete lines 16 through 24 of Part I (whether or not you have to complete lines 12 through 28), and ignore the note under line 16. Your limitation for line 30b is the sum of $1,500 plus (1) the loss on line 24 of Part I, and (2) the loss on line 39 of Part I. Your total limitation must not exceed $3,000.

☆ U.S. Government Printing Office: 1986—493-249 23-0916750

Form **4852** (Revised September 1986)

Dept. of the Treasury Internal Revenue Service

SUBSTITUTE FOR FORM W-2, WAGE AND TAX STATEMENT OR FORM W-2P, STATEMENT FOR RECIPIENTS OF ANNUITIES, PENSIONS, RETIRED PAY, OR IRA PAYMENTS

◀ **Attach to Form 1040, 1040A, 1040EZ or 1040X**

OMB No. 1545-0458
Expires 5–31–87

1. NAME *(First, middle, last)*	**2. SOCIAL SECURITY NUMBER**

3. ADDRESS *(Number, street, city, State, ZIP code)*

4. PLEASE FILL IN THE YEAR AT THE END OF THIS STATEMENT:
I have been unable to obtain or have received an Incorrect Form W-2, Wage and Tax Statement, or Form W-2P, Statement for Recipients of Annuities, Pensions, Retired Pay, or IRA Payments, from my employer or payer named below, and have so notified the Internal Revenue Service. The amounts shown below are my best estimates of all wages or payments paid to me and the Federal taxes withheld by this employer or payer during 19______ .

5. EMPLOYER'S OR PAYER'S NAME, ADDRESS, AND ZIP CODE	**6. EMPLOYER'S OR PAYER'S IDENTIFICATION NUMBER** *(If known)*

7. ADVANCE EIC (Earned Income Credit) PAYMENTS RECEIVED	**8. FEDERAL INCOME TAX WITHHELD**	**9. WAGES, TIPS, OTHER COMPENSATION OR PAYMENTS (See Note Below)**	**10. SOCIAL SECURITY TAX WITHHELD**	**11. SOCIAL SECURITY WAGES**	**12. SOCIAL SECURITY TIPS**

NOTE: Include the total of (1) wages paid, (2) noncash payments, (3) tips/reported, and (4) all other compensation before deductions for taxes, insurance, etc.

13. How did you determine the amounts in items 7 through 12 above?

14. Give reason Form W-2, W-2P (or W-2C, Statement of Corrected Income and Tax Amounts) was not furnished by employer, or payer, if known, and explain your efforts to get it.

Paperwork Reduction Notice

We ask for this information to carry out the Internal Revenue laws of the United States. We need it to ensure that taxpayers are complying with these laws and to allow us to figure and collect the right amount of tax. You are required to give us this information.

IMPORTANT NOTICE: If your employer has ceased operations or filed for bankruptcy, you may wish to send a copy of this form to the Social Security Administration, 13–D–6 Metro West Tower, 301 N. Green Street, Baltimore, Maryland 21201, Attn: Lewis Oppenheimer, to ensure proper social security credit.

Under penalties of perjury, I declare that I have examined this statement, and to the best of my knowledge and belief, it is true, correct, and complete.

15. Your signature	16. Date

★U.S.GPO:1986-0-181-457/54461

Form **4852** (Rev. 9-86)

Form **4868**
Department of the Treasury
Internal Revenue Service (O)

Application for Automatic Extension of Time To File U.S. Individual Income Tax Return

OMB No. 1545-0188

1986

Please Type or Print	Your first name and initial (if joint return, also give spouse's name and initial) Last name	**Your social security number**
	Present home address (number and street or rural route). (If you have a P.O. Box, see the instructions.)	**Spouse's social security no.**
	City, town or post office, state, and ZIP code	

Note: *File this form with the Internal Revenue Service Center where you must file your income tax return and pay the amount shown on line 6 below.* ***This is not an extension of time for payment of tax.*** *You will be charged a penalty for late payment of tax and late filing unless you show reasonable cause for not paying or filing on time (see instructions).*

If you expect to file a gift tax return (Form 709 or Form 709-A) for 1986, generally due by April 15, 1987, check this box . . . . ▶ ☐

I request an automatic 4-month extension of time to August 17, 1987, to file Form 1040A or Form 1040 for the calendar year 1986 (or if a fiscal year Form 1040 to ________________________, 19______, for the tax year ending __________________________, 19_____).

1	Total income tax liability for 1986. (You may estimate this amount.) . . . . **Note:** *You **must** enter an amount on line 1. If you do not expect to owe tax, enter zero (0).*		1
2	Federal income tax withheld	2	
3	1986 estimated tax payments (include 1985 overpayment allowed as a credit) .	3	
4	Other payments and credits you expect to show on Form 1040A or Form 1040 .	4	
5	Add lines 2, 3, and 4		5
6	Income tax balance due (subtract line 5 from line 1). Pay in full with this form. (If line 5 is more than line 1, enter zero (0).) . . . . ▶		6
7	Total gift tax and generation-skipping transfer tax you expect to owe for 1986 (see instructions) . . . ▶		7

If you send only one check for income, gift, and generation-skipping transfer taxes due, attach a statement showing how much of the check applies to each type of tax.

Signature and Verification

Under penalties of perjury, I declare that I have examined this form, including accompanying schedules and statements, and to the best of my knowledge and belief, it is true, correct, and complete; and, if prepared by someone other than the taxpayer, that I am authorized to prepare this form.

Signature of taxpayer ▶ ______________________________ Date ▶ ______________

Signature of spouse ▶ ______________________________ Date ▶ ______________
(If filing jointly, BOTH must sign even if only one had income)

Signature of preparer other than taxpayer ▶ Date ▶

General Instructions

Paperwork Reduction Act Notice.—We ask for this information to carry out the Internal Revenue laws of the United States. We need it to ensure that taxpayers are complying with these laws and to allow us to figure and collect the right amount of tax. You are required to give us this information.

Purpose of Form.—Use Form 4868 to ask for an automatic 4-month extension of time to file **Form 1040A** or **Form 1040.** The 4-month extension period includes the automatic 2-month extension granted to U.S. citizens and resident aliens who are living or traveling outside the United States and Puerto Rico on the due date for filing their returns. Do not file this form if:

- You want the IRS to figure your tax, or
- You are under a court order to file your return by the regular due date.

The extension will be granted if you complete this form properly, file it on time, **and pay with it the amount of tax shown on line 6.** We will notify you only if your request for an extension is denied.

Note: *Any extension of time granted for filing your 1986* ***calendar*** *year income tax return also extends the time for filing a gift tax return for 1986.*

Filing Form 2688.—Except in cases of undue hardship, we will not accept Form 2688, Application for Additional Extension of Time To File U.S. Individual Income Tax Return, until you have first used Form 4868.

If you have filed Form 4868 and still need more time, use Form 2688 or write a letter of explanation. You must show reasonable cause. Send Form 2688 or the letter to the Internal Revenue Service Center where you file your Form 1040A or Form 1040. (See **Where To File.**)

If you need a further extension, ask for it early so that, if denied, you can still file your return on time.

Form **4868** (1986)

When To File.—File Form 4868 by April 15, 1987. If you are filing a fiscal year Form 1040, file Form 4868 by the regular due date of your return. If you were granted the automatic 2-month extension explained above, file this form by the end of the 2-month period (June 15, 1987, for a 1986 calendar year return).

You may file Form 1040A or Form 1040 any time before the 4-month period ends.

Where To File.—Mail this form to the **Internal Revenue Service Center** for the place where you live.

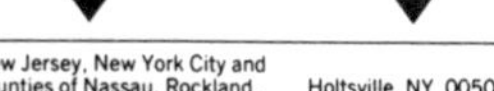

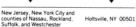

If you are located in:	Use this address:
New Jersey, New York City and counties of Nassau, Rockland, Suffolk, and Westchester	Holtsville, NY 00501
New York (all other counties), Connecticut, Maine, Massachusetts, Minnesota, New Hampshire, Rhode Island, Vermont	Andover, MA 05501
Delaware, District of Columbia, Maryland, Pennsylvania	Philadelphia, PA 19255
Alabama, Florida, Georgia, Mississippi, South Carolina	Atlanta, GA 31101
Kentucky, Michigan, Ohio, West Virginia	Cincinnati, OH 45999
Kansas, Louisiana, New Mexico, Oklahoma, Texas	Austin, TX 73301
Alaska, Arizona, California (counties of Alpine, Amador, Butte, Calaveras, Colusa, Contra Costa, Del Norte, El Dorado, Glenn, Humboldt, Lake, Lassen, Marin, Mendocino, Modoc, Napa, Nevada, Placer, Plumas, Sacramento, San Joaquin, Shasta, Sierra, Siskiyou, Solano, Sonoma, Sutter, Tehama, Trinity, Yolo, and Yuba), Colorado, Idaho, Montana, Nebraska, Nevada, North Dakota, Oregon, South Dakota, Utah, Washington, Wyoming	Ogden, UT 84201
California (all other counties), Hawaii	Fresno, CA 93888
Illinois, Iowa, Missouri, Wisconsin	Kansas City, MO 64999
Arkansas, Indiana, North Carolina, Tennessee, Virginia	Memphis, TN 37501
American Samoa	Philadelphia, PA 19255
Guam	Commissioner of Revenue and Taxation Agana, GU 96910
Puerto Rico (or if excluding income under section 933) Virgin Islands: Nonpermanent residents	Philadelphia, PA 19255
Virgin Islands: Permanent residents	V.I. Bureau of Internal Revenue P.O. Box 3186 St. Thomas, VI 00801
Foreign country: U.S. citizens and those filing Form 2555 or Form 4563, even if you have an A.P.O. or F.P.O. address	Philadelphia, PA 19255
A.P.O. or F.P.O. address of:	Miami—Atlanta, GA 31101 New York—Holtsville, NY 00501 San Francisco—Fresno, CA 93888 Seattle—Ogden, UT 84201

Penalties.—You may be charged one or both of the following penalties.

Late payment penalty.—Form 4868 does not extend the time to pay income, gift or generation-skipping transfer taxes. Generally, a penalty of 1/2 of 1% of any tax (other than estimated tax) not paid by the regular due date is charged for each month, or part of a month, that the tax remains unpaid. The penalty will not be charged if you can show reasonable cause for not paying on time. The penalty is limited to 25%.

You are considered to have reasonable cause for the period covered by this automatic extension if the amount you owe on Form 1040A, line 27, or Form 1040, line 67 (minus any estimated tax penalty):

- Is not more than 10% of the amount shown as total tax on Form 1040A, line 23, or Form 1040, line 55, and
- Is paid with Form 1040A or Form 1040.

If both of the above conditions are not met, the late payment penalty will apply, unless you show reasonable cause.

If you have reasonable cause, attach a statement to your return giving your reason.

If you cannot show reasonable cause, figure the penalty on the total tax due on Form 1040A, line 27, or Form 1040, line 67, from the regular due date of your return to the date of payment.

Late filing penalty.—A penalty is charged if your return is filed after the due date (including extensions), unless you can show reasonable cause for filing late. The penalty is 5% of the tax not paid by the regular due date for each month, or part of a month, that your return is late, but not more than 25%. If your return is more than 60 days late, the penalty will not be less than $100 or the balance of tax due on your return, whichever is smaller. If you file your return late, attach a full explanation with the return.

Interest.—Interest is charged from the regular due date of the return until the tax is paid. It will be charged even if:

- You have been granted an extension, or
- You show reasonable cause for not paying the tax on time.

Specific Instructions

Name, address, and social security numbers.—At the top of this form, fill in the spaces for your name, address, social security number, and spouse's social security number if you are filing a joint return. If the post office does not deliver mail to your street address and you have a P.O. Box, enter your P.O.Box number on the line for your present home address instead of your street address.

If you expect to file a gift tax return **(Form 709** or **Form 709-A)** for 1986, generally due by April 15, 1987, check the box on the front of this form. Below that, if you are on a fiscal year, fill in the date on which your 4-month extension will end and the date your tax year ends.

Note: *If you were granted the automatic 2-month extension because you were a U.S. citizen or resident alien outside the country and are filing Form 4868 to ask for an additional 2-month extension, write "Taxpayer Abroad" across the top of this form.*

Line 1.—Enter the total amount of income tax you expect to owe for 1986 (the amount you expect to enter on Form 1040A, line 23, or Form 1040, line 55, when you file your return). Be sure to estimate the amount correctly. If you underestimate this amount, you may be charged a penalty as explained earlier under **Penalties.**

Line 6.—Form 4868 does not extend the time to pay your income tax. Therefore, you must pay the amount of income tax shown on line 6 in full with this form.

Line 7.—If you plan to use the extension of time to file your gift tax return, enter the amount of gift tax and generation-skipping transfer tax (GST tax) you expect to owe for 1986. To avoid the late payment penalty, you must pay this amount in full with Form 4868 unless you specifically request an extension to pay these taxes. To request an extension to pay the gift tax and GST tax only, you must attach a statement to this form that paying these taxes on the due date would cause you undue hardship (not merely inconvenience).

If your spouse is filing a separate Form 4868, enter on your form only the total gift tax and GST tax you expect to owe.

If you are filing Form 4868 with your spouse, enter on line 7 the total gift tax and GST tax the two of you expect to owe. However, if each of you expects to file a gift tax return, also show in the space to the right of line 7 how much gift tax and GST tax each expects to owe for 1986.

Signature by Taxpayers.—Generally, both spouses must sign this form for the extension to be valid if a joint return is to be filed. But if one spouse cannot sign because of illness, absence, or other good cause, the other spouse may sign for both, provided a proper explanation is attached explaining why that spouse cannot sign this form.

Signature by Other than Taxpayer.—Persons who may sign for the taxpayers include attorneys or certified public accountants qualified to practice before the IRS, enrolled agents, or any person holding a power of attorney. If the taxpayer cannot sign because of illness, absence, or other good cause, a person in close personal or business relationship to the taxpayer may sign provided a proper explanation is attached as to why the taxpayer cannot sign this form. It is not necessary that such person hold a power of attorney.

How To Claim Credit for Payment Made With This Form.—If you file Form 1040A, include the amount paid (line 6) with this form in the total on Form 1040A, line 25. Also write "Form 4868" and the amount paid in the space to the left of line 25. If you file Form 1040, enter the amount paid (line 6) with this form on Form 1040, line 59.

If you and your spouse file separate Forms 4868 for 1986, but file a joint income tax return for the year, enter on the appropriate line of your Form 1040A or Form 1040, the total of the amounts paid on the separate Forms 4868. Also enter the social security numbers of both spouses in the spaces on your return.

If you and your spouse file a joint Form 4868 for 1986, but file separate income tax returns for the year, you may claim the total tax payment (line 6) on your separate return or on your spouse's separate return or you may divide it in any agreed amounts. Be sure to enter the social security numbers of both spouses on the separate returns.

☆ U.S. Government Printing Office: 1986—493-252 23-0916750

Form **4952**

Department of the Treasury
Internal Revenue Service

Investment Interest Expense Deduction

▶ See instructions on back.
▶ Attach to your tax return.

OMB No. 1545-0191
1986
Attachment Sequence No. 72

Name(s) as shown on return | Identifying number

Kind of return . . . ▶ ☐ Individual ☐ Estate ☐ Trust

Part I Interest on Investment Debts Incurred Before December 17, 1969

Note: *Use Part I only if you have investment interest expense on debts incurred before December 17, 1969, in addition to debts incurred on or after that date.*

1	Interest expense on investment debts incurred before December 17, 1969	1	
2	Total net investment income	2	
3	Net investment income allocable to the period before December 17, 1969: $\frac{\text{Line 1}}{\text{Line 1 + Line 7 + Line 15 + Line 27}}$ x Line 2	3	
4	Subtract line 3 from line 2—Enter here and on line 10(a)	4	

Part II Interest on Investment Debts Incurred After September 10, 1975

5	Interest expense on investment debts incurred after September 10, 1975			5	
6	Carryover—Enter amount from 1985 Form 4952, line 14 (see instructions)			6	
7	Total investment interest expense (add lines 5 and 6)			7	
8a	Individuals enter $10,000 ($5,000 if married filing separately)	8a			
b	Additional limitation	8b			
9	Estates enter $10,000; trusts enter zero	9			
10a	Total net investment income (amount from line 4 if Part I is used) 10a				
b	$\frac{\text{Line 7}}{\text{Line 7 + Line 15 + Line 27}}$ x Line 10(a)	10b			
11	Excess expenses from "net lease property"	11			
12	Limitation on deduction (add lines 8(a), (b), 9, 10(b) and 11)			12	
13	Allowable investment interest deduction—Enter the smaller of line 7 or line 12 (see instructions)			13	
14	Disallowed investment interest to be carried over to 1987 (subtract line 13 from line 7)			14	

Part III Interest on Investment Debts Incurred Before September 11, 1975, and After December 16, 1969

15	Interest expense on investment debts incurred before September 11, 1975, and after December 16, 1969			15	
16	Individuals enter $25,000 ($12,500 if married filing separately)	16			
17	Estates enter $25,000; trusts enter zero	17			
18	Net investment income (subtract line 10(b) from line 10(a))	18			
19	Excess expenses from "net lease property"	19			
20	Net long-term capital gain minus net short-term capital loss from sale or exchange of property held for investment	20			
	Note: *To adjust this gain on Schedule D or Form 4798, see Schedule D (Form 1040) instructions.*				
21	Tentative limitation (add lines 16 through 20)			21	
22	Subtract line 21 from line 15. If line 21 is more than line 15, enter zero			22	
23	Additional deduction (50% of line 22)			23	
24	Limitation on deduction (add lines 21 and 23)			24	
25	Allowable investment interest deduction—Enter the smaller of line 15 or line 24 (see instructions)			25	
26	Disallowed investment interest to be carried over to 1987 (subtract line 25 from line 15)			26	

Part IV Investment Interest Expense Carryover From Earlier Years—Incurred Before September 11, 1975

27	Carryover—Enter the sum of the amounts from your 1985 Form 4952, lines 26 and 35 (see instructions)			27	
28	Enter amount reportable on line 18 plus $25,000*	28			
29	Enter the larger of line 15 or $25,000*	29			
30	Subtract line 29 from line 28. If line 29 is larger than line 28, enter zero	30			
31	Enter 50% of line 30			31	
32	Allowable investment interest deduction (enter the smaller of line 27 or line 31)			32	
33	Interest carryover from earlier years disallowed in 1986 (subtract line 32 from line 27)			33	
34	Enter the 60% capital gain deduction from your 1986 Schedule D or 1986 Form 4798			34	
35	Interest carryover to 1987 (subtract line 34 from line 33)			35	

*$12,500, if married filing separately; zero, if a trust.

For Paperwork Reduction Act Notice, see back of form. Form **4952** (1986)

General Instructions

(Section references are to the Internal Revenue Code)

Paperwork Reduction Act Notice.—We ask for this information to carry out the Internal Revenue laws of the United States. We need it to ensure that taxpayers are complying with these laws and to allow us to figure and collect the right amount of tax. You are required to give us this information.

Purpose of Form.—If you paid or accrued interest during 1986 on debts you incurred to buy or hold investment property, the amount of interest you can deduct may be limited. The term "interest" for this purpose includes any allowable deduction in connection with personal property used in a short sale. Property held for investment includes all investments held for producing taxable income or gain. This includes rental property that is net lease property. It does not include property used in a trade or business.

Use Form 4952 to figure your allowable deduction for investment interest expense if a, b, or d apply.

a. Fill in Part II if in 1986, you paid or accrued more than $10,000 in interest ($5,000 if married filing separately; zero if a trust) on investment debts incurred after September 10, 1975.

b. Fill in Part III if in 1986, you paid or accrued more than $25,000 in interest ($12,500 if married filing separately; zero if a trust) on investment debts incurred before September 11, 1975, and after December 16, 1969.

c. Fill in Part I if in 1986, a, b, or d applies, and you also paid or accrued interest on investment debts incurred before December 17, 1969.

d. Fill in Part IV if in 1985, you had interest from Parts III or IV not allowed due to the limitations.

Source of Amounts to Include.—

a. Your own investment interest expense and other items used in the computation.

b. Partnership and S Corporation.—Your pro-rata share of investment interest expense and other items used in the computation, as reported on the Schedule K-1 (Form 1065 or 1120S) that you get from the partnership or corporation.

c. Estates and Trusts.—When there is distributable net income, include your share of: (1) the net investment income, and (2) the excess of net long-term capital gain over net short-term capital loss from the sale or exchange of investment property.

Net lease property.—Rental income is to be considered trade or business income unless it is from net lease property. Then it is treated as investment income. Rental property is net lease property if:

(a) You (the lessor) either are guaranteed a specific return of income or are guaranteed in whole or in part against loss of income; or

(b) Your 1986 deductions for the property that are allowable **only** because of section 162 (except rents and reimbursed amounts) are less than 15% of the rental income produced by the property. For this 15% test, you may elect to: (1) treat all leased portions of a parcel of real property as subject to a single lease, and (2) exempt real property that has been in use for more than 5 years.

In figuring your section 162 deduction for purposes of (b), do not include expenses such as depreciation, taxes, interest, etc.

Line-by-Line Instructions

Identifying Number.—Individuals, enter your social security number. Estates and trusts, enter your employer identification number.

Preparing Form 4952.—First complete lines 1, 5 through 7, 15, and 27. Then complete the form in numerical sequence starting with line 2, if applicable.

Line 1.—Enter your total investment interest expense from all sources, on debts created before December 17, 1969, from a specific item of property for a specified term. Also include debts in existence after December 16, 1969, if a binding contract was in effect on that date. Enter only the interest you paid or accrued in 1986, depending on your method of accounting.

Lines 2, 10, and 18.—Enter your net investment income from all sources required to be reported on your tax return for 1986. This cannot be less than zero.

If you have an entry on line 1 and had net investment income in 1986, complete lines 2, 3, and 4. Then enter the figure from line 4 on line 10(a). If you do not have an entry on line 1, enter your total net investment income on line 10(a).

Allocate your net investment income for all periods before December 17, 1969, before September 11, 1975 and after December 16, 1969, and after September 10, 1975. The formulas on lines 3 and 10(b) are for this purpose.

Net investment income is the amount by which investment income exceeds investment expenses. Investment income and expenses do not include any amounts connected with a trade or business.

Investment income includes the following that are includible in gross income: Interest, dividends, rents from net lease property, royalties, net short-term capital gains from investment property, and amounts recaptured as ordinary income from the sale or exchange of investment property subject to sections 1245, 1250 and 1254.

Investment expenses are those deductions directly connected with the production of investment income. Interest is not included in investment expenses for this purpose. You may figure depreciation using the straight line method. You may figure depletion based on cost.

Line 5.—Enter your total investment interest expense from all sources, for obligations incurred after September 10, 1975. Do not include those obligations for which a binding contract was in effect on September 11, 1975. Enter only the interest you paid or accrued in 1986, depending on your method of accounting.

Lines 6 and 27.—Enter interest disallowed in 1985 because of the limitations, but do not include any amount which would have reduced taxable income below zero and would not have increased a net operating loss available for carryback or carryover. The carryover retains its same character. For example, treat interest on investment debts incurred after September 10, 1975, when carried over as if it were incurred after that date and subject to the same limitations.

Line 8(b).—If you incurred investment interest in connection with acquiring stock in a corporation or a partnership interest, and you, your spouse, and children own 50% or more of the stock or the capital interest in that enterprise, enter the smaller of $15,000 ($7,500 if married filing separately) or the amount of this interest.

Lines 11 and 19.—Excess expenses from net lease property is the amount by which the expenses allowable under sections 162, 163 (without any reduction for the limitations of section 163(d)), 164(a)(1) or (2), and 212 attributable to property subject to a net lease, are more than the income produced by this property.

Lines 13 and 25.—This is the allowable investment interest expense. Deduct it as an itemized deduction on Schedule A (Form 1040) unless part or all of it is from net lease property. Deduct that part on Schedule E (Form 1040), Part I.

Deduct the pro-rata share of allowable investment interest from a partnership or S corporation on Schedule A (Form 1040), unless the partnership or corporation notifies you that all or part of it relates to net lease property. Deduct that part on Schedule E (Form 1040), Part II, column (e).

Estates and trusts, deduct the allowable part of investment interest on the interest line of your tax return.

Figure the allowable parts for each of the above by the following formula:

$$\frac{\text{Part of investment interest}}{\text{Total investment interest}} \times \text{Total allowable investment interest}$$

All interest on investment debts incurred before December 17, 1969 is allowed without limitation.

Caution: *If you (1) paid or accrued investment interest for any activity you engaged in for the production of income, except the holding of real property (other than mineral property) placed in service before 1987, and (2) you have amounts for which you are not "at risk" in the activity, you must also use Form 6198, Computation of Deductible Loss From an Activity Described in Section 465(c), to figure your deductible investment interest. After you figure the allowable investment interest, carry the applicable portion to line 4 of Form 6198. You must reduce your interest deduction that you carry from this form to Schedule A or E, by the amount you carry to Form 6198. See Form 6198 and its separate instructions for more information, especially the instructions for line 4 of that form.*

Line 15.—Enter your total investment interest expense from all sources, from a specific item of property for a specified term, and from debts incurred before September 11, 1975, and after December 16, 1969. Also include obligations incurred after September 10, 1975, but subject to a written contract or commitment in effect on September 11, 1975. Enter only the interest you paid or accrued in 1986, depending on your method of accounting.

Line 32.—This is the investment interest from earlier years that is allowable this year. Allocate this amount according to the formula in the instructions for lines 13 and 25. Use the percentages obtained in years in which the carryovers were created.

Form **5305**
(Rev. November 1983)
Department of the Treasury
Internal Revenue Service

Individual Retirement Trust Account

(Under Section 408(a) of the Internal Revenue Code)

OMB No. 1545-0365

Do NOT File with Internal Revenue Service

State of ▶ .... } SS ☐ Amendment

County of ▶

Grantor's name .... Grantor's date of birth .... Grantor's social security number .... Grantor's address ....
Trustee's name .... Trustee's address or principal place of business ....

The Grantor whose name appears above is establishing an individual retirement account (under section 408(a) of the Internal Revenue Code) to provide for his or her retirement and for the support of his or her beneficiaries after death.

The Trustee named above has given the Grantor the disclosure statement required under the Income Tax Regulations under section 408(i) of the Code.

The Grantor has assigned the trust .... dollars ($ ....) in cash.

The Grantor and the Trustee make the following agreement:

Article I

The Trustee may accept additional cash contributions on behalf of the Grantor for a tax year of the Grantor. The total cash contributions are limited to $2,000 for the tax year unless the contribution is a rollover contribution described in section 402(a)(5), 402(a)(7), 403(a)(4), 403(b)(8), 405(d)(3), 408(d)(3), or 409(b)(3)(C) of the Code or an employer contribution to a simplified employee pension plan as described in section 408(k).

Article II

The Grantor's interest in the balance in the trust account is nonforfeitable.

Article III

1. No part of the trust funds may be invested in life insurance contracts, nor may the assets of the trust account be commingled with other property except in a common trust fund or common investment fund (within the meaning of section 408(a)(5) of the Code).

2. No part of the trust funds may be invested in collectibles (within the meaning of section 408(m) of the Code).

Article IV

1. The Grantor's entire interest in the trust account must be, or begin to be, distributed before the end of the tax year in which the Grantor reaches age 70½. By the end of that tax year, the Grantor may elect, in a manner acceptable to the trustee, to have the balance in the trust account distributed in:

(a) A single sum payment.

(b) An annuity contract that provides equal or substantially equal monthly, quarterly, or annual payments over the life of the Grantor. The payments must begin by the end of that tax year.

(c) An annuity contract that provides equal or substantially equal monthly, quarterly, or annual payments over the joint and last survivor lives of the Grantor and his or her spouse. The payments must begin by the end of the tax year.

(d) Equal or substantially equal monthly, quarterly, or annual payments over a specified period that may not be longer than the Grantor's life expectancy.

(e) Equal or substantially equal monthly, quarterly, or annual payments over a specified period that may not be longer than the joint life and last survivor expectancy of the Grantor and his or her spouse.

Even if distributions have begun to be made under option (d) or (e), the Grantor may receive a distribution of the balance in the trust account at any time by giving written notice to the trustee. If the grantor does not choose any of the methods of distribution described above by the end of the tax year in which he or she reaches age 70½, distribution to the Grantor will be made before the end of that tax year by a single sum payment. If the Grantor elects as a means of distribution (b) or (c) above, the annuity contract must satisfy the requirements of section 408(b)(1), (3), (4), and (5) of the Code. If the Grantor elects as a means of distribution (d) or (e) above, figure the payments made in tax years beginning in the tax year the Grantor reaches age 70½ as follows:

(i) For the minimum annual payment, divide the Grantor's entire interest in the trust account at the beginning of each year by the life expectancy of the Grantor (or the joint life and last survivor expectancy of the Grantor and his or her spouse, or the period specified under (d) or (e), whichever applies). Determine the life expectancy in either case on the date the Grantor reaches 70½ minus the number of whole years passed since the Grantor became 70½.

(ii) For the minimum monthly payment, divide the result in (i) above by 12.

(iii) For the minimum quarterly payment, divide the result in (i) above by 4.

2. If the Grantor dies before his or her entire interest in the account is distributed to him or her, or if distribution is being made as provided in (e) above to his or her surviving spouse, and the surviving spouse dies before the entire interest is distributed, the entire remaining undistributed interest will, within 5 years after the Grantor's death or the death of the surviving spouse, be distributed to the beneficiary or beneficiaries of the Grantor or the Grantor's surviving spouse. However, the preceding distribution is not required if distributions over a specified term began before the death of the Grantor and the term is for a period permitted under (d) or (e) above and distributions continue over that period.

If the Grantor dies before his or her entire interest has been distributed and if the beneficiary is other than the surviving spouse, no additional cash contributions or rollover contributions may be accepted in the account.

Article V

Unless the Grantor dies, is disabled (as defined in section 72(m) of the Code), or reaches age 59½ before any amount is distributed from the trust account, the Trustee must receive from the Grantor a statement explaining how he or she intends to dispose of the amount distributed.

For Paperwork Reduction Act Notice, see back of this form.

Article VI

1. The Grantor agrees to provide the Trustee with information necessary for the Trustee to prepare any reports required under section 408(i) of the Code and related regulations.

2. The Trustee agrees to submit reports to the Internal Revenue Service and the Grantor as prescribed by the Internal Revenue Service.

Article VII

Notwithstanding any other articles which may be added or incorporated, the provisions of Articles I through III and this sentence will be controlling. Any additional articles that are not consistent with section 408(a) of the Code and related regulations will be invalid.

Article VIII

This agreement will be amended from time to time to comply with the provisions of the Code and related regulations. Other amendments may be made with the consent of the persons whose signatures appear below.

Note: *The following space (Article IX) may be used for any other provisions you wish to add. If you do not wish to add any other provisions, draw a line through this space. If you add provisions, they must comply with applicable requirements of State law and the Internal Revenue Code.*

Article IX

Grantor's signature ....

Trustee's signature ....

Date ....

Witness ....
(Use only if signature of the Grantor or the Trustee is required to be witnessed.)

Instructions

(Section references are to the Internal Revenue Code unless otherwise noted.)

Paperwork Reduction Act Notice

The Paperwork Reduction Act of 1980 says that we must tell you why we are collecting this information, how it is to be used, and whether you have to give it to us. The information is used to determine if you are entitled to a deduction for contributions to this trust. Your completing this information is only required if you want a qualified individual retirement account.

Purpose of Form

This model trust may be used by an individual who wishes to adopt an individual retirement account under section 408(a). When fully executed by the Grantor and the Trustee not later than the time prescribed by law for filing the Federal income tax return for the Grantor's tax year (including any extensions thereof), an individual will have an individual retirement account (IRA) trust which meets the requirements of section 408(a). This trust must be created in the United States for the exclusive benefit of the Grantor or his/her beneficiaries.

Definitions

Trustee.—The trustee must be a bank or savings and loan asociation, as defined in section 408(n), or other person who has the approval of the Internal Revenue Service to act as trustee.

Grantor.—The grantor is the person who establishes the trust account.

IRA for Non-Working Spouse

Contributions to an IRA trust account for a non-working spouse must be made to a separate IRA trust account established by the non-working spouse.

This form may be used to establish the IRA trust for the non-working spouse.

An employee's social security number will serve as the identification number of his or her individual retirement account. An employer identification number is not required for each individual retirement account, nor for a common fund created for individual retirement accounts.

For more information, get a copy of the required disclosure statement from your trustee or get **Publication 590,** Individual Retirement Arrangements (IRA's).

Specific Instructions

Article IV.—Distributions made under this Article may be made in a single sum, periodic payment, or a combination of both. The distribution option should be reviewed in the year the Grantor reaches age 70½ to make sure the requirements of section 408(a)(6) have been met. For example, if a Grantor elects distributions over a period permitted in (d) or (e) of Article IV, the period may not extend beyond the life expectancy of the Grantor at age 70½ (under option (d)) or the joint life and last survivor expectancy of the Grantor (at age 70½) and the Grantor's spouse (under option (e)). For this purpose, life expectancies must be determined by using the expected return multiples in section 1.72-9 of the Income Tax Regulations (26 CFR Part 1). The balance in the account as of the beginning of each tax year beginning on or after the Grantor reaches age 70½ will be used in computing the payments described in (d) and (e) of Article IV. Article IV does not preclude a mode of distribution different from those described in (a) through (e) of Article IV prior to the close of the tax year of the Grantor in which he/she reaches age 70½.

Article IX.—This Article and any that follow it may incorporate additional provisions that are agreed upon by the grantor and trustee to complete the agreement. These may include, for example: definitions, investment powers, voting rights, exculpatory provisions, amendment and termination, removal of trustee, trustee's fees, State law requirements, beginning date of distributions, accepting only cash, treatment of excess contributions, prohibited transactions with the grantor, etc. Use additional pages if necessary and attach them to this form.

Note: *This form may be reproduced and reduced in size for adoption to passbook or card purposes.*

☆U.S. Government Printing Office: 1984—461-495/10064

Form **5305-SEP**
(Rev December 1985)
Department of the Treasury
Internal Revenue Service

Simplified Employee Pension-Individual Retirement Accounts Contribution Agreement

(Under Section 408(k) of the Internal Revenue Code)

OMB No. 1545-0499
Expires 10-31-88

Do NOT File with Internal Revenue Service

______________________________ makes the following agreement under the terms of section 408(k) of
(Business name—employer)
the Internal Revenue Code and the instructions to this form.

The employer agrees to provide for discretionary contributions in each calendar year to the Individual Retirement Accounts or Individual Retirement Annuities (IRA's) of all eligible employees who are at least ________ years old (not over 25 years old) (see instruction "Who May Participate") and worked in at least ________ years (not over 3 years) of the immediately preceding 5 calendar years (see instruction "Who May Participate"). This ☐ includes ☐ does not include employees covered under a collective bargaining agreement and ☐ includes ☐ does not include employees whose total compensation during the tax year is less than $200.

The employer agrees that contributions made on behalf of each eligible employee will:

- Be made only on the first $200,000 of compensation (as adjusted per Code section 408(k)(3)(C)).
- Be made in an amount that is the same percentage of total compensation for every employee.
- Be limited to the smaller of 15% of compensation or $30,000 as adjusted per section 415(d)(1)(B) for cost of living changes.
- Be paid to the employee's IRA trustee, custodian, or insurance company (for an annuity contract).

______________________________ Signature of employer ______________ Date

______________________________ By

Instructions for the Employer

(Section references are to the Internal Revenue Code, unless otherwise noted.)

Paperwork Reduction Act Notice.—The Paperwork Reduction Act of 1980 says we must tell you why we are collecting this information, how it is to be used, and whether you have to give it to us. The information is used to determine if you are entitled to a deduction for contributions made to a SEP. Your completing this form is only required if you want to establish a Model SEP.

Purpose of Form.— Form 5305-SEP (Model SEP) is used by an employer to make an agreement to provide benefits to all employees under a Simplified Employee Pension (SEP) plan described in section 408(k). This form is NOT to be filed with IRS.

What Is a SEP Plan?— A SEP provides an employer with a simplified way to make contributions toward an employee's retirement income. Under a SEP the employer is permitted to contribute a certain amount (see below) to an employee's Individual Retirement Account or Individual Retirement Annuity (IRA's). The employer makes contributions directly to an IRA set up by an employee with a bank, insurance company, or other qualified financial institution. When using this form to establish a SEP, the IRA must be a model IRA established on an IRS form or a master or prototype IRA for which IRS has issued a favorable opinion letter. Making the agreement on Form 5305-SEP does not establish an employer IRA as described under section 408(c).

This form may not be used by an employer who:

- Currently maintains any other qualified retirement plan.
- Has maintained in the past a defined benefit plan, even if now terminated.
- Has any eligible employees for whom IRA's have not been established.
- Uses the services of leased employees (as described in section 414(n)).
- Is a member of an affiliated service group (as described in section 414(m)), a controlled group of corporations (as described in section 414(b)), or trades or businesses under common control (as described in section 414(c)), UNLESS all eligible employees of all the members of such groups, trades or businesses, participate under the SEP.

Who May Participate.— Any employee who is at least 25 years old and has performed "service" for you in at least 3 years of the immediately preceding 5 calendar years must be permitted to participate in the SEP. However, you may establish less restrictive eligibility requirements if you choose. "Service" is any work performed for you for any period of time, however short. Further, if you are a member of an affiliated service group, a controlled group of corporations, or trades or businesses under common control, "service" includes any work performed for any period of time for any other member of such group, trades or businesses. Generally, to make the agreement, all eligible employees (including all eligible employees, if any, of other members of an affiliated service group, a controlled group of corporations, or trades or businesses under common control) must participate in the plan. However, employees covered under a collective bargaining agreement and certain nonresident aliens may be excluded if section 410(b)(3)(A) or 410(b)(3)(C) applies to them. Employees whose total compensation for the tax year is less than $200 may be excluded.

Amount of Contributions.— You are not required to make any contributions to an employee's SEP-IRA in a given year. However, if you do make contributions, you must make them to the IRA's of all eligible employees, whether or not they are still employed at the time contributions are made. The contributions made must be the same percentage of each employee's total compensation (up to a maximum compensation base of $200,000 as adjusted per section 408(k)(3)(C) for cost of living changes). The contributions you make in a calendar year for any one employee may not be more than the smaller of $30,000 or 15% of that employee's total compensation (figured without considering the SEP-IRA contributions).

For this purpose, compensation includes:

- Amounts received for personal services actually performed (see section 1.219-1(c) of the Income Tax Regulations); and
- Earned income defined under section 401(c)(2).

In making contributions, you may not discriminate in favor of any employee who is an officer, a more than 10% shareholder, a self-employed individual, or an employee who is highly compensated.

Under this form you may not integrate your SEP contributions with, or offset them by, contributions made under the Federal Insurance Contributions Act (FICA).

How to Report Contributions.— You must include the amount you contribute to the SEP-IRA of an employee in the employee's gross income on Form W-2 for the calendar year for which the amount is contributed. Report the amount of the SEP contributions in the "Employer's use" box on Form W-2. For example, for an employee with annual compensation of $22,000 which includes $2,000 of SEP contributions, enter "$22,000" in the box on Form W-2 labeled "Wages, tips, and other compensation." In the "Employer's use" box, enter "$2,000-SEP" to indicate the SEP contributions for the year.

You may choose to treat contributions made in the first 3½ months of a calendar year as made in the prior year, even though a Form W-2 was already issued for the prior year. To do so, you must complete an additional Form W-2 for the prior year and show the SEP contributions made in the first 3½ months of the following year. For example, if you treat $150 of contributions made in the first 3½ months of a year as additional contributions for the prior year, you would issue a new Form W-2 showing $150 of wages, tips, and other compensation and "$150-SEP" in the "Employer's use" box.

Currently, employers who have established a SEP using this agreement and have provided each participant with a copy of this form, including the questions and answers, are not required to file the annual information returns, Forms 5500, 5500-C, or 5500-R for the SEP.

Deducting Contributions.— You may deduct all allowable contributions under section 404(h). If your tax year is the calendar year, you may take the employer deductions for that tax year, subject to the limits of section 404, for contributions made either during the year or by April 15 of the following year. If the tax year and calendar year do not coincide, you may only deduct contributions made for a calendar year for the tax year in which the calendar year ends. If you use a fiscal year, contributions for a calendar year must be made no later than 3½ months after the end of that calendar year.

Making the Agreement.— This agreement is considered made when IRA's have been established for all of your eligible employees, you have completed all blanks on the agreement form without modification, and you have given all your eligible employees copies of the agreement form, instructions, and questions and answers.

Keep the agreement form with your records; do not file it with IRS.

Information for the Employee

The information provided explains what a Simplified Employee Pension plan is, how contributions are made, and how to treat your employer's contributions for tax purposes.

Please read the questions and answers carefully. For more specific information, also see the agreement form and instructions to your employer on this form.

Questions and Answers

1. Q. What is a Simplified Employee Pension, or SEP?

A. A SEP is a retirement income arrangement under which your employer may contribute any amount each year up to the smaller of $30,000 or 15% of your compensation into **your own** Individual Retirement Account/Annuity (IRA).

Your employer will provide you with a copy of the agreement containing participation requirements and a description of the basis upon which employer contributions may be made to your IRA.

All amounts contributed to your IRA by your employer belong to you, even after you separate from service with that employer.

2. Q. Must my employer contribute to my IRA under the SEP?

A. Whether or not your employer makes a contribution to the SEP is entirely within the employer's discretion. If a contribution is made under the SEP, it must be allocated to all the eligible employees according to the SEP agreement. The Model SEP specifies that the contribution on behalf of each eligible employee will be the same percentage of compensation (excluding compensation higher than $200,000) for all employees.

3. Q. How much may my employer contribute to my SEP-IRA in any year?

A. Under the Model SEP **(Form 5305-SEP)** that your employer has adopted, your employer will determine the amount of contribution to be made to your IRA each year. However, the contribution for any year is limited to the smaller of $30,000 or 15% of your compensation for that year. The compensation used to determine this limit does not include any amount which is contributed by your employer to your IRA under the SEP. The agreement does not require an employer to maintain a particular level of contributions. It is possible that for a given year no employer contribution will be made on an employee's behalf.

Also see Question 5.

4. Q. How do I treat my employer's SEP contributions for my taxes?

A. The amount your employer contributes will be included in your gross income reported on Form W-2. The amount of the employer's SEP contribution will be shown in the "Employer's use" box on Form W-2. For example, an employee with annual compensation of $27,000 which includes $3,500 of SEP contributions, would receive a Form W-2 for the year showing $27,000 of wages, tips, and other compensation. In the "Employer's use" box "$3,500-SEP" would be shown. You will be entitled to an offsetting deduction on your tax return for this amount. (If your employer contributes more than the limit on your behalf see Question 12.) Because contributions for a particular calendar year may be made through April 15 following that calendar year, it is possible that your employer may make a contribution that is not reflected on your original W-2. In that case, your employer must provide you with an additional W-2 which includes the amount of that contribution.

5. Q. May I also contribute to my IRA if my employer has a SEP?

A. Yes, you may contribute an amount up to your normal IRA limitation.

Also see Question 12.

6. Q. Are there any restrictions on the IRA I select to deposit my SEP contributions in?

A. Under the Model SEP that is approved by IRS, contributions must be made to either a Model IRA which is executed on an IRS form or a master or prototype IRA for which IRS has issued a favorable opinion letter.

Also see Question 7.

7. Q. My spouse and I both have IRA's. Can my employer contribute the SEP contribution to my spouse's IRA?

A. Although there is no prohibition against this, it may result in adverse tax consequences. Your employer's entire contribution will be included in your income for that year, but all or part of the offsetting deduction may be disallowed. A transaction of this sort could result in complex tax consequences requiring professional advice.

8. Q. What if I don't want a SEP-IRA?

A. Your employer may require that you become a participant in such an arrangement as a condition of employment. However, if the employer does not require all eligible employees to become participants and an eligible employee elects not to participate, all other employees of the same employer are prohibited from entering into a SEP-IRA arrangement with that employer. If one or more eligible employees do not participate and the employer attempts to establish a SEP-IRA agreement with the remaining employees, the resulting arrangement will not result in any tax advantage and may in fact result in adverse tax consequences to the participating employees.

9. Q. Can I move funds from my SEP-IRA to another tax-sheltered IRA?

A. Yes, it is permissible for you to withdraw, or receive, funds from your SEP-IRA, and no more than 60 days later, place such funds in another IRA, or SEP-IRA. This is called a "rollover" and may not be done without penalty more frequently than at one-year intervals. However, there are no restrictions on the number of times you may make "transfers" if you arrange to have such funds transferred between the trustees, so that you never have possession.

10. Q. What happens if I withdraw my employer's contribution from my IRA?

A. If you don't want to leave the employer's contribution in your IRA, you may withdraw it at any time, but any amount withdrawn is includible in your income. Also, if withdrawals occur before attainment of age 59 ½, and not on account of death or disability, you may be subject to a penalty tax.

11. Q. May I participate in a SEP even though I'm covered by another plan?

A. An employer may not adopt this IRS Model SEP **(Form 5305-SEP)** if the employer maintains another qualified retirement plan or has ever maintained a qualified defined benefit plan. However, if you work for several employers, you may be covered by a SEP of one employer and a pension or profit-sharing plan of another employer.

Also see Questions 12 and 13.

12. Q. What happens if too much is contributed to my SEP-IRA in one year?

A. Any contribution by you or by your employer that is more than the yearly deduction limitations may be withdrawn without penalty by the due date (plus extensions) for filing your tax return (normally April 15th). Excess contributions left in your SEP-IRA account after that time are subject to a 6% excise tax. Withdrawals of those contributions may be taxed as premature withdrawals.

Also see Question 10.

13. Q. What happens if I have two or more employers who maintain SEP's?

A. If you are employed by two or more employers who maintain SEP's, the amount that you can deduct will depend upon the compensation received from each employer. For example, if employer A maintains a SEP and your compensation from employer A is $20,000, the maximum amount that you will be able to deduct is $3,000 (15% × $20,000) for contributions under employer A's SEP. If employer B maintains a SEP and your compensation from employer B is $10,000, the maximum amount that you will be able to deduct is $1,500 (15% × $10,000) for contributions under employer B's SEP. Therefore, your total SEP deduction would be no greater than $4,500.

14. Q. Do I need to file any additional forms with IRS because I participate in a SEP?

A. No.

15. Q. Is my employer required to provide me with information about SEP-IRA's and the SEP agreement?

A. Yes, your employer must provide you with a copy of the executed SEP agreement **(Form 5305-SEP)**, these Questions and Answers, and provide a statement each year showing any contribution to your IRA.

Also see Question 4.

16. Q. Is the financial institution where I establish my IRA also required to provide me with information?

A. Yes, it must provide you with a disclosure statement which contains the following items of information in plain, nontechnical, language:

(1) the statutory requirements which relate to your IRA;

(2) the tax consequences which follow the exercise of various options and what those options are;

(3) participation eligibility rules, and rules on the deduction for retirement savings;

(4) the circumstances and procedures under which you may revoke your IRA, including the name, address, and telephone number of the person designated to receive notice of revocation **(this explanation must be prominently displayed at the beginning of the disclosure statement);**

(5) explanations of when penalties may be assessed against you because of specified prohibited or penalized activities concerning your IRA; and

(6) financial disclosure information which:

(a) either projects value growth rates of your IRA under various contribution and retirement schedules, or describes the method of computing and allocating annual earnings and charges which may be assessed;

(b) describes whether, and for what period, the growth projections for the plan are guaranteed, or a statement of the earnings rate and terms on which the projection is based;

(c) states the sales commission to be charged in each year expressed as a percentage of $1,000; and

(d) states the proportional amount of any nondeductible life insurance which may be a feature of your IRA.

See **Publication 590,** Individual Retirement Arrangements (IRA's), available at most IRS offices, for a more complete explanation of the disclosure requirements.

In addition to this disclosure statement, the financial institution is required to provide you with a financial statement each year. It may be necessary to retain and refer to statements for more than one year in order to evaluate the investment performance of the IRA.

☆ U.S.G.P.O.: 1986-491-473/20082

Form **5329**

Department of the Treasury
Internal Revenue Service

Return for Individual Retirement Arrangement Taxes

(Under Sections 408(f), 4973, and 4974 of the Internal Revenue Code)
▶ Attach to Form 1040.

OMB No. 1545-0203
1986
Attachment Sequence No. 28

Name | Your social security number

Address (number and street)

City or town, state, and ZIP code

Part I Excess Contributions Tax for Individual Retirement Arrangements

Complete this part if, either in this year or in earlier years, you have contributed more to your IRA than is or was allowable as a deduction and you have an excess contribution subject to tax.

1 Excess contributions for 1986 (see Instructions for line 1). Do ***not*** include this amount on Form 1040, line 26 . . . 1

2 Earlier year excess contributions not previously eliminated (see Instructions for line 2) . . . 2

3 Contribution credit. (If your maximum allowable deduction for 1986 is more than your actual contribution, see instructions for line 3; otherwise, enter zero.) . . . 3

4a 1986 distributions out of your account that are taxable income . . . 4a

b 1985 tax year excess contributions (if any) withdrawn after the due date (including extensions) of your 1985 income tax return, and 1984 and earlier tax year excess contributions withdrawn in 1986 . . . 4b

Do ***not*** enter any withdrawn excess contributions on line 4b if in the tax year that the excess contributions were made:

- your total IRA contributions (other than rollover contributions) were more than $2,250 (or if the total contributions for the year include employer contributions to a SEP, $2,250 increased by the lesser of the amount of the employer contributions to the SEP or $30,000); or
- you took a deduction for the excess contributions on your Form 1040.

Instead, enter these withdrawn excess contributions on line 4a of Form 5329 and also on line 16 of Form 1040.

c Add lines 3 through 4b . . . 4c

5 Adjusted earlier year excess contributions (line 2 minus line 4c but not less than zero) . . . 5

6 Total excess contributions (add lines 1 and 5) . . . 6

7 Tax (6% of line 6 or 6% of the value of your IRA on the last day of 1986, whichever is smaller). Enter tax on Form 1040, line 54 . . . 7

Part II Tax on Premature Distributions

Complete this part if you received a distribution from your IRA before you reached age 59½. Also, enter the amount of the distribution on Form 1040, line 16.

8a If you entered into a prohibited transaction as described in the Instructions, borrowed any amount from one of your individual retirement annuities, or pledged any part of your individual retirement annuity contracts, enter 10% of the value of the account or annuity at the beginning of the year . . . 8a

b If in 1986 any part of your arrangement was invested in collectibles (see Instructions for line 8b), include 10% of the cost of the collectibles here . . . 8b

9 Enter 10% of the amount of the premature distributions from your arrangement during the year (see Instructions for line 9 for items that are not considered taxable distributions) . . . 9

10 Enter 10% of the amount from your individual retirement savings accounts that you pledged as security for a loan . . . 10

11 Total tax (add lines 8a through 10). Enter here and on Form 1040, line 54 . . . 11

Part III Tax on Excess Accumulation in Individual Retirement Accounts and Annuities

12 Tax based on current year distribution method (see worksheet in Instructions) . . . 12

13 Tax based on aggregate distribution method (see worksheet in Instructions) . . . 13

14 Tax due. Enter amount from line 12 or, if aggregate distribution method is applicable, enter the smaller of line 12 or line 13. Also include this amount on Form 1040, line 54 . . . 14

Please Sign Here

Under penalties of perjury, I declare that I have examined this return, including accompanying schedules and statements, and to the best of my knowledge and belief, it is true, correct, and complete. Declaration of preparer (other than taxpayer) is based on all information of which preparer has any knowledge.

▶ Your signature ▶ Date

Paid Preparer's Use Only

Preparer's signature ▶ | Date | Check if self-employed ▶ ☐ | Preparer's social security no.

Firm's name (or yours, if self-employed) and address ▶ | E.I. No. ▶ | ZIP code ▶

For Paperwork Reduction Act Notice, see page 1 of Instructions.

U.S. GPO: 1986-493-259

Form **5329** (1986)

1986  Department of the Treasury Internal Revenue Service

Instructions for Form 5329

Return for Individual Retirement Arrangement Taxes

(Section references are to the Internal Revenue Code.)

General Instructions

Paperwork Reduction Act Notice.— We ask for this information to carry out the Internal Revenue laws of the United States. We need it to ensure that taxpayers are complying with these laws and to allow us to figure and collect the right amount of tax. You are required to give us this information.

Purpose of Form.—Use this form to report any excise tax or additional income tax you owe in connection with your individual retirement account and individual retirement annuity. These two types of individual retirement arrangements are collectively referred to as an IRA in the following instructions.

Who Must File.—You must file a Form 5329 if you owe taxes on:

(i) excess contributions to your IRA under section 4973,

(ii) premature distributions from your IRA under section 408(f), or

(iii) excess accumulations in your individual retirement account or annuity under section 4974.

Do ***not*** file Form 5329 to report your deduction for contributions to your IRA. Report this deduction only on your **Form 1040** or **Form 1040A**, U.S. Individual Income Tax Return.

If you need any information about your IRA not covered in these instructions, see **Publication 590,** Individual Retirement Arrangements (IRAs).

Also, individuals who redeem their individual retirement bonds, see Publication 590.

When and Where to File.—Attach a 1986 Form 5329 to your 1986 Form 1040 and file both of them at the time (including any extension) and place for filing Form 1040. If you are paying tax for prior years, use a separate Form 5329 for the year you are paying tax. For example, if you made an excess contribution to your IRA in 1985, you must complete a separate 1985 Form 5329 and not a 1986 Form 5329 to determine the excess contributions tax that is owed for 1985.

If you do not have to file Form 1040 because you do not have enough income to require filing an income tax return or you are filing for prior years, file only a completed Form 5329 with the Internal Revenue Service at the time and place you are required to file Form 1040. Include a check or money order payable to the Internal Revenue Service for any tax due shown on lines 7, 11, or 14.

Sign and Date Form 5329.—This form is not considered a return unless you sign it. It must be signed whether it is being filed separately or attached to Form 1040.

Note: *If you are filing a joint return on Form 1040 and you are attaching Form 5329 to your return, only the name and signature of the spouse who is required to file Form 5329 should be shown on this form.*

Preparer's Number.—The paid preparer's number is needed only if you owe a tax on premature distributions. For further information about a paid preparer's signing responsibilities, see instructions for Form 1040.

Definitions

Compensation.—Compensation includes wages, salaries, professional fees, and other pay you receive for services you perform. It also includes sales commissions, commissions on insurance premiums, pay based on percent of profit, tips, and bonuses. It includes *net earnings* from self-employment, but only for a trade or business in which your personal services are a material income-producing factor. In addition, all taxable alimony received by a former or current spouse under a decree of divorce or separate maintenance is treated as compensation.

The term "compensation" does not include any amounts received as a pension or annuity and does not include any amount received as deferred compensation.

Rollover Contribution.—Generally, a rollover contribution to an IRA is an allowable contribution which is not deductible on your income tax return. See section 402(a)(6)(F) and section 402(e)(4)(M) for more information regarding distributions pursuant to qualified domestic relations orders. There are two types of rollover contributions to an IRA:

(1) transferring a distribution from a pension plan to an IRA;

(2) transferring a distribution from one IRA to another IRA.

Note: *If you instruct the trustee of your IRA to transfer funds directly to another IRA, the transfer is not considered a rollover. Do **not** include the amount transferred in income and do **not** deduct the amount transferred as a contribution to your IRA.*

(1) The first type of rollover contribution is a transfer of all or part of your interest in a qualified pension plan, profit-sharing plan, stock bonus plan, or 403(b) annuity arrangement to an IRA. To be considered as a rollover from a qualified pension, profit-sharing, or stock bonus plan, the contribution must meet requirement (a) and requirement (b), (c), or (d) below. To be considered as a rollover from a section 403(b) annuity arrangement, the contribution must meet requirement (a) and requirement (c) or (d). To be considered as a rollover from a bond purchase plan, the contribution must meet requirement (a) only.

(a) You must transfer the amount of the plan or annuity arrangement distribution you want to roll over to an IRA (other than an endowment contract) within 60 days after you receive the distribution. If the distribution is other than money, transfer to the IRA the property that you received in the distribution or the money you get from selling the property. No amount of the rollover contribution to your IRA can come from contributions you have made to the plan other than accumulated deductible employee contributions. Accumulated deductible employee contributions means any qualified voluntary contributions defined in section 219(e).

(b) Your employer ends the plan and because of this your entire interest in the plan is paid to you during one tax year (ending of contributions to a profit-sharing or stock bonus plan is considered ending a plan).

(c) You receive your entire interest in the plan or section 403(b) annuity arrangement in a lump-sum distribution.

(d) You receive a distribution of part of your interest in the plan (equal to at least 50% of your interest in the plan) and such distribution is not one of a series of periodic payments nor a qualified total distribution. You elect, as prescribed in regulations under section 402(a)(5), to treat this distribution as a rollover to your IRA. You acknowledge that the making of this election prohibits you from using the special 10-year averaging and capital gains treatment on any subsequent distributions from this plan or any other plan that meets the aggregation rules of section 402(e)(4)(C).

To have a lump-sum distribution from a plan or section 403(b) annuity arrangement, the following two conditions must be met:

(a) you must receive within one tax year the distribution to you of the total amount credited to you in a qualified pension, profit-sharing, stock bonus plan, or section 403(b) annuity arrangement, and

(b) this distribution must occur on or after the day you reach age 59½ or upon the end of your employment.

If you are self-employed, a distribution due to ending of employment applies only if it is due to disability as described in section 72(m)(7).

Do not include in your income the amount of the distribution you roll over to an IRA. See Form 1040 instructions for line 17.

Special rollover of deceased spouse's interest in a qualified pension, profit-sharing, or stock bonus plan.—If you receive all of your deceased spouse's interest in one of these qualified plans within one tax year either because the employer ends the plan or as a lump-sum distribution, you may roll over the distribution into an IRA. Transfer the part of the distribution you want to roll over to an IRA within 60 days from the date you receive it. If the part of the distribution you wish to transfer is property other than money, you must transfer to the IRA the property or the money you get from selling the property.

(2) The second type of rollover contribution occurs when you receive a distribution from one IRA (other than an inherited account or annuity) and transfer all or part of the distribution to another IRA (other than an endowment contract or an inherited account or annuity) within 60 days after you receive the distribution. However, any part of the distribution you do not transfer to the second IRA within 60 days is taxable income. If in the past you have received other nontaxable distributions like this, at least one year must have passed before you can receive this distribution and not be taxed. Based on proposed regulations, the 1-year rollover distribution rule applies to each separate IRA you own.

Premature Distribution.—Generally, any distribution from your IRA that you receive before you are age 59½ is a premature distribution.

The following are exceptions to the above general rule and are not considered premature distributions:

(1) Amount distributed because of disability (defined in section 72(m)(7)) or death; and

(2) Amount transferred to a former spouse under a divorce decree or current spouse under a separate maintenance agreement.

See Specific Instructions, Part II, for the tax on premature distributions.

Prohibited Transactions.— Transactions such as borrowing from your individual retirement account or annuity or using your account or annuity as a basis for obtaining a benefit are prohibited transactions. They cause the individual retirement account or annuity to no longer be considered an individual retirement account or annuity under section 408 as of the first day of your tax year in which the transaction occurs. Further, the entire value of your account or annuity is considered distributed to you as of the first day of your tax year. See Specific Instructions, Part II, line 8(a).

Pledging of Account.—

(1) If, during the tax year, you use any part of your account as security for a loan, that part is treated as being distributed to you.

(2) If, during the tax year, you use all or any part of your individual retirement annuity contract as security for a loan, the total value of that contract is treated as being distributed to you as of the first day of your tax year.

Also, if you are under age 59½ at the time the account or annuity is treated as being distributed to you, these distributions are subject to the tax on premature distributions. See Specific Instructions, Part II, lines 8(a) and 10.

Note: *Report any distributions received or considered to be received from your IRA as a fully taxable pension on Form 1040, line 16, except:*

(a) *Rollover contributions to another plan or IRA.*

(b) *Excess current year contributions that you withdraw from your IRA before the due date of your income tax return for the year the excess contributions were made and for which you took no deduction.*

(c) *Any excess contributions from earlier years that you withdraw, if the total contributions for the year in which the excess contributions were made are not more than $2,250 (or if the total contributions for the year include employer contributions to a SEP, increased by the lesser of the amount of the employer contributions to the SEP or $30,000) and you took no deduction for the excess contributions.*

(d) *Amounts transferred (by transfer of ownership of an IRA) to a former spouse under a divorce decree or current spouse under a separate maintenance agreement.*

(e) *Any individual retirement annuity contracts distributed to you. However, report on your income tax return any payments you received from these annuities as fully taxable annuity payments.*

Specific Instructions

Part I—Excess Contributions Tax for Individual Retirement Arrangements

If you have contributed, either this year or in earlier years, more to your IRA than is allowable as a deduction on your Form 1040 or Form 1040A, you may have to pay an excess contributions tax.

However, if you withdrew your current year excess IRA contributions before the due date (including any extension) of your current year's income tax return, the excess will not be taxable as excess IRA contributions if:

(1) you do not claim a deduction for the amount of the excess contributions withdrawn, and

(2) the withdrawal from your IRA includes any income earned on the excess contributions.

Do not include such withdrawn excess contributions on line 1, Form 5329.

However, you must include the income earned on the excess contributions withdrawn before the due date of your income tax return on Form 1040 for the year in which the contribution was made. Also report 10% of the income on line 9, Form 5329, for the year of the distribution if you have not reached age 59½ at the time you received the distribution of income.

Line 1.—Enter the excess contributions you made in 1986. You can figure this amount from the worksheet in the instructions for line 26 of Form 1040. The amount of taxable excess contributions is the difference you get by subtracting your limitation on line 4 or 10 of that worksheet from your actual contributions.

Note: *Any distribution of current year excess contributions will not be subject to the tax on premature distributions (see Part II) if you withdraw them and any income earned on them before the due date of your income tax return; if you do not take a deduction for them; and if you included all the income earned on the excess contributions withdrawn on Form 1040, line 16, and 10% of the income on Form 5329, line 9. All other withdrawals of excess contributions will not be subject to the tax on premature distributions if the total contribution for the year in which the excess contributions were made is not more than $2,250 (or if the total contributions for the year include employer contributions to a SEP, increased by the lesser of the amount of the employer contributions to the SEP or $30,000) and you did not take a deduction for the excess contributions.*

Line 2.—Enter the 1985 excess contributions not withdrawn from your IRA before the due date of your 1985 income tax return. Also enter 1984 and earlier excess contributions not withdrawn or otherwise eliminated before January 1, 1986.

Line 3.—If your maximum limitation is larger than the amount actually contributed to your IRA, and you have excess contributions from earlier years which have not been eliminated, complete the worksheet below to see if you have a contribution credit.

Line 4(a).—If you have withdrawn any money from your IRA in 1986 that must be included in your income for 1986, write the amount on line 4(a). Do not include in this amount any excess contributions withdrawn that will be reported on line 4(b).

Line 4(b).—Enter on this line any excess contributions to your IRA for 1976 through 1984 that you withdrew in 1986 and also enter any 1985 excess contributions that you withdrew after the due date (including any extensions) for your 1985 income tax return if:

(1) you did not claim a deduction for the excess contributions, and

(2) the total contributions to your IRA for the tax year for which the excess contributions were made were not more than $2,250 (or if the total contributions for the year include employer contributions to a SEP, increased by the lesser of the amount of the employer contributions to the SEP or $30,000).

Worksheet for line 3	
1 Enter amount from line 2 of the IRA worksheet in Form 1040 Instructions for line 26, but not more than $2,000 ($2,250 if you contributed to your non-working spouse's account)	
2 Enter amount that is deductible under section 219 and is contributed either to your account or to your and your nonworking spouse's accounts. (Do not include contributions under section 219(f)(6).)	
3 Contribution credit—subtract line 2 from line 1. Put this amount on line 3 of Form 5329. Also include on line 4 or 10, whichever is applicable, of the worksheet in Form 1040 Instructions for line 26 either (i) this amount or (ii) your earlier years' excess contributions not previously eliminated, whichever is smaller (see section 219(f)(6))	

Part II—Tax on Premature Distributions

Line 8(a).—If you engage in a prohibited transaction (see definition on page 2), borrow any amount from your individual retirement annuity or pledge any or all of your annuity contract as security for a loan, the account or annuity is considered ended. You are considered to have received a distribution of the entire value of your account or annuity as of the first day of the year in which any of these transactions take place. If you are under age 59½ on the first day of the year, report 10% of the distribution on line 8(a) unless the distribution is because of a disability you have incurred. If you enter an amount on line 8(a), do not fill in line 9 or 10 for this IRA.

Line 8(b).—The cost of any collectible (defined below) in which you invested funds of your arrangement in 1986 is deemed to be a distribution to you in 1986. The cost is includible in your 1986 income. Enter the total cost of the collectible on Form 1040, line 16. If you are under age 59½ when the funds were invested, enter 10% of the cost of the collectible on Form 5329, line 8(b).

For this tax a collectible is:

(1) any work of art,
(2) any rug or antique,
(3) any metal or gem,
(4) any stamp or coin,
(5) any alcoholic beverage, or
(6) any other tangible personal property specified by regulations under section 408(m).

Line 9.—The following distributions are not to be taken into account on line 9:

(a) 1986 excess contributions withdrawn during the year or 1985 excess contributions withdrawn in 1986 before the filing date (including extensions) of your 1985 income tax return;

(b) "Rollover contributions" to another retirement arrangement or plan;

(c) Amount distributed because of disability;

(d) Amount transferred to a former spouse under a divorce decree;

(e) Amount from an arrangement for which you made an entry on line 8;

(f) Amount distributed from an arrangement because it was pledged as security for a loan (use this amount for line 10 purposes);

(g)1976 and 1977 excess contributions withdrawn in 1986 if no deduction was allowed for the excess contributions; or

(h) 1978 through 1984 excess contributions withdrawn in 1986 and 1985 excess contributions withdrawn after the due date (including extensions) of your 1985 income tax return if no deduction was allowed for the excess contributions and the total IRA contributions for the tax year for which the excess contributions were made were not more than $2,250 (or if the total contributions for the year include employer contributions to a SEP, increased by the lesser of the amount of the employer contributions to the SEP or $30,000).

Line 10.—If you pledge any portion of your individual retirement account as security for a loan, enter 10% of the amount pledged on Form 5329, line 10, and the total of the amount pledged on Form 1040, line 16.

Part III—Tax on Excess Accumulations in Individual Retirement Accounts and Annuities

For tax years ending in 1986, you must start receiving a distribution of your individual retirement account or annuity on or before April 1, 1987, if you reached age 70½ during 1986. This distribution may be either:

(a) the entire interest in your account;

(b) an annuity which provides for non-increasing payments payable during your life or the lives of you and your designated beneficiary;

(c) approximately equal payments at least annually over a period of years not greater than your life expectancy (see Table I, on page 4); or

(d) approximately equal payments at least annually over a period of years not greater than the joint life and last survivor expectancy of you and your designated beneficiary (see Table II, on page 4).

If the initial payment was not received, or if the payments you received were not made according to (a) through (d) above, complete the worksheet on page 4 to see if you have to pay any excise tax.

Note: *The IRS may waive this tax on excess accumulations. The waiver of the tax is conditional upon evidence you submit that any shortfall in the amount of withdrawals from your IRA was due to reasonable error, and that appropriate steps have been or are being taken to remedy the shortfall. If you believe you qualify for this waiver, file Form 5329, pay this excise tax, and attach your letter of explanation. If your waiver request is granted, we will send you a refund.*

Worksheet for Tax on Excess Accumulations in Individual Retirement Accounts and Annuities

A. Current year distribution method:

1 Value of your account/annuity* as of the first day of this year

2 **(a)** Multiple from Table I or II below, whichever is applicable

(b) Number of years since the last day of the tax year in which you became age 70½

(c) Adjusted life expectancy multiple (subtract line 2(b) from 2(a))

3 Minimum required distribution (divide line 1 by line 2(c) and enter the result here)

4 Amount actually distributed to you from your individual retirement account/annuity this year

5 If line 3 is greater than line 4, enter the difference here; otherwise enter zero

6 Tax on underdistributed amount (50% of line 5). Enter here and on Form 5329, line 12

B. Aggregate distribution method.—This method is not applicable to you if you are filing this return for the year you reach age 70½ or if you have not received any distribution from your IRA since you reached age 70½:

7 Total of all minimum annual amounts required to be distributed starting with the year you reached age 70½ through the end of this year. Compute lines A.1 through 3 for each year starting with the year you reached age 70½. Enter the total of all line A.3 computations here

8 Total of all distributions made starting with the year you reached age 70½ through the end of the year covered by this return

9 If line 7 is greater than line 8, enter the difference here; otherwise enter zero

10 Tax on undistributed amount (50% of line 9). Enter here and on Form 5329, line 13

* The value of your annuity for this computation is the reserve under the contract. You can get this information from the insurance company that issued your contract.

Table I

One Life—Expected Return Multiples

To be used for distributions described in Part III, (c), on page 3

Owner of Individual Retirement Arrangement	Multiple
Female	15.0
Male	12.1

Table II

Two Lives—Joint Life and Last Survivor—Expected Return Multiples

(For designated beneficiaries other than the spouse, see the annuity tables in **Publication 575**, Pension and Annuity Income, for the appropriate life expectancy multiple.)

To be used for distributions described in Part III, (d), on page 3

Owner of Individual Retirement Arrangement	Age of Spouse (in year you became age 70½)												
	61	62	63	64	65	66	67	68	69	70	71	72	73
Female-Multiple	21.6	21.1	20.7	20.3	19.9	19.6	19.2	18.9	18.6	18.3	18.0	17.8	17.5
Male-Multiple	23.0	22.4	21.8	21.2	20.7	20.2	19.7	19.2	18.7	18.3	17.9	17.5	17.1

Owner of Individual Retirement Arrangement	Age of Spouse (in year you became age 70½)											
	74	75	76	77	78	79	80	81	82	83	84	85
Female-Multiple	17.3	17.1	16.9	16.7	16.6	16.4	16.3	16.2	16.0	15.9	15.8	15.8
Male-Multiple	16.7	16.4	16.1	15.8	15.5	15.2	14.9	14.7	14.5	14.3	14.1	13.9

☆ U.S. Government Printing Office: 1986—493-260 23-0916750

Form **5695**

Department of the Treasury
Internal Revenue Service

Residential Energy Credit Carryforward

► Attach to Form 1040.

OMB No. 1545-0214

1986

Attachment Sequence No. **30**

Name(s) as shown on Form 1040 | **Your social security number**

Enter the address of your principal residence on which the credit is claimed if it is different from the address shown on Form 1040.

Part I **Fill in this part to figure the residential energy credit for 1986.**

1	Enter your energy credit carryforward from a previous tax year but only if it is $10 or more. (This should be the amount on line 32 of your 1985 Form 5695. **Caution**—You do not have a carryforward if your 1985 Form 1040, line 50, shows an amount of more than zero.)	1		
2	Enter the amount of tax shown on Form 1040, line 40	2		
3	Add lines 41, 42, and 43 from Form 1040 and enter the total	3		
4	Subtract line 3 from line 2. If zero or less, enter zero	4		
5	Residential energy credit. Enter the amount shown on line 1 or line 4, whichever is less. Also, add this amount to the total on Form 1040, line 44. Write "REC" and show the amount on the dotted line next to that total.	5		

Part II **Fill in this part to figure your carryforward to 1987 (complete only if line 5 is less than line 1).**

6	Enter amount from Part I, line 1	6		
7	Enter amount from Part I, line 5	7		
8	Credit carryforward to 1987 (subtract line 7 from line 6). (If less than $10, you do not have a carryforward to 1987.)	8		

General Instructions

Paperwork Reduction Act Notice.—We ask for this information to carry out the Internal Revenue laws of the United States. We need it to ensure that taxpayers are complying with these laws and to allow us to figure and collect the right amount of tax. You are required to give us this information.

A Change You Should Note.—1985 was the last year that expenditures made for energy saving items qualified for the residential energy credit. No carryforward will be allowed for taxable years beginning after December 31, 1987.

Purpose of Form.—Use this form to claim your residential energy credit carryforward from 1985 to 1986. If your energy credit is more than your tax minus lines 41, 42, and 43 of Form 1040, you may carryforward the excess energy credit to 1987.

Specific Instructions

Part I, Line 1.—Generally, your energy credit carryforward will be computed on your prior year Form 5695. **Exception**—If the alternative minimum tax applied, see **Publication 909,** Alternative Minimum Tax.

Part II.—Complete this part only if line 5 is less than line 1. You can carryforward the amount entered on line 8 to 1987, if it is $10 or more.

Form **5695** (1986)

Form **6251**
Department of the Treasury
Internal Revenue Service

Alternative Minimum Tax Computation

▶ Attach to Forms 1040, 1040NR, 1041 or 990-T (Trust).

OMB No. 1545-0227
1986
Attachment Sequence No. 32

Name(s) as shown on tax return | Identifying number

1	Adjusted gross income (see instructions)			1
2	Deductions (Individuals, attach Schedule A (Form 1040))(see instructions):			
a (1)	Medical and dental expense from Schedule A, line 5	2a(1)		
(2)	Multiply Form 1040, line 33, by 5% (.05)	2a(2)		
(3)	Subtract line 2a(2) from line 2a(1). (If zero or less, enter zero.)		2a(3)	
b	Contributions from Schedule A, line 18, **OR** Form 1040, line 34d		2b	
c	Casualty and theft losses from Schedule A, line 19		2c	
d	Qualified interest on property used as a residence (see instructions)		2d	
e (1)	Interest, other than line 2d above, from Schedule A, line 14	2e(1)		
(2)	Net investment income (If zero or less, enter zero)	2e(2)		
(3)	Enter the smaller of line 2e(1) or line 2e(2)		2e(3)	
f	Gambling losses to the extent of gambling winnings from Schedule A, line 22		2f	
g	Estate tax allowable under section 691(c) from Schedule A		2g	
h	Estates and trusts only: Charitable deduction and income distribution deduction		2h	
i	Add lines 2a(3), b, c, d, e(3), f, g, and h			2i
3	Subtract line 2i from line 1			3
4	Tax preference items:			
a	Dividend exclusion		4a	
b	60% capital gain deduction		4b	
c	Accelerated depreciation on nonrecovery real property or 15-, 18-, or 19-year real property		4c	
d	Accelerated depreciation on leased personal property or leased recovery property other than 15-, 18-, or 19-year real property		4d	
e	Amortization of certified pollution control facilities		4e	
f	Mining exploration and development costs		4f	
g	Circulation and research and experimental expenditures		4g	
h	Reserves for losses on bad debts of financial institutions		4h	
i	Depletion		4i	
j	Incentive stock options		4j	
k	Intangible drilling costs		4k	
l	Add lines 4a through 4k			4l
5	Alternative minimum taxable income (add lines 3 and 4(l)) (short period returns, see instructions)			5
6	Enter: $40,000, if married filing joint return or Qualifying widow(er); $30,000, if single or head of household; $20,000, if married filing separate return or estate or trust			6
7	Subtract line 6 from line 5. If zero or less, do not complete the rest of this form			7
8	Enter 20% of line 7			8
9	Amount from Form 1040, line 49, or Form 1040NR, line 49. (Do not include Form 1040, line 39, or Form 1040NR, line 40.) (Estates and trusts, see instructions.)			9
10	Subtract line 9 from line 8. If zero or less, enter zero			10
11	Foreign tax credit			11
12	ALTERNATIVE minimum tax (subtract line 11 from line 10). Enter on your tax return, on the line identified as alternative minimum tax			12

Instructions

(Section references are to the Internal Revenue Code)

Paperwork Reduction Act Notice.— We ask for this information to carry out the Internal Revenue laws of the United States. We need it to ensure that taxpayers are complying with these laws and to allow us to figure and collect the right amount of tax. You are required to give us this information.

Who Must File.—File this form if : (a) You are liable for the alternative minimum tax; **or** (b) you have one or more tax preference items on lines 4c through 4k; **or** (c) your adjusted gross income is more than line 6 and you have an amount on line 2e(3), and line 2e(2) includes income other than interest and dividend income.

Individuals, estates or trusts may be liable if their adjusted gross income plus tax preference items listed on line 4 total more than line 6.

For more information, see **Publication 909,** Alternative Minimum Tax.

Minimum Tax Deferred From Earlier Year(s).—If a net operating loss carryover from an earlier year(s) reduces taxable income for 1986 and the net operating loss giving rise to the carryover resulted in the deferral of minimum tax in that earlier year(s), all or part of the deferred minimum tax may be includible as tax liability for 1986. Figure the deferred minimum tax in the worksheet in Publication 909 and enter it on Form 1040, line 51, or Form 1041, line 31. Write "Deferred Minimum Tax."

Partners, Beneficiaries, etc.—If you are a:

(1) Partner or shareholder of an S corporation, take into account separately your distributive share of items of income and deductions that enter into the computation of tax preference items.

(2) Beneficiary of an estate or trust, see section 58(c) and the line 4(l) instructions.

(3) Participant in a common trust fund, see section 58(e).

(4) Shareholder or holder of beneficial interest in a regulated investment company or a real estate investment trust, see section 58(f).

Carryback and Carryover of Unused Credits.—It may be necessary to figure the carryback or carryover of certain unused credits. See section 55(c)(3).

Note : *If you have an earned income credit, you must reduce that credit by any alternative minimum tax.*

Line-by-Line Instructions

Line 1, Estates and Trusts.—Adjusted gross income is figured in the same way as for an

Form **6251** (1986)

individual except that the costs of the administration of the estate or trust are allowed in figuring adjusted gross income.

All taxpayers.—Do not deduct any interest expense incurred to purchase or carry a limited business interest in a partnership or S corporation, in figuring adjusted gross income. Instead, include in line 2(e)(1).

Do not include in line 1 any alcohol fuel credit included in income.

Add to adjusted gross income any net operating loss deduction taken, and reduce the result by any alternative tax net operating loss deduction. See **Publication 909**, Alternative Minimum Tax, for details and attach a computation.

Lines 2(a) through 2(h).—Do not include on these lines any deduction that can be carried back or forward as a net operating loss or forward as a charitable contribution.

Individuals.—Complete and attach Schedule A (Form 1040) for any deduction listed on these lines, whether or not you completed it in figuring Form 1040, line 34. If you did not use Schedule A to figure Form 1040, line 34, write **"Alt Min Tax"** in the top margin of Schedule A.

Estates and Trusts.—Enter on the applicable line any deduction listed on these lines allowable to the estate or trust. Include on line 2h, any itemized deduction not allowable on lines 2a to 2g, and allocated to the beneficiaries of the estate or trust.

Line 2(d).—Enter on line 2(d) your qualified interest from Schedule A, line 11. Include allowable points from line 13.Enter the part of the interest that is from debts you incurred in acquiring, constructing, or substantially rehabilitating property, other than a houseboat, which you, or certain family members listed in section 267(c)(4), use as a residence.

If the interest expense is on debts incurred before July 1, 1982, the following applies. At the time you incurred the debt, it must have been secured by property which you, or certain family members listed in section 267(c)(4), used as a residence.

Line 2(e)(2).—Enter your investment income minus investment expenses.

Investment income is your gross income from interest, dividends, rents, and royalties, and any amount treated as ordinary income under sections 1245, 1250, and 1254. Do not include income from a trade or business. Include as investment income, your capital gain net income from the sale or exchange of property held for investment, and the amount to be entered on line 4(a). Add or subtract from investment income, any income or loss from a limited business interest.

Investment expenses are those expenses allowable against the production of investment income provided they are allowed in figuring adjusted gross income and not includible in line 4.

Line 4(b), 60% Capital gain deduction.—Individuals.—Enter your 60% capital gain deduction from your Schedule D (Form 1040), line 20, or Form 4798, line 9. If you had an entry on Form 1040, line 14, enter 60% of your capital gain distributions. Do not include the capital gain deduction attributable to a sale or exchange of a principal residence.

Certain insolvent farmers may reduce their capital gain tax preference item on a farm insolvency transaction. See Publication 909 for more information. Indicate any reduction on the dotted portion of line 4(b), and write "Section 13208 Relief."

Estates and Trusts.—Enter the capital gain deduction taken into account on Forms 1041 or 990-T. However, an amount paid or permanently set aside for a charitable purpose is not a tax preference item.

Lines 4(c) and 4(d), Accelerated depreciation on real property; Accelerated depreciation on leased personal property or leased recovery property other than 15, 18, or 19-year real property.—If you use the Class Life Asset Depreciation Range (CLADR) System, use the asset guideline period as the straight-line useful life to figure lines 4(c) and (d).

For (c) but not (d), use any variance in useful life under section 167(m)(1) as the straight-line useful life.

Line 4(c).—For property other than recovery property, enter the amount you get (never less than zero) by subtracting the depreciation that would have been allowable for the year if you had used the straight-line method, from the depreciation or amortization actually allowable. Figure this amount separately for each property.

For 15, 18, or 19-year real property, or low income housing, enter the amount by which the deduction allowed under section 168(a) (or section 167 for section 167(k) property) is more than the deduction which would have been allowable had the property been depreciated using a 15, 18, or 19-year period and the straight-line method without salvage value.

Line 4(d).—For leased property other than recovery property, enter the amount you get (never less than zero) by subtracting the depreciation that would have been allowable for the year if you had used the straight-line method, from the depreciation or amortization actually allowable. Figure this amount separately for each property.

For leased recovery property other than 15,18, or 19-year real property, or low income housing, enter the amount by which your deduction under section 168(a) is more than the deduction allowable using the straight-line method with a half-year convention, no salvage value, and the following recovery period:

3 year property	5 years
5 year property	8 years
10 year property	15 years
15 year public utility property	22 years

Note: *If the recovery period actually used is longer than the recovery period in 4(c) or 4(d), do not complete lines 4(c) or 4(d).*

Line 4(e), Amortization of certified pollution control facilities.—Enter the amount by which the amortization allowable under section 169 is more than the depreciation deduction otherwise allowable.

Line 4(f), Mining exploration and development costs.—For each mine or other natural deposit (other than an oil or gas well), enter the amount by which the deductions allowable under section 616(a) or 617 are more than the amount that would have been allowable if you had amortized the expenses over a 10-year period.

Line 4(g), Circulation and research and experimental expenditures.—Enter the amount by which the deductions allowable for circulation and research and experimental expenditures under sections 173 or 174(a) are more than the amount that would have been allowable if you had amortized the circulation expenses over a 3-year period and the research and experimental expenditures over a 10-year period.

Line 4(h), Reserves for losses on bad debts of financial institutions.—Enter your share of the excess of the addition to the reserve for bad debts over the reasonable addition to the reserve for bad debts that would have been allowable if you had maintained the bad debt reserve for all tax years based on actual experience.

Line 4(i), Depletion.—In the case of mines, wells, and other natural deposits, enter the amount by which the deduction for depletion under section 611 (including percentage depletion for geothermal deposits), is more than the adjusted basis of such property at the end of the tax year. Figure the adjusted basis without regard to the depletion deduction and figure the excess separately for each property.

Line 4(j), Incentive stock options.—If you received stock by the exercise of an incentive stock option, enter the amount by which the fair market value of the shares at the time of exercise was more than the option price. See sections 57(a)(10) and 422A.

Line 4(k), Intangible drilling costs.—Intangible drilling costs are a tax preference item to the extent that the excess intangible drilling costs are more than your net income from oil, gas, and geothermal properties.

Figure excess intangible drilling costs as follows: from the allowable intangible drilling and development costs (except for costs in drilling a non-productive well), subtract the amount that would have been allowable if you had capitalized these costs and either amortized them over the 120 months that started when production began, or treated them according to any election you made under section 57(d)(2).

Your net income from oil, gas, and geothermal properties is your gross income from them, minus the deductions allocable to them, except for excess intangible drilling costs and nonproductive well costs.

Figure the line 4(k) amount separately for oil and gas properties which are not geothermal deposits and for all properties which are geothermal deposits.

Line 4(1), Special Tax Preference Item for Estate and Trust Beneficiaries. Some itemized deductions of the estate or trust (such as state and local taxes) are deducted by the estate or trust in figuring the income passed through to you, but are not allowed as itemized deductions on this form. These amounts must be treated as a tax preference item allocated to you. The estate or trust should separately show these amounts on the Schedule K-1 it sends you. Add any such amounts to the total of your other tax preference items on line 4(1). Also, on the dotted line to the left of the entry space for line 4(1), write "Section 58(c)" and indicate the amount.

Lines 5 and 8.—If this is a short period return, use the formula in section 443(d)(1) to determine the amount to enter on these lines.

Nonresident Alien Individuals.—If you disposed of U.S. real property interests at a gain, see Form 1040NR instructions for a special rule in figuring line 8.

Line 9, Estates and trusts.—Enter your tax after credits. Do not include any tax from Forms 4970, 4972 or 5544.

Line 11, Foreign Tax Credit.—If line 10 is more than zero, and you incurred foreign taxes and elect to take them as a credit, enter on line 11 the foreign tax credit allowed against the alternative minimum tax. Figure this credit as follows:

(1) Use and attach a separate Form 1116 for each type of income specified at the top of Form 1116.

(2) Print across the top of each Form 1116 used: "ALT MIN TAX."

(3) Part I.—Fill in a new Part I using that portion of your income, deductions and tax preference items from Form 6251, attributable to sources outside the U.S.

(4) Part III.—Complete only the following lines:

(a) Insert on line 5 the result of the following:

- *(i)* the amount from Part III, line 5 of the Form 1116 used to figure the credit allowed against your regular tax, minus
- *(ii)* the amount from Part III, line 15 of that Form 1116, plus
- *(iii)* the smaller of (A) the amount from Part III, line 15 of that Form 1116, or (B) Form 6251, line 10 (or if more than one Form 1116 is being used, an allocable portion of Form 6251, line 10).

(b) Complete lines 6 through 8, using the result of step 3 for line 6.

(c) Line 11.—Enter Form 6251, line 5.

(d) Complete line 12 as indicated in Part III.

(e) Line 13.—Enter Form 6251, line 8.

(f) Complete lines 14 and 15 as indicated in Part *III.*

(5) Part IV.—Enter on line 11, Form 6251, the amount from line 7, Part IV of this Form 1116 (but not more than the amount on Form 6251, line 10).

☆ U.S. GOVERNMENT PRINTING OFFICE 1986 493-284

Form **8283** (Rev. October 1986)
Department of the Treasury Internal Revenue Service

Noncash Charitable Contributions

► **Attach to your Federal income tax return if the total claimed value of all property contributed exceeds $500.**

OMB No. 1545-0908 Expires 9-30-88

Attachment Sequence No. **55**

Name(s) as shown on your income tax return | **Identification number**

Section A Include in Section A **only** items (or groups of similar items) which have a claimed value of $5,000 or less per item or group and certain publicly traded securities (see instructions).

Part I Information on Donated Property

1	**(a)** Name and address of the donee organization	**(b)** Description of donated property (attach a separate sheet if more space is needed)
A		
B		
C		
D		
E		

Note: *Columns (d), (e), and (f) do not have to be completed for items with a value of $500 or less.*

	(c) Date of the contribution	**(d)** Date acquired by donor (mo., yr.)	**(e)** How acquired by donor	**(f)** Donor's cost or adjusted basis	**(g)** Fair market value	**(h)** Method used to determine the fair market value
A						
B						
C						
D						
E						

Part II Other Information—Complete questions 2 and 3 only if you gave less than the entire interest in property or if restrictions were attached to the contribution.

2 If less than the entire interest in the property is contributed during the year, complete the following:

(a) Enter letter from Part I which identifies the property ________. (Attach a separate statement if Part II applies to more than one property.)

(b) Total amount claimed as a deduction for the property listed in Part I for this tax year ________________; for any prior tax year(s) ________________.

(c) Name and address of each organization to which any such contribution was made in a prior year (complete only if different from the donee organization above).

Charitable organization (donee) name

Number and street

City or town, state, and ZIP code

(d) The place where any tangible property is located or kept. ________________

(e) Name of any person, other than the donee organization, having actual possession of the property. ________________

3 If conditions were attached to the contribution, answer the following questions:	Yes	No
(a) Is there a restriction either temporarily or permanently on the donee's right to use or dispose of the donated property?		
(b) Did you give to anyone (other than the donee organization or another organization participating with the donee organization in cooperative fundraising) the right to the income from the donated property or to the possession of the property, including the right to vote donated securities, to acquire the property by purchase or otherwise, or to designate the person having such income, possession, or right to acquire?		
(c) Is there a restriction limiting the donated property for a particular use?		

For Paperwork Reduction Act Notice, see separate instructions. Form **8283** (Rev. 10-86)

Form 8283 (Rev. 10-86) Page **2**

Name(s) as shown on your income tax return. (Do not enter name and identification number if shown on the other side.)	**Identification number**

Section B **Appraisal Summary**—Include in Section B only items (or groups of similar items) which have a claimed value of more than $5,000 per item or group. *(Report contributions of certain publicly traded securities only in Section A.)*

Part I **Donee Acknowledgment** *(To be completed by the charitable organization.)*

1 This charitable organization acknowledges that it is a qualified organization under section 170(c) and that it received the donated property as described in Part II on ______________________ (Date).

Furthermore, this organization affirms that in the event it sells, exchanges, or otherwise disposes of the property (or any portion thereof) within two years after the date of receipt, it will file an information return (**Form 8282,** Donee Information Return) with the IRS and furnish the donor a copy of that return. This acknowledgment does not represent concurrence in the claimed fair market value.

Charitable organization (donee) name	Employer identification number	
Number and street	City or town, state, and ZIP code	
Authorized signature	Title	Date

Part II **Information on Donated Property** *(To be completed by the taxpayer and/or appraiser.)*

2 Check type of property:

☐ Art* ☐ Real Estate ☐ Gems/Jewelry

☐ Stamp Collections ☐ Coin Collections ☐ Books ☐ Other

**Art includes paintings, sculpture, watercolors, prints, drawings, ceramics, antique furniture, decorative arts, textiles, carpets, silver, rare manuscripts, historical memorabilia, and other similar objects.*

3	**(a)** Description of donated property (attach a separate sheet if more space is needed)	**(b)** Date acquired by donor (mo., yr.)	**(c)** How acquired by donor	**(d)** Donor's cost or adjusted basis	**(e)** Appraised fair market value
A					
B					
C					
D					

4 If tangible property was donated, write a brief summary of the overall physical condition of the property at the time of the gift.

....

....

....

Part III **Taxpayer (Donor) Statement** *(To be completed for items listed in Section B, Part II, with appraised value of $500 or less per item.)*

I declare that item(s) (enter letter(s) identifying property) __________ listed in Part II above has (have) to the best of my knowledge and belief an appraised value of not more than $500 (per item).

Signature of taxpayer (donor) ▶ Date ▶

Part IV **Certification of Appraiser** *(To be completed by the appraiser of the above donated property.)*

I declare that I am not the donor, the donee, a party to the transaction in which the donor acquired the property, employed by or related to any of the foregoing persons, or a person whose relationship to any of the foregoing persons would cause a reasonable person to question my independence as an appraiser.

Also, I declare that I hold myself out to the public as an appraiser and that because of my qualifications as described in the appraisal, I am qualified to make appraisals of the type of property being valued. I certify the appraisal fees were not based upon a percentage of the appraised property value. Furthermore, I understand that a false or fraudulent overstatement of the property value as described in the qualified appraisal or this appraisal summary may subject me to the civil penalty under section 6701(a) (aiding and abetting the understatement of tax liability). I affirm that I have not been barred from presenting evidence or testimony by the Director of Practice.

Please Sign Here Signature ▶ Title ▶ Date of appraisal ▶

Business address	Identification number
City or town, state, and ZIP code	

☆ U.S. Government Printing Office: 1986—493-352 23-0916750

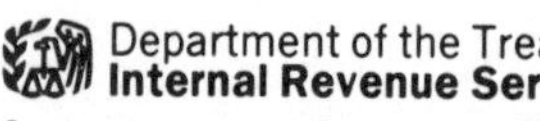

Instructions for Form 8283

(Revised October 1986)

Noncash Charitable Contributions

(Section references are to the Internal Revenue Code, unless otherwise noted.)

General Instructions

Paperwork Reduction Act Notice.—We ask for this information to carry out the Internal Revenue laws of the United States. We need it to ensure that taxpayers are complying with these laws and to allow us to figure and collect the right amount of tax. You are required to give us this information.

Purpose of Form

You must attach Form 8283 to your return if you claim a deduction for a charitable contribution of property other than cash if the total claimed value of all property contributed exceeds $500. Depending on the value and type of property, you may need to complete Section A, Section B, or both.

Who Must File

- Individuals.
- Closely held corporations.
- Personal service corporations.
- Partnerships.
- S corporations.

When To File

File this form with your tax return for the tax year in which you contributed the property and first deducted it on your return.

Which Sections To Complete

Section A.—Include in Section A only items (or groups of similar items) with a fair market value of $5,000 or less per item (or group of similar items) and certain publicly traded securities (even if their value exceeds $5,000).

The publicly traded securities that are reportable in Section A even if their value exceeds $5,000 are securities which are:

1. Listed on a stock exchange in which quotations are published on a daily basis; or

2. Regularly traded in a national or regional over-the-counter market for which published quotations are available.

Section B.—Include in Section B only items (or groups of similar items) with a fair market value of more than $5,000 (except for certain publicly traded securities reportable in Section A).

Similar items of property are items of the same generic category or type, such as stamp collections, coin collections, lithographs, paintings, books, nonpublicly traded stock, land, or buildings.

Example. *A taxpayer donated clothing valued at $400, publicly traded securities (quotations for which are published daily) valued at $7,000, and a collection of 15 books to a charitable organization. Each book in the collection is valued at $400 ($6,000 total). The taxpayer should report the clothing and the securities in Section A and the books (which are a group of similar items) in Section B.*

With certain exceptions, items reported in Section B will require information based on a written appraisal by a qualified appraiser.

Specific Instructions

Identification Number.—Donors who are individuals must enter their social security number; all other donors should enter their employer identification number.

Partnerships and S Corporations.—A partnership (S corporation) that makes contributions of property with a total claimed fair market value over $500 must file Form 8283 with Form 1065 (1120S). If the claimed fair market value of any item or group of similar items exceeds $5,000, the partnership (S corporation) must complete Section B of Form 8283 even if the amount allocated to each partner (shareholder) does not exceed $5,000.

The partnership (S corporation) is required to give a copy of the complete Form 8283 to every partner (shareholder) who receives an allocation of a deduction for donated property shown on the partnership's (S corporation's) Section B.

Partners and Shareholders.—The partnership (S corporation) will provide you with information on your share of the value of contributed property with your Schedule K-1 (Form 1065 or Form 1120S).

In some cases, the partnership (S corporation) is required to give you a copy of the partnership's (S corporation's) Form 8283. In these cases attach a copy of the Form 8283 you received to your tax return. Be sure to deduct the amount shown on your Schedule K-1, not the amount shown on the Form 8283.

If the partnership is not required to give you a copy of Form 8283, combine the amount of noncash contributions shown on Schedule K-1 with any noncash contributions you made to see if you must file Form 8283. If you need to file Form 8283, you do not have to complete all the information requested in Section A for your share of the partnership (S corporation) contributions. Do not complete line 1, columns (a)–(f) and (h). Instead, write "From Schedule K-1 (Form 1065 or 1120S)" across columns (c)–(f). Enter your share of the contribution on line 1, column (g).

Section A

Part I, Information on Donated Property

Line 1, column (a).—Enter the name and address of the donee organization to which the property was contributed.

Line 1, column (b).—Describe the property in reasonably sufficient detail. The greater the value of the property, the more detail is needed. For example, a car should be described in greater detail than a contribution of pots and pans.

For securities, the description should include:

- Name of the issuer;
- Kind of security; and
- Whether or not the security is regularly traded on a stock exchange or in an over-the-counter market.

Note: *Columns (d), (e), and (f) do not have to be completed for items with a value of $500 or less.*

Line 1, column (d).—Enter the approximate date you acquired the property. If the property was created, produced, or manufactured by or for you, enter the date the property was substantially completed.

Line 1, column (e).—State how you acquired the property, i.e., by purchase, gift, inheritance, or exchange.

Line 1, column (f).—You do not have to complete this column for:

- Publicly traded securities; or
- Property held six months or more for which the information is not available.

If you do not have to complete column (f), be sure to keep your records regarding the property's cost or other basis.

Note: *If you have reasonable cause for not providing the acquisition date in column (d) or the cost basis when required in column (f), attach an explanation.*

Line 1, column (g).—Enter the fair market value of the property on the date you contributed it. The fair market value is the price a willing buyer would pay a willing seller when neither has to buy or sell and both are aware of the conditions of the sale. If you donate property, other than certain publicly traded stock, with a fair market value that is more than your basis in it, you may have to reduce the fair market value by all or part of the increase in value when you figure your deduction. The amount of the reduction depends on whether the property is ordinary income property or capital gain property.

Property is ordinary income property if its sale on the date it was contributed would have resulted in ordinary income or in short-term capital gain. Examples of ordinary income property are inventory, works of art created by the donor, and capital assets held for six months or less . The deduction for a gift of ordinary income property is limited to the fair market value less the amount that would be ordinary income if the property were sold at its fair market value.

Capital gain property is property that would result in long-term capital gain if it were sold at its fair market value on the date of contribution. It includes certain real property and depreciable property used in your trade or business, and generally held for more than 6 months. You usually may deduct gifts of capital gain property at their fair market value. However, you must reduce the fair market value by 40% (100% for tax years beginning after 1986) of the appreciation if: the capital gain property is contributed to certain private nonoperating foundations; you choose the 50% limit instead of the special 30% limit; or the contributed property is tangible personal property that is put to an unrelated use by the charity.

Attach a computation showing your reduction to the fair market value. For more information, get **Publication 526**, Charitable Contributions. If you contribute depreciable property, also get **Publication 544**, Sales and Other Dispositions of Assets.

If your donation qualifies as a "qualified conservation contribution" under section 170(h), attach a statement that shows the claimed fair market value of the underlying property before and after the gift and the conservation purpose furthered by the gift.

Line 1, column (h).—Enter the method(s) you used to determine the fair market value of your donation. The fair market value of used household goods and clothing is usually much lower than the price paid when new. For this reason, standard formulas or methods to value this kind of property are generally not appropriate. A good measure of value for this kind of property might be the price that buyers of these used items actually pay in consignment or thrift shops.

Examples of entries to make in this column include:

- "Appraisal."
- "Thrift Shop Value" (for clothing or household goods).
- "Catalog" (for stamp or coin collections, etc.).
- "Comparable Sales" (for real estate and other kinds of assets).

See **Publication 561**, Determining the Value of Donated Property, for more information on methods of valuing different kinds of property.

Part II, Other Information

Attach a separate statement if there is more than one property to which Part II applies. Give the information which the form requires for each property separately and identify which property listed in Part I the information relates to.

Line 2.—Complete lines 2(a)–2(e) only if you contributed less than the entire interest in the donated property during the tax year. Enter on line 2(b) the amount claimed as a deduction for this year and in any earlier tax years for gifts of a partial interest in the same property. If the organization that received the prior interest in the property is the same as the one listed on line 1, column (a), you do not have to complete line 2(c).

Line 3.—Complete lines 3(a)–3(c) only if you attached restrictions to the right to the income, use, or disposition of the donated property. Attach a statement explaining:

- The terms of any agreement or understanding that relates to the income, use, sale, or other disposition of the property; and
- Whether the property is designated for a particular use, e.g., the use of donated furniture in the reading room of the organization's library.

Section B

Part I, Donee Acknowledgment

The donee organization must complete Part I. Before submitting Form 8283 to the donee for acknowledgment, complete at least your name, identification number, and description of the donated property (line 3, column (a)). If tangible property is donated, you must also describe the physical condition of the property (line 4) at the time of the gift. Complete the Taxpayer (Donor) Statement in Part III, if it is applicable, before submitting Form 8283 to the donee. See the instructions for Part III.

The person acknowledging the gift must be an official authorized to sign the tax returns of the organization, or a person specifically designated to sign Form 8283. After completing Part I, the organization must return Form 8283 to you, the donor. A copy of this form must be provided to the donee organization for its records. You may then complete any remaining information required in Part II. Also, Part IV may be completed at this time by the qualified appraiser.

Note: *If the donee organization sells, exchanges, transfers, or otherwise disposes of the property within two years after the date of the receipt of the contribution, the organization must file an information return on* ***Form 8282****, Donee Information Return, with the IRS and send a copy to the donor. However, an exception applies to items having a value of $500 or less which are part of a group of similar items contributed. For these items, a donee organization does not have to file Form 8282 if the donor completed and signed the statement in Part III (Section B) of Form 8283. This rule applies only to items clearly identified in Part II as having a value of $500 or less.*

Part II, Information on Donated Property

The information provided in Part II must be based on a written appraisal by a qualified appraiser, unless the property donated is:

- Nonpublicly traded stock valued at $10,000 or less; or
- Securities for which market quotations are considered to be readily available because the issue satisfies the five requirements explained in Announcement 86-4, 1986-4 I.R.B. 51. At the time this form went to print, final regulations for section 170 were being written that will incorporate the information in this Announcement.

Use Part II to summarize your appraisal or appraisals. You do not need to attach the appraisals, but you should keep them for your records.

The appraisal must be made not earlier than 60 days before the date you contribute the property. It must be received by you before the due date (including extensions) of the return on which the deduction is first claimed. For a deduction first claimed on an amended return, the appraisal must be received before the date the amended return was filed.

A separate qualified appraisal and a separate Form 8283 is required for each item of property except for an item which is part of a group of similar items of property. Only one qualified appraisal is required for a group of similar items of property contributed in the same tax year, provided the appraisal includes all the required information for each item.

The appraiser may select any items whose aggregate value is appraised at $100 or less for which a group description rather than a specific description of each item will suffice.

If similar items of property are given to more than one donee and the total is more than $5,000, a separate Form 8283 must be attached for each donee. For example, if you deduct $2,000 for books given to College A, and $2,500 for books given to College B, and $900 for books given to a public library, you must attach a separate Form 8283 for each donee.

See temporary regulations section 1.170A-13T(c)(3)(i)–(ii) for a definition of a qualified appraisal and for information to be included in the appraisal.

Line 3.—In column (a) describe the property in enough detail so that a person who is not familar with the type of property could determine that the property appraised is the property that was contributed.

Include in column (e) the fair market value from the qualified appraisal. For property for which a qualified appraisal was not required, include the fair market value you determine to be correct.

If you have reasonable cause for being unable to provide the information for columns (b), (c), and (d), attach an appropriate explanation to Form 8283 to prevent your deduction from being automatically disallowed.

Part III, Taxpayer (Donor) Statement

If you (the donor) complete Part III, the donee is relieved of filing Form 8282, Donee Information Return, for items having a value of $500 or less. See the **Note** in the Part I instructions of this section for more information on the filing of Form 8282 by the donee.

Complete Part III only for donated items which are included in Section B and which have an appraised value of $500 or less per item. Be sure to also clearly identify these items in Part II.

All shares of nonpublicly traded stock, or items that form a set, are considered one item. For example, a collection of books written by the same author, components of a stereo system, or six place settings of a pattern of silverware are considered one item for the $500 test.

Example. *A taxpayer donated 15 books to a charitable organization. The value of each book is $400 ($6,000 total). Ten of the books are by the same author. The taxpayer should report all 15 books in Part II. The taxpayer should also complete Part III for the 5 books which are by different authors.*

Part IV, Certification of Appraiser

You must have an appraiser complete Part IV for any property for which an appraisal is required. This section **MUST** be completed in order for the individual to be considered a qualified appraiser. See temporary regulations section 1.170A-13T(c)(5) for a definition of a qualified appraiser.

Persons who cannot be qualified appraisers are listed in the Certification of Appraiser (Part IV) of Form 8283. Usually, a party to the transaction will not qualify to sign the certification. However, a person who sold, exchanged, or gave the property to the donor may sign the certification if the property is donated within two months of the date the donor acquired it and the property's appraised value does not exceed its acquisition price.

An appraiser may not be considered qualified if the donor had knowledge of facts which would cause a reasonable person to expect the appraiser to overstate falsely the value of the donated property. An indication that this is true is an agreement between the donor and the appraiser concerning the amount at which the property will be valued and such an amount exceeds the fair market value of the property.

Usually, appraisal fees cannot be based on a percentage of the appraised property value unless the fees were paid to certain not-for-profit associations. See temporary regulations section 1.170A-13T(c)(6)(ii) for the requirements which have to be met.

Failure To File Form 8283, Section B.—If you give property required to be reported in Section B and you fail to attach the form to your return, the deduction will not be allowed unless your failure was due to a good faith omission. If the IRS requests that you submit this form because you had not attached it to your return, you have 90 days to submit a completed Section B of Form 8283 before the charitable deduction is disallowed.

☆ U.S. Government Printing Office: 1986—493-353 23-0916750

Appendix B

Guide To Tax-Free Services

Reprinted from Publication 910 (11-86)
Department of the Treasury, Internal Revenue Service

Of all the sources, resources, workbooks, guides, handbooks, and other self-help materials available, to help you with your tax forms, perhaps none contains more information than those produced by the Internal Revenue Service itself. Millions upon millions of your tax dollars pay for the collecting of taxes as well as for enforcement of the tax laws. So it follows that some of those millions have been used to help you, the taxpayer, not only understand the tax laws but to fill out the forms required by the IRS.

Chapter 2 explains the steps to take in filling out the simplest of all tax returns, the Form 1040EZ. Chapter 3 explains "That Tax Return under Tax Reform."

Listed here are all the free "Taxpayer Information Publications" offered by the IRS. You may either order these publications directly from the IRS, or see them at your local library. Public libraries have received reproducible copies of all publications available from the IRS, and you are free to photo-copy them.

1. "Your Federal Income Tax" takes you through a tax return line by line. It will also help you in filling out any schedules your particular situation may require.
2. "Highlights of the 1986 Tax Changes" will be especially helpful in tax planning.
3. "Federal Estate and Gift Taxes" is for you senior citizens who want to start a program of giving assets to your children

and grandchildren. It explains the federal estate and gift tax rules.

4. "Tax Withholding and Estimated Tax" will help you correctly figure your withheld taxes and estimated taxes.
5. "Educational Expenses" explains which expenses may be deducted, how to report expenses, and how to adjust income to include those expenses.
6. "Tax Calendars" is that all-important list of dates when the IRS expects you to submit certain forms or send in certain payments.
7. "Tax Information on Selling Your Home" will be useful if and when you move and sell your house.
8. "Tax Information for Owners of Homes, Condominiums, and Co-operative Apartments" tells how to determine your basis, how to treat closing costs, improvements and repairs, and how to figure deductions for mortgage interest, local property taxes, and theft.
9. "Tax Information for Older Americans" discusses selling your house; credit for the elderly; and pension and annuity income.
10. "Alternative Minimum Tax" discusses how this tax affects individuals, trusts, and estates.

Guide To Tax-Free Services

This list highlights some of the hundreds of publications available. Please refer to the following:

How to Get IRS Forms and Publications

You can order tax forms and publications from the IRS Forms Distribution Center for your state at the address below. Or, if you prefer, you can photocopy tax forms from reproducible copies kept at many participating public libraries. In addition, many of these libraries have reference sets of IRS publications which you can read or copy.

If you are located in:	Send to "Forms Distribution Center" for your state
Alaska, Arizona, California, Colorado, Hawaii, Idaho, Montana, Nevada, Oregon, Utah, Washington, Wyoming	P.O. Box 12626, Fresno, CA 93778
Illinois, Indiana, Iowa, Kansas, Kentucky, Michigan, Minnesota, Missouri, Nebraska, New Mexico, North Dakota, Ohio, Oklahoma, South Dakota, Texas, Wisconsin	P.O. Box 9903, Bloomington, IL 61799
Alabama, Arkansas, Connecticut, Delaware, District of Columbia, Florida, Georgia, Louisiana, Maine, Maryland, Massachusetts, Mississippi, New Hampshire, New Jersey, New York, North Carolina, Pennsylvania, Rhode Island, South Carolina, Tennessee, Vermont, Virginia, West Virginia	P.O. Box 25866, Richmond, VA 23260

Foreign Addresses—Taxpayers with mailing addresses in foreign countries should send this order blank to either: Forms Distribution Center, P.O. Box 25866, Richmond, VA 23260; or Forms Distribution Center, P.O. Box 12626, Fresno, CA 93778, whichever is closer. Send letter requests for other forms and publications to: Forms Distribution Center, P.O. Box 25866, Richmond, VA 23260.

Puerto Rico—Forms Distribution Center, P.O. Box 25866, Richmond, VA 23260.

Virgin Islands—V.I. Bureau of Internal Revenue, P.O. Box 3186, St. Thomas, VI 00801

Taxpayer Information Publications

The Internal Revenue Service publishes many free publications to help you with your taxes. These publications are listed here, generally in numerical order. The list describes the ones used most often and indicates the main related forms and schedules. A form or schedule shown in italics appears as a filled-in example in the publication. You may order these free publications and forms by calling IRS. You may find it convenient to obtain copies of many forms and schedules at public libraries, which have been furnished reproducible copies. A reference set entitled Taxpayer Information Publications may also be found at most libraries.

The four publications listed first give general information about taxes for individuals, small businesses, farming, and the fishing industry. You may want to order one of these publications, and then, if you need detailed information on any subject, order the specific publication about it. The fifth publication listed here highlights recent tax changes.

---

17 Your Federal Income Tax

This publication can help you prepare your own return. It takes you through the return and explains the tax laws that cover salaries and wages, interest and dividends, itemized deductions, rental income, gains and losses and adjustments to income (such as alimony, moving expenses, employee business expenses, and the deduction for a married couple when both work).

Examples illustrate typical situations. Filled-in forms and schedules show how to report income and deductions.

The Tax Table, Tax Rate Schedules, sales tax tables and earned income credit tables are included in this publication.

Forms *1040, 1040A, 1040EZ*, Schedules *A, B, D, E, G, R, W, SE*, Forms *W-2, 2106, 2119, 2441, 3903*.

334 Tax Guide for Small Business

This book explains some federal tax laws that apply to businesses. It describes the four major forms of business organizations—sole proprietorship, partnership, corporation, and S corporation—and explains the tax responsibilities of each.

This publication is divided into eight parts. The first part contains general information on business organization and accounting practices. Part II discusses the tax aspects of accounting for the assets used in a business.

Parts III and IV explain how to figure your business income for tax purposes. They describe the kinds of income you must report and the different types of business deductions you can take.

Part V discusses the rules that apply when you sell or exchange business assets or investment property. It includes chapters on the treatment of capital gains and losses, and on involuntary conversions, such as theft and casualty losses. The chapters in Part VI bring together some specific tax considerations for each of the four major forms of business organizations.

Part VII looks at some of the credits that can reduce your income tax, and some of the other taxes you may have to pay in addition to income tax. It also discusses the information returns that may have to be filed. The last part shows how to fill out the main income tax forms businesses use.

Schedule C (Form 1040), Forms *1065, 1120, 1120-A*, Form *1120S*, Schedule *K-1* (Form 1065), Forms *4562 and 4797*.

225 Farmer's Tax Guide

This publication explains how the federal tax laws apply to farming. It gives examples of typical farming situations and discusses the kinds of farm income you must report and the different deductions you can take.

Form *1040*, Schedule *F* (Form 1040), Schedules *A, D, SE, W*, (Form 1040), Forms *3468, 4136, 4255, 4562, 4684, 4797*, and *6251*.

595 Tax Guide for Commercial Fishermen

This publication will familiarize you with the federal tax laws as they apply to the fishing business. It is intended for sole proprietors who use Schedule C (Form 1040) to report profit or loss from fishing. This guide does not cover corporations or partnerships.

The publication's 16 chapters each give tax information about a different aspect of the fishing business. The last chapter gives an example of a fisherman's recordkeeping system and sample tax forms.

Schedule *C* (Form 1040), Forms *1099—MISC, 4562*, and *4797*.

553 Highlights of 1986 Tax Changes

This publication discusses the more important changes in the tax rules brought about by recent legislation, rulings, and administrative decisions. It does not discuss all new tax rules or detail all changes. It highlights the important recent changes that taxpayers should know about when filing their 1986 tax forms and when planning for 1987.

---

15 Circular E, Employer's Tax Guide

Every employer automatically receives this publication on its revision and every person who applies for an employer identification number receives a copy.

Forms 940, 941, and 941E.

17 Your Federal Income Tax

(Described at the beginning of this list)

51 Circular A, Agricultural Employer's Tax Guide

Form 943.

54 Tax Guide for U.S. Citizens and Resident Aliens Abroad

This publication discusses the tax situations of U.S. citizens and resident aliens who live and work abroad, or who have income from foreign countries. In particular, it explains the rules for excluding income and excluding or deducting certain housing costs. Answers are provided to questions that taxpayers ask most often about taxes for people living overseas.

Forms *2555, 1116*, and *1040*, Schedule SE (Form 1040).

80 Circular SS, Federal Tax Guide for Employers in the Virgin Islands, Guam, and America Samoa

Forms 940, 941SS and 943.

179 Circular PR, Guia Contributiva Federal Para Patronos Puertorriqueños (Federal Tax Guide for Employers in Puerto Rico)

Forms W-3PR, 940PR, 941PR, 942PR, and 943PR.

225 Farmer's Tax Guide

(Described at the beginning of this list)

334 Tax Guide for Small Business

(Described at the beginning of this list)

349 Federal Highway Use Tax on Heavy Vehicles

This publication explains what trucks, truck-tractors, and buses are subject to the federal use tax on heavy highway motor vehicles, which is one source of funds for the national highway construction program. The tax is due from the person in whose name the vehicle is either registered or required to be registered. The publication tells how to figure and pay the tax due.

The Highway Revenue Act of 1982 and the Tax Reform Act of 1984 amended the highway use tax, effective July 1, 1984. The 1986 revision of this publication discusses the new law.

Form 2290.

378 Fuel Tax Credits

This publication explains the credit or refund allowed for the federal excise taxes paid on certain fuels, and the income tax credit available when alcohol is used as a fuel.

Forms 4136 and 6478.

Guide To Tax-Free Services

448 Federal Estate and Gift Taxes

This publication explains the federal estate and gift taxes.

Forms 706 and 709.

463 Travel, Entertainment, and Gift Expenses

This publication explains what expenses you may deduct for business-related travel, entertainment, and gifts. It also discusses the reporting and recordkeeping requirements for these expenses.

The publication summarizes the deduction and substantiation rules for employees, self-employed persons (including independent contractors), and employers (including corporations and partnerships).

Form 2106.

501 Exemptions

This publication explains when you can take exemptions. Each one you have lowers your taxable income. Besides your personal exemption, you may be able to take additional exemptions for your husband or wife and for your or your spouse's age or blindness. You may also take an exemption for each person who qualifies as your dependent.

Form 2120.

502 Medical and Dental Expenses

This publication tells you how to figure your deduction for medical and dental expenses. You may take this deduction only if you itemize your deductions on Schedule A (Form 1040).

Specific expense items and examples are given to make the discussions easier to understand. Tax tips on many pages remind you of deductions that you may have overlooked.

Schedule A (Form 1040).

503 Child and Dependent Care Credit, and Employment Taxes for Household Employers

This publication explains the credit you may be able to take if you pay someone to care for your dependent who is under 15, for your disabled dependent, or for your disabled spouse. For purposes of the credit, "disabled" refers to a person physically or mentally unable to care for himself or herself.

The expenses must be paid so you can work or look for work.

It also explains the employment taxes you may have to pay if you are a household employer.

Forms *W-2, W-3, 940, 942,* Schedule 1 (Form 1040A), and *2441.*

504 Tax Information for Divorced or Separated Individuals

This publication explains tax rules of interest to divorced or separated individuals. It covers filing status, dependency exemptions, and the treatment of alimony and property settlements.

505 Tax Withholding and Estimated Tax

This publication explains the two methods of paying tax under our pay-as-you-go system.

They are:

1. Withholding. Your employer will withhold income tax from your pay. Tax is also withheld from other types of income. You can have more or less withheld, depending on your circumstances.

2. Estimated tax. If you do not pay your tax through withholding, or do not pay enough tax that way, you might have to pay estimated tax.

This publication also explains how to take credit on your 1986 return for your tax withholding and estimated tax payments.

Forms *W-4,* W-4P, W-5, W-4S, *1040-ES, 2210,* and *2210F.*

506 Income Averaging

This publication explains the rules for using the income averaging method to compute your tax, which may help you if your income increased substantially this year. Under this method, part of an unusually large amount of taxable income can be taxed at lower rates.

Schedule G (Form 1040).

508 Educational Expenses

This publication explains what work related educational expenses qualify for deduction, how to report your expenses and any reimbursement you receive, and which forms and schedules to use. You deduct some of these expenses as adjustments to income and others as itemized deductions. You may not deduct educational expenses on Form 1040EZ or 1040A.

Form *2106.*

509 Tax Calendars for 1987

510 Excise Taxes for 1987

Form 720.

513 Tax Information for Visitors to the United States

This publication can familiarize you with the general requirements of U.S. income tax laws for foreign visitors. You may have to file a U.S. income tax return during your visit. Most visitors who come to the United States are not allowed to work in this country. Please check with the Immigration and Naturalization Service before you take a job.

Forms 1040C, 1040NR, 2063, and 1040-ES(-NR).

514 Foreign Tax Credit for U.S. Citizens and Resident Aliens

This publication may help you if you paid foreign income tax. You may be able to take a foreign tax credit or deduction to avoid the burden of double taxation. The pamphlet explains what foreign taxes qualify and how to figure your credit or deduction.

Form *1116.*

515 Withholding of Tax on Nonresident Aliens and Foreign Corporations

Forms 1042 and 1042S.

516 Tax Information for U.S. Government Civilian Employees Stationed Abroad

This publication covers the tax treatment of allowances, reimbursements, and business expenses that U.S. government employees, including Foreign Service Officers, are likely to receive or incur.

517 Social Security for Members of the Clergy and Religious Workers

This publication discusses social security coverage and self-employment tax for the clergy.

It also tells you how, as a member of the clergy (minister, member of a religious order, or Christian Science practitioner), you may apply for an exemption from the self-employment tax that would otherwise be due for the services you perform in the exercise of your ministry.

Net earnings from self-employment are explained and sample forms are shown.

Form *2106,* Form 4361, Form *1040,* Schedule *SE* (Form 1040), and *Schedule C* (Form 1040).

518 Foreign Workers, Scholars, and Exchange Visitors

This publication gives federal tax information for foreign visitors who are in the United States on an "F," "J," "H," "L," or "M" visa. It also provides information about tax treaty provisions that apply to various kinds of earned income from U.S. sources.

Forms 1040NR and 2063.

519 U.S. Tax Guide for Aliens

This publication gives guidelines on how to determine your U.S. tax status and figure your U.S. tax.

Resident aliens, like U.S. citizens, generally are taxed on income from all sources, both in and outside the United States. Nonresident aliens generally are taxed only on income from sources in the United States. This income may be from investments or from business activities such as performing personal services in the United States. An income tax treaty may reduce the standard 30% tax rate on nonresident alien's investment income. Their business income is taxed at the same graduated rates that apply to U.S. citizens or residents.

Aliens admitted to the United States with permanent immigration visas generally are resident aliens, while temporary visitors generally are nonresident aliens. Aliens with other types of visas may be resident aliens or nonresident aliens, depending on the length and nature of their stay.

Forms *1040, 1040C, 1040NR, 2063,* and Schedule *A* (Form 1040).

520 Scholarships and Fellowships

This publication explains U.S. tax laws as they apply to U.S. citizens and resident aliens who study, teach, or conduct research in the United States or abroad under scholarships and fellowship grants.

521 Moving Expenses

This publication explains how, if you changed job locations last year, or started a new job, you may be able to deduct your moving expenses. You may qualify for a deduction whether you are self-exployed or an employee. The expenses must be connected with starting work at your new job location. You must meet a distance test and a time test. You also may be able to deduct expenses of moving to the United States if you retire while living and working overseas or if you are a survivor or dependent of a person who died while living and working overseas.

You may deduct your allowable moving expenses even if you do not itemize your

deductions. You should use Form 3903, Moving Expense Adjustment, if your move is within or to the United States or its possessions. You should use Form 3903F, Foreign Moving Expense Adjustment, if your move is outside the United States or its possessions.
Forms *3903, 3903F,* and *4782.*

523 Tax Information on Selling Your Home

This publication explains how you report gain from selling your home, how you may postpone the tax on part or all of the gain on the sale of your home, and how you may exclude part of all of the gain from your gross income if you are 55 or over.
Form *2119.*

524 Credit for the Elderly or for the Permanently and Totally Disabled

This publication explains how to figure the credit for the elderly or for the permanently and totally disabled. You may be able to claim this credit if you are 65 or over, or if you are under 65 and retired on disability and were permanently and totally disabled when you retired. Figure the credit on Schedule R, (Form 1040), Credit for the Elderly or for the Permanently and Totally Disabled. To take the credit you must file a Form 1040.
Schedule *R* (Form 1040).

525 Taxable and Nontaxable Income

This publication discusses wages, salaries, fringe benefits and other compensation received for services as an employee. In addition, it discusses items of miscellaneous taxable income, as well as items that are exempt from tax.

526 Charitable Contributions

If you make a charitable contribution or gift to, or for the use of, a qualified organization, you may be able to claim a deduction on your tax return. This publication explains how the deduction is claimed by taxpayers who itemize their deductions and by taxpayers who do not itemize. The limitations that apply to these deductions are also explained.
Schedule A (Form 1040)

527 Rental Property

This publication defines rental income, discusses rental expenses, and explains how to report them both on your return. It also covers casualty losses on rental property and the sale of rental property.
Schedule *E* (Form 1040), *4562* and *4797.*

529 Miscellaneous Deductions

This publication discusses expenses you generally may take as miscellaneous deductions on Schedule A (Form 1040), such as employee expenses and expenses of producing income. It does not discuss other itemized deductions, such as the ones for charitable contributions, interest, taxes, or medical and dental expenses.
Schedule A (Form 1040).

530 Tax Information for Owners of Homes, Condominiums, and Cooperative Apartments

This publication gives information about home ownership and federal taxes. It explains how to determine basis, how to treat settlement and closing costs, and how to treat repairs and improvements you make. The publication discusses itemized deductions for mortgage interest, real estate taxes, and casualty and theft losses. It also explains the mortgage interest credit and the residential energy credit carryforward.

531 Reporting Income from Tips

This publication gives advice about keeping track of cash and charge tips and explains that all tips received are subject to federal income tax. Social security or railroad retirement tax may also be due if tips total more than $20 a month. The publication also explains the rules about the information that employers must report to the Internal Revenue Service about their employees' tip income.
Forms *4070* and *4070A.*

533 Self-Employment Tax

This publication explains the self-employment tax, which is a social security tax for people who work for themselves. It is similar to the social security tax withheld from the pay of wage earners.

Social security benefits are available to people who are self-employed just as they are to wage earners. Your payments of self-employment tax contribute to your coverage under the social security system.
Schedule *SE* (Form 1040).

534 Depreciation

This publication discusses the various methods of depreciation, including the accelerated cost recovery system (ACRS). This publication covers:

—What can be depreciated
—ACRS-assets placed in service after 1980
—Section 179 deduction
—The limitations for passenger automobiles and other "listed property" placed in service after June 18, 1984
—Methods used for assets placed in service before 1981 and for assets not qualifying for ACRS
—Example with a filled-in Form 4562

Form *4562.*

535 Business Expenses

This publication discusses such business expenses as pay for your employees; fringe benefits; rental expenses; interest; taxes; insurance; employee benefit plans; and certain education expenses of yourself and your employees. It also outlines the choice to capitalize certain business expenses; discusses amortization and depletion; covers some business expenses that may be deductible in some circumstances and not deductible in others; and points out some expenses that are not deductible.

536 Net Operating Losses and the At-Risk Limits

537 Installment Sales

This publication discusses sales arrangements that provide for part or all of the selling price to be paid in a later year. These arrangements are "installment sales." If you finance the buyer's purchase of your property, instead of having the buyer get a loan or mortgage from a bank, you probably have an installment sale.

You must report depreciation recapture income, to the extent of the gain, in the year of sale. You may use the installment method to report any gain in excess of depreciation recapture income.

Gain on an installment sale is reported only as the payments are actually received, whether you use the cash or accrual method of accounting. You are taxed only on the part of each payment that represents your profit on the sale.
Form *6252.*

538 Accounting Periods and Methods

This publication explains what accounting periods and methods can be used for figuring federal taxes, and how to apply for approval to change from one period or method to another. Almost all individual taxpayers have the calendar year as their tax period and use the cash method.
Forms 1128 and 3115.

539 Employment Taxes

This publication explains the responsibility you may have, if you have employees, to withhold federal income tax from their wages. You may also have to pay social security taxes (FICA) and federal unemployment tax (FUTA). The publication also discusses the rules for advance payment of the earned income credit and the rules for reporting and allocating tips.
Forms *940* and *941.*

541 Tax Information on Partnerships

Forms *1065, 4797* and Schedules *D, K,* and *K-1* (Form 1065).

542 Tax Information on Corporations

Forms 1120 and 1120-A.

544 Sales and Other Dispositions of Assets

This publication explains how to figure gain and loss on various transactions, such as trading or selling an asset, and it explains the tax results of different types of gains and losses. Not all transactions result in taxable gains or deductible losses, and not all gains are taxed the same way.
Schedule *D* (Form 1040), and Form *4797.*

545 Interest Expense

This publication explains what items may and may not be deducted as interest, which is an amount paid for the use of borrowed money. Where on the return you deduct interest depends on whether you borrowed the money for personal use, for rental or royalty property, or for your business.
Schedule A (Form 1040).

547 Nonbusiness Disasters, Casualties and Thefts

This publication explains when you can deduct a disaster, casualty, or theft loss. Casualties are events such as hurricanes, earthquakes, tornadoes, fires, floods, vandalism, and car accidents. The publication also explains how to treat the amount you receive from insurance or other sources.
Form *4684.*

548 Deduction for Bad Debts

This publication explains that if someone owes you money and you cannot collect on the debt, you may be able to claim a deduction for a bad debt. For a bad debt to qualify for the deduction, there must be a true creditor-debtor relationship between you and the person or organization that owes you the money. There must be a legal obligation to pay you a fixed sum of money. You must realize a loss because of your inability to collect the money owed to you.

549 Condemnations and Business Casualties and Thefts

This publication can help you figure your gain or loss if you have property that is condemned or if you sell or exchange it under threat or imminence of condemnation. Condemnation is the process by which private property is legally taken, for public use and in exchange for money or property, by the federal government, a state government, or a political subdivision.

The publication also explains the deduction for casualties and thefts to business property. Casualties are events such as hurricanes, earthquakes, tornadoes, fires, floods, vandalism, and car accidents.

Forms *4797* and *4864*.

550 Investment Income and Expenses

This publication explains which types of investment income are and are not taxable, when the income is taxed, and how to report it on your tax return. The publication discusses the treatment of tax shelters and investment related expenses. The publication also explains how to figure your gain or loss when you sell or trade your investment property.

Schedules B and D (Form 1040).

551 Basis of Assets

This publication explains how to determine the basis of property. The basis of property you buy is usually its cost. If you received property in some other way, such as by gift or inheritance, you normally must use a basis other than cost.

552 Recordkeeping for Individuals and a List of Tax Publications

This publication can help you decide what records to keep and how long to keep them for tax purposes. These records will help you prepare your income tax returns so that you will pay only your correct tax. If you keep a record of your expenses during the year, you may find that you can reduce your taxes by itemizing your deductions. Deductible expenses include medical and dental bills, interest, contributions, and taxes.

553 Highlights of 1986 Tax Changes

(Described at the beginning of this list)

554 Tax Information for Older Americans

This publication gives tax information of special interest to older Americans. An example takes you through completing a tax return and explains such items as the sale of a home, credit for the elderly and permanently and totally disabled, and pension and annuity income. The publication includes filled-in forms and schedules that show how these and other items are reported.

Schedules *B, D,* and *R* (Form 1040), Forms *1040* and *2119*.

555 Community Property and the Federal Income Tax

This publication may help married taxpayers who are domiciled in one of the following community property states: Arizona, California, Idaho, Louisiana, Nevada, New Mexico, Texas, or Washington. If you wish to file a separate tax return, you should understand how community property laws affect the way you figure your tax before completing your federal income tax return. Effective January 1, 1986, Wisconsin became a marital property state with property laws similar to those of community property states.

556 Examination of Returns, Appeal Rights, and Claims for Refund

This publication may be helpful if your return is examined by the Internal Revenue Service. It explains that returns are normally examined to verify the correctness of reported income, exemptions, or deductions, and it describes what appeal rights you have if you disagree with the results of the examination.

The publication also explains the procedures for the examination of items of partnership income, deduction, gain, loss, and credit. Information is given on how to file a claim for refund, the time for filing a claim for refund, and the limit on the amount of refund.

Forms 1040X and 1120X.

556S Revisión de las Declaraciones de Impuesto, Derecho de Apelación y Reclamaciones de Reembolsos (Examination of Returns, Appeal Rights, and Claims for Refund)

Forms 1040X and 1120X.

557 Tax-Exempt Status for Your Organization

This publication discusses how organizations become recognized as exempt from federal income tax under section 501(a) of the Internal Revenue Code. (These include organizations described in section 501(c).) The publication explains how to get an appropriate ruling or determination letter recognizing the exemption, and it gives other information that applies generally to all exempt organizations.

Forms 990, 1023, and 1024.

559 Tax Information for Survivors, Executors, and Administrators

This publication can help you report and pay the proper federal income and estate taxes if you have the responsibility for settling an estate. The publication answers many questions that a spouse or other survivor faces when a person dies. They include:

What was the decedent's tax liability for the year of death? When is the last return due? How does the survivor (or beneficiary) treat bequests or inheritances received from the estate of a decedent? How is the income taxed from the date of the decedent's death to the distribution of the estate? Who is responsible for the decedent's tax? What are the tax problems of the heirs?

Form *1040*, Schedules *A, B, E* (Form 1040), Form *1041*, Schedule *D* (Form 1041), and Form *4562*.

560 Self-employed Retirement Plans

This publication discusses retirement plans for self-employed persons and certain partners in partnerships. These retirement plans are sometimes called Keogh plans or HR-10 plans.

If you set up a retirement plan that meets certain legal requirements, you may be able to deduct your payments to the plan. In addition, income earned by the plan will be tax free until it is distributed.

561 Determining the Value of Donated Property

This publication can help donors and appraisers determine the value of property (other than cash) that is given to qualified organizations. It explains what kind of information you need to support a charitable deduction you claim on your return.

Form *8283*.

564 Mutual Fund Distributions

This publication discusses the federal income tax treatment of distributions paid or allocated to you as an individual shareholder of a mutual fund. A comprehensive example shows distributions made by a mutual fund with illustrations of Form 1099-DIV and Form 1040.

Form *1040*, Schedule *B* (Form 1040), and Form *1099-DIV*.

567 U.S. Civil Service Retirement and Disability

This publication explains the federal tax rules that apply to your civil service annuity. Items discussed include:

—How to figure the taxable part of your annuity
—How to report the annuity income on your Form 1040
—Liability for the federal gift tax

Form 1040.

570 Tax Guide for U.S. Citizens Employed in U.S. Possessions

Forms *4563* and *5074*.

571 Tax-Sheltered Annuity Programs for Employees of Public Schools and Certain Tax-Exempt Organizations

This publication explains the rules concerning employers qualified to buy tax sheltered annuities, eligible employees who may participate in the program, the amounts that may be excluded from income, and the taxation of benefits when they are received.

Form 5330.

572 Investment Credit

This publication explains how the regular investment credit, the business energy investment credit, and the investment credit for rehabilitated buildings are figured; what type of property is eligible; what limits the amount; and other rules about the investment credit.

Forms *3468, 3800* and *4255*.

575 Pension and Annuity Income

This publication explains how to report pension and annuity income on your federal income tax return. It also explains the special tax treatment for lump-sum distributions from pensions, stock bonus plans, or profit-sharing plans.

Forms *1040, 1099-R* and *4972*.

Guide To Tax-Free Services

578 Tax Information for Private Foundations and Foundation Managers

Form 990PF.

579S Cómo preparar la declaración de impuesto federal (How to Prepare the Federal Income Tax Return)

Forms *1040*, *1040A*, 1040EZ, 1040NR, 1040X, Schedules *A*, *B*, and *W* (Form 1040). Form *W-2*.

583 Information for Business Taxpayers

This publication shows sample records that a small business can use if it operates as a sole proprietorship. Records like these will help you prepare complete and accurate tax returns and make sure you pay only the tax you owe. This publication also discusses the taxpayer identification number businesses must use, information returns businesses may have to file, and the kinds of business taxes businesses may have to pay.

Schedule *C* (Form 1040), and *4562*.

584 Nonbusiness Disaster, Casualty, and Theft Loss Workbook

This workbook can help you figure your loss from a disaster, casualty or theft. It will help you most if you use it now to help establish the value of your property **before** any losses occur. The workbook has schedules to help you figure the loss on your home and its contents. There is also a schedule to help you figure the loss on your car, truck, or motorcycle.

585 Voluntary Tax Methods to Help Finance Political Campaigns

586A The Collection Process (Income Tax Accounts)

This booklet explains your rights and duties as a taxpayer who owes tax. It also explains the legal obligation of the Internal Revenue Service to collect overdue taxes, and the way we fulfill this obligation. It is not intended to be a precise and technical analysis of the law in this area.

586S Proceso de cobro (Deudas del Impuesto sobre Ingreso) (The Collection Process (Income Tax Accounts))

587 Business Use of Your Home

This publication can help you decide if you qualify to deduct certain expenses for using part of your home in your business. You must meet specific tests and your deduction is limited. Deductions for the business use of a home computer are also discussed.

Schedule *C* (Form 1040), and *4562*.

588 Tax Information for Homeowners Associations

This publication gives tax information for homeowners associations. There are discussions about what associations can elect to be tax-exempt homeowners associations, how to make the election, and what tax obligations there are for organizations that are not exempt. There is also an example with a filled-in return for homeowners associations.

Form *1120-H*.

589 Tax Information on S Corporations

Form *1120S* and Schedule *K-1* (Form 1120S).

590 Individual Retirement Arrangements (IRAs)

This publication explains the benefits of having an individual retirement arrangement (IRA) and provides information on current deductions, tax responsibilities, and the "rollover" from one IRA to another. An IRA is a savings plan that lets you set aside money for your retirement. Your contributions to an IRA are tax deductible and the earnings in your IRA are not taxed until they are distributed to you.

Topics covered include:

- Who is eligible?
- Setting Up An IRA
- Deduction for contributions
- Excess contributions
- Distributions
- Rollovers

Form *5329*.

593 Income Tax Benefits for U.S. Citizens Who Go Overseas

This publication briefly reviews various U.S. tax provisions that apply to U.S. citizens or resident aliens who live or work abroad and expect to receive income from foreign sources.

594 The Collection Process (Employment Tax Accounts)

This booklet explains your rights and duties as a taxpayer who owes employer's quarterly federal taxes. It also explains how we fulfill the legal obligation of the Internal Revenue Service to collect these taxes. It is not intended as a precise and technical analysis of the law.

595 Tax Guide for Commercial Fishermen

(Described at the beginning of this list)

596 Earned Income Credit

This publication discusses who may receive the earned income credit, and how to figure and claim the credit. It also discusses how to receive advance payments of the earned income credit.

Forms *W-5*, *1040*, and *1040A*.

597 Information on the United States-Canada Income Tax Treaty

598 Tax on Unrelated Business Income of Exempt Organizations

Form 990-T.

686 Certification for Reduced Tax Rates in Tax Treaty Countries

721 Comprehensive Tax Guide to U.S. Civil Service Retirement Benefits

This publication explains how the federal income tax rules apply to the benefits that retired federal employees or their survivors receive under the U.S. Civil Service Retirement Act. There is also information on estate and gift taxes.

Form 1040.

794 Favorable Determination Letter

850 English-Spanish Glossary of Words and Phrases Used in Publications Issued by the Internal Revenue Service

901 U.S. Tax Treaties

904 Interrelated Computations for Estate and Gift Taxes

Forms 706 and 709.

905 Tax Information on Unemployment Compensation

906 Jobs and Research Credits

This publication discusses two credits that may be available to businesses. The first, the targeted jobs credit, is based on a percentage of wages paid to qualified employees. The second, the research credit, is based on qualifying expenses of a business for research and experimental purposes.

Forms *5884* and *6765*.

907 Tax Information for Handicapped and Disabled Individuals

This publication explains tax rules of interest to handicapped and disabled people and to taxpayers with disabled dependents. For example, a tax credit is available for certain disability payments, medical expenses can be deducted, and a credit is available for expenses of care for disabled dependents.

Schedule *A* (Form 1040), Schedule *R* (Form 1040), Form 2441.

908 Bankruptcy

This publication expains the income tax aspects of bankruptcy and discharge of debt for individuals and small businesses.

Forms 1040, 1041, 1120.

909 Alternative Minimum Tax

This publication discusses the alternative minimum tax, which applies to individuals, trusts and estates.

Forms 1116 and *6251*.

911 Tax Information for Direct Sellers

This publication may help you if you are a "direct seller," a person who sells consumer products to others on a person-to-person basis. Many direct sellers sell door-to-door, at sales parties, or by appointment in someone's home. Information on figuring your income from direct sales as well as the kinds of expenses you may be entitled to deduct is also provided.

Schedules *C* and *SE* (Form 1040) and Form 4562.

915 Social Security Benefits and Equivalent Railroad Retirement Benefits

This publication explains when you may have to include part of your social security or tier 1 railroad retirement benefits in income on Form 1040. It also explains how to figure the amount to include.

Forms *SSA-1099* and *RRB-1099*, *Social Security Benefits Worksheet*, Notice 703, Forms SSA-1042S and RRB-1042S.

916 Information Returns

This publication provides general information about the rules for reporting payments to nonemployees and transactions with other persons. This publication also provides information on taxpayer identification numbers, information on backup withholding, and an explanation of the penalties relating to information returns.

Forms 1099 Series; W-2G; 1098, 4789; 5498; 8300; 8308; 8362.

917 Business Use of a Car

This publication explains the expenses that you may deduct for the business use of your car. Car expenses that are deductible include only those expenses necessary to drive and maintain a car that you use to go from one workplace to another. They do not include the cost of commuting expenses (driving from your home to your regular workplace). The publication also discusses the taxability of the use of a car provided by an employer.

1004 Identification Numbers Under ERISA

1048 Filing Requirements for Employee Benefit Plans

Forms 5500, 5500-C, and 5500-R.

1212 List of Original Issue Discount Instruments

This publication explains the tax treatment of original issue discount (OID). It describes how:

—Brokers and other middlemen, who may hold the debt instruments as nominees for the owners, should report OID to IRS and to the owners on Forms 1099-OID or 1099-INT; and

—Owners of OID debt instruments should report OID on their income tax returns.

The publication gives rules for figuring the discount amount to report each year, if required. It also gives tables that IRS has compiled regarding certain publicly-traded OID debt instruments, including short-term U.S. Treasury securities.

Schedule B (Form 1040) and Forms 1099-OID and 1099-INT.

1244 Employee's Daily Record of Tips (Form 4070-A) and Employee's Report of Tips to Employer (Form 4070)

This publication explains how you must report tips if you are an employee who receives tips. Copies of the monthly tip report you must give your employer are included, as well as a daily list you can use for your own records.

Forms *4070* and *4070-A*.

Subject Matter Index to Publications

This index is listed alphabetically by subject. The main publication numbers are shown in bold type.

Guide To Tax-Free Services

Guide To Tax-Free Services

Guide To Tax-Free Services

Guide To Tax-Free Services

Guide To Tax-Free Services

Guide To Tax-Free Services

To Call Tele-Tax Toll-Free, Use Only The Numbers Listed Below For Your Area

Recorded Tax Information has about 150 topics of tax information that answer many Federal tax questions and a topic for local information such as the location of VITA and TCE sites. You can hear up to three topics on each call you make.

Automated Refund Information is available after March 15. If it has been 10 weeks since you mailed your 1986 tax return, we will be able to check the status of your refund.

Long-distance charges apply if you call from outside the local dialing area of the numbers listed below. **Do not dial 800 when using a local number.** A complete list of these topics and instructions on how to use Tele-Tax are on the next page.

Note: *Cities with a* ***1*** *before them have only Recorded Tax Information and can only be called if you have a push-button (tone signalling) phone. Cities with a* ***2*** *before them have Recorded Tax Information, including topic 999 for local information, and Automated Refund Information and can be called by using any type of phone.*

ALABAMA
1 Birmingham, 251-9454
1 Huntsville, 534-5203
1 Mobile, 433-6993
1 Montgomery, 262-8304

ALASKA
1 Anchorage, 562-1848

ARIZONA
2 Phoenix, 252-4909

ARKANSAS
1 Little Rock, 372-3891

CALIFORNIA
1 Bakersfield, 861-4105
1 Carson, 632-3555
2 Counties of Amador, Calaveras, Contra Costa, Marin, and San Joaquin, 1-800-428-4032
2 Los Angeles, 617-3177
2 Oakland, 839-4245
1 Oxnard, 485-7236
1 Riverside, 351-6769
1 Sacramento, 448-4367
1 San Diego, 293-5020
1 San Jose, 293-5606
1 Santa Ana, 836-2974
1 Santa Maria, 928-7503
1 Santa Rosa, 528-6233
1 Stockton, 463-6005
1 Visalia, 733-8194

COLORADO
1 Colorado Springs, 597-6344
2 Denver, 592-1118
1 Ft. Collins, 221-0658

CONNECTICUT
1 Bridgeport, 335-0070
1 Hartford, 547-0015
1 New Haven, 777-4594
1 Waterbury, 754-4235

DELAWARE
1 Dover, 674-1118
1 Wilmington, 652-0272

DISTRICT of COLUMBIA
2 Call 628-2929

FLORIDA
1 Daytona Beach, 253-0669
1 Ft. Lauderdale, 523-3100
2 Jacksonville, 353-9579
1 Miami, 374-5144
1 Orlando, 422-0592
1 St. Petersburg, 578-0424
1 Tallahassee, 222-0807
1 Tampa, 229-0815
1 West Palm Beach, 655-1996

GEORGIA
1 Albany, 435-1415
2 Atlanta, 331-6572
1 Augusta, 722-9068
1 Columbus, 327-0298
1 Macon, 745-2890
1 Savannah, 355-9632

HAWAII
1 Honolulu, 541-1185

IDAHO
2 Call 1-800-554-4477

ILLINOIS
1 Aurora, 851-2718
1 Bloomington, 828-6116
1 Champaign, 398-1779
2 Chicago, 886-9614
1 East St. Louis, 875-4050
1 Ottawa, 433-1568
1 Peoria, 637-9305
1 Quad Cities, 326-1720
1 Rockford, 987-4280
1 Springfield, 789-0489

INDIANA
1 Evansville, 422-1026
1 Fort Wayne, 484-3065
1 Gary, 884-4465
2 Indianapolis, 634-1550
1 South Bend, 232-5459

IOWA
1 Cedar Rapids, 399-2210
1 Des Moines, 284-4271
1 Quad Cities, 326-1720
1 Waterloo, 234-0817

KANSAS
1 Wichita, 264-3147

KENTUCKY
1 Erlanger, 727-3338
1 Lexington, 233-2889
1 Louisville, 582-5599

LOUISIANA
1 New Orleans, 529-2854

MAINE
1 Portland, 775-0465

MARYLAND
2 Baltimore, 244-7306
1 Cumberland, 722-5331
1 Frederick, 663-5798
1 Hagerstown, 733-6815
1 Salisbury, 742-9458

MASSACHUSETTS
2 Boston, 523-8602
1 Springfield, 739-6624

MICHIGAN
1 Ann Arbor, 665-4544
2 Detroit, 961-4282
1 Flint, 238-4599
1 Grand Rapids, 451-2034
1 Kalamazoo, 343-0255
1 Lansing, 372-2454
1 Mt. Clemens, 463-9550
1 Pontiac, 858-2336
1 Saginaw, 753-9911

MINNESOTA
1 Duluth, 722-5494
1 Rochester, 288-5595
2 St. Paul, 224-4288

MISSISSIPPI
1 Gulfport, 863-3302
1 Jackson, 965-4168

MISSOURI
1 Jefferson City, 636-8312
1 Kansas City, 421-3741
1 Springfield, 883-3419
2 St. Louis, 241-4700

MONTANA
1 Billings, 656-1422
1 Great Falls, 727-4902
1 Helena, 443-7034

NEBRASKA
1 Lincoln, 471-5450
1 Omaha, 221-3324

NEVADA
2 Call 1-800-554-4477

NEW HAMPSHIRE
1 Manchester, 623-5778
1 Portsmouth, 431-0637

NEW JERSEY
1 Atlantic City, 348-2636
1 Camden, 966-3412
1 Hackensack, 487-1817
2 Newark, 624-1223
1 Paterson, 278-5442
1 Trenton, 599-2150

NEW MEXICO
1 Albuquerque, 766-1102

NEW YORK
1 Albany, 465-8318
1 Binghamton, 722-8426
2 Brooklyn, 858-4461
2 Buffalo, 856-9320
2 Manhattan, 406-4080
1 Mineola, 248-6790
1 Poughkeepsie, 452-1877
1 Rochester, 454-3330
1 Smithtown, 979-0720
2 Staten Island, 406-4080
1 Syracuse, 471-1630
1 White Plains, 683-0134

NORTH CAROLINA
1 Asheville, 254-3044
1 Charlotte, 567-9885
1 Durham, 541-5283
1 Fayetteville, 483-0735
1 Greensboro, 378-1572
1 Raleigh, 755-1498
1 Winston-Salem, 725-3013

NORTH DAKOTA
1 Bismarck, 258-8210
1 Fargo, 232-9360
1 Grand Forks, 746-0324
1 Minot, 838-1234

OHIO
1 Akron, 253-1170
1 Canton, 455-6061
2 Cincinnati, 421-0329
2 Cleveland, 522-3037
1 Columbus, 469-2266
1 Dayton, 225-7237
1 Lima, 224-0341
1 Mansfield, 525-3474
1 Toledo, 255-3743
1 Youngstown, 744-4200

OKLAHOMA
1 Oklahoma City, 235-3434
1 Tulsa, 599-0555

OREGON
2 Portland, 294-5363

PENNSYLVANIA
1 Bethlehem, 861-0325
1 Harrisburg, 236-1356
1 Jenkintown, 887-1261
1 Lancaster, 392-0980
1 Norristown, 275-0242
2 Philadelphia, 592-8946
2 Pittsburgh, 281-3120
1 Reading, 373-4568
1 Scranton, 961-0325
1 Wilkes-Barre, 823-9552
1 Williamsport, 323-4242

RHODE ISLAND
1 Providence, 861-5220

SOUTH CAROLINA
1 Charleston, 722-0369
1 Columbia, 254-4749
1 Greenville, 235-8093

SOUTH DAKOTA
1 Rapid City, 348-3454
1 Sioux Falls, 335-7081
1 Watertown, 882-4979

TENNESSEE
1 Chattanooga, 892-5577
1 Jackson, 664-1858
1 Johnson City, 282-1917
1 Knoxville, 521-7478
1 Memphis, 525-2611
2 Nashville, 242-1541

TEXAS
1 Austin, 479-0391
2 Dallas, 767-1792
1 El Paso, 534-0260
1 Ft. Worth, 334-3888
2 Houston, 850-8801
1 San Antonio, 680-9591

UTAH
1 Salt Lake City, 355-9328

VERMONT
1 Burlington, 658-0007

VIRGINIA
1 Bristol, 669-0565
1 Charlottesville, 296-8558
1 Danville, 797-2223
1 Hampton, 826-8071
1 Lynchburg, 845-6052
1 Norfolk, 441-3623
2 Richmond, 771-2369
1 Roanoke, 982-6062
1 Staunton, 886-3541

WASHINGTON
2 Seattle, 343-7221
1 Spokane, 455-9213

WEST VIRGINIA
1 Charleston, 343-3597
1 Huntington, 523-0104

WISCONSIN
1 Eau Claire, 834-6121
1 Green Bay, 433-3884
1 Madison, 264-5349
2 Milwaukee, 291-1783
1 Racine, 886-1615

WYOMING
1 Cheyenne, 634-1198

Note: *If there is no number listed for your specific area, call* ***1-800-554-4477.***

Guide To Tax-Free Services

To Call IRS Toll-Free for Answers to Your Federal Tax Questions, Use Only the Number Listed Below for Your Area.

Caution: *"Toll-free" is a telephone call for which you pay only local charges with no long-distance charge. Please use a local city number only if it is not a long-distance call for you.* ***Do not dial 800 when using a local city number.*** Otherwise, *use the general toll-free number given.*

We are happy to answer questions to help you prepare your return. But you should know that you are responsible for the accuracy of your return. If we do make an error, you are still responsible for the payment of the correct tax.

To make sure that IRS employees give courteous responses and correct information to taxpayers, a second IRS employee sometimes listens in on telephone calls. No record is kept of any taxpayer's name, address, or social security number.

If you find it necessary to write instead of calling, please address your letter to your IRS District Director for a prompt reply. Make sure you include your social security number or taxpayer identifying number when you write.

The IRS has a telephone service called Tele-Tax. It provides automated refund information and recorded tax information on about 150 topics covering such areas as filing requirements, dependents, itemized deductions, and tax credits. Tele-Tax is available 24 hours a day, 7 days a week, to taxpayers using push-button (tone signalling) telephones, and Monday through Friday, during office hours, to taxpayers using push-button (pulse dial) or rotary (dial) phones. See Tele-Tax Information in the index for the page numbers that contain telephone numbers, available topics, and instructions describing how to use this service.

ALABAMA
Call 1-800-424-1040

ALASKA
Anchorage, 561-7484
Elsewhere in Alaska, call 1-800-478-1040

ARIZONA
Phoenix, 257-1233

ARKANSAS
Call 1-800-424-1040

CALIFORNIA
Please call the telephone number shown in the white pages of your local telephone directory under U.S. Government, Internal Revenue Service, Federal Tax Assistance

COLORADO
Denver, 825-7041

CONNECTICUT
Call 1-800-424-1040

DELAWARE
Call 1-800-424-1040

DISTRICT of COLUMBIA
Call 488-3100

FLORIDA
Jacksonville, 354-1760

GEORGIA
Atlanta, 522-0050

HAWAII
Oahu, 541-1040
All other islands, 1-800-232-2511

IDAHO
Call 1-800-424-1040

ILLINOIS
Chicago, 435-1040

INDIANA
Indianapolis, 269-5477

IOWA
Des Moines, 283-0523

KANSAS
Call 1-800-424-1040

KENTUCKY
Call 1-800-424-1040

LOUISIANA
Call 1-800-424-1040

MAINE
Call 1-800-424-1040

MARYLAND
Baltimore, 962-2590
Montgomery County, 488-3100
Prince George's County, 488-3100

MASSACHUSETTS
Boston, 523-1040

MICHIGAN
Detroit, 237-0800

MINNESOTA
Minneapolis, 291-1422
St. Paul, 291-1422

MISSISSIPPI
Call 1-800-424-1040

MISSOURI
St. Louis, 342-1040

MONTANA
Call 1-800-424-1040

NEBRASKA
Omaha, 422-1500

NEVADA
Call 1-800-424-1040

NEW HAMPSHIRE
Call 1-800-424-1040

NEW JERSEY
Newark, 622-0600

NEW MEXICO
Call 1-800-424-1040

NEW YORK
Bronx, 732-0100
Brooklyn, 596-3770
Buffalo, 855-3955
Manhattan, 732-0100
Nassau, 222-1131
Queens, 596-3770
Rockland County, 997-1510
Staten Island, 732-0100
Suffolk, 724-5000
Westchester County, 997-1510

NORTH CAROLINA
Call 1-800-424-1040

NORTH DAKOTA
Call 1-800-424-1040

OHIO
Cincinnati, 621-6281
Cleveland, 522-3000

OKLAHOMA
Call 1-800-424-1040

OREGON
Eugene, 485-8286
Portland, 221-3960
Salem, 581-8721

PENNSYLVANIA
Philadelphia, 574-9900
Pittsburgh, 281-0112

PUERTO RICO
San Juan Metro Area, 753-4040
Isla DDD, 753-4549

RHODE ISLAND
Call 1-800-424-1040

SOUTH CAROLINA
Call 1-800-424-1040

SOUTH DAKOTA
Call 1-800-424-1040

TENNESSEE
Nashville, 259-4601

TEXAS
Austin, 472-1974
Corpus Christi, 888-9431
Dallas, 742-2440
El Paso, 532-6116
Ft. Worth, 263-9229
Houston, 965-0440
San Antonio, 229-1700

UTAH
Call 1-800-424-1040

VERMONT
Call 1-800-424-1040

VIRGINIA
Bailey's Crossroads, 557-9230
Richmond, 649-2361

WASHINGTON
Seattle, 442-1040

WEST VIRGINIA
Call 1-800-424-1040

WISCONSIN
Milwaukee, 271-3780

WYOMING
Call 1-800-424-1040

Note: *If there is no number listed for your specific area, please call* ***1-800-424-1040.***

Telephone Assistance Services for Deaf Taxpayers Who Have Access to TV / Telephone—TTY Equipment.

Hours of Operation

8:00 A.M. to 6:45 P.M. EST (Filing Season)

8:00 A.M. to 4:30 P.M. EST (Nonfiling Season)

Indiana residents, 1-800-382-4059

Elsewhere in U.S., including Alaska, Hawaii, Virgin Islands, and Puerto Rico, 1-800-428-4732

Toll-Free "Forms Only" Telephone Numbers

If you only need to order tax forms and publications and do not have any tax questions, call the number listed below for your area.

ALASKA
Anchorage, 563-5313
Elsewhere in Alaska, call 1-800-478-1040

ARIZONA
Phoenix, 257-1233
Tucson, 882-0730

CALIFORNIA
Please call the telephone number shown in the white pages of your local telephone directory under U.S. Government, Internal Revenue Service, Federal Tax Forms.

COLORADO
Denver, 825-7041

HAWAII
Honolulu, 541-1180
All other islands, 1-800-232-2511

ILLINOIS
Bloomington, 662-2515

OREGON
Eugene, 485-8286
Portland, 221-3933
Salem, 581-8721

PUERTO RICO
San Juan Metro Area, 753-4040
Isla DDD, 753-4549

VIRGINIA
Richmond, 329-1052

WASHINGTON
Seattle, 442-5100

Note: *If there is no number listed for your state or specific area, call* ***1-800-424-FORM (3676).***

Guide To Tax-Free Services

IRS Information and Assistance

Most taxpayers should be able to meet the requirements of the tax laws by using information such as tax package instructions, publications, taxpayer education programs, films, and library programs. If further information and assistance are needed, services are available as indicated in the following paragraphs.

Toll-free telephone and walk-in assistance is available to answer questions on taxpayer accounts, IRS procedures, or technical inquiries on tax-related matters.

Telephone Service

Toll-free telephone assistance is available in all 50 states, the District of Columbia, Puerto Rico and the Virgin Islands. Under this system you pay only local charges, with no long-distance charge for your call. Through the toll-free system you may obtain assistance on your tax questions.

To help us provide courteous responses and accurate information, an IRS employee occasionally listens in on telephone calls. No record is made of the taxpayer's name, address or social security number except where a follow-up telephone call must be made.

During periods of peak demand for telephone assistance you may encounter busy signals when trying to call. Generally, demand is lower early in the morning and later in the week so you may want to call at those times.

Tele-Tax

The IRS provides a toll-free telephone service called Tele-Tax. This service has both Automated Refund Information and Recorded Tax Information.

Automated Refund Information can be used to check on the status of your current year's refund. If it has been ten weeks since you mailed your 1986 tax return, we will then be able to check the status of your refund. Automated Refund Information is available after March 15th, Monday through Friday from 6:30 a.m. to 7:00 p.m. (hours may vary in your area) to taxpayers using a push-button (tone signalling) phone. It is also available Monday through Friday during normal business hours to taxpayers using a rotary (dial) or push-button (pulse dial) phone.

Recorded Tax Information is available on about 150 topics covering such areas as filing requirements, dependents, itemized deductions and tax credits. Recorded Tax Information is available 24 hours a day, 7 days a week to taxpayers using a push-button (tone signalling) phone. It is also available during normal business hours to taxpayers using a rotary (dial) or push-button (pulse dial) phone.

Telephone Service for Deaf Taxpayers

Toll-free telephone assistance for deaf taxpayers is available for those who have access to TV/Telephone-TTY equipment. The hours of operation of this service are 8:00 a.m. to 6:45 p.m. Eastern Standard Time for January thru April and 8:00 a.m. to 4:30 p.m. for May thru December. Residents of Indiana may call 1-800-382-4059. Residents elsewhere in the U.S. including Alaska, Hawaii, Puerto Rico, and the Virgin Islands may call 1-800-428-4732.

Information for the Blind

Braille materials are available at Regional Libraries for the Blind and Physically Handicapped in conjunction with the Library of Congress. These materials include Publications 17 and 334, Forms 1040, 1040A, and 1040EZ and Schedules A and B, W, and instructions.

Walk-In Service

While the Internal Revenue Service will not prepare your tax return for you, assistors are available in most IRS offices throughout the country to help you as you prepare your own individual federal tax return. You will be expected to help yourself to the maximum extent possible. However, you will be provided assistance and at the same time, provided the opportunity of learning how to research and prepare your own tax return. An assistor will "walk-through" a return with you and a number of other taxpayers in a group setting.

In many IRS Offices a walk-in counter is available to assist you with inquiries that do not involve preparation of a return at the time of your visit such as receipt of an IRS notice or bill. You may also obtain certain technical information or publications at most IRS offices.

If you wish assistance with your tax return, you should bring in your tax package, your Forms W-2 and 1099 and any other information (such as a copy of last year's return) which will enable us to help you.

Computer Tax Database

The IRS has prepared a database of tax information that is available through several commercial information retrieval (videotex) services. These services are accessible on a subscription basis by computer terminals that are equipped with modems.

The database consists of selected Taxpayer Information Publications, answers to the most commonly asked tax related questions, and other items that are prepared for information retrieval. The database covers many topics that can be used in preparing Federal tax returns and as a reference source for year-round tax planning.

Taxpayer Education Programs

The Internal Revenue Service has a number of programs designed to educate the public about our nation's voluntary compliance tax system and each citizen's share in it so that the system works as smoothly as possible. The more that citizens understand their role in this tax system, the better they will be able to carry out their responsibilities with a minimum of intrusion in their lives by the government. All of these taxpayer education programs offer opportunity for citizen involvement through service as volunteers.

Understanding Taxes

This is a tax education program that begins in the schools, where young people are taught about their tax rights and responsibilities under our voluntary compliance tax system. They also learn how to fill out basic tax returns. Since many of them already are working, often at their first jobs, this learning has immediate practical value. They also learn about the history of taxes and current issues in taxation, such as tax reform. All materials teachers need are available free of charge, including a six-part film series, "Tax Whys: Understanding Taxes." These films were produced in cooperation with the states. Workshops are conducted during the year to help prepare teachers for course instruction.

Small Business Workshops

These workshops help people start small businesses by providing them with the information they need to carry out their tax responsibilities, including tax withholding, making correct and timely tax deposits and filing a business return. Some sessions focus on the needs of the self-employed, minority entrepreneurs and specialized business groups.

Volunteer Income Tax Assistance

The Volunteer Income Tax Assistance program (VITA) provides free tax assistance to lower income, elderly, non-English-speaking and handicapped people and also to members of the military. Generally those who receive these services can't afford professional tax assistance. After completing IRS training, volunteers provide free help at special locations.

Tax Counseling for the Elderly

Tax Counseling for the Elderly (TCE) provides free tax assistance to people 60 or older, especially those who are disabled or have other special needs. Non-profit organizations under cooperative agreements with the IRS provide local assistance.

Both VITA and TCE sites usually are located in neighborhood centers, libraries, churches and other places in the community.

Student Tax Clinics

Another program, Student Tax Clinic, uses volunteer law and graduate accounting students who have received permission from the Treasury Department to represent taxpayers before the IRS. They provide free assistance to taxpayers during IRS examination and appeals proceedings.

Community Outreach Tax Assistance

This is a year-round program of assistance to groups who need help understanding the tax laws, especially as they apply to members of their profession or group, such as teaching or business or farming. Seminars are conducted at times and locations in the community that are convenient for members of the group.

For all of these programs, contact your local IRS office for more information and locations of sites or presentations in your areas.

Taxpayer Information Program

The Taxpayer Information Program is designed to give taxpayers the information they need to understand their rights and comply with their responsibilities under the tax laws.

To reach the greatest number of taxpayers, the Taxpayer Information Program provides print and audio-visual public service materials directly to the public, and to the news media for dissemination to the public. In cooperation with public television stations IRS also produces programs for broadcast which take taxpayers step-by-step through Forms 1040A and 1040EZ and highlight Form 1040 and Schedules A and B.

The IRS provides local libraries with audio cassettes and videocassettes, for loan to the public, on how to fill out Forms 1040EZ, 1040A, 1040 and Schedules A and B. These tax tapes contain simple, step-by-step instructions through the forms, tax tips, and special rules for the military.

Guide To Tax-Free Services

How To Use Tele-Tax

Recorded Tax Information

1. Select, by number, the topic you wish to hear
2. Have paper and pencil handy to take notes
3. Call the appropriate phone number
4. • If you have a push-button (tone signalling) phone, follow the recorded instructions, or

   • If you have a rotary (dial) or push-button (pulse dial) phone, ask the IRS operator for the topic number you want to hear
5. • Push-button (tone signalling) service is available 24 hours a day, 7 days a week

   • Rotary (dial)/push-button (pulse dial) service is available Monday through Friday during regular office hours. (In Hawaii, from 6:30 A.M. to 1:00 P.M.)

Automated Refund Information

1. Have a copy of your tax return available since you will need to know the first social security number shown on your return, the filing status, and the exact amount of your refund
2. Call the appropriate phone number
3. Follow the recorded instructions
4. • Push-button (tone signalling) service is available Monday through Friday from 6:30 A.M. to 6 P.M. (Hours may vary in your area.)

   • Rotary (dial)/push-button (pulse dial) service is available Monday through Friday during regular office hours. (In Hawaii, from 6:30 A.M. to 1:00 P.M.)

Tele-Tax Topic Numbers and Subjects

Topic No.	Subject
	IRS Procedures and Services
100	IRS help available—Volunteer tax assistance programs, toll-free telephone, walk-in assistance, and outreach program
101	Tax assistance for handicapped individuals and the deaf
102	Small business tax workshops—Tax help for the new business person
103	Problem resolution program—Special help for problem situations
104	Public libraries—Tax information tapes and reproducible tax forms
105	Examination procedures and how to prepare for an audit
106	The collection process
107	Tax fraud—How to report
108	Special enrollment examination to practice before IRS
109	Organizations—How to apply for exempt status
999	Local Information
	Filing Requirements, Filing Status, Exemptions
110	Who must file?
111	Which form—1040, 1040A, or 1040EZ?
112	When, where, and how to file
113	Filing requirements for a dependent child
114	Filing as single
115	Filing joint or separate
116	Filing as head of household
117	Filing as qualifying widow/widower
118	Filing status for separated individuals
119	Exemptions for age and blindness
120	Dependent—Who can be claimed?
121	Dependent child—Divorced or separated parents
122	Dependent—Items to include in determining support
126	Estimated tax
127	Amended returns
128	Decedents
	Types of Income
130	Wages and salaries
131	Tips
132	Interest received
133	Dividends and dividend exclusion
134	Refund of state and local taxes
135	Alimony received
136	Business income
137	Sole proprietorship
138	Capital gains and losses
139	Pensions and annuities
140	Pensions—The general rule
141	Lump sum distributions—Profit-sharing plans
143	Rental income and expenses
200	Renting vacation property/Renting to relatives
201	Royalties
202	Farming and fishing income
203	Earnings for clergy members
204	Unemployment compensation
205	Gambling income and expenses
206	Bartering income
207	Scholarships, fellowships, and grants
208	Nontaxable income
209	Social security and tier 1 railroad retirement taxability
210	Social Security Benefit Statement—Form SSA-1099
	Adjustments to Income
211	Charitable contributions deduction for those who do not itemize
212	Deduction for married couples when both work
213	Moving expenses
214	Employee business expenses
215	Business use of car
216	Business travel expenses
217	Business entertainment expenses
218	Individual retirement arrangements (IRA's)
219	Alimony paid
225	Bad debt deduction
226	Tax shelters
	Itemized Deductions
227	Should I itemize?
228	Medical and dental expenses
229	Medical insurance
231	Taxes
232	Sales tax
233	Interest expense
234	Contributions
235	Casualty losses
236	Miscellaneous expenses
237	Business use of your home
238	Educational expenses
	Tax Computation
240	Tax table/Tax rate schedules
243	Tax and credits figured by IRS
244	Income averaging
300	Self-employment tax
301	Ten-year averaging for lump sum distributions
303	Alternative minimum tax
304	Gift tax
305	Estate tax
	Tax Credits
306	Child care credit
307	Earned income credit
308	Residential energy credit
309	Credit for the elderly or for the permanently and totally disabled
310	Tax credit for contributions to candidates for public office
311	Investment credit
312	Qualified royalty owners exemption (windfall profit tax)
	General Information
314	Substitute tax forms
315	Highlights of 1986 tax changes
316	Refunds—How long they should take
317	Copy of your tax return—How to get one
318	Forms/Publications—How to order
319	Tax shelter registration
320	Extensions for time to file your tax return
325	Form W-2—What to do if not received
326	Highlights of the Tax Reform Act
327	IRS notices and bills/Penalty and interest charges
328	Tax benefits for low income Americans
329	Penalty for underpayment of estimated tax—Form 2210
330	Recordkeeping
331	How to choose a tax preparer
332	Audit appeal rights
333	Failure to pay child/spousal support and other Federal obligations
335	Withholding on interest and dividends
336	Highway use tax
337	Checklist/Common errors when preparing your tax return
338	Withholding on pensions and annuities
339	Your tax form is overdue—Let us hear from you
340	Second request for information about your tax form
341	Notice of intent to levy
342	Notice of underreported income—CP2000
	Basis of Assets, Depreciation, Sale of Assets
343	Sale of personal residence—General
344	Sale of personal residence—How to report gain
400	Sale of personal residence—Exclusion of gain, age 55 and over
401	Basis of assets
402	Depreciation—General
403	Depreciation—Accelerated cost recovery system
404	Installment sales
	Employer Tax Information
406	Social security withholding rates
407	Form W-2—Where, when and how to file
408	Form W-4—Employee's Withholding Allowance Certificate
409	Federal tax deposits—General
410	Employer identification number—How to apply
412	Form 942—Employer's Quarterly Tax Return for Household Employees
413	Form 941—Deposit requirements
414	Form 941—Employer's Quarterly Federal Tax Return
415	Form 940—Deposit requirements
416	Form 940—Employer's Annual Federal Unemployment Tax Return
417	Targeted jobs credit
418	Tips—Withholding and reporting
	Tax Information for Aliens and U.S. Citizens Living Abroad
420	Resident and nonresident aliens
425	Dual-status alien
426	Alien tax clearance
428	Foreign earned income exclusion—General
429	Foreign earned income exclusion—Who qualifies?
430	Foreign earned income exclusion—What income qualifies?
431	Foreign tax credit
	The following topics are in Spanish
433	Who must file?
434	Which form to use?
435	Filing status—Single, married filing jointly, and married filing separately
436	Filing status—Head of household and qualifying widow/widower
437	Earned income credit
438	Highlights of 1986 tax changes
439	Forms and publications—How to order
440	Alien tax clearance
441	Refunds—How long they should take
442	IRS help available—Volunteer tax assistance programs, toll-free telephone, walk-in assistance, and outreach program
443	Social security and tier 1 railroad retirement taxability
444	Social Security Benefit Statement—Form SSA-1099

Guide To Tax-Free Services

IRS-produced films and videotapes are available for loan directly from the IRS, without charge, to groups or interested organizations. To order the film of your choice, call your local office and ask for the Public Affairs Officer.

"How to Fill Out Your Tax Return"

A line-by-line guide on how to fill out Forms 1040EZ, 1040A, 1040 and Schedules A and B. It explains how to choose the right tax return and discusses filing status, deductions, tax law changes, tax credits, and tax computations as well as other topics pertaining to your tax returns. (60 mins.) (¾", ½" Beta and VHS) (Updated versions available by January of each year.)

"Why Us, the Lakens?"

This film, narrated by Lyle Waggoner, highlights taxpayers' rights during a tax audit and their Appeal rights. It follows Jeff and Kathy Laken, whose tax return has been selected for an IRS audit. Unhappy with the audit finding, the Lakens appeal and the viewer learns not only how the audit procedure works but the appeals system as well. (28 mins.) (16mm film and ¾" videocassettes)

"A Trip Down the Pipeline"

The 14-minute film, narrated by Terry Carter who appeared in such popular TV programs as *Battlestar Galactica* and *McCloud*, shows how a tax return is processed at an IRS Service Center. The film depicts the various steps that occur in the processing cycle, or along the pipeline. (14 mins.) (16mm film)

"A Vital Service"

People helping people with their federal taxes is what "A Vital Service" is all about. It aims at enlisting groups and organizations into the Volunteer Income Tax Assistance (VITA) Program in which IRS trains volunteers to help the low-income, elderly, non-English speaking and the handicapped with their tax forms. (9½ mins.) (16mm film and ¾" videocassettes)

"Helping to Recover"

Focuses on how to claim disaster, casualty and theft losses. (13 mins.) (¾" videocassette)

"Hey, We're in Business"

A couple just starting their own restaurant business—and encountering the related tax problems—are the focus of this dramatized presentation. Jim Backus, David Hedison, Pat Crowley, and Nehemiah Persoff, form the cast of this production about good recordkeeping, tax deadlines, and free IRS assistance to business persons. (27½ mins.) (16mm film) (English and Spanish)

Guide To Tax-Free Services

The following pages will give you some Tax Return Filing Tips, provided by the IRS to make the process of paying your taxes as painless as possible. Keep a copy of this section with the packet of materials you receive from the IRS and refer to it as you prepare and then submit your return.

Your Tax Package

In most cases after you file your first federal income tax return the IRS will mail you a tax package containing either Form 1040 and related schedules or Form 1040A and 1040EZ. You should receive this package in late December or early January. If you do not receive one, you should pick up forms at IRS, the library or a bank.

Your tax package contains a coded, peel-off address label. Attaching this label to your return will speed up the processing of your return and the issuing of any refund. If any of the information on the label is incorrect, make the necessary change right on the label. Even if you don't use the tax form in the tax package you receive in the mail, you should attach the label to the tax return you file. If you take your return to a tax return preparer, VITA site, etc. for completion, have the person who prepares your return use your address label.

Your tax package also contains an addressed envelope for mailing your return. Using this envelope will also speed up the processing of your return because this envelope is coded for electronic sorting by type of tax return before opening. If you do not have an addressed envelope or if you moved during the year, mail your return to the Internal Revenue Service Center for the area where you now live.

Social Security Number

Your social security number, which the IRS uses as your taxpayer identification number (TIN), must appear on every individual tax return, statement or other document. You should include it on your check or money order for payment of tax you pay when you file your return with the IRS. If the social security number shown on the preprinted address label on the individual tax return package is wrong, mark through it and make the correction on the label. If you do not have a tax return with the preprinted label, write the social security number in the appropriate space on the form.

If you are married, provide the social security numbers for both yourself and your spouse, whether you file jointly or separately. If you are filing a joint return, list your social security numbers in the same order that you show your first names.

If your name changes for reasons such as marriage or divorce, you should notify the Social Security Administration so that the name on our records is the same as the Social Security Administration has on its records. If you don't notify the Social Security Administration, processing your return and issuing your refund may be delayed.

Wage and Tax Statement—Form W-2

If you work for an employer during the year, your employer must provide you with a Form W-2 showing wages and other compensation paid you and amounts deducted from the pay for federal, state, local (if applicable) and social security (FICA) taxes. If you filed Form W-5, Earned Income Credit Advance Payment Certificate, with your employer, the amount of the advance earned income credit paid to you during the year will also be included on your Form W-2.

If you work for an employer for only part of a year, your employer may provide you with a Form W-2 at the time you leave your job or wait until the end of the year. If you worked for more than one employer during the year, you should receive a Form W-2 from each employer. If you change jobs and move and your employer(s) have not give you a Form W-2, you should provide the employer(s) with your new address so the Form(s) W-2 can be mailed to you.

Copy B of each Form W-2 should be filed with your federal income tax return. If you receive a Form W-2 on which any of the entries are incorrect, ask your employer for a corrected form. Your employer should mark the corrected form "Corrected by Employer". Copy B of the corrected form should be filed with your federal income tax return.

If you do not receive your Form W-2 from any employer by January 31, you should contact that employer and ask for the form. If after contacting your employer you do not receive your Form W-2 by February 15, call the IRS number for your area and request assistance. You will be asked to provide your name, address, social security number, and the name and Employer Identification Number of your employer who failed to furnish you with a Form W-2 along with an estimate of your wages and tax withheld.

Do not delay filing your return by the due date even if you have not received a Form W-2 from your employer. File your individual tax return and attach Form 4852, Substitute for Form W-2, Wage and Tax Statement or Form W-2P, Statement for Recipients of Annuities, Pensions, Retired Pay or IRA Payments, or a statement giving your name and social security number, the employer's name, address and Employer Identification Number, the total wages you received, and the amount of federal income tax withheld from your pay. If you are not sure of these amounts you should estimate them to the best of your knowledge.

If after you file your return you receive a Form W-2 and find that the income you reported on your return does not agree with the amount shown on the Forms W-2, you must file an amended return (Form 1040X, Amended U.S. Individual Income Tax Return) to correct the error.

Tax Credits

Taxpayers meeting the necessary qualifications will be able to claim certain credits against the amount of tax they owe. Some of these credits are earned income credit, child and dependent care credit, residential energy credit carryover, credit for the elderly and the permanently and totally disabled and credit for political contributions. These credits are discussed in various taxpayer information publications.

Employee's Withholding Allowance Certificate—Form W-4

Each time you start working for a new employer you will be asked to complete a Form W-4. Using information provided by you on the form your employer will know how much money to withhold from your wages for federal income tax so that by the end of the year the amount of federal income tax withheld should be about the same as your federal income tax liability. If any of the information changes, such as the number of allowances claimed on your Form W-4, it is your responsibility to go to the employer and ask to complete a new Form W-4 so that the correct amount of federal income tax will be withheld from your wages.

Estimated Tax

If you are self-employed or have other income not subject to income tax withholding, you may be required to make estimated tax payments during the year. In general, estimated tax is the amount of tax that you are going to owe that will not be paid through the withholding system.

You may pay the entire amount you estimate your tax to be by April 15 when the first payment is due or you may pay the tax in four installments with the first payment due by April 15. Because you may be charged a penalty for underpayment of estimated tax, it is important that you pay your estimated tax timely.

For additional information on who must pay estimated taxes and how and when to make payments, please see IRS Publication 505, Estimated Tax and Tax Withholding.

Recordkeeping

A well-organized system for your records will make preparing your tax return easier and will also help you to answer questions if your return is selected for examination or if you are billed for additional tax.

You should keep these records as long as there is a possibility that an entry on your return may be questioned by the IRS. You should keep records such as receipts, cancelled checks and other documents that prove an item of income or deduction appearing on your return until the statute of limitations expires for the return. Usually this is three years from the date the return was due or filed, or two years from the date the tax was paid, whichever is later. There is no statute of limitations when a return is false or fraudulent or when no return is filed.

Some records, such as property records, should be retained indefinitely since they may be needed to prove the amount of gain or loss if the property is sold. These income tax returns should also be kept indefinitely. They will help you prepare future tax returns and will also help you if you later file a claim for refund.

For additional information on the importance of recordkeeping, please see Publication 552, Recordkeeping Requirements and a List of IRS Publications, and Publication 583, Recordkeeping for a Small Business.

Checklist Before Mailing Your Return

Before you mail your individual income tax return, check to be sure you have done all these things:

1. Transferred the address label to your return, and made any necessary corrections to your name, address, and social security number;
2. Attached Copy B of all your Forms W-2;
3. Attached all required forms and related schedules;
4. Reported all your taxable income;
5. Rechecked your return to make sure you have made no mistake in your arithmetic;
6. Signed and dated your return (on a joint return, both husband and wife must sign);
7. Attached your check or money order payable to "Internal Revenue Service," if you owe additional tax, and have written your social security number, tax form number and tax year on your check or money order;
8. Used the envelope that came with the package or addressed the return to the Internal Revenue Service Center for your state;
9. Made a copy of the return for your records.

If you file early you may expect to receive your refund within four to six weeks. If you do not get your refund within 10 weeks after filing your return, call your Internal Revenue Office.

Common Errors

Following is a list of the most common errors taxpayers have made on their Forms 1040, 1040EZ and 1040A. Explanations are provided to help you avoid making these errors. Be sure to double check your tax return because errors such as those listed below may delay the issuance of any refund you may be expecting.

1. Computation error in computing medical and dental expenses on Schedule A.
   — Form 1040 through the Adjusted Gross Income line must be completed before you can figure Medical and Dental Expenses on Schedule A. Read carefully the instructions on how to deduct these expenses and double check your math for these entries.
2. Incorrect amount of Earned Income Credit
   — You may be entitled to a credit of up to $550 if your Adjusted Gross Income is less than $11,000. The Earned Income Credit Worksheet is used to determine eligibility. If your Adjusted Gross Income is $6,500 or less, find your credit in the Earned Income Credit Table and place that amount on the proper line of your Form 1040 or 1040A. If your Adjusted Gross Income is over $6,500, use your earned income amount to find your credit in the table. Then use your Adjusted Gross Income to find your credit in the table. Enter the smaller amount of the two as your credit on the proper line of your Form 1040 or 1040A.
3. Incorrect amount of tax entered from tax tables.
   — Make sure you use the correct tax table for your filing status. Take the amount shown on the taxable income line of your Form 1040 or 1040A and go to the tax table column showing that amount. Find the column for your marital status (married filing jointly, single, etc.) and read down the column. The amount shown where the income line and filing status column meet is your tax.
4. Social Security Tax, instead of your Federal Income Tax Withheld, was entered on your tax return.
   — When entering the amount from your Form W-2, recheck to make sure that you have entered the Federal Income Tax Withheld and *not* the FICA (Social Security Tax) amount.
5. Incorrect computation of taxable amount of Unemployment Compensation.
   — You should receive a statement, Form 1099-G showing the total unemployment compensation paid to you during the year. Enter this amount on the proper line of Form 1040 or Form 1040A. Use the Unemployment Compensation Worksheet in the instructions to determine if it is taxable by using the formula given for your filing status. Enter the computed amount, which is the taxable amount of your unemployment compensation, on the appropriate line of Form 1040 or Form 1040A.
6. Computation error made on Form 2441, Credit for Child and Dependent Care Expenses.
   — Verify your addition, subtractions and multiplication. Use the correct percentage for line 8 as shown on the back of Form 2441.
7. Incorrect computation of refund or balance due.
   — Verify your addition and subtraction. You are due a "Refund" if your tax from the tax table and any other taxes you are liable for are less than the amounts you have paid (such as the amount withheld shown on your form W-2). A "Balance Due" is computed when the above items total more than the amounts you have already paid.
8. Earned Income Credit not claimed when qualification met.
   — Refer to your tax package to determine if you meet the qualifications for the Earned Income Credit and then use the Earned Income Credit Worksheet to determine your refund.
9. Computation error made on page 1 of your tax return when figuring your dividends.
   — You can exclude (subtract) up to $100 of qualifying dividend income. If a joint return is filed, you can subtract up to $200, regardless of which spouse received the dividends.
10. Computation error on page 1 of the tax return when income amounts were totalled.
    — Verify the addition of all income amounts on the front of your return.

Where To File

Please use the address envelope that came with your return. If you do not have an addressed envelope or if you moved during the year, mail your return to the Internal Revenue Service Center for the area where you live.

If you are requesting copies of prior year returns, you should send the request to the service center where the original return was filed. No street address is needed.

Where To File

If an addressed envelope came with your return, please use it. If you do not have one, or if you moved during the year, mail your return to the **Internal Revenue Service Center** for the place where you live. No street address is needed.

If you are located in:	Use this address:
Alabama, Florida, Georgia, Mississippi, South Carolina	Atlanta, GA 31101
New Jersey, New York City and counties of Nassau, Rockland, Suffolk, and Westchester	Holtsville, NY 00501
Connecticut, Maine, Massachusetts, Minnesota, New Hampshire, New York (all other counties), Rhode Island, Vermont	Andover, MA 05501
Illinois, Iowa, Missouri, Wisconsin	Kansas City, MO 64999
Delaware, District of Columbia, Maryland, Pennsylvania	Philadelphia, PA 19255
Kentucky, Michigan, Ohio, West Virginia	Cincinnati, OH 45999
Kansas, Louisiana, New Mexico, Oklahoma, Texas	Austin, TX 73301
Alaska, Arizona, California (counties of Alpine, Amador, Butte, Calaveras, Colusa, Contra Costa, Del Norte, El Dorado, Glenn, Humboldt, Lake, Lassen, Marin, Mendocino, Modoc, Napa, Nevada, Placer, Plumas, Sacramento, San Joaquin, Shasta, Sierra, Siskiyou, Solano, Sonoma, Sutter, Tehama, Trinity, Yolo, and Yuba), Colorado, Idaho, Montana, Nebraska, Nevada, North Dakota, Oregon, South Dakota, Utah, Washington, Wyoming	Ogden, UT 84201
California (all other counties), Hawaii	Fresno, CA 93888
Arkansas, Indiana, North Carolina, Tennessee, Virginia	Memphis, TN 37501
American Samoa	Philadelphia, PA 19255
Guam	Commissioner of Revenue and Taxation, Agana, GU 96910
Puerto Rico (or if excluding income under section 933), Virgin Islands: Nonpermanent residents	Philadelphia, PA 19255
Virgin Islands: Permanent residents	V. I. Bureau of Internal Revenue, P.O. Box 3186, St. Thomas, VI 00801
Foreign country: U.S. citizens and those filing Form 2555 or Form 4563, even if you have an A.P.O. or F.P.O. address	Philadelphia, PA 19255
A.P.O. or F.P.O. address of:	Miami—Atlanta, GA 31101 New York—Holtsville, NY 00501 San Francisco—Fresno, CA 93888 Seattle—Ogden, UT 84201

After You File

Refunds

If it has been at least 10 weeks since you mailed your tax return, you can call a telephone number to find out the status of your refund. When you call, you should have available a copy of your tax return since you will need to know the first social security number shown on the return, the filing status, and the exact amount of the refund.

Problem Resolution Program

The Problem Resolution Program (PRP) is for taxpayers who have been unable to resolve their problems through normal Internal Revenue Service channels. Someone with a tax problem should first contact IRS taxpayer assistance, or in the case of a letter or notice from the IRS, call the number provided. Generally, questions are answered and problems solved right then—but not always. That's when PRP steps in. Each of the IRS's 64 district offices has a PRP office whose specialty is assisting taxpayers who previously contacted the IRS with their tax problems but could not get them resolved. People in the PRP office have the authority to cut through the red tape and handle problems promptly. The taxpayer generally deals with one person and is kept informed of the case's progress. Taxpayers can contact PRP by calling the IRS assistance number or writing to their local Internal Revenue Service District Director and asking for Problem Resolution assistance. While PRP offices do everything they can to help taxpayers, there are some things they cannot do. Appeals of decisions made in tax examinations, Freedom of Information Act requests, Privacy Act inquiries and complaints about hiring practices are all outside of PRP's authority.

Amending Your Return

After you have filed your return, if you discover that you did not report some income, did not claim deductions or credits you could have claimed, or claimed deductions or credits you should not have claimed, you can correct your return by filing a Form 1040X, Amended U.S. Individual Income Tax Return. Generally, this form must be filed within three years from the date you filed your original return or within two years from the date you paid your tax, whichever is later.

File Form 1040X with the IRS Service Center for the area in which you live. See the listing of these service centers at the top of this page.

Your state tax liability may be affected by a change made on your federal income tax return. For more information on this you should contact your state tax agency.

Copies of Prior Year Returns

You can obtain a copy of your prior year tax return by completing Form 4506, Request for Copy of Tax Form or Tax Account Information, and mailing it to the service center where you filed the return you are requesting. Service center addresses are listed on the back of Form 4506. There is a charge for each copy of a return. This fee must be sent to the service center along with your Form 4506 or written request. If you are unable to act on your own behalf, your authorized representative may request a copy of your return. Your representative must sign the request and attach a copy of Form 2848, Power of Attorney, or other document authorizing him or her to act for you.

If you do not have a Form 4506, you can send the service center a written request containing the following information: your name, the social security number, and, if you filed a joint return, the name and social security number of your spouse; the form number; the tax period; and your current address. You must sign this request. If you filed a joint return, only one of you must sign this request. You should allow 45 days to receive your copy.

If you need tax account information but do not need a copy of your prior year tax return, you can get it also by using Form 4506. The tax account information you will receive includes: marital status, type of return filed, tax shown on return, adjusted gross income, self-employment tax and the number of exemptions. Generally, there is a charge for this information.

IRS Examination of Returns

Examination of a tax return does not suggest any wrongdoing. Usually a return is selected for examination to verify that the income, exemptions and deductions that are reported on the return are correct.

If the IRS selects your return for examination, you may be asked to produce such records as cancelled checks, receipts or other documents to prove entries on your return. You may act on your own behalf or you may have an attorney, a certified public accountant, or an individual enrolled to practice before the IRS represent or accompany you. Any other person who prepared your return and signed it as the preparer may accompany you to an examination, but must have a power of attorney to represent you.

Not all examinations result in changes in tax liability. If the examination of your return shows that you overpaid your tax, you will receive a refund. If the examination of your return shows that you owe additional tax, payment will be expected. Should you disagree with the findings of the examination, you can appeal.

As mentioned in an earlier section of this publication, under Volunteer Assistance Programs, Student Tax Clinics are available in some IRS districts to help taxpayers during examinations and appeals proceedings.

Collection of Unpaid Taxes

Each tax return filed with the Internal Revenue Service is checked for mathematical accuracy and to see if the correct payment has been made. If tax is owing, the IRS will send a notice of tax due. Generally, you are then required by law to make payment within 10 days of the date of the bill.

If the tax is not paid on time, the law provides for charging interest and penalties for late payment of tax. There is also a penalty for failure to file the return by the due date.

If you believe the bill is wrong, be prepared to provide records to help correct the mistake. We will make any required adjustment to your tax account.

If you cannot pay the amount due in full, contact the local IRS office. In certain cases, depending on your financial condition, Installment payments or delayed collection action may be arranged.

If you neglect the notice of tax due or refuse to make payments, the tax may be collected by levy on income or seizure and sale of property. For further information on the collection process and on your rights in collection matters, please see Publication 586A, "The Collection Process (Income Tax Accounts)," or Publication 594, "The Collection Process (Employment Tax Accounts)."

Exempt Organization Returns

Certain exempt organization returns and approved applications for recognition of exemption from federal income tax are available for public inspection and copying upon request. Requests to inspect the exempt organization returns must be submitted in writing and must include the name and address of the organization that filed the return, the type (number) of the return, and the year(s) involved. The request should be sent to the District Director (Attention: Disclosure Officer) for the district in which the requester desires to inspect the return(s). If inspection at the IRS National Office is desired, the request should be sent to the Commissioner of Internal Revenue, Attention: Freedom of Information Reading Room, 1111 Constitution Avenue, N.W., Washington, DC 20224. Similar procedures apply in the case of requests to inspect approved exemption applications except that the application form number and years involved do not have to be indicated. You will be advised when and where the material will be made available for inspection. The Service may limit the number of returns or exemption applications made available to any person for inspection on a given date. For more information on inspecting exempt organization returns and exemption applications, contact IRS using your toll-free number.

Guide To Tax-Free Services

Where To File

If an addressed envelope came with your return, please use it. If you do not have one, or if you moved during the year, mail your return to the **Internal Revenue Service Center** for the place where you live. No street address is needed.

If you are located in:	Use this address:
Alabama, Florida, Georgia, Mississippi, South Carolina	Atlanta, GA 31101
New Jersey, New York City and counties of Nassau, Rockland, Suffolk, and Westchester	Holtsville, NY 00501
Connecticut, Maine, Massachusetts, Minnesota, New Hampshire, New York (all other counties), Rhode Island, Vermont	Andover, MA 05501
Illinois, Iowa, Missouri, Wisconsin	Kansas City, MO 64999
Delaware, District of Columbia, Maryland, Pennsylvania	Philadelphia, PA 19255
Kentucky, Michigan, Ohio, West Virginia	Cincinnati, OH 45999
Kansas, Louisiana, New Mexico, Oklahoma, Texas	Austin, TX 73301
Alaska, Arizona, California (counties of Alpine, Amador, Butte, Calaveras, Colusa, Contra Costa, Del Norte, El Dorado, Glenn, Humboldt, Lake, Lassen, Marin, Mendocino, Modoc, Napa, Nevada, Placer, Plumas, Sacramento, San Joaquin, Shasta, Sierra, Siskiyou, Solano, Sonoma, Sutter, Tehama, Trinity, Yolo, and Yuba), Colorado, Idaho, Montana, Nebraska, Nevada, North Dakota, Oregon, South Dakota, Utah, Washington, Wyoming	Ogden, UT 84201
California (all other counties), Hawaii	Fresno, CA 93888
Arkansas, Indiana, North Carolina, Tennessee, Virginia	Memphis, TN 37501
American Samoa	Philadelphia, PA 19255
Guam	Commissioner of Revenue and Taxation Agana, GU 96910
Puerto Rico (or if excluding income under section 933) Virgin Islands Nonpermanent residents	Philadelphia, PA 19255
Virgin Islands Permanent residents	V. I. Bureau of Internal Revenue P.O. Box 3186 St. Thomas, VI 00801
Foreign country U.S. citizens and those filing Form 2555 or Form 4563, even if you have an A.P.O. or F.P.O. address	Philadelphia, PA 19255
A.P.O. or F.P.O. address of	Miami—Atlanta, GA 31101 New York—Holtsville, NY 00501 San Francisco—Fresno, CA 93888 Seattle—Ogden, UT 84201

After You File

Refunds

If it has been at least 10 weeks since you mailed your tax return, you can call a telephone number to find out the status of your refund. When you call, you should have available a copy of your tax return since you will need to know the first social security number shown on the return, the filing status, and the exact amount of the refund.

Problem Resolution Program

The Problem Resolution Program (PRP) is for taxpayers who have been unable to resolve their problems through normal Internal Revenue Service channels. Someone with a tax problem should first contact IRS taxpayer assistance, or in the case of a letter or notice from the IRS, call the number provided. Generally, questions are answered and problems solved right then—but not always. That's when PRP steps in. Each of the IRS's 64 district offices has a PRP office whose specialty is assisting taxpayers who previously contacted the IRS with their tax problems but could not get them resolved. People in the PRP office have the authority to cut through the red tape and handle problems promptly. The taxpayer generally deals with one person and is kept informed of the case's progress. Taxpayers can contact PRP by calling the IRS assistance number

or writing to their local Internal Revenue Service District Director and asking for Problem Resolution assistance. While PRP offices do everything they can to help taxpayers, there are some things they cannot do. Appeals of decisions made in tax examinations, Freedom of Information Act requests, Privacy Act inquiries and complaints about hiring practices are all outside of PRP's authority.

Amending Your Return

After you have filed your return, if you discover that you did not report some income, did not claim deductions or credits you could have claimed, or claimed deductions or credits you should not have claimed, you can correct your return by filing a Form 1040X, Amended U.S. Individual Income Tax Return. Generally, this form must be filed within three years from the date you filed your original return or within two years from the date you paid your tax, whichever is later.

File Form 1040X with the IRS Service Center for the area in which you live. See the listing of these service centers at the top of this page.

Your state tax liability may be affected by a change made on your federal income tax return. For more information on this you should contact your state tax agency.

Copies of Prior Year Returns

You can obtain a copy of your prior year tax return by completing Form 4506, Request for Copy of Tax Form or Tax Account Information, and mailing it to the service center where you filed the return you are requesting. Service center addresses are listed on the back of Form 4506. There is a charge for each copy of a return. This fee must be sent to the service center along with your Form 4506 or written request. If you are unable to act on your own behalf, your authorized representative may request a copy of your return. Your representative must sign the request and attach a copy of Form 2848, Power of Attorney, or other document authorizing him or her to act for you.

Common Errors

Following is a list of the most common errors taxpayers have made on their Forms 1040, 1040EZ and 1040A. Explanations are provided to help you avoid making these errors. Be sure to double check your tax return because errors such as those listed below may delay the issuance of any refund you may be expecting.

1. Computation error in computing medical and dental expenses on Schedule A.
   — Form 1040 through the Adjusted Gross Income line must be completed before you can figure Medical and Dental Expenses on Schedule A. Read carefully the instructions on how to deduct these expenses and double check your math for these entries.
2. Incorrect amount of Earned Income Credit
   — You may be entitled to a credit of up to $550 if your Adjusted Gross Income is less than $11,000. The Earned Income Credit Worksheet is used to determine eligibility. If your Adjusted Gross Income is $6,500 or less, find your credit in the Earned Income Credit Table and place that amount on the proper line of your Form 1040 or 1040A. If your Adjusted Gross Income is over $6,500, use your earned income amount to find your credit in the table. Then use your Adjusted Gross Income to find your credit in the table. Enter the smaller amount of the two as your credit on the proper line of your Form 1040 or 1040A.
3. Incorrect amount of tax entered from tax tables.
   — Make sure you use the correct tax table for your filing status. Take the amount shown on the taxable income line of your Form 1040 or 1040A and go to the tax table column showing that amount. Find the column for your marital status (married filing jointly, single, etc.) and read down the column. The amount shown where the income line and filing status column meet is your tax.
4. Social Security Tax, instead of your Federal Income Tax Withheld, was entered on your tax return.
   — When entering the amount from your Form W-2, recheck to make sure that you have entered the Federal Income Tax Withheld and *not* the FICA (Social Security Tax) amount.
5. Incorrect computation of taxable amount of Unemployment Compensation.
   — You should receive a statement, Form 1099-G showing the total unemployment compensation paid to you during the year. Enter this amount on the proper line of Form 1040 or Form 1040A. Use the Unemployment Compensation Worksheet in the instructions to determine if it is taxable by using the formula given for your filing status. Enter the computed amount, which is the taxable amount of your unemployment compensation, on the appropriate line of Form 1040 or Form 1040A.
6. Computation error made on Form 2441, Credit for Child and Dependent Care Expenses.
   — Verify your addition, subtractions and multiplication. Use the correct percentage for line 8 as shown on the back of Form 2441.
7. Incorrect computation of refund or balance due.
   — Verify your addition and subtraction. You are due a "Refund" if your tax from the tax table and any other taxes you are liable for are less than the amounts you have paid (such as the amount withheld shown on your form W-2). A "Balance Due" is computed when the above items total more than the amounts you have already paid.
8. Earned Income Credit not claimed when qualification met.
   — Refer to your tax package to determine if you meet the qualifications for the Earned Income Credit and then use the Earned Income Credit Worksheet to determine your refund.
9. Computation error made on page 1 of your tax return when figuring your dividends.
   — You can exclude (subtract) up to $100 of qualifying dividend income. If a joint return is filed, you can subtract up to $200, regardless of which spouse received the dividends.
10. Computation error on page 1 of the tax return when income amounts were totalled.
    — Verify the addition of all income amounts on the front of your return.

Where To File

Please use the address envelope that came with your return. If you do not have an addressed envelope or if you moved during the year, mail your return to the Internal Revenue Service Center for the area where you live.

If you are requesting copies of prior year returns, you should send the request to the service center where the original return was filed. No street address is needed.

Tax Credits

Taxpayers meeting the necessary qualifications will be able to claim certain credits against the amount of tax they owe. Some of these credits are earned income credit, child and dependent care credit, residential energy credit carryover, credit for the elderly and the permanently and totally disabled and credit for political contributions. These credits are discussed in various taxpayer information publications.

Employee's Withholding Allowance Certificate—Form W-4

Each time you start working for a new employer you will be asked to complete a Form W-4. Using information provided by you on the form your employer will know how much money to withhold from your wages for federal income tax so that by the end of the year the amount of federal income tax withheld should be about the same as your federal income tax liability. If any of the information changes, such as the number of allowances claimed on your Form W-4, it is your responsibility to go to the employer and ask to complete a new Form W-4 so that the correct amount of federal income tax will be withheld from your wages.

Estimated Tax

If you are self-employed or have other income not subject to income tax withholding, you may be required to make estimated tax payments during the year. In general, estimated tax is the amount of tax that you are going to owe that will not be paid through the withholding system.

You may pay the entire amount you estimate your tax to be by April 15 when the first payment is due or you may pay the tax in four installments with the first payment due by April 15. Because you may be charged a penalty for underpayment of estimated tax, it is important that you pay your estimated tax timely.

For additional information on who must pay estimated taxes and how and when to make payments, please see IRS Publication 505, Estimated Tax and Tax Withholding.

Recordkeeping

A well-organized system for your records will make preparing your tax return easier and will also help you to answer questions if your return is selected for examination or if you are billed for additional tax.

You should keep these records as long as there is a possibility that an entry on your return may be questioned by the IRS. You should keep records such as receipts, cancelled checks and other documents that prove an item of income or deduction appearing on your return until the statute of limitations expires for the return. Usually this is three years from the date the return was due or filed, or two years from the date the tax was paid, whichever is later. There is no statute of limitations when a return is false or fraudulent or when no return is filed.

Some records, such as property records, should be retained indefinitely since they may be needed to prove the amount of gain or loss if the property is sold. These income tax returns should also be kept indefinitely. They will help you prepare future tax returns and will also help you if you later file a claim for refund.

For additional information on the importance of recordkeeping, please see Publication 552, Recordkeeping Requirements and a List of IRS Publications, and Publication 583, Recordkeeping for a Small Business.

Checklist Before Mailing Your Return

Before you mail your individual income tax return, check to be sure you have done all these things:

1. Transferred the address label to your return, and made any necessary corrections to your name, address, and social security number;
2. Attached Copy B of all your Forms W-2;
3. Attached all required forms and related schedules;
4. Reported all your taxable income;
5. Rechecked your return to make sure you have made no mistake in your arithmetic;
6. Signed and dated your return (on a joint return, both husband and wife must sign);
7. Attached your check or money order payable to "Internal Revenue Service," if you owe additional tax, and have written your social security number, tax form number and tax year on your check or money order;
8. Used the envelope that came with the package or addressed the return to the Internal Revenue Service Center for your state;
9. Made a copy of the return for your records.

If you file early you may expect to receive your refund within four to six weeks. If you do not get your refund within 10 weeks after filing your return, call your Internal Revenue Office.

Guide To Tax-Free Services

Your Tax Package

In most cases after you file your first federal income tax return the IRS will mail you a tax package containing either Form 1040 and related schedules or Form 1040A and 1040EZ. You should receive this package in late December or early January. If you do not receive one, you should pick up forms at IRS, the library or a bank.

Your tax package contains a coded, peel-off address label. Attaching this label to your return will speed up the processing of your return and the issuing of any refund. If any of the information on the label is incorrect, make the necessary change right on the label. Even if you don't use the tax form in the tax package you receive in the mail, you should attach the label to the tax return you file. If you take your return to a tax return preparer, VITA site, etc. for completion, have the person who prepares your return use your address label.

Your tax package also contains an addressed envelope for mailing your return. Using this envelope will also speed up the processing of your return because this envelope is coded for electronic sorting by type of tax return before opening. If you do not have an addressed envelope or if you moved during the year, mail your return to the Internal Revenue Service Center for the area where you now live.

Social Security Number

Your social security number, which the IRS uses as your taxpayer identification number (TIN), must appear on every individual tax return, statement or other document. You should include it on your check or money order for payment of tax you pay when you file your return with the IRS. If the social security number shown on the preprinted address label on the individual tax return package is wrong, mark through it and make the correction on the label. If you do not have a tax return with the preprinted label, write the social security number in the appropriate space on the form.

If you are married, provide the social security numbers for both yourself and your spouse, whether you file jointly or separately. If you are filing a joint return, list your social security numbers in the same order that you show your first names.

If your name changes for reasons such as marriage or divorce, you should notify the Social Security Administration so that the name on our records is the same as the Social Security Administration has on its records. If you don't notify the Social Security Administration, processing your return and issuing your refund may be delayed.

Wage and Tax Statement—Form W-2

If you work for an employer during the year, your employer must provide you with a Form W-2 showing wages and other compensation paid you and amounts deducted from the pay for federal, state, local (if applicable) and social security (FICA) taxes. If you filed Form W-5, Earned Income Credit Advance Payment Certificate, with your employer, the amount of the advance earned income credit paid to you during the year will also be included on your Form W-2.

If you work for an employer for only part of a year, your employer may provide you with a Form W-2 at the time you leave your job or wait until the end of the year. If you worked for more than one employer during the year, you should receive a Form W-2 from each employer. If you change jobs and move and your employer(s) have not give you a Form W-2, you should provide the employer(s) with your new address so the Form(s) W-2 can be mailed to you.

Copy B of each Form W-2 should be filed with your federal income tax return. If you receive a Form W-2 on which any of the entries are incorrect, ask your employer for a corrected form. Your employer should mark the corrected form "Corrected by Employer". Copy B of the corrected form should be filed with your federal income tax return.

If you do not receive your Form W-2 from any employer by January 31, you should contact that employer and ask for the form. If after contacting your employer you do not receive your Form W-2 by February 15, call the IRS number for your area and request assistance. You will be asked to provide your name, address, social security number, and the name and Employer Identification Number of your employer who failed to furnish you with a Form W-2 along with an estimate of your wages and tax withheld.

Do not delay filing your return by the due date even if you have not received a Form W-2 from your employer. File your individual tax return and attach Form 4852, Substitute for Form W-2, Wage and Tax Statement or Form W-2P, Statement for Recipients of Annuities, Pensions, Retired Pay or IRA Payments, or a statement giving your name and social security number, the employer's name, address and Employer Identification Number, the total wages you received, and the amount of federal income tax withheld from your pay. If you are not sure of these amounts you should estimate them to the best of your knowledge.

If after you file your return you receive a Form W-2 and find that the income you reported on your return does not agree with the amount shown on the Forms W-2, you must file an amended return (Form 1040X, Amended U.S. Individual Income Tax Return) to correct the error.

In addition to all of the publications available directly from the IRS, a wide range of services for you, the taxpayer, can be had by picking up the telephone and asking for help—direct assistance available almost any day of the year:

For the deaf who have access to TV/Telephone-TTY equipment.

In Braille for the blind and physically handicapped.

An "assistor" from the IRS who will walk you through the return. Through computer terminals equipped with modems.

Through taxpayer education programs.

To the elderly, non-speakers of English, and handicapped, through VITA.

For people over 60 especially if disabled.

At tax clinics for students.

It is even possible to obtain a series of video tapes covering:

1. "How to Fill Out Your Tax Return."
2. Your rights when your return is audited.
3. How your return is processed.
4. How to claim losses.
5. Your taxes and your business.

IRS Information and Assistance

Most taxpayers should be able to meet the requirements of the tax laws by using information such as tax package instructions, publications, taxpayer education programs, films, and library programs. If further information and assistance are needed, services are available as indicated in the following paragraphs.

Toll-free telephone and walk-in assistance is available to answer questions on taxpayer accounts, IRS procedures, or technical inquiries on tax-related matters.

Telephone Service

Toll-free telephone assistance is available in all 50 states, the District of Columbia, Puerto Rico and the Virgin Islands. Under this system you pay only local charges, with no long-distance charge for your call. Through the toll-free system you may obtain assistance on your tax questions.

To help us provide courteous responses and accurate information, an IRS employee occasionally listens in on telephone calls. No record is made of the taxpayer's name, address or social security number except where a follow-up telephone call must be made.

During periods of peak demand for telephone assistance you may encounter busy signals when trying to call. Generally, demand is lower early in the morning and later in the week so you may want to call at those times.

Tele-Tax

The IRS provides a toll-free telephone service called Tele-Tax. This service has both Automated Refund Information and Recorded Tax Information.

Automated Refund Information can be used to check on the status of your current year's refund. If it has been ten weeks since you mailed your 1986 tax return, we will then be able to check the status of your refund. Automated Refund Information is available after March 15th, Monday through Friday from 6:30 a.m. to 7:00 p.m. (hours may vary in your area) to taxpayers using a push-button (tone signalling) phone. It is also available Monday through Friday during normal business hours to taxpayers using a rotary (dial) or push-button (pulse dial) phone.

Recorded Tax Information is available on about 150 topics covering such areas as filing requirements, dependents, itemized deductions and tax credits. Recorded Tax Information is available 24 hours a day, 7 days a week to taxpayers using a push-button (tone signalling) phone. It is also available during normal business hours to taxpayers using a rotary (dial) or push-button (pulse dial) phone.

Telephone Service for Deaf Taxpayers

Toll-free telephone assistance for deaf taxpayers is available for those who have access to TV/Telephone-TTY equipment. The hours of operation of this service are 8:00 a.m. to 6:45 p.m. Eastern Standard Time for January thru April and 8:00 a.m. to 4:30 p.m. for May thru December. Residents of Indiana may call 1-800-382-4059. Residents elsewhere in the U.S. including Alaska, Hawaii, Puerto Rico, and the Virgin Islands may call 1-800-428-4732.

Information for the Blind

Braille materials are available at Regional Libraries for the Blind and Physically Handicapped in conjunction with the Library of Congress. These materials include Publications 17 and 334, Forms 1040, 1040A, and 1040EZ and Schedules A and B, W, and instructions.

Walk-In Service

While the Internal Revenue Service will not prepare your tax return for you, assistors are available in most IRS offices throughout the country to help you as you prepare your own individual federal tax return. You will be expected to help yourself to the maximum extent possible. However, you will be provided assistance and at the same time, provided the opportunity of learning how to research and prepare your own tax return. An assistor will "walk-through" a return with you and a number of other taxpayers in a group setting.

In many IRS Offices a walk-in counter is available to assist you with inquiries that do not involve preparation of a return at the time of your visit such as receipt of an IRS notice or bill. You may also obtain certain technical information or publications at most IRS offices.

If you wish assistance with your tax return, you should bring in your tax package, your Forms W-2 and 1099 and any other information (such as a copy of last year's return) which will enable us to help you.

Computer Tax Database

The IRS has prepared a database of tax information that is available through several commercial information retrieval (videotex) services. These services are accessible on a subscription basis by computer terminals that are equipped with modems.

The database consists of selected Taxpayer Information Publications, answers to the most commonly asked tax related questions, and other items that are prepared for information retrieval. The database covers many topics that can be used in preparing Federal tax returns and as a reference source for year-round tax planning.

Taxpayer Education Programs

The Internal Revenue Service has a number of programs designed to educate the public about our nation's voluntary compliance tax system and each citizen's share in it so that the system works as smoothly as possible. The more that citizens understand their role in this tax system, the better they will be able to carry out their responsibilities with a minimum of intrusion in their lives by the government. All of these taxpayer education programs offer opportunity for citizen involvement through service as volunteers.

Understanding Taxes

This is a tax education program that begins in the schools, where young people are taught about their tax rights and responsibilities under our voluntary compliance tax system. They also learn how to fill out basic tax returns. Since many of them already are working, often at their first jobs, this learning has immediate practical value. They also learn about the history of taxes and current issues in taxation, such as tax reform. All materials teachers need are available free of charge, including a six-part film series, "Tax Whys: Understanding Taxes." These films were produced in cooperation with the states. Workshops are conducted during the year to help prepare teachers for course instruction.

Small Business Workshops

These workshops help people start small businesses by providing them with the information they need to carry out their tax responsibilities, including tax withholding, making correct and timely tax deposits and filing a business return. Some sessions focus on the needs of the self-employed, minority entrepreneurs and specialized business groups.

Volunteer Income Tax Assistance

The Volunteer Income Tax Assistance program (VITA) provides free tax assistance to lower income, elderly, non-English-speaking and handicapped people and also to members of the military. Generally those who receive these services can't afford professional tax assistance. After completing IRS training, volunteers provide free help at special locations.

Tax Counseling for the Elderly

Tax Counseling for the Elderly (TCE) provides free tax assistance to people 60 or older, especially those who are disabled or have other special needs. Non-profit organizations under cooperative agreements with the IRS provide local assistance.

Both VITA and TCE sites usually are located in neighborhood centers, libraries, churches and other places in the community.

Student Tax Clinics

Another program, Student Tax Clinic, uses volunteer law and graduate accounting students who have received permission from the Treasury Department to represent taxpayers before the IRS. They provide free assistance to taxpayers during IRS examination and appeals proceedings.

Community Outreach Tax Assistance

This is a year-round program of assistance to groups who need help understanding the tax laws, especially as they apply to members of their profession or group, such as teaching or business or farming. Seminars are conducted at times and locations in the community that are convenient for members of the group.

For all of these programs, contact your local IRS office for more information and locations of sites or presentations in your areas.

Taxpayer Information Program

The Taxpayer Information Program is designed to give taxpayers the information they need to understand their rights and comply with their responsibilities under the tax laws.

To reach the greatest number of taxpayers, the Taxpayer Information Program provides print and audio-visual public service materials directly to the public, and to the news media for dissemination to the public. In cooperation with public television stations IRS also produces programs for broadcast which take taxpayers step-by-step through Forms 1040A and 1040EZ and highlight Form 1040 and Schedules A and B.

The IRS provides local libraries with audio cassettes and videocassettes, for loan to the public, on how to fill out Forms 1040EZ, 1040A, 1040 and Schedules A and B. These tax tapes contain simple, step-by-step instructions through the forms, tax tips, and special rules for the military.

Guide To Tax-Free Services

To Call IRS Toll-Free for Answers to Your Federal Tax Questions, Use Only the Number Listed Below for Your Area.

Caution: *"Toll-free" is a telephone call for which you pay only local charges with no long-distance charge. Please use a local city number only if it is not a long-distance call for you.* ***Do not dial 800 when using a local city number.*** Otherwise, *use the general toll-free number given.*

We are happy to answer questions to help you prepare your return. But you should know that you are responsible for the accuracy of your return. If we do make an error, you are still responsible for the payment of the correct tax.

To make sure that IRS employees give courteous responses and correct information to taxpayers, a second IRS employee sometimes listens in on telephone calls. No record is kept of any taxpayer's name, address, or social security number.

If you find it necessary to write instead of calling, please address your letter to your IRS District Director for a prompt reply. Make sure you include your social security number or taxpayer identifying number when you write.

The IRS has a telephone service called Tele-Tax. It provides automated refund information and recorded tax information on about 150 topics covering such areas as filing requirements, dependents, itemized deductions, and tax credits. Tele-Tax is available 24 hours a day, 7 days a week, to taxpayers using push-button (tone signalling) telephones, and Monday through Friday, during office hours, to taxpayers using push-button (pulse dial) or rotary (dial) phones. See Tele-Tax Information in the index for the page numbers that contain telephone numbers, available topics, and instructions describing how to use this service.

ALABAMA
Call 1-800-424-1040

ALASKA
Anchorage, 561-7484
Elsewhere in Alaska, call 1-800-478-1040

ARIZONA
Phoenix, 257-1233

ARKANSAS
Call 1-800-424-1040

CALIFORNIA
Please call the telephone number shown in the white pages of your local telephone directory under U.S. Government, Internal Revenue Service, Federal Tax Assistance.

COLORADO
Denver, 825-7041

CONNECTICUT
Call 1-800-424-1040

DELAWARE
Call 1-800-424-1040

DISTRICT of COLUMBIA
Call 488-3100

FLORIDA
Jacksonville, 354-1760

GEORGIA
Atlanta, 522-0050

HAWAII
Oahu, 541-1040
All other islands, 1-800-232-2511

IDAHO
Call 1-800-424-1040

ILLINOIS
Chicago, 435-1040

INDIANA
Indianapolis, 269-5477

IOWA
Des Moines, 283-0523

KANSAS
Call 1-800-424-1040

KENTUCKY
Call 1-800-424-1040

LOUISIANA
Call 1-800-424-1040

MAINE
Call 1-800-424-1040

MARYLAND
Baltimore, 962-2590
Montgomery County, 488-3100
Prince George's County, 488-3100

MASSACHUSETTS
Boston, 523-1040

MICHIGAN
Detroit, 237-0800

MINNESOTA
Minneapolis, 291-1422
St. Paul, 291-1422

MISSISSIPPI
Call 1-800-424-1040

MISSOURI
St. Louis, 342-1040

MONTANA
Call 1-800-424-1040

NEBRASKA
Omaha, 422-1500

NEVADA
Call 1-800-424-1040

NEW HAMPSHIRE
Call 1-800-424-1040

NEW JERSEY
Newark, 622-0600

NEW MEXICO
Call 1-800-424-1040

NEW YORK
Bronx, 732-0100
Brooklyn, 596-3770
Buffalo, 855-3955
Manhattan, 732-0100
Nassau, 222-1131
Queens, 596-3770
Rockland County, 997-1510
Staten Island, 732-0100
Suffolk, 724-5000
Westchester County, 997-1510

NORTH CAROLINA
Call 1-800-424-1040

NORTH DAKOTA
Call 1-800-424-1040

OHIO
Cincinnati, 621-6281
Cleveland, 522-3000

OKLAHOMA
Call 1-800-424-1040

OREGON
Eugene, 485-8286
Portland, 221-3960
Salem, 581-8721

PENNSYLVANIA
Philadelphia, 574-9900
Pittsburgh, 281-0112

PUERTO RICO
San Juan Metro Area, 753-4040
Isla DDD, 753-4549

RHODE ISLAND
Call 1-800-424-1040

SOUTH CAROLINA
Call 1-800-424-1040

SOUTH DAKOTA
Call 1-800-424-1040

TENNESSEE
Nashville, 259-4601

TEXAS
Austin, 472-1974
Corpus Christi, 888-9431
Dallas, 742-2440
El Paso, 532-6116
Ft. Worth, 263-9229
Houston, 965-0440
San Antonio, 229-1700

UTAH
Call 1-800-424-1040

VERMONT
Call 1-800-424-1040

VIRGINIA
Bailey's Crossroads, 557-9230
Richmond, 649-2361

WASHINGTON
Seattle, 442-1040

WEST VIRGINIA
Call 1-800-424-1040

WISCONSIN
Milwaukee, 271-3780

WYOMING
Call 1-800-424-1040

Note: *If there is no number listed for your specific area, please call* ***1-800-424-1040.***

Telephone Assistance Services for Deaf Taxpayers Who Have Access to TV / Telephone—TTY Equipment.

Hours of Operation

8:00 A.M. to 6:45 P.M. EST (Filing Season)

8:00 A.M. to 4:30 P.M. EST (Nonfiling Season)

Indiana residents, 1-800-382-4059

Elsewhere in U.S., including Alaska, Hawaii, Virgin Islands, and Puerto Rico, 1-800-428-4732

Toll-Free "Forms Only" Telephone Numbers

If you only need to order tax forms and publications and do not have any tax questions, call the number listed below for your area.

ALASKA
Anchorage, 563-5313
Elsewhere in Alaska, call 1-800-478-1040

ARIZONA
Phoenix, 257-1233
Tucson, 882-0730

CALIFORNIA
Please call the telephone number shown in the white pages of your local telephone directory under U.S. Government, Internal Revenue Service, Federal Tax Forms.

COLORADO
Denver, 825-7041

HAWAII
Honolulu, 541-1180
All other islands, 1-800-232-2511

ILLINOIS
Bloomington, 662-2515

OREGON
Eugene, 485-8286
Portland, 221-3933
Salem, 581-8721

PUERTO RICO
San Juan Metro Area, 753-4040
Isla DDD, 753-4549

VIRGINIA
Richmond, 329-1052

WASHINGTON
Seattle, 442-5100

Note: *If there is no number listed for your state or specific area, call* ***1-800-424-FORM (3676).***

Guide To Tax-Free Services

To Call Tele-Tax Toll-Free, Use Only The Numbers Listed Below For Your Area

Recorded Tax Information has about 150 topics of tax information that answer many Federal tax questions and a topic for local information such as the location of VITA and TCE sites. You can hear up to three topics on each call you make.

Automated Refund Information is available after March 15. If it has been 10 weeks since you mailed your 1986 tax return, we will be able to check the status of your refund.

Long-distance charges apply if you call from outside the local dialing area of the numbers listed below. **Do not dial 800 when using a local number.** A complete list of these topics and instructions on how to use Tele-Tax are on the next page.

Note: *Cities with a **1** before them have only Recorded Tax Information and can only be called if you have a push-button (tone signalling) phone. Cities with a **2** before them have Recorded Tax Information, including topic 999 for local information, and Automated Refund Information and can be called by using any type of phone.*

ALABAMA
1 Birmingham, 251-9454
1 Huntsville, 534-5203
1 Mobile, 433-6993
1 Montgomery, 262-8304

ALASKA
1 Anchorage, 562-1848

ARIZONA
2 Phoenix, 252-4909

ARKANSAS
1 Little Rock, 372-3891

CALIFORNIA
1 Bakersfield, 861-4105
1 Carson, 632-3555
2 Counties of Amador, Calaveras, Contra Costa, Marin, and San Joaquin, 1-800-428-4032
2 Los Angeles, 617-3177
2 Oakland, 839-4245
1 Oxnard, 485-7236
1 Riverside, 351-6769
1 Sacramento, 448-4367
1 San Diego, 293-5020
1 San Jose, 293-5606
1 Santa Ana, 836-2974
1 Santa Maria, 928-7503
1 Santa Rosa, 528-6233
1 Stockton, 463-6005
1 Visalia, 733-8194

COLORADO
1 Colorado Springs, 597-6344
2 Denver, 592-1118
1 Ft. Collins, 221-0658

CONNECTICUT
1 Bridgeport, 335-0070
1 Hartford, 547-0015
1 New Haven, 777-4594
1 Waterbury, 754-4235

DELAWARE
1 Dover, 674-1118
1 Wilmington, 652-0272

DISTRICT of COLUMBIA
2 Call 628-2929

FLORIDA
1 Daytona Beach, 253-0669
1 Ft. Lauderdale, 523-3100
2 Jacksonville, 353-9579
1 Miami, 374-5144
1 Orlando, 422-0592
1 St. Petersburg, 578-0424
1 Tallahassee, 222-0807
1 Tampa, 229-0815
1 West Palm Beach, 655-1996

GEORGIA
1 Albany, 435-1415
2 Atlanta, 331-6572
1 Augusta, 722-9068
1 Columbus, 327-0298
1 Macon, 745-2890
1 Savannah, 355-9632

HAWAII
1 Honolulu, 541-1185

IDAHO
2 Call 1-800-554-4477

ILLINOIS
1 Aurora, 851-2718
1 Bloomington, 828-6116
1 Champaign, 398-1779
2 Chicago, 886-9614
1 East St. Louis, 875-4050
1 Ottawa, 433-1568
1 Peoria, 637-9305
1 Quad Cities, 326-1720
1 Rockford, 987-4280
1 Springfield, 789-0489

INDIANA
1 Evansville, 422-1026
1 Fort Wayne, 484-3065
1 Gary, 884-4465
2 Indianapolis, 634-1550
1 South Bend, 232-5459

IOWA
1 Cedar Rapids, 399-2210
1 Des Moines, 284-4271
1 Quad Cities, 326-1720
1 Waterloo, 234-0817

KANSAS
1 Wichita, 264-3147

KENTUCKY
1 Erlanger, 727-3338
1 Lexington, 233-2889
1 Louisville, 582-5599

LOUISIANA
1 New Orleans, 529-2854

MAINE
1 Portland, 775-0465

MARYLAND
2 Baltimore, 244-7306
1 Cumberland, 722-5331
1 Frederick, 663-5798
1 Hagerstown, 733-6815
1 Salisbury, 742-9458

MASSACHUSETTS
2 Boston, 523-8602
1 Springfield, 739-6624

MICHIGAN
1 Ann Arbor, 665-4544
2 Detroit, 961-4282
1 Flint, 238-4599
1 Grand Rapids, 451-2034
1 Kalamazoo, 343-0255
1 Lansing, 372-2454
1 Mt. Clemens, 463-9550
1 Pontiac, 858-2336
1 Saginaw, 753-9911

MINNESOTA
1 Duluth, 722-5494
1 Rochester, 288-5595
2 St. Paul, 224-4288

MISSISSIPPI
1 Gulfport, 863-3302
1 Jackson, 965-4168

MISSOURI
1 Jefferson City, 636-8312
1 Kansas City, 421-3741
1 Springfield, 883-3419
2 St. Louis, 241-4700

MONTANA
1 Billings, 656-1422
1 Great Falls, 727-4902
1 Helena, 443-7034

NEBRASKA
1 Lincoln, 471-5450
1 Omaha, 221-3324

NEVADA
2 Call 1-800-554-4477

NEW HAMPSHIRE
1 Manchester, 623-5778
1 Portsmouth, 431-0637

NEW JERSEY
1 Atlantic City, 348-2636
1 Camden, 966-3412
1 Hackensack, 487-1817
2 Newark, 624-1223
1 Paterson, 278-5442
1 Trenton, 599-2150

NEW MEXICO
1 Albuquerque, 766-1102

NEW YORK
1 Albany, 465-8318
1 Binghamton, 722-8426
2 Brooklyn, 858-4461
2 Buffalo, 856-9320
2 Manhattan, 406-4080
1 Mineola, 248-6790
1 Poughkeepsie, 452-1877
1 Rochester, 454-3330
1 Smithtown, 979-0720
2 Staten Island, 406-4080
1 Syracuse, 471-1630
1 White Plains, 683-0134

NORTH CAROLINA
1 Asheville, 254-3044
1 Charlotte, 567-9885
1 Durham, 541-5283
1 Fayetteville, 483-0735
1 Greensboro, 378-1572
1 Raleigh, 755-1498
1 Winston-Salem, 725-3013

NORTH DAKOTA
1 Bismarck, 258-8210
1 Fargo, 232-9360
1 Grand Forks, 746-0324
1 Minot, 838-1234

OHIO
1 Akron, 253-1170
1 Canton, 455-6061
2 Cincinnati, 421-0329
2 Cleveland, 522-3037
1 Columbus, 469-2266
1 Dayton, 225-7237
1 Lima, 224-0341
1 Mansfield, 525-3474
1 Toledo, 255-3743
1 Youngstown, 744-4200

OKLAHOMA
1 Oklahoma City, 235-3434
1 Tulsa, 599-0555

OREGON
2 Portland, 294-5363

PENNSYLVANIA
1 Bethlehem, 861-0325
1 Harrisburg, 236-1356
1 Jenkintown, 887-1261
1 Lancaster, 392-0980
1 Norristown, 275-0242
2 Philadelphia, 592-8946
2 Pittsburgh, 281-3120
1 Reading, 373-4568
1 Scranton, 961-0325
1 Wilkes-Barre, 823-9552
1 Williamsport, 323-4242

RHODE ISLAND
1 Providence, 861-5220

SOUTH CAROLINA
1 Charleston, 722-0369
1 Columbia, 254-4749
1 Greenville, 235-8093

SOUTH DAKOTA
1 Rapid City, 348-3454
1 Sioux Falls, 335-7081
1 Watertown, 882-4979

TENNESSEE
1 Chattanooga, 892-5577
1 Jackson, 664-1858
1 Johnson City, 282-1917
1 Knoxville, 521-7478
1 Memphis, 525-2611
2 Nashville, 242-1541

TEXAS
1 Austin, 479-0391
2 Dallas, 767-1792
1 El Paso, 534-0260
1 Ft. Worth, 334-3888
2 Houston, 850-8801
1 San Antonio, 680-9591

UTAH
1 Salt Lake City, 355-9328

VERMONT
1 Burlington, 658-0007

VIRGINIA
1 Bristol, 669-0565
1 Charlottesville, 296-8558
1 Danville, 797-2223
1 Hampton, 826-8071
1 Lynchburg, 845-6052
1 Norfolk, 441-3623
2 Richmond, 771-2369
1 Roanoke, 982-6062
1 Staunton, 886-3541

WASHINGTON
2 Seattle, 343-7221
1 Spokane, 455-9213

WEST VIRGINIA
1 Charleston, 343-3597
1 Huntington, 523-0104

WISCONSIN
1 Eau Claire, 834-6121
1 Green Bay, 433-3884
1 Madison, 264-5349
2 Milwaukee, 291-1783
1 Racine, 886-1615

WYOMING
1 Cheyenne, 634-1198

Note: *If there is no number listed for your specific area, call **1-800-554-4477.***

Guide To Tax-Free Services

How To Use Tele-Tax

Recorded Tax Information

1. Select, by number, the topic you wish to hear.
2. Have paper and pencil handy to take notes.
3. Call the appropriate phone number.
4. • If you have a push-button (tone signalling) phone, follow the recorded instructions, or
   • If you have a rotary (dial) or push-button (pulse dial) phone, ask the IRS operator for the topic number you want to hear.
5. • Push-button (tone signalling) service is available 24 hours a day, 7 days a week.
   • Rotary (dial)/push-button (pulse dial) service is available Monday through Friday during regular office hours. (In Hawaii, from 6:30 A.M. to 1:00 P.M.)

Automated Refund Information

1. Have a copy of your tax return available since you will need to know the first social security number shown on your return, the filing status, and the exact amount of your refund.
2. Call the appropriate phone number.
3. Follow the recorded instructions.
4. • Push-button (tone signalling) service is available Monday through Friday from 6:30 A.M. to 6 P.M. (Hours may vary in your area.)
   • Rotary (dial)/push-button (pulse dial) service is available Monday through Friday during regular office hours. (In Hawaii, from 6:30 A.M. to 1:00 P.M.)

Tele-Tax Topic Numbers and Subjects

Topic No.	Subject
	IRS Procedures and Services
100	IRS help available—Volunteer tax assistance programs, toll-free telephone, walk-in assistance, and outreach program
101	Tax assistance for handicapped individuals and the deaf
102	Small business tax workshops—Tax help for the new business person
103	Problem resolution program—Special help for problem situations
104	Public libraries—Tax information tapes and reproducible tax forms
105	Examination procedures and how to prepare for an audit
106	The collection process
107	Tax fraud—How to report
108	Special enrollment examination to practice before IRS
109	Organizations—How to apply for exempt status
999	Local Information
	Filing Requirements, Filing Status, Exemptions
110	Who must file?
111	Which form—1040, 1040A, or 1040EZ?
112	When, where, and how to file
113	Filing requirements for a dependent child
114	Filing as single
115	Filing joint or separate
116	Filing as head of household
117	Filing as qualifying widow/widower
118	Filing status for separated individuals
119	Exemptions for age and blindness
120	Dependent—Who can be claimed?
121	Dependent child—Divorced or separated parents
122	Dependent—Items to include in determining support
126	Estimated tax
127	Amended returns
128	Decedents
	Types of Income
130	Wages and salaries
131	Tips
132	Interest received
133	Dividends and dividend exclusion
134	Refund of state and local taxes
135	Alimony received
136	Business income
137	Sole proprietorship
138	Capital gains and losses
139	Pensions and annuities
140	Pensions—The general rule
141	Lump-sum distributions—Profit-sharing plans
143	Rental income and expenses
200	Renting vacation property/Renting to relatives
201	Royalties
202	Farming and fishing income
203	Earnings for clergy members
204	Unemployment compensation
205	Gambling income and expenses
206	Bartering income
207	Scholarships, fellowships, and grants
208	Nontaxable income
209	Social security and tier 1 railroad retirement taxability
210	Social Security Benefit Statement—Form SSA-1099
	Adjustments to Income
211	Charitable contributions deduction for those who do not itemize
212	Deduction for married couples when both work
213	Moving expenses
214	Employee business expenses
215	Business use of car
216	Business travel expenses
217	Business entertainment expenses
218	Individual retirement arrangements (IRA's)
219	Alimony paid
225	Bad debt deduction
226	Tax shelters
	Itemized Deductions
227	Should I itemize?
228	Medical and dental expenses
229	Medical insurance
231	Taxes
232	Sales tax
233	Interest expense
234	Contributions
235	Casualty losses
236	Miscellaneous expenses
237	Business use of your home
238	Educational expenses
	Tax Computation
240	Tax table/Tax rate schedules
243	Tax and credits figured by IRS
244	Income averaging
300	Self-employment tax
301	Ten-year averaging for lump-sum distributions
303	Alternative minimum tax
304	Gift tax
305	Estate tax
	Tax Credits
306	Child care credit
307	Earned income credit
308	Residential energy credit
309	Credit for the elderly or for the permanently and totally disabled
310	Tax credit for contributions to candidates for public office
311	Investment credit
312	Qualified royalty owners exemption (windfall profit tax)
	General Information
314	Substitute tax forms
315	Highlights of 1986 tax changes
316	Refunds—How long they should take
317	Copy of your tax return—How to get one
318	Forms/Publications—How to order
319	Tax shelter registration
320	Extensions for time to file your tax return
325	Form W-2—What to do if not received
326	Highlights of the Tax Reform Act
327	IRS notices and bills/Penalty and interest charges
328	Tax benefits for low income Americans
329	Penalty for underpayment of estimated tax—Form 2210
330	Recordkeeping
331	How to choose a tax preparer
332	Audit appeal rights
333	Failure to pay child/spousal support and other Federal obligations
335	Withholding on interest and dividends
336	Highway use tax
337	Checklist/Common errors when preparing your tax return
338	Withholding on pensions and annuities
339	Your tax form is overdue—Let us hear from you
340	Second request for information about your tax form
341	Notice of intent to levy
342	Notice of underreported income—CP2000
	Basis of Assets, Depreciation, Sale of Assets
343	Sale of personal residence—General
344	Sale of personal residence—How to report gain
400	Sale of personal residence—Exclusion of gain, age 55 and over
401	Basis of assets
402	Depreciation—General
403	Depreciation—Accelerated cost recovery system
404	Installment sales
	Employer Tax Information
406	Social security withholding rates
407	Form W-2—Where, when and how to file
408	Form W-4—Employee's Withholding Allowance Certificate
409	Federal tax deposits—General
410	Employer identification number—How to apply
412	Form 942—Employer's Quarterly Tax Return for Household Employees
413	Form 941—Deposit requirements
414	Form 941—Employer's Quarterly Federal Tax Return
415	Form 940—Deposit requirements
416	Form 940—Employer's Annual Federal Unemployment Tax Return
417	Targeted jobs credit
418	Tips—Withholding and reporting
	Tax Information for Aliens and U.S. Citizens Living Abroad
420	Resident and nonresident aliens
425	Dual-status alien
426	Alien tax clearance
428	Foreign earned income exclusion—General
429	Foreign earned income exclusion—Who qualifies?
430	Foreign earned income exclusion—What income qualifies?
431	Foreign tax credit
	The following topics are in Spanish
433	Who must file?
434	Which form to use?
435	Filing status—Single, married filing jointly, and married filing separately
436	Filing status—Head of household and qualifying widow/widower
437	Earned income credit
438	Highlights of 1986 tax changes
439	Forms and publications—How to order
440	Alien tax clearance
441	Refunds—How long they should take
442	IRS help available— Volunteer tax assistance programs, toll-free telephone, walk-in assistance, and outreach program
443	Social security and tier 1 railroad retirement taxability
444	Social Security Benefit Statement—Form SSA-1099

Guide To Tax-Free Services

IRS-produced films and videotapes are available for loan directly from the IRS, without charge, to groups or interested organizations. To order the film of your choice, call your local office and ask for the Public Affairs Officer.

"How to Fill Out Your Tax Return"

A line-by-line guide on how to fill out Forms 1040EZ, 1040A, 1040 and Schedules A and B. It explains how to choose the right tax return and discusses filing status, deductions, tax law changes, tax credits, and tax computations as well as other topics pertaining to your tax returns. (60 mins.) (¾", ½" Beta and VHS) (Updated versions available by January of each year.)

"Why Us, the Lakens?"

This film, narrated by Lyle Waggoner, highlights taxpayers' rights during a tax audit and their Appeal rights. It follows Jeff and Kathy Laken, whose tax return has been selected for an IRS audit. Unhappy with the audit finding, the Lakens appeal and the viewer learns not only how the audit procedure works but the appeals system as well. (28 mins.) (16mm film and ¾" videocassettes)

"A Trip Down the Pipeline"

The 14-minute film, narrated by Terry Carter who appeared in such popular TV programs as *Battlestar Galactica* and *McCloud*, shows how a tax return is processed at an IRS Service Center. The film depicts the various steps that occur in the processing cycle, or along the pipeline. (14 mins.) (16mm film)

"A Vital Service"

People helping people with their federal taxes is what "A Vital Service" is all about. It aims at enlisting groups and organizations into the Volunteer Income Tax Assistance (VITA) Program in which IRS trains volunteers to help the low-income, elderly, non-English speaking and the handicapped with their tax forms. (9½ mins.) (16mm film and ¾" videocassettes)

"Helping to Recover"

Focuses on how to claim disaster, casualty and theft losses. (13 mins.) (¾" videocassette)

"Hey, We're in Business"

A couple just starting their own restaurant business—and encountering the related tax problems—are the focus of this dramatized presentation. Jim Backus, David Hedison, Pat Crowley, and Nehemiah Persoff, form the cast of this production about good recordkeeping, tax deadlines, and free IRS assistance to business persons. (27½ mins.) (16mm film) (English and Spanish)

Appendix C

Glossary: The Language Of Taxation ...In Words Of One Syllable

Abatement: See TAX ABATEMENT.

Ability-to-pay principle of taxation: One should be taxed on his or her ability to pay and not on the cost or value of public services actually used. This is sometimes called the "faculty principle of taxation."

Abusive Tax Shelters: Schemes or promotions involving extreme or improper interpretation of the tax laws in order to obtain substantial benefits.

Acquisition date: For tax purposes, the date you actually got the asset.

1. A stock: On the settlement date, the stock is owned by the buyer.
2. A gift: The date of purchase by the donor is considered to be the acquisition date of the gift.
3. A bequest: This is considered to be owned on the date of death of the deceased.

Ad Valorem: A tax based on the assessed value of the property. The township has an ad valorem tax of 50 mills per dollar of assessed valuation ($.050). See also ASSESSMENT.

Adjusted basis: The cost of property reduced for depreciation or increased for capital improvements for the purpose of computing gains or losses.

Adjusted gross income: Total income received minus adjustments to income. This amount, as reported on IRS Form 1040, is used in the calculation of federal income taxes.

After-tax basis: An expression of the return on an investment that would allow the investor to compare this after-tax yield with the non-taxable yield on a municipal bond. In the case of a bond bought at a discount, this term would express the return after federal tax on the income and the capital gain.

After-tax income: Income left over after taxes are paid, also known as "net income," "disposable income" and "take-home pay."

Alimony: Monies paid by one spouse to the other following a divorce. It is considered income by the recipient and is deductible by the payer.

Alternative minimum tax: A tax designed to affect taxpayers who have used all of the rules to reduce their tax burden to nothing or almost nothing. Under reform, a tax rate of 21% (the alternative minimum tax rate) applies to those "preference items" added onto wages, interest, dividends, other income, and investments, minus certain deductions.

American Municipal Bond Assurance Corporation (AMBAC): An insurer who guarantees payment of the principal and interest on insured municipal bonds. The premiums are paid by the issuer of the bond.

Amortization: The gradual reduction of debt by regular payments that exceed the interest costs of that debt.

Annual exclusion: Any person can give any other person $10,000 every year and have that gift excluded from gift taxes. For example, a husband and wife could give their son and daughter-in-law $40,000 in one year and not pay any gift tax.

Appreciation: 1. Increase in the value of a piece of real property, usually a result of changing neighborhood or stock market conditions.
2. Increase in the value of an asset that is not taxed or subject to taxation until it is sold. If your stock goes from $10 to $20 per share, it has appreciated but would not be taxed.

Arrears: An amount of money that you owe but have not paid.

You could owe taxes, mortgage payments, loan payments, or the like, and be in arrears in each case.

Assessment: A value placed on property for the purposes of a tax levy. It may or may not relate to fair market value.

Assessed valuation: A value put on a piece of property for taxing purposes. See also AD VALOREM; ASSESSMENT.

Attachment: The taking of property by court order. The IRS will frequently attach the property of a taxpayer until the taxes due are paid. If the taxes remain unpaid, the IRS can then sell the property; pay itself the taxes, penalties, and interest due, and remit the balance to the taxpayer.

Audit: An examination of your tax return, at the request of the IRS, that may be conducted at your offices, in your home, at the local IRS offices, or by mail. The IRS simply wants the taxpayer to prove what has been shown on the tax returns submitted.

Bad debt: Monies lent that cannot be recovered. Bad debts may be deductible.

Barter: Payment by means of goods and services instead of money. The mechanic fixes your car because you fixed his teeth. One of the first questions asked by an IRS auditor is, "Do you engage in barter?" The IRS will put a dollar value on that barter and call it income.

Bearer bond: Usually a tax-free municipal bond that is unregistered. It belongs to the bearer.

Bequest: A gift of personal property willed by a person now dead. The heir receives the property free of any tax, although it may have been taxed as part of the gross estate before distribution. Of course, any gains or income made on the bequest by the heir, subsequent to the inheritance, are taxed accordingly.

Betterment tax: A special assessment usually levied on landowners for a resulting direct benefit from governmental improvements.

BIG MAC: Nickname for the Municipal Assistance Corporation for the City of New York, one of the largest issuers of tax-exempt bonds.

Bracket-creep: Moving up into higher tax brackets as your income increases. As a result of inflation, your income goes up, thereby raising your tax bracket and increasing the government's income without legislating a tax increase.

Broker's loan: A loan made from a brokerage house against securities held by them for you. Such loans used to be deductible, but under tax reform you may offset only the interest expense on the loan against the income (interest) from the securities.

Business expenses: Ordinary, necessary, and reasonable expenses incurred in the day-to-day operation of your business or profession. These expenses are deductible.

CPA (Certified Public Accountant): A professional who has met the licensing requirements of the state in which he or she works and prepares tax returns for corporations as well as for individuals.

Calendar-year taxpayers: Those whose tax year begins on January 1 and ends on December 31. Taxpayers using any other tax year are fiscal-year taxpayers and their year could begin on June 30 of one year and end on May 31 of the next.

Capital contribution: The sum of all of the investor's contributed capital in a real estate investment, without deduction of selling expenses.

Cash flow: May be called positive cash flow, in which case it is taxable income; flat cash flow, all consumed by expenses, and there is nothing to tax; or may be called negative cash flow, in which case certain deductions may be taken against income.

Capital gain: The difference between the cost of a capital asset and its selling price. Capital gains no longer receive the favorable tax treatment they once enjoyed. In 1987 these gains are taxed at the rate of 28%.

Capital improvement: An improvement made to a capital asset (real estate) that is expected to produce benefits beyond one year, adding to the cost basis of the property.

Carry-over: A provision in the tax law that allows benefits (deductions, contributions, etc.) that cannot be used in one tax year to be used in the next or until used up. Also known as a "carry-forward."

Charitable deduction: A contribution made to a recognized charitable organization and which results in an allowable tax deduction. Excess charitable contributions may be carried forward. See also CARRY-OVER.

Closing costs: A laundry list of items that must be paid by the buyer at the closing of a real estate transaction, including bank charges, bank's attorney fees, escrow account for insurance and taxes, heating oil in the tank, title insurance, points, and the like. These costs are variously deductible items and amounts added to the cost basis of the property.

Collectible: Gold coins, pictures (paintings), antique automobiles, stamps, toy trains, and other rare items that are bought and sold by investors. As any other asset does, they have a cost basis and a selling price and the difference will result in either a capital gain or a capital loss. Unlike other investments, they don't pay dividends.

Compound interest: Interest paid on accumulated interest as well as on the principal sum owned. This interest is taxed as ordinary income.

Conduit theory: Income that is "piped down" from a mutual fund to the fundholder and which is taxed at the level of the recipient rather than of the fund earning the income.

Included are interest, income, and capital gains generated by the fund.

Construction loan: A short-term loan from a bank, usually above the bank's mortgage rates, to be used to build a new house. Upon completion of the construction phase, the loan is usually converted into a traditional mortgage with the same lender. These loans have relatively short terms and may be renewed. The interest is, of course, tax deductible.

Cost approach: A method for determining, by talking with local building contractors, the cost of replacing a building at current prices.

Cost basis: What it cost you to buy something: the purchase price, plus the out-of-pocket expenses associated with the purchase, plus any improvements made subsequent to that purchase. See also CAPITAL IMPROVEMENTS and CLOSING COSTS.

Coupon bond: A debt instrument that carries the interest with it (the coupon). See also BEARER BOND.

Debt service: The regular payment of principal and interest under the terms of a note or mortgage obligation.

Deduction: An expense allowed by the IRS as a subtraction from adjusted gross income; the remainder is called taxable income. Such deductions include a portion of interest expenses on consumer debt; mortgage interest on your principal residence and a second home; and certain other business expenses.

Deferral of taxes: Moving the tax obligation from one year to another. In the case of IRA contributions, the income isn't taxed until the year it is taken from the account. The tax is deferred until you are age 59½ or 62 or even older.

Deficiency: Any and all additional income taxes owed by the taxpayer.

Depreciation: Tax and accounting deductions allowed for the amortization of the actual cost of improved properties over their useful life.

Dependent: A person who is supported, at least in part, by the taxpayer and who meets certain standards relating to support, income, citizenship, and other factors. May include others than just your children and spouse.

Disposable income: Whatever monies an individual has left over after the payment of all taxes due. The more you use the tax laws and reduce your taxes, the more disposable income you will have available.

District Court (U.S.): A federal court that handles unusual tax cases. There is a jury.

Dividend exclusion: Under the old tax law, a certain portion of dividend income was exempt from taxation. Under the Tax Reform Act, the dividend exclusion allowance has been repealed.

Domicile: A term fixing the place in which a person may be taxed—a country, state, and city.

Double-tax-free bond: A bond whose interest payments are not subject to federal and state taxation. This exemption usually applies if the recipient of the interest lives in the same state in which the bond was issued. See also TRIPLE-TAX-FREE-BONDS.

Double taxation: The taxation of a corporation's income and a further taxation of that money when distributed to the shareholders as dividends.

Earned income: Income received as a result of the work of the taxpayer, not from passive sources. Includes wages and salary. See also PASSIVE INCOME.

Equivalent taxable yield: Compares what yield you would have to get on a taxable corporate bond with the tax-free yield on a municipal bond. For someone in the 28% tax bracket, an 8% municipal bond would have a taxable equivalent of 11.1%.

Estate tax: A tax on property which is left to another, levied on the testator. The federal government and some state governments impose this tax on the value of the assets owned by the deceased at the time of death, less certain statutory deductions.

Estimated tax: Taxes which the taxpayer anticipates paying for the current year. Estimated taxes are paid quarterly to the IRS.

Excise tax: A tax on goods and services, not on income.

Exemption: An adjustment or deduction made from adjusted gross income, as specified in the law.

Field audit: An IRS audit conducted at your place of business or at your home rather than at the offices of the IRS. See also AUDIT.

Filing status: The factor that determines the tax table or tax rate schedule you must use to compute your tax liability. It's another name for your family situation: "Single", "Head of Household", "Married, Filing Joint Return," etc.

Fiscal year: For tax and bookkeeping purposes, a period of time other than from January 1 through December 31. Many companies operate on a fiscal rather than a calendar year because of the seasonal nature of their business. See also CALENDAR-YEAR TAXPAYERS.

Flower bonds: Bonds issued by the United States Treasury which can be used to pay federal estate taxes. These bonds, regardless of their market value, are credited at par, their face value, when tendered to pay those taxes.

401 (k) plan: A type of tax-deferred retirement plan for people other than those covered by the 403(b)-type plans, allowing pre-tax dollars to grow, with tax deferred until retirement. This plan is also known as a "salary reduction plan." See also 403 (B) PLAN.

403 (b) plan: A type of tax-deferred retirement plan for people employed by non-profit organizations or public schools. The employer will make contributions from withheld salary into various investment vehicles, and the income taxes on those contributions are deferred until the retirement of the employee.

Fully tax-exempt security: A municipal security whose interest is received free of federal, state, and local taxes. Also known as "triple-tax-free."

Gift tax: A tax levied on you for the privilege of giving your assets to another. Any individual can give any other individual $10,000 per year free of tax, but on larger amounts, a progressive tax is levied. Gift taxes, when due, are paid by the donor of the gift.

Graduated income tax: Another word for "progressive tax." The percentage paid rises as income rises. The federal system is graduated. Some of the states use either the graduated system or have a flat tax paid by all regardless of income.

Gross estate: The sum of all property that can be taxed at the estate tax rates.

Gross income: The total amount of all income received from taxable sources—wages, salary, income from self-employment, interest, and the like.

HR-10: Another name for a retirement plan for self-employed individuals. See also KEOGH PLAN.

Head of household: A family status recognized by the IRS to classify an individual who maintains a home for dependent relatives. This classification allows individuals to use a lower tax bracket than they could if they filed as single or as married and filing separately.

Heir: A person who inherits property as the result of a will. Estate taxes are not paid by the heirs but are deducted from the estate prior to distribution.

Holding period: Under the old tax laws, the period of time an asset was owned. If owned less than six months, a gain or loss was treated as short term. If owned longer than six months and one day, the gain or loss was treated as long term. Long-term gains received favorable tax treatment.

IRA Rollover Account: An arrangement whereby an individual leaving the retirement plan at one company and moving on to another, or simply retiring, may take all the money in that retirement plan and roll it over into another tax-deferred account. Even though the IRA annual limits are $2,000, or 100% of earned income, whichever is less, you could roll over any amount from a qualified source into an IRA rollover account.

Income: The most common types of income are:

Wages	Dividends
Bonuses	Pension Income
Commissions	Annuity Income
Rent	Alimony
Royalties	Gains from the sale of property
Interest	Business Income
Bequests	Gambling Winnings

Income-producing property: Investment property that has been rented for an amount that exceeds expenses and thereby produces income for the owner.

Individual Retirement Account (IRA): A savings plan that allows you to set aside money out of gross income in an account that grows with tax deferred until withdrawn by you at retirement. Under tax reform, certain taxpayers are no longer entitled to the deduction but may still make the annual contributions from after-tax dollars and have the account grow tax-deferred.

Industrial revenue bond: A debt instrument issued by a municipality to finance, construct, or purchase facilities which are leased to private corporations. The interest on these bonds is tax-exempt but under tax reform not all industrial revenue projects fall into that category.

Inheritance tax: A tax levied on property being inherited, known also as a "succession tax." The monies are paid by the estate of the deceased and the heirs inherit their shares with the tax already deducted.

Interest: Money paid for the use of money. Under the old law, all interest expenses could be considered deductions but since tax reform, the deductions have been limited. In general, home mortgage interest is deductible to the extent of the cost basis on the property. Consumer interest will gradually lose its deductibility over the next four years.

Internal Revenue Manual: A document setting forth all the policies, guidelines, and official procedures followed by agents of the IRS.

Internal Revenue Service: That division of the United States Treasury Department charged with the collection of federal taxes.

Investment grade: A system of rating municipal bonds that includes the top four categories developed by the major rating services:
Standard & Poor's: AAA, AA, A, BBB.
Moody's: Aaa, Aa, A, Baa.

Investment property: Property other than one's principal residence, including property, land, commercial, or residential real estate bought for gain and/or income instead of as a place to live. Tax reform has changed many of the advantages of owning investment property.

Itemized deductions: Separately-listed amounts that are not among the standard deductions that reduce your tax burden. Some interest, medical expenses, charitable contributions, and miscellaneous deductions would all fall into this classification.

Joint return: The income tax filing by a husband and wife.

Keogh Plan: Designed for self-employed people, this retirement plan allows investment in most instruments, for tax-deferred income and growth. See also HR-10.

Levy: The taking of property held by someone else. If you fail to pay your income taxes and if the IRS serves the bank holding your savings with a levy, the bank must turn over your assets to the IRS.

Limited tax bond: A type of municipal bond that pays tax-free interest and which is secured by a tax that is limited as to rate and amount.

Living trust: A trust that you create while you are alive. An Inter Vivos Trust.

Long-term capital gain or loss: Gain or loss resulting from holding an asset six months and one day, or longer. Under the old tax laws a long-term capital gain received favorable tax treatment. This advantage has been phased out under tax reform.

Loophole: Use of the letter of the tax law to evade or violate its intent. Tax shelters legally allow taxpayers to avoid paying some taxes.

Luxury tax: A tax levied on things that are not necessary for daily living, as an excise tax on jewelry, furs, and the like.

Margin account: An account maintained at a brokerage house that allows you to buy stock without paying the full purchase price and to borrow against the value of stocks already owned. Under the old law, all of the interest expense for this type of borrowing was deductible. Under tax reform, the interest expense is deductible from the investment income earned in the account.

Marginal tax rate: The rate of tax paid on the next dollar earned. The marginal tax rate increases as income increases in a progressive tax system such as the one we have in this country.

Marital deduction: A deduction for purposes of estate and gift tax on the property that passes to one's spouse.

Mill: One-tenth (1/10) of one cent and used commonly to express town tax rates. If your town has a tax rate of 10 mills per dollar of assessed value and your house is assessed at $100,000, the tax on that house will be $1,000 per year.

Mortgage: Debt against real property. In the case of a mortgage on a principal residence, the interest paid on that mortgage is tax-deductible. Under tax reform this applies to mortgages that do not exceed the cost basis of the property.

Municipal bond funds: Mutual funds whose portfolios are substantially invested in tax-exempt bonds. The interest received from such funds is free of federal income taxes to the extent of the law. These funds make it possible for small investors to share in the advantages previously enjoyed only by big investors.

Municipal bonds: Interest-bearing securities issued by states, towns, local governments, and other municipalities to finance public needs. The interest from municipal bonds is exempt from federal income taxes but may be subject to state and local income taxes as well as to the alternative minimum tax.

Net estate: What actually passes to the heirs after deducting funeral expenses, estate taxes, administration expenses, and other deductions.

Net income: Gross revenues or income minus all expenses.

Non-taxable income: Tax-free income, not subject to federal, state, or local income taxes. Income from municipal bonds is an example of non-taxable income.

Notice of deficiency: Sent before the IRS can seize payments. This notice tells the taxpayer the amount of tax claimed to be due, the reason the tax is being assessed, and why, if it is not contested, it will be assessed.

Notice of seizure: The last resort in the collection process by the IRS, it is the taking of your personal property or residence to pay taxes due.

Offer in compromise: Payment of a fraction of the tax due, following a long case with the IRS. Since this rarely happens, don't expect to compromise all of the tax obligations you have.

Office audit: An audit of your tax returns conducted in the offices of the IRS instead of your home or office. See also FIELD AUDIT.

Office in home: Use of a portion of your residence exclusively and regularly as a place of business or as a place to meet with clients. If the office qualifies as an office in home, deductions for interest, utilities, and property taxes may be taken.

Ordinary income: Income that is reduced only by allowable deductions before being taxed. Includes salary, wages, tips, etc. See also INCOME.

Original-issue discount bonds: A designation given an issuer of bonds by the IRS. The difference between the discounted offer price of the issue and its face value does not constitute capital gain but is treated as ordinary income.

Overlapping debt: In the case of municipal bond issues, the co-issuing of debt securities by two or more municipalities which share responsibility for an issue.

Paper profit: A gain that hasn't been taken. You purchased an asset and it went up in value by $10,000. You have realized a paper profit but don't owe any tax since the profit has not been realized (exists only on paper).

Penalty: Additional monies assessed by the IRS for late filing, failure to file, paying your tax late, or breaking other IRS rules.

Points: A loan-origination fee based on a percentage of the money borrowed. If you borrowed $100,000 and had to pay three points to the lender, your loan-origination fee would be $3,000. Points are a deductible item and are amortized over the life of the mortgage.

Pre-tax rate of return: The rate of return earned on an investment before taking into account any tax consequences.

Preference items: Intangible costs such as depreciation that are subject to a special add-on tax. See also ALTERNATIVE MINIMUM TAX.

Premium bond: An issue you bought knowing that it would mature at a lower price than the premium you paid. Since you were aware of the possibility of loss before you bought it, the IRS will not allow any tax benefits for that loss.

Problems-Resolution Office: A service offered by the IRS when conventional efforts to resolve problems do not suffice. If the IRS makes a mistake and you have tried every reasonable way to resolve it, the Problems-Resolution Office will act as liaison between you and the IRS.

Progressive tax: A system whereby the more you make, the higher your tax bracket will be. Our federal income tax is still a progressive tax even though under tax reform there are far fewer brackets than before.

Project notes: Short-term tax-exempt securities backed by the United States Department of Housing and Urban Development (HUD) for local housing and renewal projects.

Property tax: A tax on real property based on a percentage of the assessed value of that property and levied by local government to pay for schools, police and fire protection, street-cleaning, and the like.

Public housing authority bonds: Longer-term tax-exempt municipal bonds used to finance the construction of public housing and guaranteed by the full faith and credit of the United States Government.

Qualified annuity: A type of annuity that meets the requirements of the IRS for inclusion in IRAs and in Keogh and pension plans.

Qualified retirement plans: Plans primarily funded by employees that meet criteria set by the IRS. Contributions to such plans grow, tax deferred.

Realized gain: A gain actually taken as the result of the sale of an appreciated asset. By realizing the gain, the monies are now subject to tax.

Revenue anticipation notes (RANs): Short-term borrowings by a municipality to be repaid from future revenues. The income earned by the owner is tax exempt. Also TANs—tax anticipation notes, repaid from taxes to be collected, and BANs—bond anticipation notes, repaid from bonds to be issued in the future.

Revenue bonds: Municipal bonds that are repaid from specific revenues earned from the facility financed. Toll-road bonds are repaid from tolls paid by the users. The interest received by the owner is tax exempt.

Revenue officer: A representative of the IRS who handles your case when a settlement couldn't be reached by mail.

Revenue sharing: A large governmental unit takes some of the taxes collected and shares them with a small unit of government.

Rollover: A tax-free transfer of funds from one tax-deferred account to another. If you leave your job and move to another company, you may take the retirement funds that have been building up for you at the first job and roll them over into an IRA rollover account without their being treated as income. They remain tax-deferred in the new account.

Salary reduction plans: As in savings plans, a portion of your before-tax salary is withheld and the money is allowed to grow, tax deferred. Like a 401 (k) plan. See also IRA and KEOGH PLANS.

Sales tax: A tax levied by states, cities, or towns at the point of purchase of certain goods, a form of regressive tax in that those with smaller incomes are most affected.

Savings bond: A tax-deferred vehicle for saving that is guaranteed by the full faith and credit of the United States Government. Known also as a Series EE bond, it is bought at a discount from face value and may be further tax-deferred if exchanged for Series HH bonds.

Self-directed IRA: Similar in every way to a standard IRA except that the account is managed by the account-holder, you.

Simplified Employee-Pension Plan (SEPP IRA): A retirement savings plan similar to an IRA that allows higher amounts to be contributed. It differs from an IRA in that it is available only to employees, but the contributions are still made before taxes and they grow, tax deferred.

Sin tax: An excise tax levied against those who wish to "sin," a sales or excise tax on tobacco, entertainment, and alcoholic beverages, even though it is perfectly legal to sell and to use them.

Small-tax-case procedure: An informal trial procedure where some of the rules are relaxed so that you can have your tax case tried more comfortably. Small-tax-case procedures cannot be appealed.

Special tax bond: A municipal revenue bond paying tax-exempt interest that will be repaid through excise taxes on gasoline, tobacco, and liquor. These bonds are not backed by the full faith and credit of the municipality.

Spousal IRAs: Designed for the household in which one spouse goes to work and the other stays home. The working spouse makes a full $2,000 contribution and the non-working spouse contributes $250. These amounts can be credited to either spouse's IRA so long as neither account receives more than $2,000 in any one year.

Standard deduction: Taxpayers may elect to take a suggested deduction based on national averages and computed by the IRS instead of itemizing their own deductions.

Subchapter S corporation: A corporation that pays no taxes itself but passes all profits and losses on to its shareholders. Used by many self-employed individuals.

Surtax: A tax added to a tax. If an individual or corporation reaches a certain level of income, the government may add a surtax of, say, 10% on top of the already-computed tax.

TEFRA: The Tax Equity and Fiscal Responsibility Act of 1982 was federal legislation designed to raise taxes by closing some of the loopholes in the tax law and instituting tougher procedures of enforcement.

Tax: A charge levied by Government to help pay the cost of doing its work. There are sales taxes, excise taxes, property taxes, and of course income taxes.

Tax avoidance: A legal way of reducing your taxes, not to be confused with tax evasion which is reducing tax illegally.

Tax credit: Dollar for dollar reduction of the amount of tax due. This is not to be confused with a tax deduction which simply lowers the percentage of tax due by a percentage of the deduction.

Tax deferred: Delaying the tax consequences. By taking untaxed dollars away from income and depositing them in an IRA account, you have merely moved the taxation of those dollars from this year to the year when they are taken out of the IRA.

Tax havens: Foreign countries that have favorable tax laws for foreign investors.

Tax lien: A claim filed by the IRS against real property for unpaid taxes.

Tax loss carry-forward: Unused losses that could not be deducted in one year may be carried forward into future years until used up. This concept of carry-forward also applies to excess charitable contributions.

Tax selling: Securities transactions made during the last trading days of the year so as to create gains and losses for tax purposes.

Tax shelter: An interpretation of the tax regulations providing a legal means of avoiding paying taxes on income, sometimes referred to as tax loopholes, tax incentives and even tax savers. Under tax reform these methods of reducing taxes have been severely limited.

Taxable income: Income after deductions, adjustments, and exemptions.

Tax-deductible: Expenses that reduce one's taxable income. Medical expenses, interest expenses, and charitable contributions are some tax deductions.

Tax-exempt money funds: A type of mutual fund that invests in short-term municipal securities, pays out tax-exempt profit, and is very liquid. Smaller investors can use these instruments to shelter their money from taxes and still have the advantage of check-writing in many cases.

Transfer tax: A tax levied by various governments (federal, state and local) on:

Gifts	Transfer of documents
Estates	Transfer of deeds
Sale of bonds	Transfer of securities
Sale of stocks	Transfer of licenses
	Transfer of property

Triple-tax-exempt: The income from a triple-tax-exempt security is free of federal, state, and local taxation for the residents of the issuing municipality. A resident of New York City would pay no income taxes on the income from New York City General Obligation Bonds.

Underground economy: Cash businesses conducted by people who don't bother to report their sales or income and don't bother to collect sales taxes, a form of tax evasion, not tax avoidance.

Unearned income: Taxable income from sources other than work. Dividends and interest income are considered unearned.

Unified credit: A tax credit allowed by the federal government toward either gift or estate taxes.

Uniform Gifts to Minors Act: Allows certain property to be held by a custodian for a minor until the minor reaches majority. It is in force in most states.

Unlimited tax bonds: Bonds which are not limited in rate or amount and which are secured by the pledge of real property taxes. The income received by bondholders is tax-free.

Unrealized profit or loss: Gains or losses that have not yet been taken. See also PAPER PROFITS.

Vacation home: A second home that is not rented out for income purposes but is used by family members for their personal recreation. Under tax reform, this home is treated as a personal residence for tax purposes.

Value-added tax: A tax added to manufactured goods at each stage of production. As each producer processes the product, the added value is taxed.

WHOOPS: Nickname for bonds of the Washington Public Power Supply System. This was a very large issue of tax-exempt bonds issued to finance a series of nuclear power plants in the northwest corner of the country that went into partial default or slipped up . . . whoops . . .

Wages: Compensation for employment, so many dollars per hour for so many hours of employment per week. Blue-collar workers earn wages, white-collar workers receive salaries (a set amount per week).

Wash sales: The sale of a security to establish a loss for tax purposes and the repurchase of the same or equivalent security within 30 days. You are said to have washed out the benefit of the first transaction.

Withholding taxes: Monies held back from a person's paycheck each payday and sent to the federal, state, or local governmental taxing agency.

Zero coupon investments: Typically, bonds bought at a substantial discount from their face value, growing each year in value as they approach maturity. In the case of zero corporates, that yearly growth in value is taxable shadow income even though you don't receive it. Zero municipals also produce shadow income but it is tax-free.

Appendix D

Do-It-Yourself Guides, Self-Help Workbooks, Handbooks, Answer Books, And Resources To Help You Prepare Your Own Tax Returns

All the following materials, available at your local bookstore or to be found in your public library, should be consulted before you embark on the task of preparing your income tax returns without professional help. It is suggested, however, that you have your returns prepared professionally if anything unusual occurred in your financial life during the past year, such as any of these:

The sale of your house or other real estate.

The sale of securities held for many years.

A move to another state.

A large change in income (20% or more up or down).

A change in family status.

A change in the tax laws (as this year).

BLOCK, H. & R., *H & R Block Income Tax Workbook* (New York, New York: Collier Books, Macmillan Publishing Company, latest edition).

HOLBROOK, MARTIN, E., ESQ., *Prentice-Hall 1040 Handbook* (Paramus, New Jersey: Prentice-Hall, Inc., latest edition).

KAMENSKY, DENNIS, *Winning on Your Income Taxes* (Oakland, California: Winning Publications, latest edition).

J. K. LASSER TAX INSTITUTE, *J. K. Lasser's Your Income Tax* (New York, New York: Prentice-Hall, Inc., latest edition).

PANEL PUBLISHERS, INC., *The Tax Audit Answer Book* (Greenvale, New York: Panel Publishers, Inc., 1987).

PRICE WATERHOUSE, *The Price Waterhouse Guide to the New Tax Law* (New York, New York: Bantam Books, 1986).

Do-It-Yourself Guides, Self-Help Workbooks, Handbooks, Etc.

SEBETIC, EMIL, *The IRS Practice Guidebook* (New York, New York: Richard Gallen & Company, Inc., 1984).

SPROUSE, MARY L., *Sprouse's Income Tax Handbook* (New York, New York: Penguin Books, latest edition).

STEINER, BARRY R., CPA, AND DAVID W. KENNEDY, MBS, JD, *Perfectly Legal* (New York, New York: John Wiley & Sons, latest edition).

STEINER, BARRY R., CPA, *Pay Less Taxes Legally* (New York, New York: A Signet Book, New American Library, latest edition).

WEBBER, CAROLYN, AND AARON WILDAVSKY, *A History of Taxation and Expenditure in the Western World* (New York, New York: Simon and Schuster, 1986).

WEBSTER, BRYCE, AND ROBERT L. PERRY, *The Complete Social Security Handbook* (New York, New York: Dodd, Mead & Company, 1983).

ARTHUR YOUNG & COMPANY, *The Arthur Young Tax Guide* (New York, New York: Ballantine Books, latest edition).

Appendix E

Bibliography And Selected Additional Readings

ABRAMS, RAYMOND, *Total Tax Relief* (New York, New York: Carlton Press, Inc., 1986).

ANDERSEN, ARTHUR & CO., *Tax Shelters—The Basics* (New York, New York: Harper & Row, Publishers, 1983).

ANDREW, JOHN, *Buying Municipal Bonds* (New York, New York: The Free Press, 1987).

BERG, ADRIANE G., *Your Kids, Your Money* (Englewood Cliffs, New Jersey: Prentice-Hall, Inc., 1985).

BERLIN, HOWARD M., *The Dow Jones-Irwin Guide to Buying and Selling Treasury Securities* (Homewood, Illinois: Dow Jones-Irwin, 1984).

BLAUSTEIN, RANDY BRUCE, ESQ., *How To Do Business With the IRS* (Englewood Cliffs, New Jersey: Prentice-Hall, Inc., 1984).

BLOCK, JULIAN, *Julian Block's Guide to Year-Round Tax Savings* (Homewood, Illinois: Dow Jones-Irwin, 1984, 1983, 1982, 1981).

BOVE, ALEXANDER A., JR., *Joint Property* (New York, New York: Simon and Schuster, 1982).

BROWNE, HARRY, AND TERRY COXON, *Inflation-Proofing Your Investments* (New York, New York: William Morrow and Company, Inc., 1981).

CERAMI, CHARLES A., *More Profit, Less Risk* (New York, New York: McGraw-Hill Book Company, 1982).

CLAIRMONT, GEORGE B., AND KIRIL SOKOLOFF, *Street-Smart Investing* (New York, New York: Random House, 1983).

CORRIGAN, ARNOLD, *How Your IRA Can Make You a Millionaire* (New York, New York: Harmony Books, 1984).

COSTALES, S. B., *The Guide to Understanding Financial Statements* (New York, New York: McGraw-Hill Book Company, 1979, 1970).

CRESTOL, JACK, AND HERMAN M. SCHNEIDER, *Tax Planning for Investors* (Homewood, Illinois: Dow Jones-Irwin, 1983 and 1985).

CRUMBLEY, LARRY, AND JERRY CURTIS, *Donate Less to the IRS* (Vestal, New York: The Vestal Press Ltd.).

Bibliography and Selected Additional Readings

DARST, DAVID M., *The Handbook of Bond and Money Markets* (New York, New York: McGraw-Hill Book Company, 1981).

DUNNAN, NANCY, *Financial Savvy For Singles* (New York, New York: Rawson Associates, 1983).

DUNTON, LOREN, *Financial Planning Can Make You Rich* (Englewood Cliffs, New Jersey: Prentice-Hall, Inc., 1987).

ESPERTI, ROBERT A., AND RENNO L. PETERSON, *The Handbook of Estate Planning* (New York, New York: McGraw-Hill Book Company, 1983).

FABRICAND, BURTON P., PH.D., *Abolish the Income Tax* (Mt. Dora, Florida: Documentary Photo Aids, 1985).

FIERRO, ROBERT DANIEL, *Tax Shelters in Plain English* (New York, New York: Penguin Books, 1981, 1983).

GARBER, ROBERT, *The Only Tax Book You'll Ever Need* (New York, New York: Harmony Books, 1983, 1984).

GORDON, ROBERT D., CPA, *Tax-Planning Handbook: Strategies and Applications* (New York, New York: The New York Institute of Finance, 1982).

HEERWAGEN, PETER D., *Self-Directed IRA's for the Active Investor* (Chicago, Illinois: Probus Publishing Company, 1986).

JORGENSEN, JAMES, *How to Stay Ahead in the Money Game* (New York, New York: Stein and Day, 1984).

————, *Your Retirement Income* (New York, New York: Charles Scribner's Sons, 1982).

KALISH, GERALD I., *Compensating Yourself* (Chicago, Illinois: Probus Publishing Company, 1985).

KRASS, STEPHEN J., AND RICHARD L. KESCHNER, *The Pension Answer Book, Third Edition* (Greenvale, New York: Panel Publishers, Inc., 1984).

KREFETZ, GERALD, *Leverage: The Key to Multiplying Money* (New York, New York: John Wiley and Sons, 1986).

LAMB, ROBERT, *How to Invest in Municipal Bonds* (New York, New York: Franklin Watts, 1984).

LAMB, ROBERT, AND STEPHEN P. RAPPAPORT, *Municipal Bonds* (New York, New York: McGraw-Hill Book Company, 1987, 1980).

LASSER, J. K., *J. K. Lasser's All You Should Know about IRA, Keogh and Other Retirement Plans* (New York, New York: Simon and Schuster, 1983, 1984, 1985).

LESKO, MATTHEW, *How To Get Free Tax Help* (New York, New York: Bantam Books, 1983).

LOCHRAY, PAUL J., *The Financial Planner's Guide to Estate Planning* (Englewood Cliffs, New Jersey: Prentice-Hall, Inc., 1987).

MADDEN, ROBERT E., *Tax Planning for Highly Compensated Individuals* (New York, New York: Warren, Gorham and Lamont, 1983).

MCQUOWN, JUDITH H., *How to Profit after You INC. Yourself* (New York, New York: Warner Books, Inc., 1985).

MENDLOWITZ, EDWARD, CPA, *The Biggest Mistakes Taxpayers Make and How to Avoid Them* (Englewood Cliffs, New Jersey: Prentice-Hall, Inc., 1984).

MILTON, ARTHUR, *You Are Worth a Fortune* (Secaucus, New Jersey: Citadel Press, 1977).

NICHOLS, DONALD R., *The Dow Jones-Irwin Guide to Zero Coupon Investments* (Homewood, Illinois: Dow Jones-Irwin, 1986).

PANEL PUBLISHERS, INC., *The Real Estate Transaction Answer Book* (Greenvale, New York: Panel Publishers, Inc., 1987).

PLOTNICK, CHARLES K., AND STEPHAN R. LEIMBERG, *The Executor's Manual* (Garden City, New York: Doubleday and Company, Inc., 1986).

PUBLIC SECURITIES ASSOCIATION, *Fundamentals of Municipal Bonds* (New York, New York: Public Securities Association Publishers, 1981, 1982).

REILLY, JIM, *Bonds as Investments in the Eighties* (New York, New York: Van Nostrand Reinhold Company, 1982).

RICHARDS, ROBERT W., *Maximize Your Gains: Tax Strategies for Today's Investor* (Chicago, Illinois: Probus Publishing Company, 1985).

RICHELSON, HILDY AND STAN, *Income Without Taxes* (New York, New York: Carroll & Graff Publishers, Inc., 1985).

SCAVUZZO, JOHN J., *The Real Estate IRA* (New York, New York: Dodd, Mead & Company, 1987).

SHENKMAN, MARTIN M., *Real Estate after Tax Reform* (New York, New York: John Wiley & Sons, 1987).

SKIBA, JONATHAN W., AND JOSEPH P. SULLIVAN, *The Tax Shelter Answer Book* (Greenvale, New York: Panel Publishers, Inc., 1984).

SPROUSE, MARY L., *How to Survive a Tax Audit* (New York, New York: Penguin Books, 1981, 1982).

———, *Taxable You: Every Woman's Guide to Taxes* (New York, New York: Penguin Books, 1984).

STRASSELS, PAUL N., AND WILLIAM B. MEAD, *Strassels' Tax Savers* (New York, New York: The New York Times Book Company, Inc., 1985).

TANNER, BEVERLY, MARVIN PHEFFER, AND ALEX LAURINS, *Shelter What You Make, Minimize the Take* (Reston, Virginia: Reston Publishing Company, Inc.—A Prentice-Hall Company, 1982).

VAN CASPEL, VENITA, *Money Dynamics for the New Economy* (New York, New York: Simon and Schuster, 1986).

WADE, JACK WARREN, JR., *When You Owe the IRS* (New York, New York: Macmillan Publishing Company, Inc., 1983).

WHITE, WILSON, *The Municipal Bond Market Basics* (Jersey City, New Jersey: The Financial Press, 1985).

WESTIN, RICHARD A., AND ALAN H. NEFF, *Tax, Attacks and Counterattacks* (New York, New York: Harcourt Brace Jovanovich Publishers, 1983).

WINDISH, DAVID F., *Tax-Advantaged Investments* (New York, New York: The New York Institute of Finance—A Prentice-Hall Company, 1983).

ZABALAOUI, JUDITH COWAN, *How to Use Your Business or Profession as a Tax Shelter* (Reston, Virginia: Reston Publishing Company, Inc.—A Prentice-Hall Company, 1983).

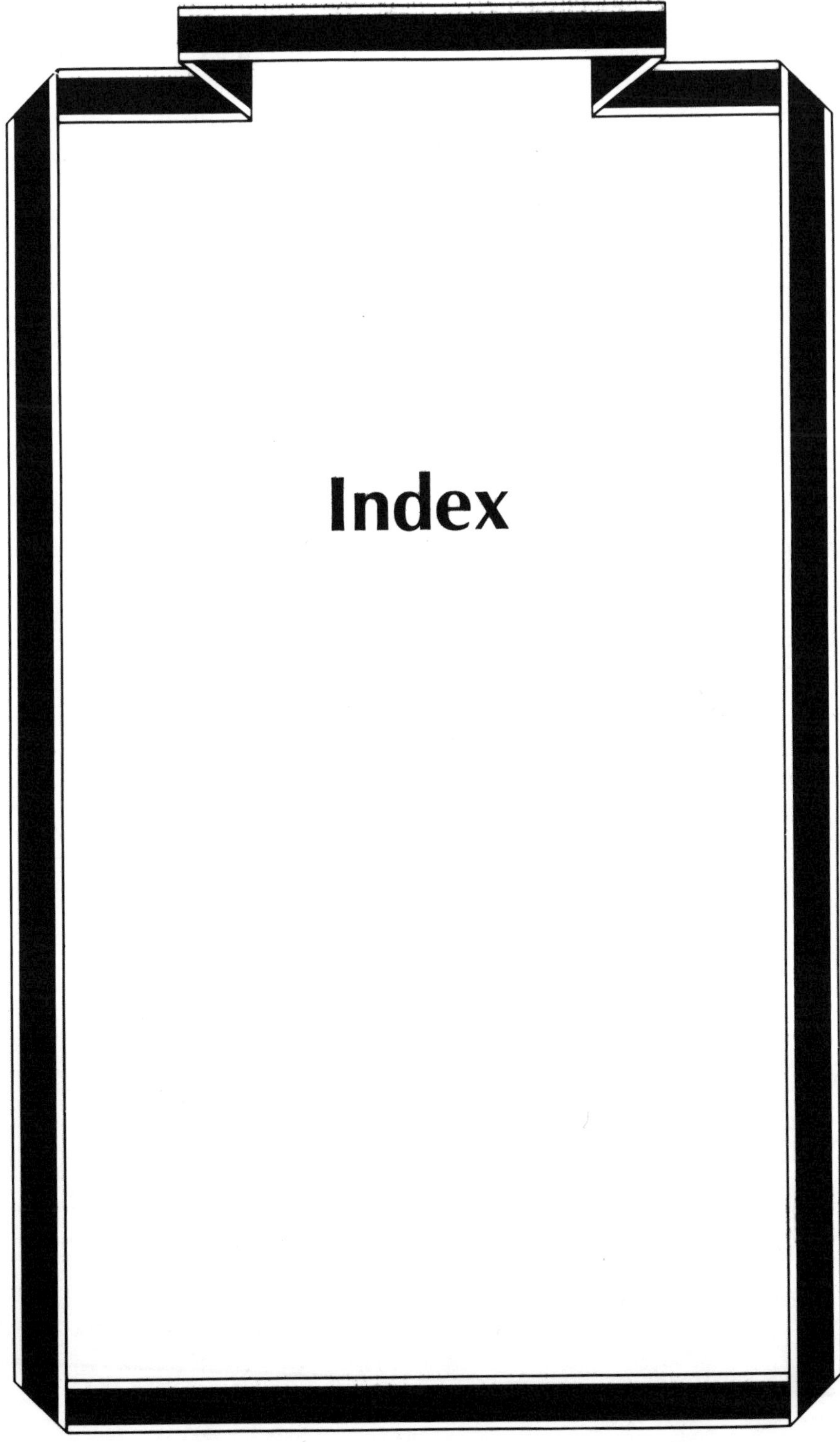

Index

Index